Floridian of His Century

THE FLORIDA HISTORY AND CULTURE SERIES

UNIVERSITY OF
SOUTH FLORIDA

USF LIBRARIES' FLORIDA STUDIES CENTER

UNIVERSITY PRESS OF FLORIDA

Florida A&M University, Tallahassee
Florida Atlantic University, Boca Raton
Florida Gulf Coast University, Ft. Myers
Florida International University, Miami
Florida State University, Tallahassee
University of Central Florida, Orlando
University of Florida, Gainesville
University of North Florida, Jacksonville
University of South Florida, Tampa
University of West Florida, Pensacola

Floridian
OF HIS CENTURY

THE COURAGE OF GOVERNOR LEROY COLLINS

University Press of Florida

GAINESVILLE
TALLAHASSEE
TAMPA
BOCA RATON
PENSACOLA
ORLANDO
MIAMI
JACKSONVILLE
FT. MYERS

125505

Martin A. Dyckman

FOREWORD BY
GARY R. MORMINO AND
RAYMOND ARSENAULT

UNIVERSITY OF
SOUTH FLORIDA

Published in cooperation with USF Libraries' Florida Studies Center
Copyright 2006 by Martin A. Dyckman
Printed in the United States of America on acid-free paper

11 10 09 08 07 06   6 5 4 3 2 1

A record of cataloging-in-publication data is available from the Library of Congress.
ISBN 0-8130-2969-4

The University Press of Florida is the scholarly publishing agency for the State
University System of Florida, comprising Florida A&M University, Florida Atlantic
University, Florida Gulf Coast University, Florida International University, Florida
State University, University of Central Florida, University of Florida, University
of North Florida, University of South Florida, and University of West Florida

University Press of Florida
15 Northwest 15th Street
Gainesville, FL 32611-2079
http://www.upf.com

To Ivy

For bearing with this endeavor for five years
And with me for much longer

Contents

Foreword

Floridian of His Century: The Courage of Governor LeRoy Collins is the latest volume in a series devoted to the study of Florida history and culture. During the past half century, the burgeoning growth and increased national and international visibility of Florida have sparked a great deal of popular interest in the state's past, present, and future. As the favorite destination of hordes of tourists and as the new home for millions of retirees, immigrants, and transplants, modern Florida has become a demographic, political, and cultural bellwether.

A state of vast distances and distant strangers, Florida needs more citizens who care about the welfare of this special place and its people. We hope this series helps newcomers and old-timers appreciate and understand Florida. The University Press of Florida established the Florida History and Culture Series in an effort to provide an accessible and attractive format for the publication of works related to the Sunshine State.

As coeditors of the series, we are deeply committed to the creation of an eclectic but carefully crafted set of books that will provide the field of Florida studies with a fresh focus and encourage Florida researchers and writers to consider the broader implications and context of their work. The series includes monographs, memoirs, anthologies, and travelogues. And, while the series features books of historical interest, we encourage authors researching Florida's environment, politics, and popular or material culture to submit their manuscripts as well. We want each book to retain a distinct personality and voice, but at the same time we hope to foster a sense of community and collaboration among Florida scholars.

Floridian of His Century is history at its best. In this much-anticipated study, Martin Dyckman has crafted a stirring account of the life and times of Thomas LeRoy Collins, widely regarded as the greatest Floridian of the twentieth century. As governor of Florida from 1955 to 1961, Collins led the state during the tumult of racial and social change. An unapologetic segregationist in 1955, Collins pleaded for "moral, simple justice" and racial reconciliation in 1960. A contemporary of George Wallace and Orval Faubus, Collins earned a reputation for integrity and moderation in an era of demagoguery and extremism.

When Collins died at his beloved Tallahassee home in March 1991, newspapers and politicians praised the former governor and state legislator for his wisdom and courage. During the preceding decades, the silver-haired gentleman with a contagious smile had become a beloved statesman, writing and lecturing about the state's past and future. Few Floridians knew or remembered that a much-reviled Collins had left the governor's office in 1961, or that he was blamed for the 1965 march across Selma's Edmund Pettis Bridge, or that he was humiliated in the 1968 U.S. senatorial race by Edward Gurney.

Written with passion and clarity, *Floridian of His Century* is a study that will serve as a model for future biographers. A lifetime of experiences prepared Dyckman for this challenge. He began his journalistic career as a young reporter for the *Clearwater Sun* and the Florida State University *Flambeau* in the early 1950s. For a half century, he has earned a reputation for uncompromising integrity while covering state and local politics for the *St. Petersburg Times*. As veteran journalist and historian, Dyckman has the rare opportunity to write the first and second drafts of history.

Gary Mormino and Raymond Arsenault
University of South Florida, St. Petersburg
Series Editors

Acknowledgments

This book owes much to the financial and moral support of my employer, the *St. Petersburg Times*, and most notably to the inspiration of James W. Apthorp, director of the LeRoy Collins Institute at Florida State University, who perceived that the time had come and persuaded my editors, Andy Barnes and Phil Gailey, to underwrite the project as a meritorious public service. I am deeply grateful to Mary Call Collins, Florida's First Lady of the twentieth century, for her infinite courtesies and patience in the course of many interviews; to Ed H. Price Jr. and Gary Mormino, for their encouragement and their faith that Florida history is worth the telling; to all the librarians and archivists whose assistance has been indispensable, particularly Kitty Bennett and Mary Mellstrom of the *Times*, Gail Penner and Paul E. Camp at the University of South Florida, Burt Altman at the Florida State University, Joan Morris at the State Archives of Florida, and Joann Mrazek, Pam Thompson, and Delbra McGriff of the Legislative Library at the Capitol. Dr. Tom Wagy, LeRoy Collins's first biographer, and Julia Sullivan Waters graciously shared their tape recordings of interviews that I could not have replicated. The late Donn Dughi volunteered splendid photographs. Lucy Morgan and Steve Bousquet, colleagues at the *Times*, shared valuable notes. I have had also the great benefit of interviews, many on multiple occasions, with Robert Akerman, George Allen, Reubin Askew, Jane Collins Aurell, John Aurell, Duby Ausley, Loranne Ausley, John F. Banzhaf III, Tom Barkdull, Gloria Barton, George Bedell, Raymond Bellamy, Jerry Blizin, Canter Brown Jr., Jeb Bush, Susan Cary, Roger Collar, Darby Collins, LeRoy Collins Jr., LeRoy Collins III, Doyle Conner, James Corbin, Sandy D'Alemberte, Norman Davis, Earl Dobert, Harry Douglas, W. Dexter Douglass, Bill Durden, Hildy Ellis, the late Richard W. Ervin, Robert Ervin, Ruth Espey-Romero, Judge Seymour Gelber, John Germany, the late Martha Gibbons, Sam Gibbons,

Bob Graham, Bill Harris, Judge Joseph Hatchett, Harley Herman, Mallory Horne, Clark Hoyt, Charles Intriago, Judge Jim Joanos, Wilbur Jones, Arthenia Joyner, Fred Karl, Burke Kibler, Bill Killian, Lewis Killian, Claude R. Kirk Jr., Mary Kumpe, Manny Lucoff, Buddy MacKay, the late Bob Mann, William Manness, Jim Martin, Bob Martinez, Judge Guyte McCord Jr., Miles McGrane, John Robert Middlemas, Dan Millott, Newton Minow, Jon Moyle, Tom Orr, Justice Ben Overton, Gary Pajcic, Robert Parks, Gene Patterson, Durrell Peaden, Jack Peeples, John Perry, Dick Pettigrew, Ted Phelps, the late Paul Piccard, Bob Pittman, Ed Price, Mary Call Collins Proctor, Nathaniel P. Reed, Janet Reno, Vince Rio, Elston Roady, Leo Sandon, the late Robert Saunders, the late Judge Robert Shevin, Paul Skelton, Bruce Smathers, Jim Schnur, C. U. Smith, Jim Smith, Jim Southerland, George Starke, David Susskind, Pat Tornillo, Ralph Turlington, Marjorie Turnbull, Steve Uhlfelder, Margaret Vandiver, Will Varn, Murray Wadsworth, Louis Wainwright Sr., Ann Waldron, Edward K. Walker, Julia Sullivan Waters, Tommy Warren, Roger Wilkins, Bonnie Williams, the late J. D. Williamson, and the late Leo Wotitzky. To Susan Albury, my project editor, and Susan Brady, a most patient copyeditor, and to all the others who contributed generously of their time and counsel, a heartfelt "Thank you."

Chapter 1

"I Will Do the Right Thing"

A few Southerners had seen it coming. Ralph McGill, editor of the *Atlanta Constitution*, warned of it in a column he entitled "One Day It Will Be Monday." On that Monday, he wrote, "The Supreme Court of the United States is going to hand down a ruling which may, although it is considered by some unlikely, outlaw the South's dual school system, wholly or in part." The South's most influential editor was vacationing in London on May 17, 1954, when Eugene C. Patterson, London bureau chief of the United Press, called for his reaction to the desegregation decision he had anticipated. McGill hesitated, fearing to inflame the Southern outrage he expected. "I'm just surprised that it was unanimous," he said at last.[1]

Among the South's politicians, some were relieved that the Court had postponed putting the decision into effect pending further hearings on when to begin desegregation and how to do it. Florida's senior U.S. senator, Spessard Holland, called the ruling "revolutionary" but seemed to take it for granted that Florida would comply. George Smathers, the junior senator, said, "It would be a mistake to rush into hasty decisions, or to make inflammatory statements based on anger or resentment."[2]

Other Southern voices were not so temperate. South Carolina governor James W. Byrnes, a former Supreme Court justice and Franklin D. Roosevelt protégé, said he was "shocked" that the Court had reversed *Plessy v. Ferguson*, its 1896 decision embodying the doctrine of "separate but equal." Georgia governor Herman Talmadge, who had said repeatedly that "there never will be mixed schools while I am governor," accused the Court of having "reduced our Constitution to a mere scrap of paper." Lieutenant Governor Marvin Griffin declared flatly, "The races will not be mixed, come hell or high water." In Mississippi, Rep. John Bell Williams, a future governor, said the decision meant "the probable end of public education in the South." Sen. James O. Eastland, who would soon become chairman of the Senate Judiciary Committee, overseeing all civil rights legislation and the appointments of federal judges, vowed that the South "will not abide by nor obey" the decision.[3]

Florida was in the toils of a political campaign. In just eight days, Democratic Party voters would nominate (and, in effect, elect) someone to serve out the last two years of the term of Governor Dan McCarty, who had died the previous September. State senator LeRoy Collins and acting governor Charley Johns, each a veteran of eighteen years in the Legislature, were in a runoff that, while hard-fought and increasingly nasty, had been largely free of racial issues. The segregation issue had scarcely been raised; when asked, Collins had said he favored segregation as "a part and parcel of our way of life," and the subject had not come up again. Two months earlier, *St. Petersburg Times* reporter John Perry had asked what he intended to do about the segregation issue. Collins pondered the question at a traffic light while it cycled from red to green to red and to green again and car horns began to sound behind them. At last, Collins said to Perry, "I'm going to do the right thing." It seemed to Perry that Collins did not know what the right thing would be, and he did not use the quotation. At the time, Collins did not expect the Court to outlaw segregation.[4]

The ensuing election would be critical to Florida's future. The state was on the cusp of phenomenal growth for which its infrastructure and antique political institutions were grossly inadequate. It was the worst of times for a racial crisis, or to elect a governor predisposed to exploiting one.

Collins and Johns were very dissimilar, though both were North Floridians. Collins, a forty-five-year-old lawyer, represented Leon County; though relatively small and deeply Southern in culture, the county contained the state capital and two state universities, which made for a more sophisticated electorate than in any of the neighboring counties bordering Georgia. Collins had long wanted to be governor. Johns, forty-nine, represented Union and Bradford, small and rural counties where people usually farmed or worked at the Florida State Prison and often did both. He was a former railroad conductor who had become a successful insurance agent and was happy to call himself "this Cracker boy from Bradford County." He had reached the limit of his ambition with his selection as president of the Florida Senate, which put him in the governor's office, as the constitutional successor, when Mc-Carty died. The Supreme Court required an election for the final two years of the term, and so for the first time since Reconstruction the governor's race featured an incumbent.[5]

Both candidates reacted mildly, by standards of the day, to the desegregation decision, but there was one difference that augured trouble. Johns's off-the-cuff reaction was that he might have to call a special session of the Legislature, the likely business of which would be to defy the Court. Collins's response was simply to warn against overreaction.[6]

"As I have stated repeatedly in this campaign, I favor segregation in our public schools," Collins said in a three-paragraph statement. "It is a part of Florida's custom and law. I will use all the lawful power of the governor's office to preserve this custom and law." He cautioned that Florida "cannot find a solution to the problem arising from the U.S. Supreme Court decision in an atmosphere of hysteria and political demagoguery. We should call together the best brains in our state to study the situation and meet it calmly and properly."[7] Richard W. Ervin, the attorney general, and Thomas D. Bailey, the superintendent of public instruction, spoke just as cautiously. A day later, Johns said that he would not convene a session immediately but "wouldn't hesitate" if necessary.[8]

Collins, who had run second to Johns in the first primary, won the runoff with 380,323 votes to his opponent's 314,198 on the strength of huge majorities in six of the eight most populous counties. The Democratic nomination was the only election that mattered, so Collins was already assured of victory when the Republican nominee died before the election. In 1956, Collins became the first Florida governor to be reelected—the state Supreme Court having waived a constitutional one-term limit—and the first candidate for governor to be nominated without a runoff.[9]

He subsequently made more history by fiercely resisting radical measures advocated by Johns and others that would have closed schools and otherwise aligned Florida with the "massive resistance" of Virginia, Georgia, Louisiana, Alabama, and Mississippi, and by becoming the first Southern governor to renounce segregation. The governor who had promised to use all his lawful power on behalf of segregation—and whose measured responses helped to keep all but two of Florida's public schools segregated through the end of his term—would come to be remembered as a liberal on issues of race.

As governor, he adjourned the Legislature to delay passage of a resolution defying the Supreme Court. During a bus boycott in Tallahassee, he said he did not think the average white citizen objected to sitting next to black people on public conveyances.[10] And in March 1960, in the last year of his term, with Florida in turmoil over sit-in demonstrations by Negroes seeking service at lunch counters, Collins went on statewide television to say that he considered it "unfair and morally wrong" for a merchant to take a black person's money at one counter but not at another; that while the merchant "has a legal right to do that . . . I don't think he can square that right with simple, moral justice."[11]

Constitutionally barred from running again in 1960, Collins became president of the National Association of Broadcasters, where he outraged members by denouncing tobacco advertising aimed at children. President Lyndon Johnson recruited him to be the first director of the federal Community Relations Service, established under the 1964 Civil Rights Act to assist peaceful desegregation. In that role, ten years after his promise to support segregation, Collins declared civil rights to be "the most important moral issue of our time."[12]

In 1965, Johnson sent Collins to Selma, Alabama, where state and local police had brutally beaten civil rights demonstrators. Collins prevented more bloodshed, but a photograph that made it appear he was marching with them contributed to his defeat when he returned to Florida to run for the U.S. Senate in 1968. Collins, who had lost only his first campaign—for county prosecutor—was to lose his last.[13] Even Leon County considered its native son too "liberal."[14]

But when he died on March 12, 1991, two days after his eighty-second birthday, mourning was widespread and genuine. The Florida House of Representatives memorialized him as "Floridian of the Century." His reputation was luminous for civil rights, for having blazed the way for fair apportionment of the Legislature and a modern constitution, and for vast expansion of higher educational opportunities.[15] In the decade in which he served, Florida nearly doubled its population; it grew more during his six years as governor than in the ninety preceding his election to the Legislature.[16]

Political enemies who begrudged him his reputation insinuated that he had been insincere and opportunistic about segregation, but the truth, as this book will attempt to show, is simply that Collins had the rare courage to follow where his conscience and his religion led him.

Chapter 2

"This Is Where I Stood"

Thomas LeRoy Collins lived to see Florida become the nation's fourth-largest state, home to 13 million people and to world-famous tourist attractions that drew nearly 40 million visitors a year,[1] and to secure a place in history as the launching site for the first voyages to the moon. But on March 10, 1909, when Collins was born, Florida was the least-populous state in the Southeast—a frontier state with swamps rather than deserts. An open range law let livestock wander loose. Even the Capitol had to be fenced to keep cattle off its lawn. Nothing of importance had been prophesied for Florida except, oddly enough, by French novelist Jules Verne, who had selected "Tampa Town" as the launch site for his 1865 science fantasy *From the Earth to the Moon*. Collins's birthplace, the capital city of Tallahassee, had barely five thousand inhabitants and only two or three paved streets. The nearest hospital was in Thomasville, Georgia, thirty-six miles away, a day's hard journey by horse and buggy. The capital was situated in the middle of the state's so-called Plantation Belt, a region adjoining Georgia where cotton had once been king, served by human slaves, and was still home to most of Florida's 528,541 people at the dawn of the twentieth century. The region's mindsets and mores faced firmly toward the past, steeped in the mythology of a "Lost Cause" (known elsewhere as the Civil War) and Reconstruction.[2]

The future governor was the third of the six children, four boys and two girls, born to Marvin Herring Collins, a grocer, and Mattie Brandon Collins, a former schoolteacher. She had once taught at Bartow, then considered part of the Florida peninsula's vast wilderness,[3] where another future governor, Spessard L. Holland, had been her pupil.[4]

Cotton was Florida's principal crop and Leon County the largest producer, even after the Civil War, but it was declining because of an insect pest, the boll weevil. The plantations that had grown most of the cotton had been converted to tenant farming and sharecropping or to private quail-hunting preserves owned mostly by wealthy northerners.[5]

Tallahassee, Florida's antebellum social center, had acquired some minor renown as the location of a township of land Congress gave to the Revolutionary War hero the Marquis de Lafayette—he sent fifty French farmers but never visited—and as the home of the American-born widow of Prince Achille Murat, an émigré nephew of Napoleon Bonaparte, who had settled in neighboring Jefferson County.[6] The city's proudest claim to fame, however, was as the only Confederate capital east of the Mississippi not taken by Union troops during the Civil War.

A serious attempt, probably intended to reestablish a loyalist government in time to cast Florida's electoral votes for Abraham Lincoln's reelection, ended in a bloody Union defeat at Olustee, 104 miles east of the capital, in February 1864.[7] The next and last attempt came in March 1865, a month before the end of the war, when nothing but military vanity would be served by taking Tallahassee.[8] When word reached Tallahassee on March 4 that Union troops had landed at St. Marks, on the Gulf of Mexico twenty miles south of Tallahassee, the Confederate district commander quickly rallied a stronger force of militia, gray-bearded home guardsmen, and teenaged boys, "some almost too small to attend school," from the West Florida Seminary at Tallahassee. They took their stand at Natural Bridge, thirteen miles southeast of Tallahassee, where the St. Marks River goes underground, a superb defense position. The Union was repulsed, suffering 148 casualties to no more than 33 among the old men and young boys.[9]

Natural Bridge was a minor skirmish ignored by comprehensive histories of the Civil War. To the people of Tallahassee and their descendants, however, it was a glorious Confederate victory. The annual commemoration was a major event on Tallahassee's civic and social calendars. The youthful Collins never missed it "if I could possibly be there," and it became the source of a profound, if ironic, influence on his adult life.

Collins wrote and spoke often of an old man, his "beard trimmed like Robert E. Lee's," who would come to the battle site, mark a spot with his walking stick, and dance a jig as he chanted, "This is where I stood." Most children laughed, thinking him crazy. The young Collins knew better; the old man had been one of the boys in that battle, "And oh, how proud he was of what he, as one soldier, had done." Throughout his life, Collins referred to the story as an inspiration to stand up for principle. "Actually, if I live to be as old as he, I hope I can be just as proud of where I stood," he said.[10]

As in the old man's time, the North Florida of Collins's youth nurtured an intensely parochial view of American history. The Southern version scarcely acknowledged slavery as a factor let alone as the principal cause of the Civil War, which it treated as if the first shots had been fired by the North. In Southern orthodoxy, it was the "War of Southern Independence" or the "War of Northern Aggression."

"The Civil War that I had learned about was quite different from the point of view of the Civil War down here," said one of Collins's high school teachers, a woman born and educated in Minnesota.[11] The Southern point of view was rigidly enforced. The United Daughters of the Confederacy monitored textbooks for political correctness and was instrumental in the 1911 dismissal of Enoch Marvin Banks, a Georgia-born professor at the University of Florida, for writing a scholarly paper that mildly questioned the propriety of slavery and secession.[12]

In defense of slavery, the antebellum South had fashioned an elaborate racist rationalization permeating education, art, literature, and even theology. Blacks were destined for slavery, so it was said; it was to their benefit to put into practice what God had intended.[13] Though the South lost the war, it won the peace; even the North was eventually beguiled by the second great Southern myth: that Reconstruction had been a mistake and a failure. The rest of the nation rapidly became indifferent to a totalitarian regime of political, economic, and social suppression that befell the African Americans of the former Confederate and Border states.[14]

Slaves had often lived with their masters and had worshiped in their churches.[15] No longer. Throughout Reconstruction and for a while afterward, there were places in the South where blacks could patronize restaurants, hotels, and public transportation without discrimination, and where their votes were sought not only by the much-maligned carpetbaggers but also by native Southern whites running as Democrats or Populists. Beginning in the 1880s, these gains were swept away on a tide of so-called Jim Crow laws and an orgy of lynching. Black voting rights were extinguished with a variety of transparent schemes, including literacy requirements from which white men were exempt if their grandfathers had voted, poll taxes, and white primaries. The ostracism, wrote C. Vann Woodward, a leading Southern historian, "eventually extended to virtually all forms of public transportation, to sports and recreations, to hospitals, orphanages, prisons and asylums, and ultimately to funeral homes, morgues, and cemeteries." Professors called it "the maintenance of Caucasian civilization." Politicians called it "white supremacy." By whatever name, it was racism codified in law and entrenched in custom.[16] "Racial segregation in Florida was more extensive in 1900 than it had been in 1865," wrote a Florida historian.[17]

There would be little help or sympathy for Southern blacks from the public or politicians elsewhere. Racial issues were an unwelcome distraction to a nation serially preoccupied with the depression of the 1880s and with becoming a world power. The Southern myths took root even above the Mason-Dixon Line, where Reconstruction and its aftermath were represented, so far as most whites seemed to care, by *The Birth of A Nation*, a 1915 film glorifying the Ku Klux Klan that Virginia-born President Woodrow Wilson praised as "all so terribly true." All that Americans thought they needed to know about the Civil War could be learned from the 1939 film version of Margaret Mitchell's romantic novel *Gone with the Wind*.[18]

The United States Supreme Court licensed the South's institutionalized racism in the 1896 *Plessy v. Ferguson* decision upholding a Louisiana law requiring railroads to provide "equal, but separate" accommodations for whites and blacks. Such laws of discrimination, the Court said, "do not necessarily imply the inferiority of either race to the other." The lone dissent was expressed by John Marshall Harlan, the senior justice and a native Kentuckian.[19]

In Leon County, as throughout the South, white society practiced separation with no pretense of equality. Though there were some two thousand more black children than white children in Leon schools, the county in 1920 spent $66,663 to educate the whites and only $12,819 on the blacks. During the Depression, the county closed forty-four of its one-room black schools, and civic clubs provided a daily pint of milk only to needy white children.[20]

It is axiomatic of Florida that "the farther north you go, the farther south you get." Tallahassee and Leon County were as far "south" as one could get. The Plantation Belt, ranging from Jackson County on the west to Columbia County on the east, and to Alachua and Marion counties to the south, had accounted for about a third of Florida's antebellum white population, two-thirds of its slaves, most of the slave owners, and nearly two-thirds of the wealth.[21] Segregation came with the landscape, to be taken as much for granted as one's religion. There was no reason for any white child of Collins's generation to think twice about the propriety of it. Yet some saw things that would haunt them. "Many black people," Collins said in a retrospective verse he wrote as an adult,

> Lived out their deep-rutted
> Lives there too.
> We liked them.
> They did most of the heavy
> And dirty work
> At a slow pace
> And for low pay,
> Our best jokes
> Came from their funny ways
> Of shanty living,
> And graveyard ghosts.
> The black children
> Went to separate schools,
> Meager in teaching
> But strong in rules
> About it being best
> For both races,
> If they would always
> Stay in their places.
>
> *"Growing Up," stanza 3*[22]

Death was often the penalty for a black who did not stay in his "place." From 1882 to 1936, there were 281 Florida lynching victims, all but 25 of them black. From 1900 to 1930, the era in which Collins was born and came of age, Florida led the nation with 4.5 lynchings for every 100,000 blacks, a rate twice as high as that of Mississippi.[23] Massacres nearly destroyed the black community of Ocoee in 1920 and extinguished one named Rosewood, where at least twenty-four lives were lost in 1923.[24] Stetson Kennedy, a Florida author and activist who infiltrated and exposed the Ku Klux Klan, was taught as a child that "it was a civic duty to lynch."[25]

Tallahassee had a lynching the year Collins was born, when a mob stormed the jail to hang a black turpentine worker already under a death sentence for murdering the sheriff. As late as 1937, National Guardsmen with fixed bayonets had to be posted at the Leon County courthouse during the trial of a seventeen-year-old black charged with raping a white woman at Apalachicola. He was convicted without incident and electrocuted at the state prison seventeen days later.[26] Two weeks after that, two Tallahassee blacks who allegedly had confessed to stabbing a police officer during an attempted burglary were kidnapped from the county jail; their bullet-riddled corpses were left beside a main highway. The police themselves were suspect, but no one was charged even though Governor Fred P. Cone said the crime "was not a lynching, it was murder." The *Tallahassee Daily Democrat,* expressing relief that the victims had been spared the usual torture and mutilation, conceded that "it was illegal, and, as such, it cannot be condoned." It was time, the editorial added, to forget Reconstruction.[27]

After a lynching at nearby Quincy in 1941, Westbrook Pegler, a controversial syndicated columnist, wrote caustically of the crime and the perpetrators. The Florida Senate responded by decrying not the crime, but Pegler. On the motion of freshman Sen. LeRoy Collins, the Senate printed in its *Journal* Sen. Amos Lewis's denunciation of Pegler as a "soul-sick, mud-wallowing, gutter-scum columnist" who had defamed "the high honor, character, culture and patriotism of the people of this section of Florida."[28] Lewis was from Marianna, which had been the scene of a 1934 lynching described as a "carnival of sadism,"[29] victim Claude Neal's savagely mutilated corpse having been left hanging from a tree to warn blacks and entertain whites. Though news reports had announced the impending murder, Gov. David Sholtz did nothing.[30]

Florida's last lynching occurred in 1945. The victim was Jesse James Payne, a sharecropper accused (some thought framed) of sexually molesting the five-year-old daughter of the white farmer whose tobacco allotments he shared. Payne was kidnapped from the unguarded Madison County jail; his body was found seven miles away, riddled with buckshot. Gov. Millard F. Caldwell declared the sheriff guilty only of "stupid inefficiency"—no reason, as Caldwell saw it, to suspend him. When *Time* and *Collier's* criticized Caldwell for rationalizing lynchings—a fair reading of his remarks on the courtroom ordeals of young rape victims—he extracted an apology from the former and sued the other for libel. After two trials had awarded large damages, *Collier's* settled for $50,000, which Caldwell split with his lawyers and Florida's black state college.[31]

Lynchings were summary judgment not just for crime or even merely the suspicion of crime but also for any perceived insult to white supremacy. The Ocoee riot was set off by two black men attempting to vote. The year of the Neal lynching, W. Dexter Douglass, a lawyer still practicing at Tallahassee, helped his father shelter a black employee who had hit a white storekeeper for calling him a thief. They had to smuggle the man out of state.[32]

"The real way I was raised which was probably the way Roy was, you didn't mistreat black people, you never called them nigger in their presence," Douglass said. "People that worked in your house, or they worked for us, they were our responsibility, that's what I was taught. We made sure they had something to eat and clothing, and we didn't worry about their social life at all. We had the paternalistic approach."[33]

One might not call them "nigger," but neither would whites dignify them by their surnames or as "Mister" or "Miss." Blacks were addressed by their first names, even in court, unless advanced age earned them the honorific of an "Uncle Ben" or an "Aunt Sally." After Dan McCarty's death, a front-page newspaper feature on "the ghostly, silent governor's mansion" referred to its sole occupant as "Martin, the butler," never mentioning his surname.[34]

Considering the era and place of LeRoy Collins's birth, it would have been remarkable for him to mature as anything other than a proper Southern white man who took for granted all the taboos and conventions of segregation. Where differences existed among whites, they were only of degree. Some were brutal, outspoken haters. Others would deplore the violence but even the well-bred took segregation and political inequality for granted, rarely questioning the underlying racist assumptions that blacks were physically, morally, and mentally inferior. However closely together blacks and whites might live and work, there were lines never to be crossed.

As a boy, Collins closely observed this in the lives of his grandfather Thomas Jones Brandon, who owned a 300-acre farm near Miccosukee, eighteen miles from Tallahassee, and of his black tenant farmer and helper Isaac "Ike" Williams. In one sense, the young Collins thought, Grandpa Brandon and "Ike" were each other's best friends. But it was a friendship restricted to the fields where they worked.

Thomas Brandon's maternal grandparents had been prosperous slaveholders in Georgia. His father was a doctor in Thomasville, the commercial center nearest Tallahassee. Though Thomas Brandon was a farmer by choice, living from crop to crop, family tradition strongly valued education, and he made sure to send his three daughters and one of his two sons to college.[35] The oldest, Mattie, married Marvin Herring Collins in 1902. They set up housekeeping at Tampa, where he clerked in a grocery store, and moved to Tallahassee after the birth of their eldest sons, Brandon and Marvin Junior. Four more children—Alice, Thomas LeRoy, Arthur, and Mattie Sue—were born in Tallahassee between 1907 and 1913.[36]

Marvin Herring Collins was the son of William Carey Collins, a physician's son from Texas who became a preacher in the East Texas Methodist Conference, served as a chaplain in the Confederate Army, married a woman from North Carolina, and moved in 1875 to Florida, where he was to serve fifteen pastorates in twenty-five years. He died in the pulpit of Salem Church in Gadsden County of an apparent heart attack in November 1900. As the story came to his grandchildren, he had just called for the hymn "Nearer, My God, to Thee" when he was stricken.[37] Mattie Collins's fondest hope was that her middle son, Thomas LeRoy, would follow his grandfather's footsteps into the Methodist ministry and become a bishop. The ministry crossed his mind as a child, but he never pursued it.[38]

Collins, his parents, and his siblings were deeply involved Methodist laypersons. Neither parent danced, played cards, or drank alcoholic beverages. They expected their children to respect the Sabbath, when only quiet games were allowed. The annual church picnic at Lanark, a Gulf Coast resort southeast of Tallahassee, for which the church chartered a train, was a major event.[39] Revival meetings featuring visiting clergy were week-long festivities that filled dual roles in a turn-of-the-century town with little else in the way of public entertainment. It was from youth activities in the Epworth League at the Trinity Methodist Church in Tallahassee that Roy (his lifelong nickname) learned the skills of public speaking: to think on his feet and express himself to other people.[40]

His first experience augured poorly. On Children's Day, when he was five, he was to recite a poem that began "Two little eyes to look to God" while pointing to his eyes and then his ears, feet, and lips. But he could not match the words with his gestures, and the congregation was roaring in laughter by the closing line, "Two little lips to sing his praise," when he pointed to his feet. The boy wept, but it was his last such embarrassment. Collins matured into a superb public speaker.[41]

To the new teacher from Minnesota, Tallahassee was an "utterly charming" place "that couldn't have been more Southern." The charm did not extend to the unpaved red-clay streets, dusty when dry and gumbo in the rain.

Only two—at most three—were paved, and not for very far. The bolder children took their roller skates to the paved driveway and decent sidewalks at the governor's mansion.[42]

Saturdays were market days, when farmers and their families came to town. Mule-drawn wagons outnumbered automobiles, and the faces of their occupants evidenced the hardships of rural life in Florida before Franklin Roosevelt and the New Deal. Malaria, hookworm, typhoid, typhus, cholera, and pellagra were common.[43] Even the well-nourished were at risk; Collins himself suffered from malaria most of the summers of his youth, and his grandfather Brandon died from tuberculosis. As a politician, Collins took pride in fighting such diseases.[44]

To the youthful Collins, "Tallahassee was a great place to be a boy." Everyone knew everyone; the governor and other state officeholders were living civics and history lessons to be seen daily at Fain's Drug Store at the corner of Monroe Street and College Avenue.[45] Legislative debates cost nothing to hear.[46] Good hunting and fishing began where the city streets ended. His teenaged peers considered Collins a very good shot, particularly for quail.[47] Summers were for sybaritic joy, when schoolboys wore shoes only for special occasions.[48] "While strong family ties and the sense of community gave a child a feeling of security," Collins wrote in an unpublished autobiography, "nature conspired to provide a dash of freedom and wild adventure. The rolling countryside around Tallahassee was beautiful in every season and the woods abounded in dove, quail, wild turkey, duck, and other game. From any part of town, it was just a short walk to spacious fields or tangled thickets. The lakes were good for bass and bream fishing."[49]

Work at the general store he operated with a brother did not leave Marvin Collins much idle time with his children. His one indulgence, occasionally shared with Roy, was to fish for bass with cane poles on Lake Jackson north of Tallahassee. The son treasured those rare hours and grew up with lifelong passions for fishing and hunting that he shared in turn with a favorite nephew and with grandchildren.[50]

Collins also developed a passion for the shores of the Gulf of Mexico. He grew up believing that the clean, fresh salt air and sunshine had saved his life when he was a small child with an illness for which a baffled doctor could suggest only that the seashore might help.[51]

Marvin Collins's earnings as a retail grocer did not stretch far for a family of eight, though he eventually prospered in the wholesale grocery business and in real estate. When the family had moved from a rented house downtown to their own two-story suburban house built with lumber cut from trees on Thomas Brandon's farm—the house still stands in Tallahassee—the children were expected to earn spending money by growing vegetables they sold to groceries. They also kept cows raised from calves given to them by their grandfather and sold milk to households in the city. On occasion, Roy sold boiled peanuts and newspapers at the Capitol.[52]

He also hawked peanuts on the church picnic excursion trains and sold season tickets for summer Chautauqua circuit performances that were held under a large tent where William Jennings Bryan once lectured and a John Phillip Sousa concert inspired Collins to sign up for the town band.[53]

"Ours was a working family," Collins would recall, "but we gave little thought to work as something painful to endure. Our father worked, so did our mother. It just came natural for the children to do so also."[54] Collins regarded his father as a man "with a high sense of personal honor and integrity" who taught the virtues "which make a person successful in business." Though "his teachings may have omitted something of the broad social vision necessary in our own more complex times," they were at least a "sound starting point." This observation, written in 1968, hints at how far Collins and his parents eventually diverged in their attitudes on race.[55]

The family vacationed for one or two weeks most summers at a rented cottage on the Gulf coast. Collins spent the larger part of each summer at his grandparents' farm. When there was work to be done—hard, hot work for the most part, without the aid of electricity or motorized equipment—he earned the same dollar a day as the other hired hands. The Brandons grew timber, cotton, corn, and sugar cane, and kept mules, horses, cows, chickens, and hogs. Water came from a well with a hand-winched bucket. For refreshment, there was a stream on the property in which to skinny-dip and chill watermelons that had been obtained, not always legally, from a nearby field.[56]

There was no automobile. Infrequent trips to Tallahassee or Thomasville were by horse cart or mule wagon. On those occasions, Thomas Brandon would be shaved at a barber shop, keeping his mustache, but he was bearded most of the time. The boy marveled that his grandfather could work as hard as any man despite having lost most of his right hand in a cotton gin accident. "It isn't a question of what you lost, it's a question of what you can do with what you got," he told his grandson.[57] To clear land of underbrush and trees required axes, crosscut saws, shovels, digging forks, and "human and mule labor of the hardest kind," Collins wrote. "But Grandpa was our leader. He would ask nothing of his helpers that he wouldn't do himself." Collins adored his grandfather, who was probably the most influential adult in his boyhood.[58]

The democracy of farm labor did not prevail in the town. Collins's memoirs describe a three-class white society with peculiar nomenclature. The richest were "golddusters"; the middle class were "hominy huskers," a nickname evocative of the whitened corn from which grits, the ubiquitous Southern staple, are still made; and the poorest were "depot greasers, unwashed, unshaved and unschooled." The strata rarely mixed.[59]

Collins played football and baseball on neighborhood or community teams, became a leader in student activities, played a cornet in a town band, developed a long-lasting interest in drama, won a leading role in a school production of *Mail Order Brides*, and rotated the class presidency with Eleanor Mizell, a friend since elementary school who eventually became the wife of one of his law partners, Fred McMullen. He may have left some broken hearts along the way. "Everything about him is handsome," noted his senior yearbook. He was maturing into a strikingly attractive six-footer with wavy brown hair and brown eyes.[60]

The band was playing at a land auction—a frequent event during Florida's pre-Depression real estate boom—when the young cornetist impulsively called out a bid, thinking only that it would "get things going," and found himself the owner of two narrow lots for which he barely had enough money in the bank to cover the down payment. As an adult, Collins relished telling how he paid off the debt, rode his bicycle to the undeveloped property, and "got my hands down just as deep in the earth of those lots as I could and in a voice that could be heard for blocks around, I said, 'It's mine.'" Collins never said whether he made a profit on the lots, which were intended for a segregated black subdivision, but he invested regularly in real estate as an adult and told his son that half his income came from income property and land speculation.[61]

His first regular job, at the age of thirteen, was on Friday afternoons and Saturdays as a grocery clerk and delivery boy for Thomas B. Byrd and Son. The elder Byrd was well-read and widely traveled and enjoying talking with the young clerk, who began to see world vistas he had not imagined. Those vistas did not extend to Tallahassee's brothel; Byrd always sent someone older to deliver the groceries. Byrd's Grocery catered to the owners and guests of the hunting plantations, for whom it stocked gourmet foods and fancy sporting equipment not commonly found in Tallahassee. The most expensive grocery item was a two-dollar jar of pâté de foie gras; everyone wondered how something so expensive would taste. They had their answer the day Collins knocked a jar off the shelf. Knowing that he had to pay for it, he bought a ten-cent box of soda crackers and sold goose-liver sandwiches for twenty cents each. "This exercise of free enterprise brought me out even, and raised the comprehension level of all partakers," he wrote.[62]

Byrd's sold to the poor as well. Collins remembered an old black farmer in worn, tattered overalls who one afternoon bought a dime's worth of lard in a paper tray and a nickel's worth of black cane syrup. As he went to the back of the store and sat on a crate to eat it, Collins saw that the paper tray was leaking down his trouser leg. "The sight of it," he wrote,

Upset me more
Than it did him . . .
I got a cloth,
And taking the faulty tray,
Started cleaning away.
He didn't move or speak at all,
But in his eyes—
Tired and weak—
There was a tear
About to fall.
Then I gave him a new serving
In a new tray,
Of the same sweet grease,
All compliments of the store.
He seemed pleased,
Wanting nothing more.

   "Growing Up," stanza 6[63]

Collins told and retold the story late in life as a mea culpa for not having done more.

"But that is all I did, all I felt any compulsion to do," he said. "It never occurred to me to question that what this man was eating was anything but nutritious, or to question why he was so poor, or to wonder what kind of children he left back home and what opportunities they would have for a decent break in life, or how the suffering of one man like this caused all the rest of us to suffer also.... My sense of injustice went no further than stopping the hole in his paper tray."[64]

> God, help me to see
> Beyond the tear
> That needs drying,
> Also the cause of the crying.
> Keep me from feeling again,
> As that day,
> That I have done well enough,
> By just stopping
> A hole in a tray.
>
> *"Growing Up," stanza 11*[65]

Chapter 3

A Young Man in a Hurry

Marvin Collins had not attended college and did not think it essential for his sons, but he would match what they were willing to save and pay. "If you don't want it bad enough to get it this way, it won't do you any good after you get it," he said. Roy's sisters, Alice and Mattie Sue, were fortunate in having an inexpensive education within walking distance at the Florida State College for Women, but for white men the only state-supported school was the University of Florida at Gainesville, some 150 miles away. Collins apparently gave that no thought and worked full-time at Byrd's after graduating from Leon High School in 1927. Most of his classmates followed a similar path; only one in ten went to college.[1]

Collins regretted his choice long before he found himself playing catch-up with rival lawyers and politicians who had been networking since their student days at Gainesville. He believed that his lack of a baccalaureate weighed against him when he was passed over for President John F. Kennedy's Cabinet, for Florida State University's presidency, and—perhaps most hurtfully of all—for an appointment to the Florida Supreme Court. "That's the thing that Roy really was concerned about all the time," said his widow, Mary Call Collins. "[H]e always felt he should have had a stronger academic background." Collins wrote almost apologetically to the Supreme Court Judicial Nominating Commission, "Recognizing some early deficiencies in my college education, I disciplined myself to make up for shortcomings through comprehensive self-directed study, and by working especially to improve my writing and speaking skills."[2]

Leon County's schools gave him an exceptionally strong foundation in writing skills and a passion for literature. All Tallahassee revered one of his favorite teachers, Kate Sullivan, who taught English for nearly fifty years and whose death in 1953 was front-page news.[3] Collins became so fastidious that he once corrected the spelling in a letter from his wife and returned it to her. She never sent him another.[4]

By the summer of 1928 he had saved $500. Working full-time for the sophisticated Byrd family had broadened his horizons and sharpened his ambitions. He went to work for a bank but soon realized that he would need more training if he hoped to be promoted.[5] With the matching money his father had promised, there would be enough for a year at Eastman's Business School, a well-regarded institution in Poughkeepsie, New York. A year would suffice, he thought, because "I was in a hurry."[6] Roy, his brother Marvin, and a friend, John Y. Humphress, went to Eastman's together. They rode the train to Jacksonville and took a ship to New York.[7]

For the same money, Collins could have financed a full four-year education at the University of Florida. Florida residents were charged no tuition in 1928, and room, board, and book fees were modest.[8] But Collins had been out of high school for three years when he realized that, and he thought it would be embarrassing to matriculate so late. He unsuccessfully sought a political appointment to the United States Naval Academy, where his age would matter less and the education would be free.[9]

The Tallahassee trio spent only three months at Eastman's before homesickness drove them back to Tallahassee. Even so, they managed a normal six months' worth of classes in accounting, salesmanship, advertising, and penmanship, along with a full calendar of dating, football (on the school's winless team), two theater weekends in New York City, and, in Roy's case, theatrics. Vassar College, the women's school nearby, needed men for a drama production, "a chore I found rather exciting, especially with all the required evening rehearsal sessions."[10] At the Christmas holiday, Marvin went south by train. Roy and Humphress bought a Model T Ford for fifteen dollars and drove home, a major adventure about which Collins never said much.[11]

He moved back in with his parents and worked as a wholesale grocer's shipping clerk and then as a teller with the Exchange Bank of Tallahassee. He indulged his interests in amateur theatrics, hunting and fishing, and dating students at the college for women. He also took turns teaching at a nondenominational community Sunday school.[12] The Naval Academy application having failed, Collins thought he was destined to a lifelong business career.

His life-changing event was a summons from Glenn Terrell—a Florida Supreme Court justice who also taught in the Sunday school and was a distant cousin by marriage—who called him to his office to suggest he go to law school. Collins did not think he wanted to be a lawyer and was certain he could not afford it, but Terrell knew better. The school he had in mind was his own alma mater, the Cumberland School of Law in Lebanon, Tennessee, one of the few that still offered a one-year curriculum and did not require previous education at a university.[13] Terrell persuaded the young man that legal training would be an asset in any line of business. Having saved another $500, Collins claimed a matching amount from his father and set out for Cumberland in the fall of 1930. He got a job as manager of the Sigma Alpha Epsilon fraternity house, working for room and board.[14]

Collins found Cumberland to be "made to order for poor boys or boys who had difficulty making the grade in other law schools."[15] Since the Civil War it had specialized in training young Southern men who, like Collins, were poor or in a hurry.[16] The school had only two professors, but it had a good library. Collins began a fifty-year friendship with Judge Albert Williams, an inspired teacher and motivator. "He stalked his students, stimulating, challenging, demanding," Collins wrote of him. "He could be as sweet and gentle as a whisper one moment, absurd and ludicrous as a clown in a sawdust ring the next. All of his moods and gyrations were calculated to help his students learn and not forget—not just for days and months—but for all the days of their lives."[17]

Collins confessed to Williams one day that he was still uncertain about practicing law. "Well, I hope the ambitions of the rest of this class rise higher," the professor said sharply.[18]

Though some lawyers looked down on Cumberland as a trade school that taught to a test—the bar examination—the prestige of its alumni spoke well for it. By Collins's time, it numbered among alumni two justices of the Supreme Court, three judges of federal circuit courts of appeal, seven federal district judges, seven U.S. senators, fifty-five members of the House, eight governors, thirty-six justices of state supreme courts, a dean of Columbia Law School, and a future Nobel Peace Prize winner, Secretary of State Cordell Hull. The school would go through difficult times after Collins graduated,[19] but it prepared him well. He took and passed the Tennessee, Arkansas, and Florida bar examinations; at graduation in the spring of 1931, his classmates voted him the outstanding member of the student body.[20]

Collins was fortunate to have not staked his career on the Exchange Bank, which closed in 1932, not long after the president, C. L. Mizell, the father of Collins's childhood friend Eleanor Mizell, shot himself in his office. He left a note asking that his $25,000 life insurance policy be paid to the bank, to which he had pledged his home to help cover the bank's cash crisis. "Hope you let my wife keep the house. Can't put my family outdoors and not one dollar ahead," the note said.[21]

As for Collins, "I came home, boldly hung out my shingle—and proceeded to starve." There were about twenty lawyers in Tallahassee when Collins set up practice in 1931 and not nearly enough work for them. The Depression affected even divorces, the staple of many lawyers, because few couples could afford to separate. For the first six months, Collins's income ranged from as low as twenty dollars a month to a high of seventy-five. Fortunately, prices were low—a hamburger cost a dime—and Collins was still living with his parents.[22]

Collins had a potentially lucrative client soon enough, but the assignment revived his doubts about practicing law. It was to collect on liens held by a used-car dealer who had required his customers, mostly poor black tenant farmers, to pledge everything else they owned—their crops, their plows, their mules and wagons, and even their land, if they had any—as additional security on the junkyard vehicles he sold them. When they stopped paying, often because the cars had stopped running, the dealer expected Collins to seize everything his debtors needed to survive. Typically, the young lawyer would find the car "sitting in the yard of some shack" where "naked children, with hunger and ignorance dulling their eyes," peered at him from behind buildings or trees. Sickened by what he saw, Collins told the dealer he would seize only the worthless cars. The dealer wanted more, so Collins quit. "[I]f I had to practice law doing that, well, I'd just rather be doing something else," he said.[23]

He had better luck when he and Charles Ausley, a future law partner, were appointed to defend two people charged with murder. The standard fee was fifty dollars a case, for which the state did not expect many not-guilty verdicts. Yet Collins and Ausley gave it all they had, winning an acquittal in one case and a lesser verdict of manslaughter in the other. The man who went free had been accused of shooting a man with whom he had a well-known grudge, but the only evidence consisted of the sheriff's opinion—formed simply by smelling the weapon—that someone had recently fired a shotgun found in the defendant's bedroom the night of the murder. The defense attorneys presented him with two other shotguns, one freshly fired, the other idle for months. As Collins and Ausley were hoping, the sheriff's nose failed him, and the jury acquitted the defendant. In private, the judge complimented them on a fine job. "The man's as guilty as hell," he told them, "but you all did your duty."[24]

Another of Collins's early clients was a man accused of breaking into a store to steal cigarettes. The jury found him not guilty, but to his lawyer's chagrin the client offered him a few cartons of cigarettes in part payment of his fee. When Collins's practice matured, he no longer took criminal cases.[25]

In an incident typical of thousands across the South, a young Tallahassee cook walking home from work wound up in jail because a policeman assumed that a black man out late at night had to be up to no good. Someone told the prisoner's family about "a young white boy running around talking like a lawyer" who might help. It was Collins, who went to the jail, successfully demanded the man's freedom, and sent the family no bill.[26]

Collins had fallen in love and wanted to marry Mary Call Darby, whom he had known casually but had never dated in high school because she was two years younger. His interest warmed as another romance was waning. When he first asked for a date, she had other plans, but he went to her house that night with a box of candy that his sister Sue, an old friend of Mary Call's, had made for him. The next time he called for a date, she accepted.[27]

Her family was to Florida's history as the Byrds and Marshalls were to Virginia's. She was the great-granddaughter of Richard Keith Call, a dashing military protégé of Andrew Jackson who had settled in Florida after helping Jackson organize the territory's first provisional government at Pensacola in 1821. Call had to elope with Mary Letitia Kirkman of Nashville because her parents disapproved of Jackson and of Call's intent to take her to the Florida wilderness, and they were married at Jackson's home, the Hermitage, where "Old Hickory" gave away the bride. After commanding the West Florida militia and serving in the first two territorial legislative councils, Call was the territory's delegate to Congress and served as the third and fifth territorial governors. In Tallahassee, where he had settled with his bride in 1825, Call constructed a magnificent townhouse that he named "the Grove." Florida eventually built its governor's mansion next door.[28]

Collins often told of what had happened at the Grove on January 10, 1861, when a convention voted Florida's secession from the Union. Though a slaveholder, Call was also a fierce Unionist like Jackson and had published a pamphlet declaring that secession was not so much a response to Abraham Lincoln's election as the product of "a long-cherished hatred of the Union by the leading politicians of the State." The convention having disregarded all that, some of its members marched out to taunt Call: "Well, Governor, we have done it."

"And what have you done?" he replied, waving his cane. "You have opened the gates of Hell, from which shall flow the curses of the damned which shall sink you to perdition!" Call, long since a widower, died at the Grove and was buried there in September 1862, soon after learning that a favorite nephew had been killed fighting for the Confederacy.[29]

Title to the Grove had descended through another branch of the family when Mary Call Darby was growing up a block away in a home at the corner of Monroe and Brevard Streets owned by her namesake grandmother, Mary Call Brevard, the younger of Governor Call's two daughters. Jane Kirkman Brevard, her daughter, had married Thomas Arthur Darby, a former state senator from Putnam County who had become a New York City stockbroker after a freeze destroyed his Florida citrus groves. The future First Lady of Florida was born in New York City on September 11, 1911, when her father was fifty-four years old and her mother was forty-three. Fearing for the child's health in the New York climate, Darby sent his wife and daughter to Tallahassee, planning to join them there after closing one last business deal. But he was found dead in a New York City hotel room of what the newspapers reported as an "apparent heart attack." His partner left for Europe the next day; he, his ship, and the money were all lost at sea.[30]

Collins was keenly conscious that Mary Call Darby's heritage was far more prestigious than his own. His desire for an income appropriate to a perch on the Call family tree led Collins into politics. The position of Leon County prosecuting attorney carried the enormous salary of $600 a month. Collins took on a strong incumbent in the Democratic primary, which he lost by 268 votes. "If all of us who worked so hard on the campaign had been old enough to vote," said Mary Call, "he would have easily won."[31]

They had understood that they would marry only if he won the well-paid office, but just seven weeks later, on June 29, 1932, they were wed at St. John's Episcopal Church in Tallahassee. It was a simple wedding for which no invitations had been printed, but word-of-mouth filled the church. They drove to Savannah for a week-long honeymoon with a wedding cake in the back seat of the car. He was twenty-three years old. His orphan bride was not quite twenty-one.

Mary Call had withdrawn from Florida State College for Women earlier that year to care for her mother, who was terminally ill with cancer. Mary Call inherited the house, where the newlyweds could live rent-free and make some extra money by renting out an upper floor. She also inherited a share in some land, once part of General Call's plantation at Lake Jackson north of the city, which was sold so the proceeds could be invested. Even so, Collins was earning only $34 a month, and their household budget was a strict $5 a week. Collins eventually supplemented the income from his law practice with a part-time federally funded job indexing public records for $80 a month. As she had promised her mother, Mary Call returned to college.[32]

Annual editions of the college yearbook, the *Flastacowo*, had pictured an unsmiling and seemingly unhappy young woman, but her senior portrait virtually glowed. It was unusual, however, for any FSCW student to be married, and there were uncomfortable moments in a course called "Marriage and the Family." The professor conspicuously addressed her as "*Mrs.* Collins," and her classmates would turn and stare.[33]

Collins's law practice began to pay off. In a story he often told, and quite possibly embellished, a farmer had hired him to sue the railroad over a cow that had been killed by a train. Though most of his cattle were worn-out specimens that would win no ribbons, *that* cow had been a splendid animal. Collins would often say—later—that Floridians believed that "the way to produce a purebred, registered cow is to take an old range heifer and cross her with a railroad locomotive." The railroad had chosen to make a test case out of it with a battery of eloquent lawyers, and the farmer's optimism was fading fast. He told his lawyer to tell the jury "that the railroad is a great big corporation and has plenty of money to get lawyers, and I'm just a poor old farmer and can't get much." On the strength of that argument, Collins said, a sympathetic jury gave them $500, which was the equivalent of more than $7,000 today. Whatever the actual truth of how he won it, Collins impressed the railroad's lawyers as well as the jury; soon after, the railroad retained him.[34]

The 1932 campaign had whetted his appetite for politics. In 1934, he ran against State Representative George I. Martin, who was seeking a second term from Leon County. Legislative service was strictly part-time work—the Legislature met for only sixty days every other year—and paid only $360 for a two-year term. It was considered a good way, however, for young lawyers to advertise to the public and get to know other lawyers. Collins waged another homemade campaign, with hand-painted signs for cars and billboards. With four candidates in the race, Martin assumed there would be a runoff primary and held most of his campaign treasury in reserve.[35]

The June 6 newspaper reported that the election had been "signalized by the sensational race of LeRoy Collins, young Tallahassee attorney, who swept into office with almost three times the votes of his three opponents to lead the entire county ticket." The handsome young lawyer who spoke so well had carried all twenty-one precincts, winning 2,080 votes to 431 for the incumbent and 340 for the others. No Republican having filed, Collins was assured of the seat. He would have to wait nearly ten months to claim it, but there was a happy distraction to help pass the time: the birth of the couple's first child, LeRoy Collins Jr., three months after the June primary.[36]

Chapter 4

Every Man for Himself

Though nearly six out of every ten Leon County residents were black, none had voted for or against Collins. Virtually everywhere in the South blacks were barred from Democratic primaries under the fiction that the party was a private organization. This was one of several stratagems by which Florida had effectively nullified the Fifteenth Amendment to the United States Constitution. Violence and other forms of intimidation discouraged would-be black voters even while federal troops remained in the state to enforce Reconstruction. The troops left in 1877; in 1885, Florida adopted a new constitution that expressly authorized a poll tax that was levied four years later, disenfranchising poor people of both races. In 1902, the Democratic Party declared its membership open to whites only. The only common Southern technique that Florida did not adopt was the literacy test, which voters rejected in 1916. In Tampa, which was in the process of instituting a whites-only city primary, the *Tampa Morning Tribune* remarked in 1909 that the Negro "is permitted to use the ballot very infrequently and even then, his vote is a perfunctory, ineffectual exercise of an empty right." Negroes who paid their poll taxes could vote in November, but general elections were pointless because the Democratic nominees always won. African Americans who succeeded in registering were enrolled as Republicans, like it or not.[1]

The Republican Party had become so weak in the post-Reconstruction South that it rarely bothered to field candidates, and even when it did, the Democratic nomination was—as journalists learned to write by rote—"tantamount to election." Between 1876 and 1952, the Democrats lost Florida only in 1928, a consequence of anti-Catholic prejudice against presidential nominee Alfred E. Smith.[2] Some Southern Republican state organizations scarcely bothered to recruit members or voters lest it mean more people to share the spoils whenever their party won the presidency.[3]

Though Democrats were supreme, their party was irrelevant except as a barrier to black voting. The political scientist V. O. Key Jr. famously described the situation with a chapter title, "Florida: Every Man for Himself," in his landmark 1949 study *Southern Politics in State and Nation*. Florida abounded with independent political fiefdoms. A runoff primary system beckoned everyone to run on the chance that only a few votes in a crowded field might be enough to make the second round. Eight Democrats ran for governor in 1932, fourteen in 1936, and eleven in 1940. Each candidate for governor or senator had to build an individual organization that would not survive his moments of fame. The six members of Florida's elected Cabinet each maintained his own network. There were occasional courthouse cliques, centering most often on the county sheriff, but these rarely had any lasting influence at the state level. "Florida is not only unbossed," Key said, "it is unled."[4]

The nearest thing to a boss was not a politician in the conventional sense. He was an industrialist named Edward Ball, who had developed the estate in trust of his brother-in-law Alfred I. duPont into a conglomerate comprising Florida's largest banking group, a railroad, utility companies, and vast timber lands that supplied pulpwood to the estate's St. Joe Paper Company.[5] As Collins entered the Legislature, Ball began a campaign to abolish the state's tax on real property and adopt a sales tax to discourage taxes on wealth. It would take him fourteen years, but he succeeded.[6] Meanwhile, North Florida legislators who controlled the state Senate under an outdated and grotesquely unequal apportionment system were coalescing into a self-disciplined clique that would eventually be known as the Pork Chop Gang. Unlike the typical statehouse machine, the Pork Choppers cared little what happened outside their districts if their constituents did not have to pay for it.

The fragmentation of the politicians mirrored that of the government. The Constitution of 1885, a drastic reaction to Reconstruction, was more than simply a "white supremacy document,"[7] as one historian called it; it ensured also that Florida government would be weak no matter who voted. The governor could not succeed himself. There would be no lieutenant governor to perpetuate a dynasty. Executive power was shared with six officers elected independently: a secretary of state, an attorney general, a comptroller, a treasurer, a superintendent of public instruction, and a commissioner of agriculture. They could succeed themselves, which they did so often as to become, in Key's words, "something of an elective career service."[8] They became known as the Cabinet—incorrectly, "the governor's Cabinet"—because of the Legislature's habit of employing them on committees such as the Board of Education on which the governor would have only his own vote.[9]

The Legislature was allowed to meet, barring emergencies, only once every two years, and then only for sixty days. Lacking permanent staffs, the House and Senate depended on information from the executive officers and the lobbyists. A requirement to elect new presiding officers every two years created constant turnover on committees and limited institutional memory. The absence of even cursory conflict-of-interest safeguards allowed Florida's part-time lawmakers to become full-time representatives of banks, railroads, and other commercial interests that were susceptible to legislation and regulation.

Ethics was rarely the strong point of any legislature, but those of the South were particularly vulnerable to exploitation. The Southern Democratic "Bourbons" who had regained power from the Reconstruction governments were laissez-faire capitalists at heart whose natural sympathies lay with the investors of the North rather than the farmers and laborers of the South. When the Populist movement of the 1890s failed to break the power of the oligarchies, the poor whites took out their frustration on the poor blacks, much to the convenience of the elite. The existence of a voteless, powerless, despised black underclass would provide the cover, the distraction, and the pretext for nearly a century of misgovernment.[10]

By instinct and affinity, Collins was a "business progressive," sharing a prevailing Southern mindset that favored good schools and roads and competent government but "stormed no citadels of entrenched privilege."[11] Florida had only one populist governor, Sydney J. Catts (1917–21), elected on the Prohibition ticket, who was stridently anti-Catholic and racist and accomplished little.[12]

Collins came into politics at a low point in Florida's fortunes. The population had soared 68 percent from 1900 to 1920, and by 51 percent in the 1920s alone, four times the national rate of growth, to a total of 1,468,211 inhabitants.[13] The Roaring Twenties brought fanatic land speculation, first in South Florida and eventually nearly everywhere in the state. At Miami, twenty-five thousand so-called binder boys made their living selling and reselling thirty-day options on undeveloped lots. The *Miami Herald* became the world's largest newspaper in terms of total advertising lineage, and its competitor, the *Miami News*, set a record with a 22-section edition of 504 pages.[14]

As if business was not already good enough, voters overwhelmingly approved a 1924 constitutional amendment to ban taxes on incomes and inheritances. "Despite certain opposition to it here and there, there is no room for doubt that its adoption will make greatly for Florida's general development, and that is what all good Floridians seek," said the unabashedly progrowth editorial page of the *St. Petersburg Times*.[15] Though the statewide vote was four to one, it failed in fourteen counties, including most of the old Plantation Belt, where South Florida's growth frenzy did not seem like such a good idea.[16] The skeptics' suspicions were soon confirmed.

Eighty state banks, less carefully regulated than their nationally chartered cousins, failed by the close of 1925, a year in which northern newspapers began to puncture Florida's balloon. An Atlantic Coast Line Railroad strike in October overwhelmed competing lines, stranding travelers and prompting the Interstate Commerce Commission to impose a shipping embargo that left builders without materials. In January 1926, a ship sunk in Miami's harbor, exacerbating the construction backlog. The economy was already suffering when a September hurricane killed four hundred people and left fifty thousand homeless. Many new residents left, taking their bank accounts with them. In September 1928, another hurricane killed perhaps three thousand people (bodies were buried too quickly to be counted) when Lake Okeechobee overflowed its banks. In April 1929, a Mediterranean fruit fly infestation prompted an embargo on Florida citrus and vegetables. The state had already been three years in its own doldrums when the stock market crash of October 1929 inaugurated the Great Depression nationwide.[17] Florida had the nation's highest per capita debt because its cities had borrowed heavily to accommodate chimerical subdivisions and phantom settlers.[18]

The land boom collapse erased roughly a third of the property tax base for schools, local governments, and the state. Some counties forfeited bonds and closed schools. Bank failures were widespread.[19] The local governments and special taxing districts led the nation in debt, most of it in default. The state, constitutionally forbidden to borrow, could not help.[20]

Gov. Doyle E. Carlton, elected in 1928, was unable to persuade the Legislature, which was dominated by North Florida, to raise taxes to help the localities and to build roads.[21] That was an early skirmish in a cultural and political civil war that would last four decades and preoccupy Collins throughout his administration. As Florida's attorney general told Congress in a plea for federal flood control assistance, "[Y]ou must remember that a vast number of the people that come down into this particular territory are people who come from other states . . . and it is mighty hard to get people in other parts of the state interested in whether they perish or not."[22]

North Florida was more accommodating when South Florida wanted to legalize pari-mutuel wagering at horse and dog tracks. Sharing the taxes equally among the counties overcame rural social and religious scruples against gambling. There was also a strong odor of private deals. Carlton said a man told him his name would be "worth $100,000 on the racing bill." The governor thought that his name was "worth more to me than anyone else" and vetoed it. There were rumors that the gambling lobby had provided prostitutes to senators and had paid as much as $250,000 to get the veto overridden.[23]

Florida's gambling debate resumed when Collins took his seat in the House of Representatives on April 2, 1935. Collins led a losing fight against Gov. David Sholtz's bill to legalize slot machines. Collins also voted against "quickie" divorces and against allowing liquor by the drink at restaurants serving food. His own county had been dry since a referendum in 1904, long before national Prohibition.[24] Collins credited his distaste for gambling to the poverty he had observed as a grocery clerk and collection agent, which he feared the slot machines would exploit. The one-armed bandits would be in drugstores, groceries, and other places accessible to the public virtually all the time.[25] Collins thought he had killed the bill—one journalist likened his oratory to "an eruption of Vesuvius"—but Sholtz and his supporters promised enough patronage to reverse the vote and pass it.[26]

Collins also faced a major tax dispute during his first session. Voters in November 1934 had approved a constitutional amendment, proposed by the 1933 session, to exempt from taxation for heads of families the first $5,000 of appraised value on owner-occupied homes. This left the state, the schools, and local governments desperate for revenue and opened the door, some thought, to passage of a sales tax. Rep. G. Pierce Wood of Liberty County, the West Florida manager of the Ball–duPont interests, filed the sales tax bill, which failed in the House, 42 to 51, with Collins voting no.[27] The homestead exemption, meanwhile, meant that the average home would be tax-free except for millage pledged to bonded debt.[28] House members filled three *Journal* pages explaining their votes on the sales tax bill. "I am opposed to a sales tax fundamentally and only voted for this bill because of shortages created by homestead exemption . . . as a last hour and final resort to save our schools," wrote Rep. James A. Bruton Jr. of Hillsborough County.[29]

Collins's early years in the Legislature marked him as a cautious progressive devoted to good procedure; in modern terms, he was a policy wonk. He sponsored a bill giving equal property rights to women, proposed and chaired a committee to cull obsolete laws, tried unsuccessfully to expand home rule for cities and counties, and led a fight to stop a constitutional amendment proposing a state old-age pension system he considered "so vague, so indefinite and so-ill drawn that it would be impossible for us to enact a clear, concise law."[30]

He was becoming passionate about public service. He thought that "[J]ust being in the Legislature was not the important thing, but what I could do there was of tremendous importance."[31] He was reelected in 1936, again winning without a runoff. Tallahassee's first radio station had been on the air for only seven months, and Collins was one of the first politicians to put it to campaign use, buying time for an election-eve speech.[32]

In the 1937 session, Collins led a successful fight to repeal the slot machine law. Public opinion had soured on it; fifty of the sixty-seven counties, including Leon, had rejected the gambling devices by referendum.[33] The two years of experience, Collins felt, had been a "dose of moral poison," reflected in higher crime rates and an infiltration of gamblers from around the country. The final vote in the House was an emphatic 76 to 11. When Gov. Fred Cone signed the bill six days later, the press estimated that it would put some twelve thousand machines out of business.[34]

The early years found Collins on the dubious side of two issues that would seem out of character for him later. The first was a so-called Florida Recovery Act, debated in 1935 and 1937, to prohibit the A&P and other chain stores from operating in Florida. The *Tampa Tribune*, perhaps the most influential state newspaper in the 1930s, denounced it as the "Wreckovery Act." On that issue, though, Collins was the voice of his youthful employment. He said that chain stores would be "the end of the little merchant." Spessard Holland, a future governor, narrowly defeated the House-passed bill in the Senate. "He turned out to be right," Collins conceded years later.[35]

Collins also voted against 1937 legislation that effectively repealed Florida's poll tax.[36] The sponsor, Sen. Ernest Graham of Miami, complained that the gambling lobby was paying poll taxes to deliver votes for its candidates. Collins did not record why he voted as he did, but his concern could have owed to the $200,000 that would be lost to schools.[37] Race was not a factor because Florida relied on the white primary rather than the poll tax to disenfranchise blacks.[38]

The question of a personal income tax has since become a so-called third rail of Florida politics. That was not so in 1937, when Collins, as chairman of the House Committee on Constitutional Amendments, took up proposals to repeal or modify the 1924 amendment. The heavily lobbied committee killed the bills, though Collins voted for one of them.[39]

Collins's second session made him a plausible candidate for Speaker of the 1939 session. He declared his candidacy saying that many colleagues had asked him to run.[40] But he lost to Wood, whose University of Florida and Edward Ball connections were more powerful. When House members caucused in July 1938 to elect the next Speaker, Wood defeated Collins by fifty-five votes to forty. The *Tampa Tribune* captured the significance in a banner headline, "HOUSE PICKS DUPONT MAN." Collins took his defeat gracefully, making the obligatory motion that the ballot be made unanimous for Wood.[41]

Though Wood did not push the sales tax in 1939, there was something else that Ball wanted as much if not more: repeal of the taxes on real estate and personal property. Collins, Dan McCarty, and others who were "inclined to be idealists," as journalist Allen Morris described them, were able to save the property tax base for schools and local governments. But both houses voted overwhelmingly, Collins again in opposition, to bar the state from taxing land or personal property, and the voters approved the amendment in 1940. Rep. Winder H. Surrency of Sarasota protested in the *Journal*: "No other state has gone to such unreasonable extremes in this matter as we have gone, by the use of exemptions and by limitations on taxing power."[42]

Collins, who had been unopposed for reelection in 1938, meant to run again for the 1941 House Speakership and began speaking in other parts of the state. To Orlando Rotarians, he compared Florida to a boarding house with "too many boarders sitting around the table who are not paying their portion of the board bill." The *Orlando Reporter Star* remarked that Collins "could go a long way in Florida's political life, if such is his ambition."[43]

Collins's friend Daniel Thomas McCarty Jr. of St. Lucie County was elected Speaker instead. The sudden death in January 1940 of Leon County's state senator, William C. Hodges, forced Collins to decide between a shot at the Speakership and the rare opportunity to run for an open Senate seat.

He chose to run for the remaining two years of Hodges's term in the smaller, more influential, "upper chamber."[44]

He had an unexpectedly hard campaign because the senator's widow, Margaret, filed also. As owners of Goodwood Plantation, the finest antebellum estate in Leon County, Senator and Mrs. Hodges had entertained tirelessly. He had been a senator since 1923, the Senate president in 1935, and had earned the nickname "Homestead Bill" by sponsoring the enormously popular homestead tax exemption. Mrs. Hodges campaigned under the slogan "Homesteads Are Safe with Hodges," wore her widow's veil, and carried a handkerchief for her frequent tears. As the only woman in the Senate, she told voters, she could get whatever she wanted for Tallahassee and for the Florida State College for Women. The turning point, as Collins saw it, came when one of his supporters challenged one of Mrs. Hodges's to imagine that he was on a surgeon's table for an appendectomy when the doctor died of a heart attack. Would he want the doctor's widow to finish the job? Mrs. Hodges would have been the first woman to serve in the Senate and only the second in the Legislature. Without making any overt recommendation for Collins, the *Tallahassee Daily Democrat* observed editorially that she would be "at disadvantage in being unable to attend important caucuses and group meetings in smoke-filled hotel rooms."[45]

The last weekend saw a barrage of circulars and newspaper advertisements. The Hodges campaign attacked Collins for voting to keep the poll tax "against the interest of the common people," on extending homestead exemption, and other tax issues. Collins replied during what would become his campaign-ending trademark, a radio broadcast. "Every merchant in this town knows that I was a leader of the opposition in the last session of the Legislature to the plan which would have resulted in a sales tax. My vote on the final passage of the bill to repeal the gross receipts tax was 'Yes,'" he said.

On May 7, 1940, he won by more than two thousand votes.[46]

Chapter 5

The Grove

The Legislature met for only sixty days every odd-numbered year. Folk humor held that Florida would fare better if it met for only two days every sixty years.

Heavy social obligations befell the resident senator's wife. Mary Call was expected to visit each of the other legislators' wives and to entertain each member at a breakfast or dinner during the session. Formality still prevailed; women wore white gloves and carried calling cards.[1] Between sessions, LeRoy and Mary Call Collins kept busy with his law practice, their children, and social and community life.

Collins had been happy to fulfill the occasional need for a male actor in dramatics productions at the women's college. Mary Call put a stop to that not long after their marriage. As a couple they met one Sunday night a month with close friends, calling themselves the "Possum Club," to read plays. Their Shakespeare, however, "was so bad we couldn't even laugh, so we gave that up," one of the members said.[2] LeRoy and Mary Call often read to each other at home. He favored history, biography, poetry, and such fiction as *Gone with the Wind*. "[A]nd that's how he got out of washing and drying dishes," Mary Call said.[3]

With his brother Brandon and Charles Ausley, his future law partner, Collins helped organize Tallahassee's Young Democrat Club and became the first president. He was also a founder of Tallahassee's Junior Chamber of Commerce. His most significant civic venture involved another group styled after an indigenous species, the Catfish Club. "Franklin Roosevelt was our idol and we proudly thought of ourselves as New Dealers," Collins said. They were eleven young men who wanted to shake up the town, and they did it so well that one of the two physicians in the group, Dr. Edward Annis, a future president of the American Medical Association, was blackballed at the small hospital that had finally been established at Tallahassee and had to move his practice to Miami. Annis wore out his welcome in Tallahassee soon after arriving from Michigan by leading a campaign to assure the safety of the city's milk supply. His suspicions were confirmed publicly during an impromptu debate at Fain's Drug Store one Sunday morning between dairy farmers Walter Perkins and E. A. Gilbert, who had a much larger and more modern facility. "There ain't much difference really in Mr. Gilbert's milk and my milk," Perkins reportedly said. "We have the same kind of cows and the only real difference is that he keeps the manure out of his milk, and I strain it out of mine." That, said Collins, "about ended our need to crusade."[4]

LeRoy and Mary Call rented an apartment to a man whose wife, fascinated with the occult, insisted that his given name, Thomas LeRoy Collins, forebode failure. Collins was happy to humor her, as his family and others had always called him Roy or LeRoy, never Thomas. He never went by Thomas again except in the U.S. Navy, which demanded that he use his legal name.[5]

Like many young couples, the Collinses economized by sharing outgrown children's clothing with other families.[6]

Mary Call's first experience with flying inspired a lifelong preference for other means of travel. Not long after the 1938 birth of their eldest daughter, Jane Brevard, Mary Call accepted a friend's invitation for a spin in an open-cockpit airplane. She said of the experience: "I looked down on the ground and I could see the nurse holding my little girl and my little boy waving to his mother and I said, 'Lord, if you let me down I'll never want to fly again.'" Except for rare occasions, she kept the pledge. When flying was the only option, Roy and Mary Call sometimes took separate planes to accommodate her fear of leaving their children orphaned.[7]

Leon County had voted dry in 1904, remaining so until Collins was governor. But it acted wet; bootleggers operated brazenly, and liquor could be ordered legally from licensed dealers elsewhere. LeRoy and Mary Call seldom imbibed, buying alcohol in quantity only to fulfill the resident senator's social obligations. Collins never drank in public, although he did not object if staff members did. At social functions, he sometimes asked to be served water in a wine glass. As governor, Collins told an aide he chose to abstain completely from alcohol for fear it would influence a decision he might have to make.[8]

His parents promised LeRoy Jr. $500 if he abstained from alcohol until his twenty-first birthday. He kept the bargain, even questioning whether it allowed him to enjoy Mary Call's Christmas plum puddings, which were heavily laced with brandy or rum. She insisted, however, that it was just a matter of "proper flavor." A dinner guest remarked, "I see that the Collinses don't drink liquor, they just eat it."[9] The senator's only vice was cigarette smoking, which he indulged in private until his wife and son eventually prevailed on him to quit.[10]

Soon after Collins's election to the Hodges vacancy, another death allowed the family to fulfill what Mary Call had thought to be an impossible dream: owning and restoring her ancestral home, the Grove. Richard Keith Call's great townhouse had come on such hard times, most of the land having been sold, that another great-granddaughter, Reinette Long Hunt, could maintain it only by converting it into a rooming house and hotel. Rooms were divided with beaver board, sleeping quarters were built atop the back porch, and wooden bathrooms were added to the exterior of the massive brick walls. When she died in 1940, to be buried in the family cemetery behind the Grove, her estate could not afford a headstone.[11]

She had mortgaged the Grove to a cousin, John W. Ford, for $17,000, a large debt for the time, and left him the property in her will. Ford, not a Call descendent, thought that it belonged in the General's family and agreed to sell it to LeRoy and Mary Call for the sum of his investment and the estate's debts. Four prosperous Tallahasseans who could have outbid the couple deferred on learning that Mary Call wanted it. With money from the sale of the Lake Jackson land, their savings, and a large mortgage, the Grove was theirs. And so were the worries. Fourteen years later, Collins said they had been audacious; it was necessary to borrow "every single dime" that they could, and there was not enough left for furniture. "The house has just about kept us broke," he remarked. Indeed, impatient creditors occasionally had to dun him for small overdue accounts.[12]

They moved into the Grove early in 1941 and within half an hour had painted over the "Hotel Accommodations" sign on the concrete entrance posts. The partitions and exterior bathrooms remained to be removed, the roof needed repair, everything awaited scrubbing, and the grounds had become a jungle. They would have to do much of the work themselves, but domestic labor was never LeRoy Collins's strong suit. On one occasion, they were planting pine seedlings to screen the house from its neighbors. Mary

Call found that he had finished his share first by planting three seedlings to each hole.[13]

The Grove came with a boarder named Robert Aldridge, a friend of Reinette Hunt whom Mary Call exiled to a cottage on the grounds after she discovered him making wine and whiskey in the main house.[14]

Allen Morris wrote in his "Highlighting Cracker Politics" column for the *Miami Herald* that only five of the thirty-eight senators had distinguished themselves during the 1941 session. One was "genteel LeRoy Collins of Tallahassee, who may be governor some day." Collins caught other eyes as well. Reporting his announcement for reelection in 1942—he ran unopposed—the *Florida Times-Union* described him as a "legislative veteran at the age of 32" and as a "leader in public health and education." For the third time, an election year brought the birth of a new Collins. She was named Mary Call and distinguished from her mother by the nickname "Bootsie."[15]

Many of Collins's friends in the community and the Legislature went into service in World War II long before he did. "We have been having a terrible time at the house lately for the lack of servants, but I suppose this is general and we shouldn't complain about it," he wrote in December 1943. The servant shortage had serious implications; many whites suspected that their former cooks, housemaids, nannies, yardmen, and farm laborers were not only relishing military pay allotments but were also shirking in some sort of nascent civil rights movement inspired by the war effort. In drafting secret plans for martial law in Tallahassee, Jacksonville, St. Petersburg, Miami, and Tampa, state authorities cited this white antagonism as potential tinder for racial disturbances. With two major camps nearby, Tallahassee had racial incidents throughout the war, and martial law was declared briefly in April 1945, when police fought with at least 250 black soldiers.[16]

Florida's economy thrived during the war as the U.S. government established 172 military installations and leased hundreds of hotels to house troops in training. Agriculture flourished, particularly orange juice and sugar production, but often at the price of gross civil rights abuses by sheriffs who used their arrest powers to conscript unwilling laborers for private employers. In a notorious incident at Ocala, German prisoners of war who had been picking citrus were welcomed aboard a train while three black U.S. servicemen, one of them on crutches, were directed to the baggage car for lack of "colored" coaches.[17]

There was controversy in 1943 over a proposed University of South Florida to teach medicine, pharmacy, and dentistry, none of which was offered at Gainesville or Tallahassee. Despite the self-evident need, sponsors could not overcome the self-interested opposition of the University of Florida, the Florida State College for Women, and the University of Miami, a private institution that did not want state-subsidized competition. Even the *Miami Herald* opposed it. In a reversal of past and future sectional roles, legislators from North Florida passed the bill, but South Floridians nullified it by deleting the appropriation. Collins, no doubt reflecting the view from FSCW's administration building, voted against the bill. The authorization was quietly repealed several sessions later.[18]

Collins, who was never completely comfortable around some of his tobacco-chewing, backslapping, and hard-drinking political colleagues, was having second thoughts about politics. He wrote to a friend in 1943 that he did not expect to run again and "have lost what little ambition I used to have to some day run for a state-wide office." He thought it would be better for the "happiness, peace and security of my family" to quit politics. The mood soon passed.[19]

Though state legislators were exempt from the draft, many volunteered for military service. Collins did so in 1943, but the Navy rejected his application for a commission on the grounds that at thirty-four, he was too old; men over thirty were being taken only for "special qualifications." In 1944, he wrote to his brother, Brandon, that he had considered resigning from the Legislature to volunteer as a private but that the Army would not promise to accept him. "All of my friends in the Army and the Navy tell me by all means not to get in," he added. Yet he felt that he should.[20]

That spring, Collins became Leon County campaign manager for the gubernatorial campaign of his Senate colleague Ernest Graham of Miami. Another candidate was Millard Fillmore Caldwell Jr., a former congressman who had settled in Tallahassee to practice law and had developed strong local support. Collins endorsed Caldwell, the eventual runoff winner, after Graham ran third in a six-way first primary. Though Collins sponsored Caldwell's most important legislation in the 1947 session, Caldwell apparently never forgave his townsman's early opposition in 1944.[21]

Collins had just bought two hard-to-get civilian suits when he learned the Navy finally wanted him. "I feel that Uncle Sam must be getting pretty close to the bottom of the barrel when he is taking me," he wrote to a former House colleague in the Navy. "My principal concern about leaving, of course, is how Mary Call and the children will get along," he wrote to another friend. "It is going to be much harder for Mary Call then [*sic*] it will be for me and sometimes I feel like a dirty dog for leaving her, but she is a grand girl, has a lot of ability and a way of meeting problems effectively."[22]

The Navy needed people from government as military administrators of Taiwan, an intended base for the invasion of Japan. The newly commissioned Lieutenant (j.g.) Thomas L. Collins took a crash course at Princeton University in the history, economy, and society of Taiwan and was sent to Monterey, California, to study the language. But the Philippines became the proposed invasion base, and the Navy's suddenly surplus Taiwanese experts were dispersed to random assignments. Collins went to a district headquarters at Seattle, where he served as a legal officer until early 1946 and never got aboard a ship. When the American Legion offered later to make him a consultant to Florida World War II veterans, Collins declined because "I sincerely feel that the job should be given to one who had actual combat experience."[23]

Mary Call and the three children followed him to Princeton, Monterey, and Seattle. Off-duty, Collins observed California's flag flying everywhere in the state and decided to popularize Florida's flag, which needed official permission just to be displayed. "He got tired of seeing that [California] bear," Mary Call said. "Everywhere we went there was that old bear waving in the breeze."[24] They were impressed also by California's extensive state park system, which they visited on weekends in a 1934 Nash purchased for $150. When Collins wrote enthusiastically to Caldwell to propose a similar park system for Florida, the new governor replied sarcastically that Collins seemed to be enjoying California more than his own state. Collins let that pass; on returning to the Legislature he sponsored legislation that is credited for the growth of Florida's extensive state park system.[25]

The law firm of Collins, Ausley & Truitt had become profitable; the Collins income tax return for 1944 showed $13,660 from the practice and net income of $14,199, a very comfortable sum for the time. Collins, whose military base pay was just $166 a month, was eager to leave Seattle and pick up where he had left off.[26] But there was a complication. The senator who had replaced him wanted to keep the job; he happened also to be Collins's law partner.

Charles Ausley had been elected without opposition to finish Collins's four-year term. During a special reapportionment session in 1945, which began on a 100-degree day in Tallahassee and would last fifty-two days longer, Ausley wrote Collins that he was quite eager to give the job back. It had become, he said, the "toughest, bitterest, political fight that Florida has seen in many a day, a fight that may leave scars that will be many years in healing," and Ausley was uneasy as a leader of the opposition to fairer representation for South Florida.[27] But his misgivings had faded, and he wanted to run for a full term. Collins, still stationed at Seattle, insisted on taking the seat back and threatened to run against his partner if it came to that. Ausley stepped aside. "I always felt a little badly about Charles," Collins told Ausley's granddaughter, "because I think he enjoyed that Senate and he did a good job." Collins reclaimed the seat without opposition.[28]

That left time for Collins and his family to enjoy a leisurely trip home. They set out from Seattle in the 1934 Nash, nicknamed "Bouncing Betty," which needed a quart of oil with every tank of gasoline and survived the cross-country journey by only a few months. The trip home took three weeks, four days of which he spent at the El Tovar Hotel at the Grand Canyon recovering from strep throat.[29]

The family arrived home at the peak of springtime in Tallahassee, the city's best season, a welcome contrast to Seattle's notoriously damp, cloudy climate. "The weather here has been delightful," Collins wrote to one of his Navy friends. "It is warm and there hasn't been a cloud in the sky. Every morning it seems that thousands of birds are singing outside the window, and there is a beauty and fragrance to the spring flowers which seem to surpass my fondest recollection."[30]

The Grove had been unoccupied and untended for more than a year. "Mary Call has started to work on the almost impossible job of trying to wash the mold from the walls of the house," Collins wrote to a Navy friend at Seattle. "I have been begging off from undertaking any of the work personally because of an alleged sore back but I think I am going to have to find another excuse pretty soon."[31] To his friend Dan McCarty, he wrote regretfully that they would be unable to share a vacation at the coast because "we have finally gotten a crew of darkies cutting weeds out at the house who should be supervised."[32] Looking forward to more relaxed summers in the future, the couple bought lots and built a simple concrete-block cottage on the Gulf coast, an hour's drive south of Tallahassee, not far from the site of the church picnics of his youth.[33]

A few weeks before Christmas in 1946, Collins made a hard decision for the grandson of a circuit-riding Methodist preacher. He and his son joined Mary Call's church, St. John's Episcopal, so that the entire family could worship together. Collins assured his old church that he would fulfill a $500 pledge he had made to the Methodists.[34]

Still sensitive to his lack of a conventional college education, Collins took a keen interest in his son's schooling. Young Roy preferred mechanics to literature, but his father insisted he drop shop and take Latin. "He really impressed on me the importance of good communications and vocabulary," LeRoy Jr. said.[35]

The better that Collins knew people, the more he expected of them. That applied to his family as well as to his employees. "The people he was closest to, he was very, very, tough," said his son, recalling having seen a law firm secretary in tears after Collins had criticized her work. When Collins learned that his son had been ticketed for speeding 20 mph over the limit, he contacted the judge to make sure that an example would be made of him. The judge suspended his license for the month, which meant double-dating for his junior-senior prom.[36]

The family usually kept dogs at the Grove; at various times there were a Great Dane, a Labrador retriever, a collie, and a dachshund. The Grove was unfenced, and Collins frequently had to retrieve a dog from some irate neighbor's property. He considered returning the Great Dane. "He is such a friendly dog and seems to like all of us fine," Collins wrote to the breeder. "The only trouble is he likes everybody else too."[37]

As did many other prominent Tallahassee families, Mary Call and the children spent most of the summer at the coast. LeRoy drove down many nights and most weekends. The summer sojourn lasted from the end of school in June to Labor Day. Residential air-conditioning and city swimming pools had not reached North Florida, so the cool breezes of the coast were a welcome alternative to spending summers in the hottest section of a famously hot state. Friends and relatives often joined them. Coastal living was informal. Collins, who loved practical jokes, had a favorite trick for visitors: water served in a glass that dribbled down the victim's chin no matter how carefully he tried to drink from it. The joke went too far on one occasion; an embarrassed nephew from Tampa ran crying from the dinner table. Collins apologized. "We do this to everybody," he explained.[38]

The Episcopal Church had just established a summer camp nearby on the grounds of an abandoned Army base, Camp Gordon Johnston, where soldiers had trained for amphibious landings. Harry Douglas, a young seminarian, began a lifelong friendship with the Collinses during Sunday services for the summer residents at a former mess hall near the water's edge. More than fifty years later, Douglas and Mary Call disagree over his first meeting with Florida's future governor. "Mary Call looked down and he was barefooted," Douglas said; "She was horrified, and she said, 'Roy, you forgot your shoes.' And he said, 'Well, he said 'Come as you are.'" Mary Call insists that her husband never went anywhere without shoes.[39]

Chapter 6

Reform, Sales Tax, Scandals, Segregation

Caldwell ran for governor in 1944 as the candidate of Edward Ball and other conservative businessmen who were trying simultaneously to defeat Florida's most liberal politician, Sen. Claude Pepper, who had opposed a tax bill favoring the timber industry. Pepper survived that attack but lost in 1950.[1]

Caldwell opposed Ball's sales tax, however, and did not tolerate the shabby condition of Florida's public schools. His Citizens Committee on Education successfully recommended a then-record increase in state aid in 1945. In 1947, the Legislature enacted the committee's major proposal, known as the Minimum Foundation Program. Defying the historical expectation that governors got little from their lame-duck second sessions, Caldwell obtained the most comprehensive reform since Florida opened public schools. The Minimum Foundation Program created a formula to finance even poor counties adequately, boosted overall spending, required nine-month terms, committed state support for classrooms as well as salaries, consolidated tax districts countywide, and pegged teachers' salaries to their education. It also required each county superintendent to be a college graduate, a provision the state Supreme Court ruled unconstitutional.[2] At the time, barely 62 percent of Florida's teachers had four-year degrees. Two years later, nearly 80 percent did.[3] Before, Florida had no teacher standards. "Any nice old lady who liked children could teach in primary grades," recalled Leo Wotitzky, a Charlotte County representative who chaired the Education Committee in 1949.[4]

Though he was loath to admit it later, Caldwell relied on Collins, who chaired the Education Committee, to overcome serious small-county resistance in the Senate. His management of the bill earned Collins an enduring reputation as a friend of education. Charley Johns of Bradford County, his future opponent, was the only senator who voted no.[5]

Thirty years later, Caldwell maintained that there had been "a lot of noise but not a great deal of opposition," that he and Collins had not worked closely, and that Collins sponsored the bill because he was "ambitious" and "needed some help."[6] The press, however, considered Collins's contribution decisive and voted him a cowinner of the 1947 "Most Valuable Senator" award sponsored by the *St. Petersburg Times*.[7]

The 1947 reform was notable for Negro education, in which Florida performed poorly even by Southern standards. It had taken four lawsuits to win salary parity for white and black teachers. Now the state would begin to improve Negro school buildings. This reflected a spreading Southern belief that to make the long-neglected facilities "equal" to white schools would persuade the federal courts to uphold segregation. That was the reason, Ralph McGill wrote, why states were "raising taxes and spending hurriedly." Some black leaders were tempted to settle for that.[8]

Black children had been left far behind. In 1950, half of all white Floridians had completed at least 10.9 years of schooling; the nonwhite median was 5.8 years. Only Georgia, South Carolina, Kentucky, Alabama, and Mississippi showed fewer years of schooling for blacks. Fewer than 48 percent of Florida's black teachers had completed four or more years of college compared to 67 percent of the white teachers.[9]

The 1947 session also converted the women's college at Tallahassee into the Florida State University and made it and the University of Florida legally coeducational. They were already enrolling each other's students at hastily established branch campuses to accommodate a surge in enrollments from war veterans subsidized by the GI Bill of Rights.[10]

But the Legislature did not raise taxes to pay for the Minimum Foundation Program despite Caldwell's warning of a fiscal crisis. "Is the Free-Spending Legislature Opening Door for Sales Tax?" asked a *Miami Herald* headline.[11]

Departing legislators left a scandal along with the deficit. Rep. Brailey Odham, a freshman from Sanford, had charged that bribes were being offered for votes against a bill prohibiting bookmakers from leasing private wire services. The bill's defeat by a four-vote margin persuaded many that Odham had told the truth. A grand jury charged Rep. Bernie C. Papy, a veteran member from Key West and principal opponent of the antibookie bill, with offering to bribe two other legislators. Papy resigned to await his trial, was acquitted, and won reelection. Antigambling legislators had nothing to show for the session but a potent issue and a somewhat stronger bribery law.[12]

The 1947 session distinguished itself in one respect by refusing to take desperate steps to preserve the white primary, which the U.S. Supreme Court had finally declared unconstitutional in a 1944 Texas case. In Tallahassee, Sen. John E. Mathews Sr. of Jacksonville, who feared a potentially large black electorate at home, proposed that Florida follow South Carolina's eventually futile example and repeal all state election laws, allowing the Democratic Party to reestablish itself as a private club.[13] Other senators objected that this would result in massive election fraud; Mathews's two-hour summation ended with a vote of 31 to 4 against him. Among the four: Charley Johns.[14]

Mathews did persuade the Senate to approve a constitutional amendment requiring a literacy test for voting. All the other Southern states but Arkansas, Tennessee, and Texas used such tests, ingeniously interpreted, to disqualify even well-educated blacks. Florida voters, however, had rejected this in 1916 for reasons raised again in 1947: Many uneducated whites would be disenfranchised also. Collins voted for the literacy test but somehow escaped having to account for it during his subsequent campaigns and his rise to national prominence. A House committee killed the bill, as he may have assumed it would do. Mathews, meanwhile, was defeated for renomination in 1950, running a poor third. Defiant to the last, he published a campaign ad boasting in large type, "In Dixieland I'll take my stand." His defeat was attributed primarily to his support of the sales tax act of 1949. Sixteen months later, Gov. Fuller Warren appointed him to the Supreme Court.[15]

The white populations in a handful of rural Florida counties resorted to defiant registrars or Ku Klux Klan–style terrorism to suppress black registration, but most counties accepted the inevitable. In 1947, only 13 percent of Florida's voting-age Negroes were registered voters, the same ratio as in South Carolina. By 1952, black enrollment reached 33 percent of those eligible, the highest in the South, and in 1966 it was estimated at 62 percent, second in the South only to Tennessee. Florida was "an oasis of sorts in what otherwise might be classed as a political desert so far as Negro suffrage is concerned."[16] Florida politicians began to learn the difficult skill of soliciting black votes discreetly. At a Gainesville forum for black voters in 1950, another white candidate nervously asked Ralph Turlington whether he planned to shake hands. When Turlington confided that he did, the other man said, "Well, I will, too."[17]

If Florida was resigned to black voting, desegregation of education remained unthinkable despite the U.S. Supreme Court having already made clear that states could not bar blacks from law schools and other graduate programs even if they offered, as Florida did, to finance their education elsewhere.[18] Nonetheless, Florida and fourteen other Southern states agreed in 1948 to jointly subsidize a system of regional universities that Caldwell said would be the "finest in the country" but were plainly intended only for blacks. The plan evaporated after the U.S. Senate refused by a one-vote margin to approve a House-passed resolution of support.[19]

Florida's 1948 gubernatorial campaign was shaping up as the familiar free-for-all. Collins had considered it, although he wrote a friend in Seattle that he was thinking of not running for anything again. "The political road has many rough spots, and I don't like the prospect of a political career," he said.[20]

McCarty was eager to run. The prospect of a Collins candidacy ended when their circle of mutual friends informally nominated McCarty during a football weekend at Jacksonville in the fall of 1947. Though McCarty had the advantage of being a University of Florida alumnus, Collins had misgivings about him. "For a long, long time I have been telling him that he should get around more, see more people and warm up to them," Collins wrote to a friend. "He is getting out, but I still don't think he is nearly as aggressive as he should be."[21]

There was something about McCarty—citrus grower, cattleman, and war hero—that made even his admirers wonder how he eventually did get elected. George Smathers, the fast-rising congressman who would defeat Pepper in 1950, remarked in 1948 that McCarty, though the best-qualified candidate, was losing ground because he would not ask even his own friends to support him, tending to take them for granted. Collins and McCarty were so close that McCarty often stayed at the Grove on his visits to Tallahassee. "And yet there was a distance between Dan and Roy. There was a distance between Dan and most anyone," said Verle Pope, a mutual friend destined for a luminous career in the state Senate.[22] McCarty nonetheless ran a strong second in a nine-man field. The leader was Fuller Warren, a garrulous glad-hander who had run for governor once before. Warren ran well in the smaller, more rural, counties, while McCarty carried the Miami area along with most of the east coast.[23]

Florida governors typically lost influence by the ends of their terms and were unable or unwilling to influence their succession. But Warren detected Caldwell trying to help McCarty and made it an issue in the runoff campaign. He accused McCarty of being Caldwell's agent as well as the "candidate of the Southeast Coast." After narrowly defeating McCarty—the margin was 23,216 votes—Warren romped in November over a token Republican with 83.4 percent of the vote, an enduring record.[24]

Warren made two famous campaign promises: to get cows and horses off Florida's highways and to veto any general sales tax. He kept only the first. Collins voted to repeal the open-range law, twenty-five people having died in collisions with livestock during the previous two years. Johns voted no.[25] But the sales tax Warren had opposed was enacted a few months later. As they collected it from customers, many merchants segregated the proceeds in countertop cigar boxes and jars labeled "Pennies for Fuller."

Warren had spent virtually all his forty-three years plotting to be governor without planning how he would use the office. Warned by Caldwell that the state was about to exhaust its wartime surplus, Warren realized the state needed to increase its revenue by as much as 50 percent. Some legislators feared the government would have to shut down at the start of the fiscal year on October 1, 1949.[26] Addressing the Legislature in April, Warren boldly recommended sixteen new or increased taxes on commercial lodgings, banks, phosphate mining, forest products and timber lands, utilities, insurance premiums, small loan licenses, intangibles, amusements, real estate and mortgage transactions, corporate stock, and on the gross receipts of retail businesses. The poor were already taxed enough, Warren said; now it should be the turn of Florida's most powerful interests. "I trust you will listen politely to the lobbyists, and then vote according to your conscience," he concluded. "Let us so devote ourselves to our duty that if the State of Florida should endure for a thousand years, men will say this was the finest session of the Legislature."[27]

Warren's attempt to identify with Winston Churchill did not awe the lobbyists or the Legislature, which killed his entire tax program. Legislators left with the budget so deeply in the red that Warren would obviously have to recall them to enact a sales tax. (The constitution prohibited deficit spending.) Warren consented to the tax at a secret meeting with Collins and other leaders including Sen. William A. Shands of Gainesville, one of his rivals in the 1948 campaign, who had lost votes to Warren over the sales tax issue. Wotitzky, another participant, recalled that the meeting took place in a house amidst a Central Florida orange grove and that Warren said, "I'll go along with it, but don't call it a sales tax."[28]

The forbidden words did not pass Warren's lips when he addressed the Legislature in joint session on September 7, reading a speech that he had asked three Capitol reporters to write for him. The address opened and closed with the biblical admonition, "Where there is no vision, the people perish." Warren urged the legislators to raise at least $55 million but said nothing even to imply to whose pockets vision might lead them. As he knew, a joint House-Senate committee had already recommended a sales tax of three cents on the dollar with enough exemptions to stifle his conscience. Many of the details, including the specific exemptions, were decided in private at the residence of Supreme Court Justice B. K. Roberts, a close friend whom Warren had appointed to the court six days before the session convened, and who counted sales tax advocate Edward Ball as a client and best friend. The possibility that the court might have to rule on the sales tax apparently concerned no one.[29]

Collins, having defended the $240 million budget, was duty-bound to support the sales tax. He tried unsuccessfully to trim the rate to two cents on the dollar and to eliminate most of the proposed exemptions. Warren, still saying nothing in public about the tax, was privately threatening and bribing reluctant legislators over roads and patronage. The tax finally passed on September 24, with major exemptions including groceries, medicines, clothing costing less than $10, and farm machinery. On final passage there was the by-now familiar split: Collins yes, Johns no. "I voted 'aye,'" Collins explained, "because it is imperative that the state have additional revenue to carry forward a progressive program." But he conceded that "This bill has many errors, and will be difficult and expensive to administer."[30] More than a half century later, the sales tax, now six cents on the dollar with some higher local rates and hundreds of additional exemptions, remains the state's primary revenue source. It accounts for roughly three-fourths of general revenue.[31]

The joint committee also recommended an income tax. The Senate agreed—Collins voted yes—but it was unheard in the House. Warren let the sales tax become law without his signature, insisting that his campaign pledge had been to veto a "general" sales tax, not the "limited" one on his desk.[32]

Warren's administration went downhill from there, beginning with the disclosure that three friends each had secretly contributed some $150,000 or more to his campaign—for which he had reported receiving only $12,241—and that he had given them almost complete control of his patronage. They were C. V. Griffin, a citrus grower, who revealed the seamy story after falling out with Warren; Louis Wolfson, a Jacksonville industrialist who had also paid Warren's living expenses for a year while he campaigned; and William H. J. Johnston, an executive of four Florida dog tracks and a Chicago horse track. Johnston's involvement interested the Greater Miami Crime Commission and the U.S. Senate's Committee on Organized Crime, chaired by Estes Kefauver of Tennessee, which suspected him of being an ally of mobster Al Capone.[33] Warren defied Kefauver's witness subpoena on the thin ground that it intruded on state's rights, called the senator a "headline-hunting hypocrite," and challenged him to a public debate on the State Capitol steps, a stunt that the *Tampa Morning Tribune* denounced as "the despairing dirge of a deflated demagogue."[34]

The 1951 session responded by enacting what for a time was the nation's model state campaign finance code, dubbed the "Who Gave It, Who Got It" act. It set strict reporting requirements for contributions and expenses and put a $1,000 limit on individual contributions.[35]

The investigations exposed sheriffs who were tolerating gambling. Warren reluctantly suspended five of them under pressure from the press, the public, and the Legislature. One was Broward County sheriff Walter Clark, who admitted to the Kefauver committee that he owned part of a firm that was in the numbers racket and had a federal license for slot machines. "I was elected on the liberal ticket, and the people want it [gambling] and they enjoy it," he said. "I let them have what they want for the tourists down there."[36]

Holland had suspended Clark on similar grounds in 1942, but the Senate reinstated him and he was reelected twice after that. The Senate upheld his suspension by Warren, but the governor infuriated the press and many legislators by appointing the son-in-law of another of the suspended sheriffs to replace his father-in-law and by subsequently reinstating Dade sheriff Jimmy Sullivan and two others without waiting for the Senate to vote on their cases. There was an outcry for Warren's impeachment, but the House tabled the resolution.[37]

Warren became so vitriolic at his critics that Collins refused his request to introduce him at a Tallahassee function where he heard that Warren intended to denounce the management of the *Tallahassee Democrat* and other local people "who have been my friends and supporters for years."[38]

Instinctively, Warren was Florida's most liberal governor. As a young lawyer, he had helped persuade the pardon board to spare the life of a black man unfairly convicted and condemned for rape. He favored education and pensions, he was pro-labor and sympathetic to the poor, and he vetoed bills to end wartime rent control and publicly identify welfare recipients. But his weaknesses with regard to patronage and administration meant that the campaign to succeed him would be largely about restoring "good government" to Tallahassee.[39]

Warren, who had seen only six of his twenty-four recommendations passed by the 1949 session, managed just one memorable success out of the 1951 session: an enactment prohibiting the Ku Klux Klan from wearing masks in public places. Once again, Collins voted yes—he was a key supporter—and Johns voted no.[40]

Most Southerners had lost respect for the "hooded hoodlums, covered cowards and sheeted jerks," as Warren, briefly a Klansman himself in his youth, described them. Desegregation was another matter, making it a flash of courage on Warren's part to veto a 1951 appropriations restriction denying funds to any state college that integrated during the two years the budget would be in force.[41]

The House wrote it into the spending bill in response to a lawsuit filed by Virgil Hawkins and four other blacks who had been denied admission to graduate schools at the University of Florida.[42] Legislators were also incensed at members of the statewide Florida Student Government Association for adopting a resolution opposing segregation. Though the student governments at Florida State and the University of Florida repudiated the resolution as soon as it was publicized—Florida's also withdrew from the association—FSU student president Reubin Askew defended the vote he had cast.[43] Askew kept his post, but two editors of the student newspaper, the *Florida Flambeau*, were forced to resign over a column saying (apparently inaccurately) that a few black students were already taking instruction at FSU and Florida. FSU also canceled an exchange of games with an Illinois university that intended to bring several black players to Tallahassee.[44]

The vetoed restriction passed the Senate as part of a conference committee compromise on the overall budget, which Collins supported and Johns opposed. Warren's veto message said the restriction would likely be declared unconstitutional; if not, it would do "incalculable damage" to students and defame the state. Having said all that, he appointed the outspokenly racist Mathews to the Supreme Court just five months later, perhaps as compensation for the Senate seat he had lost on account of the sales tax.[45] The Legislature had adjourned when Warren signed the veto, precluding any attempt to override it.

In January 1952, Warren violated strict taboos by serving lunch at the governor's mansion to a racially mixed delegation protesting the Christmas night bombing in Brevard County that had taken the lives of Harry T. Moore, the nation's first civil rights martyr, and his wife, Harriett. Warren said proudly that his hospitality was the first such "symbol of human relations" since the mansion had been built forty-six years before. But he also prematurely exonerated the Klan, which the FBI linked strongly to the crime.[46]

That was the last Florida heard from Warren's better angels. Four years later, he ran for governor again as a strident segregationist.

Chapter 7

A Bridesmaid Again

Collins became embroiled in a contentious local issue during the summer of the sales tax session. The game commission was proposing special privileges for the private preserves in and near Leon County, where hunting would be allowed at times when it was prohibited elsewhere. The plantations would be required to record data of interest to the commission's scientists, but this did not balance the public interest as most other hunters, politicians, and editorial writers saw it. They stormed the commission's public hearing; some legislators, arriving for the special session, threatened to abolish the agency. Collins, a lawyer for some of the plantation owners, was particularly friendly with one, Walter Edge, who had been a New Jersey governor, a senator, and ambassador to France. Collins wrote to Edge that the hearing was a "civic and political debacle" at which "frankly, it looked like many of those present were ready to fight the Civil War all over again." One of the most vocal objectors was a young lawyer in Caldwell's firm, Leo Foster, a rumored opponent to Collins in 1950.[1] "My chief worry," Edge replied, "is not the curtailment of shooting, but a fear that your activity in the 'Dam Yankees' [*sic*] behalf may have put you temporarily in an embarrassing position. . . . Perhaps if various Florida plantations go on the market, some of our critics may realize the old axiom about killing the goose that laid the golden egg."[2]

It was a different Caldwell law partner, Julius Parker, a recent past president of the Florida State Bar Association, who opposed Collins in the 1950 Democratic primary. Though there had long been a political dimension to the rivalry between Tallahassee's leading law firms, Caldwell told Collins and mutual friends that he had tried to discourage Parker. The senator was skeptical, however, that Parker would run without his partners' consent. He took the threat seriously. "My biggest problem," Collins wrote to a fellow senator, "is to get my friends to realize that it will take a hard campaign."[3] He was out of practice, having had no opponent since 1940, conceded that he had "not been very political in mingling with the 'boys,'" and had offended some voters over various issues. He asked some of his friends in the Senate to solicit favorable editorials in their local papers so that he might reprint them in an advertisement. "Tallahasseans are very conscious of what outsiders think of their legislators," he said. "Naturally, I don't want the suggestion to come directly from me."[4]

His campaigning was rustier than he realized. A friend passed along a warning that some Leon County voters "felt that you assumed an air of superiority when passing them on the street" and sensed that they mattered to him only at election time. "I doubt seriously that this is true," he added, "but it may be helpful news to you. . . . [I]t may please you to know that they consider your opponent more 'high hat' than yourself."[5]

The campaign was as rough as Collins had feared. Foster made an issue of "the millionaire plantation absentee owners whom the present senator has so faithfully represented" and to whom he had sold out "for a handful of silver or a dove-shoot." He criticized Collins relentlessly for representing the Seaboard Air Line Railroad, the Southeastern Telephone Company, and Western Union, which were regulated by the state Railroad and Public Utilities Commission. "I do not believe it is humanly possible for a man to fairly represent the corporation which pays him, and the people who elect him," Parker said.[6]

Collins took offense, as he would again in his 1954 campaign for governor, because he thought himself to be highly ethical. He had declined an invitation to represent the State Welfare Board, saying he would not work for any state agency so long as he was a legislator.[7] He saw no conflict of interest, however, in representing private clients before a state agency. "Is he saying I have been doing something *wrong*?" he once asked of a friend, who replied that while such conduct was legal in Florida, federal law prohibited members of Congress from practicing before regulatory agencies. Since 1976, the Florida Constitution has contained a similar ban for state legislators.[8]

To Collins's luck and Parker's misfortune, a salesman for a legal directory showed Ausley a draft listing for Caldwell's firm that identified regulated clients such as the Greyhound bus company, two whiskey distillers, and one of the largest New York banks. Collins gleefully publicized it.[9]

When Parker made an issue of the sales tax, Collins asserted that he would have been "almost a traitor" to oppose it, considering that Leon County's economy depended on the state budget.[10] Collins sent a personal letter to Leon teachers, saying he wanted their votes more than anyone else's. The file copy bore a penciled notation, "written to all white teachers."[11]

"This is the messiest race I have ever had," Collins wrote to a former senator five weeks before the primary. He worried about Mary Call, whose fourth pregnancy was turning out to be more difficult than the others. "[P]olitics and new babies," he remarked, "don't go too well together."[12]

The pregnancy and the campaign both ended happily. Three days after the birth of Sarah Darby Collins, Collins overwhelmed Parker, 7,775 votes to 2,251, carrying every precinct. A third candidate polled only 578.[13]

"We are spoiling her [Darby] very badly," Collins wrote to a friend three months later. "After all, having a baby this late entitles us to do a little spoiling, I think."[14] Soon after, Collins recklessly took his family to their St. Teresa beach cottage to ride out a hurricane. Luckily, it made landfall nearly two hundred miles west of there and killed no one.[15]

His campaign scars took time to heal. Collins resented Parker for having "used every device known to a character assassin," as he put it in reply to a congratulatory telegram from U.S. Sen. Spessard Holland. To another friend, he wrote that "the splendid vote of confidence" was comforting and that with time, "doubtless I will feel better" toward Parker. In time, he did.[16]

Collins had scarcely settled down from the 1950 Senate campaign when he began to think seriously about running for governor in 1952. He encouraged public speculation by neither confirming nor denying it. Columnist Allen Morris wrote that a potential Collins candidacy was a reason why McCarty, the runner-up in 1952, was already "running harder for governor now than at the same time before the 1948 campaign."[17] Collins wrote that "a good many people are urging me to get into it" and that if he were ever to run for governor, "this would be the logical time." He added that it would be "impossible" for him to run against his friend McCarty but did nothing to discourage another friend from trying to persuade McCarty that he had had his chance and should now let Collins have his. "You can say nothing too good about LeRoy Collins and get any argument from me," McCarty replied to the friend in a letter that nonetheless made it plain that he intended to run even if Collins did also.[18]

John McCarty, Dan's younger brother, sent Collins a long, handwritten plea to stay out. "With the organization we have, the race we ran and the lessons we learned, plus the many new friends and supporters we have made, there is no logical explanation for Dan to withdraw now," he said. Collins, he implied, was being recruited by supporters of some other candidate who would be scheming to split McCarty's vote. Furthermore, he wrote bluntly, Collins would be as relatively unknown in 1952 as Dan McCarty had been in 1948. "For instance," McCarty said, "out of five papers that I asked to write friendly editorials for you in your [1950] race, three answered that they did not know you, nor know what to write, and the other two did not know you but would write at our request."[19]

"You may regard me as being immodest," Collins replied, "but a lot of people seem to feel that I can make a good Governor, secondly, that I can make a good candidate, and thirdly, that Dan can't win."[20] Some of Collins's family felt that McCarty was breaking an unwritten agreement that McCarty would run in 1948 and Collins in 1952. At the time, none of them thought McCarty would lose in 1948. If Collins deferred again, he would be forty-seven in 1956, and they feared his time would have passed.[21]

Collins continued to advise friends and family to count him neither out nor in, writing to one that, "this thing is building up more and more as time goes by." But there was no more correspondence in that vein after Collins and McCarty attended another November University of Florida football game. McCarty used the occasion to persuade his Tallahassee friend to be the bridesmaid yet again.[22]

Collins said nothing publicly for a long time. In July 1951, Allen Morris reported without attribution that Collins had decided to stay out of the race because it would be unfair to his family and law partners if he ran.[23] Collins confirmed his decision in a letter to Walter Edge, who expressed deep disappointment.[24] In September, Collins formally announced that he would not run and would support McCarty. "He stands for clean, efficient and progressive government," Collins said. "These are the principles I have always tried to fight for in politics. Further he has been a warm personal friend for many years. And too he seems determined to make an aggressive campaign to the people, and I believe he will win."[25]

Chapter 8

Triumph and Tragedy

McCarty's 1948 campaign had impressed so many politicians that he drew only two serious rivals four years later.[1] They were Alto Adams of Fort Pierce, who had resigned from the Florida Supreme Court to run for governor, and Brailey Odham, who had thrown the 1947 House into turmoil by shaking his finger at Bernie Papy and declaring, "That man offered me $500 and a case of scotch to take a walk on the bookie wire-service bill."[2] Despite the support of Edward Ball, who disliked McCarty and had urged Adams into the race against his fellow towns-man, Adams ran a poor third in the primary with 17.5 percent of the vote. McCarty, at 48.9 percent, fell just 7,822 votes short of making history by winning without a runoff.[3]

Odham, a large man with inexhaustible energy, relied on a strik-ingly effective radio technique. He bought time on local stations for "talkathons" that often ran twenty-four hours or longer. Odham took written questions from the audience and by telephone and answered them on the air. He liked to challenge his rivals to share a program with him and to goad their local supporters by name, hoping to lure them into arguments at his makeshift storefront studios. "Odham has merged the radio 'fireside' chat and the radio quiz program into an ef-fective method of reaching the people," wrote a reporter who marveled that Odham never ducked a question. A favorite Odham theme was that McCarty was a latecomer to the fight against the racing lobby and to other reforms Odham advocated.[4]

Odham's diligent research had discovered McCarty's cosponsorship of a 1937 House bill to decide primary elections in a fashion analo-gous to the national Electoral College. Each county a candidate carried would count for twice as many unit votes as its seats in the Florida House of Representatives. Collins had opposed that bill, which was modeled on a rural regime unique to Georgia, and it did not pass either house.[5] Fifteen years later, Odham thundered that McCarty had been willing to allow "three of the state's smallest counties [to] nullify the votes of any of the largest counties in the state," but the attack did not seem to hurt McCarty.[6] Odham broke other ground in that campaign as the first Florida gubernatorial candidate to meet with a group of Negro voters. Though he defended segregation, he promised them he would appoint a black person to the Board of Control.[7]

Odham surged in the runoff campaign, winning 104,211 more votes than he had in the primary. McCarty gained only 22,733, but they were enough. His majority of 384,200 represented 53.3 percent of the combined vote. He lost only sixteen of the sixty-seven counties and only two of the ten most populous.[8] The campaign had been sufficiently bitter that the *Tampa Tribune*, a moderately conservative newspaper that endorsed McCarty, accused Odham of "a growing attempt to put class against class." Jim Powell, its Tallahassee correspondent, wrote that it had been an "intensely bitter and violently partisan" race.[9]

McCarty paid a high price for his victory. Charles Ausley, who campaigned with him in North Florida, confided to his son that the candidate had suffered a heart attack, probably before the primary, that was never revealed to the public.[10] Though McCarty managed to conceal that, the Associated Press reported that he lost twenty-five pounds in the campaign.[11]

Collins, meanwhile, developed serious throat trouble and worried that it might be cancer. The morning after his son's graduation from high school, the family left by car for the Mayo Clinic in Minnesota. On receiving a good report from the clinic, Collins took his family to Chicago to celebrate. Father and son went to the theater, but Collins warned the boy not to tell his mother because the play was, by Collins's standards, "kind of risqué." It was the musical *Guys and Dolls*.[12]

The general election was another formality; the Republican polled barely 25 percent. McCarty was already planning his administration. Collins advised him to not depend on job-seekers and to recruit his choice of "top-grade, able and loyal" people to run his agencies. "You are going to have to go out and draft them and talk them into making substantial sacrifices," Collins wrote. He warned that legislators were "cocked and primed" by the Warren debacles and that McCarty should take the initiative in reforming the government.[13]

McCarty was inaugurated on January 6, 1953, vowing that "I will not tolerate lax law enforcement at any level. I will remove from public office any official who breaks faith with the people and is unworthy of public trust."[14]

It was his last major public speech. Seven weeks later, McCarty was hospitalized with a heart attack. This one could not be kept secret, but his doctor said it was not severe and his condition was "good."[15] His brother John, thirty-seven, a lawyer at Fort Pierce, said he would be his unpaid aide until the governor recovered.[16] But McCarty was still convalescing when the Legislature convened five weeks later. A joint session heard Secretary of State R. A. Gray read McCarty's message, which began, "Events of the past several weeks have proved beyond question that I am one governor who *really has* a heart."[17]

McCarty was in a fighting mood. He demanded that the Legislature fulfill his campaign promise to make dog tracks pay the same taxes as horse tracks. Otherwise, he would try to abolish them. "If they can continuously thwart the will of the people, then their power is too great for the good of this state," he said. He called for a new constitution incorporating one essential change: His illness dramatized why the secretary of state, as "a constitutional officer duly elected by all the people," should be the governor's emergency successor. This was not welcome advice to a Senate whose president, Charley E. Johns, was already Florida's ex officio governor-in-waiting.[18]

Johns had clinched the title over a rival Collins preferred, fulfilling a dream Johns had cherished since an older brother, Everett Markley Johns, had died while waiting to serve as president twenty years before.[19] Now Johns wanted to use the power to create a joint legislative committee to investigate crime, corruption, and suspected subversive activity. He said it was to "get these racketeers and gamblers wriggling around our back doors," but to Collins and some other senators it brought to mind the controversial tactics of U.S. Sen. Joseph McCarthy, who was at the height of his reign over a similar investigative committee. Collins objected that the Johns panel would be a "snake committee" to "grovel around in the rocks to attack unsuspecting people." The debates were bitter, with Johns denouncing his opponents as "apostles of the status quo, defenders of thieves" who were willing to ignore "the stink of corruption [that] smells to high heaven," but he was defeated, 19 votes to 17, an uncommon embarrassment for a Senate president.[20]

McCarty, meanwhile, was winning much of what he wanted, including the dog track tax increase and university status for Florida A&M College, but not his proposed commission to oversee property taxes. Johns killed the gubernatorial succession amendment by sending it to three committees.[21]

McCarty, who had kept mostly to the governor's mansion after leaving the hospital, made brief visits to his office during the session's last weeks. During one, he vetoed a bill by Johns to set racing dates for Miami's ferociously competitive horse tracks. Collins helped sustain the veto.[22] Two weeks later, a front-page *Orlando Sentinel* article said McCarty's appearance had been intended to thwart a Senate plot to declare him incapacitated and make Johns acting governor. Johns and McCarty denied knowledge of such a scheme, which Attorney General Richard Ervin said would have failed in any event because only the governor could declare himself temporarily disabled.[23]

Several weeks after the session, the Game and Fresh Water Fish Commission shifted its insurance policies, worth $40,000 a year in premiums, from Johns's insurance company to a Tallahassee agency whose owners had worked for McCarty in 1948.[24]

Collins, who had been McCarty's major Senate floor manager, won his second "Most Valuable Senator" award in the press poll conducted by the *St. Petersburg Times*. The honor for the House went to Speaker C. Farris Bryant of Ocala, his second also.[25]

In mid-July, McCarty's doctor forecast his "complete recovery" but conceded it was taking longer than expected. McCarty, still keeping mostly to the mansion, could not avoid the pressures of office. A new law made possession of a federal gambling tax stamp proof on its face that the bearer was breaking state gambling laws, and a *Tampa Tribune* editorial demanded that McCarty deal with several sheriffs who were reluctant to arrest stampholders. A series of articles focused on Jacksonville, where the newspaper charged that prostitution and bolita, an illegal numbers racket based on Cuba's national lottery, were flourishing openly. McCarty summoned the Duval County sheriff and the local prosecutors to Tallahassee for tongue-lashings and called on eight other sheriffs to report what they were or were not doing to harass stampholders. It was McCarty's first formal appearance in nearly two months, and the press reported that he still looked pale and thin but spoke in a strong voice.[26] Prosecutions began, but the Florida Supreme Court declared the stampholder law unconstitutional a year later.[27]

Collins and Bryant told friends that they would not run for reelection to the Legislature in 1954. It signified that they were preparing to run for governor in 1956. Collins confided to a Miami journalist that while he was not yet planning a campaign, "the chances that I will be in there at post time seem brighter as time goes by."[28]

There was keen local interest in a site for a new governor's mansion. After only forty-seven years, the old one was beyond reasonable repair. Collins withdrew from the site election committee because the Grove, though not under consideration, could be affected by what happened to the mansion next door. McCarty and the committee favored a site next to the Florida State University president's residence more than a mile away, an idea that was instantly unpopular in downtown Tallahassee.[29]

Early in September, McCarty made his first public appearance in seven months to lead a Shrine parade in an open red convertible. He caught a cold; it turned into pneumonia that sent him back to Tallahassee Memorial Hospital. Five days later, doctors announced a "disturbance of cardiac rhythm" and pronounced him in critical condition. Though they said the next day that he seemed to be improving, Collins and other close friends maintained a vigil at the hospital. At Starke, 145 miles away, a Florida Highway Patrol lieutenant turned up to stand watch with the governor-in-waiting. That night, with his family gathered by his bed, McCarty spoke briefly to his wife. Three minutes later, he died. The doctors said his weakened heart could not cope with the pneumonia.[30] At forty-one years old, he was the first Florida governor to die in office since April 1, 1865, when John Milton, having said that "death would be preferable to reunion," put a gun to his head.[31]

Chapter 9

"Do Not Hesitate"

Floridians instantly began speculating as to who would run for the remaining two years of McCarty's term. The press expected that Odham and John McCarty would. Reporters discounted Johns; the constitution said a legislator could not take another office "during the term for which he was elected" if he had voted to create the office or raise its pay, as Johns had done when the session raised the governor's salary from $12,000 to $15,000 a year. Johns's Senate term ran through 1956.[1]

Johns, the son of a deputy sheriff who had been killed in the line of duty, had dropped out of college to help support his family and worked as a railroad conductor before prospering in the insurance business at Starke, a rural community dependent on farming and on the Florida State Prison in neighboring Union County.[2] Until McCarty's death, no one had considered him a potential governor. But now he had the office and was not letting the fact that he was only *acting* governor—a distinction promptly emphasized by the Supreme Court—restrain how he used it. He promptly froze most purchasing and implied that he might replace McCarty's appointees. McCarty's five Road Board members quickly said they intended to stay. Four days later, Johns said that all of McCarty's major appointees should offer to resign and that "if the ones I think need to be replaced don't turn in their resignations, I'm going to ask for them." Johns also hinted that he might ask the Supreme Court to rule the pay raise illegal, clearing him to run for governor.[3]

McCarty's family and friends argued over who should run to finish his term. John McCarty said there would be a candidate to "carry out the Dan McCarty program," perhaps himself. Odham said that he likely would run with the same aim. Johns made it obvious that he would run if ruled eligible and took McCarty's comments as a cue to denounce the formation of a "political machine" among McCarty's appointees, whose resignations were now "imperative." The press called his attention to a 1934 Supreme Court ruling that a governor could suspend major appointees only for alleged misconduct. To Johns, however, it meant that he could replace the McCarty people on pretexts; there would be no session of the Senate to consider the suspensions until after the election.[4]

Johns said that he would either forgo the governor's salary or collect it only at the old rate. The campaign began, unofficially, with Johns issuing a program heavy on roads. He then set about systematically removing seventeen McCarty appointees including the entire Road Board, racing and turnpike commissions, and the hotel commissioner, all of them prominent citizens, on transparently thin charges of malfeasance or extravagance in office. Johns's new racing commissioners promptly gave a South Florida horse track some of the benefits that McCarty's veto had eliminated.[5]

Johns made Florida forget Fuller Warren. "For official arrogance and political callousness, the Johns action is unmatched in the recent history of the governorship," said a *Tampa Tribune* editorial. Among major dailies, only the *Orlando Sentinel* defended Johns.[6]

John McCarty, Odham, and Johns worked the crowds at the University of Florida homecoming, where McCarty all but declared his candidacy. Odham formally announced his three days later, saying, "the rascals are back." Collins said nothing on the record, but a *St. Petersburg Times* article that bore his fingerprints asserted that Dan McCarty's friends and supporters were not counting Collins out. The article disparaged the younger McCarty, saying that he had not discussed his chances "coldly and objectively" with anyone, that he had lost badly when he ran for St. Lucie County tax assessor, and that he had "offended many people" while assisting his ailing brother in Tallahassee.[7]

Behind the scenes, however, the McCarty faction was stubborn. Even Collins's law partners decided that he should defer for a third time. In a telephone call, Mary Call confided that news to close friends, Sen. Verle Pope of St. Johns County, and his wife, Edith. Collins was deeply hurt, she told them, and so was she. The Popes summoned them to St. Augustine, where Collins showed Pope the draft of a statement declining to run. "I took the damn thing and just tore it up in little teeny pieces," Pope recalled. "You don't fight hard enough to suit me," he told Collins, insisting that he run no matter who else did.[8]

That was typical of Pope, who became known as the "Lion of St. Johns" for his legislative battles for fair apportionment and against special interests. The son of deaf parents who taught him sign language before he learned to speak, Pope developed a distinctive booming voice. One legend describes a colleague mocking Pope during debate because his shirttail was hanging out. Without a word, Pope dropped his trousers, tucked the shirttail in, and buckled up. That was the end of the other senator's bill.[9]

Collins said he was worried less about McCarty than about Odham, whom he did not think anyone could defeat. Pope admired Odham for having "the guts to say what he thinks," but he told Collins the voters would see that "he doesn't know government and you do." At Pope's insistence, Collins telephoned Dan McCarty's widow to tell her that he intended to run. Whatever she said in reply seemed to please him.[10]

There was another reason for Collins to hesitate: Winning would likely give him only two years and one legislative session as governor. There was no self-evident exception for acting governors from the prohibition on a governor succeeding himself. The ambiguity discouraged Bryant, a potentially strong candidate, from running in 1954. He chose to wait for the anticipated shot at an open full term in 1956.[11]

Collins had discussed his ambivalence and the McCarty problem with Walter Edge, who was visiting his hunting plantation, Sunny Farm. "Listen to me," Edge said. "Do not hesitate, do not vacillate, do not procrastinate. . . . It is a great job being governor."[12]

Once again a University of Florida football weekend at Jacksonville was the venue for a political showdown. Collins told McCarty that he intended to run; if McCarty ran also they would "have to let the people decide it."[13] It took time for the ultimatum to sink in. "John does not seem aware of his limitations and appears determined to see the matter through," Collins wrote to a friend a few days later.[14] A week after the game, another unattributed article for which he was the obvious source declared that Collins "definitely will run." A few days later, McCarty met Collins again at Orlando and pledged publicly to support him.[15]

Odham was the first to file qualifying papers, which the secretary of state accepted despite the opinion of some Johns supporters that the acting governor had inherited the entire remainder of the McCarty term. A legislator who disliked Johns filed a test case in the Supreme Court. Johns, never subtle, chose the moment to propose one of the justices as a successor to the late

University of Florida president J. Hillis Miller. That idea went nowhere, but it was not the last of Johns's attempts to influence the university.[16]

On December 11, the court called unanimously for an election in 1954 but did not say whether the pay raise barred Johns from running or whether the winner would be eligible for a full term in 1956. On that day, Johns suspended the entire McCarty Road Board to clear the way for trading highways for votes and for shaking down campaign contributions from contractors. The board Johns appointed soon began buying a type of asphalt that the McCarty board had rejected as too costly.[17]

Collins announced his candidacy the day following the court's ruling, saying that "I hate despotism and dictatorship in any form." The Associated Press report described Collins as "handsome," an adjective not awarded to Odham or Johns. *Tampa Tribune* capital reporter Jim Powell paid tribute to Johns's pork-barrel populism. "No kidding," he wrote, "the man is good. When he gets to orating on his favorite topics, like checks for the old folks and the teachers, the lightning crashes and the thunder rolls."[18]

Bryant hedged. He filed a lawsuit asking for a ruling that the governor elected in 1954 could not run again two years later. The judge ruled otherwise. But there was to be no final answer because the Supreme Court pronounced the issue premature. Justice B. K. Roberts wrote separately that there were "abundant reasons" why the 1954 winner should be ineligible to succeed himself.[19]

Bryant, playing what seemed to be the safe card, chose to wait until 1956. Collins gambled, filing his qualifying papers the day after Christmas. "The need for a new governor is now, not two years from now," he said. Johns said that he would not seek reelection in 1956 even if the court said he could. Collins ducked the question, saying that the two-year term would be time enough for everything he hoped to do.[20]

Johns invoked a clause in the budget to suspend the governor's pay raise on the doubtful premise that the state might run short of money. It was too late to change his mind when the Supreme Court ruled in February, 5 to 2, that he was eligible to run regardless of the salary because it was embodied in a two-year appropriation, not permanent law.[21]

There were no nuisance candidates this time, making it the first election since 1920 when only three people contested the Democratic nomination for governor. Not since 1876, under a prior constitution, had an acting governor tried to elect himself; he had lost. For the first time, next-door neighbors were running against each other for governor: Johns from the executive mansion and Collins from the Grove. Their twelve-year-old daughters, Markleyann Johns and Mary Call Collins, rode their bicycles to school together, attended the same sixth-grade class at Sealey Memorial Elementary School, and maintained their friendship throughout what became a bitter campaign.[22]

Johns returned to Starke on March 5, two months before the primary, for a campaign kickoff rally that kept ten men busy frying three thousand pounds of fish. He bought thirty minutes on a thirty-two-station radio hookup but was only halfway through his text when the time ran out because Sen. Scott Dillworth Clarke of Monticello had used up the rest with his warm-up speech. Clarke, whose first public speech was at the 1902 rededication of a Confederate war memorial, looked over the exuberant audience at Starke and declared to them and the state at large: "Ladies and gentlemen, this is a fine crowd. I haven't seen a crowd this large since the last lynching in Jefferson County."[23]

Clarke's flip allusion to the ugliest aspect of racism reflected the clearest of differences between Johns and Collins. Both were from North Florida, but Johns appealed to agrarian regions where strong Populist instincts were deeply entwined with racism. Collins represented the moderate, increasingly urban "business progressive" wing of the Democratic Party, as political scientists and historians sometimes described it. Collins was the more fiscally conservative but had the more liberal image. Two universities and the seat of state government gave him a constituency that was more moderate than the region.[24]

But first, there was Odham, "the angry man in a hurry," as a newspaper profiled him.[25] Odham, the only candidate who had run statewide, was better known than Collins and appealed to a progressive constituency they could not afford to split.[26] Odham respected Collins but pulled no punches. He reprised Parker's 1950 attacks by assailing Collins for his "special interest" clients, for sponsoring pay raises for members of the Railroad and Public Utilities Commission before whom he practiced, and for representing the plantation owners.[27] Odham's signature issue was to abolish the Milk Commission, which fixed prices at a higher level than the unregulated market in Georgia.[28]

Collins replied that it was "logical" for big corporations to want "top-grade" counsel. "My law firm also represents the Boy and Girl Scouts, a church or two, and numerous widows and orphans," he said. Because he and

Odham differed little if at all on the Milk Commission or other fundamental reforms, Collins tried to portray Odham as a reckless and ineffective critic. "His thinking is destructive, not constructive," Collins said. "It's good to have a few men like that around the legislature, but you don't entrust the future of your state to them."[29]

The Johns campaign, apparently thinking Collins the greater danger, attacked him from the far right, asserting that he belonged to the world federalist movement, had voted against antisubversive legislation, and was "Ex-Senator Claude Pepper's candidate for Governor as part of Pepper's preparation to run for the Senate again in 1956." Echoing Odham's criticism of Collins's law clientele, Johns advertisements called Collins "father of the ten-cent telephone call."[30] Johns relentlessly denounced a Collins proposal to create a property tax oversight commission, calling it a threat to the homestead exemption. He said that "hand-picked commissioners [would] lower the assessments of the big utilities and rich plantation owners he represents and raise yours and mine."[31]

There was no truth to the Pepper connection, but it was fair to surmise that uniform tax assessments would deflate the relative benefit of homestead exemption. The world federalism issue, which dogged Collins in later campaigns, owed primarily to a single event in Tallahassee where he endorsed ticket sales for a dinner. No one ever documented that Collins had belonged to a world federalist organization.[32]

In a transparently contrived media event, Johns put on his old conductor's uniform, hopped a passenger train, and punched tickets for a day.[33]

Collins, who had dreaded the Odham radio talkathons, was relieved when Odham opted for fewer, shorter ones so that he could appear more on television, a medium that favored Collins.[34] Otherwise, the Collins campaign was not going well. Outside of Tallahassee, most voters were unfamiliar with him.[35] Apart from McCarty's immediate family, Collins was no special favorite of McCarty supporters elsewhere. Fund-raising, the part of politics Collins detested, was difficult against an incumbent. "You had to scratch it in small amounts," recalled John Germany, a volunteer supporter at Tampa. Collins tried to board with friends to spare the expense of hotels.[36]

Johns's incumbency lost some of its advantage when the attorney general warned that Florida's 1949 "Little Hatch Act," modeled on a strict federal statute, forbade people on public payroll from campaigning for anyone but themselves.[37] Much to Odham's disappointment, meanwhile, Collins was winning a large share of anti-Johns newspaper endorsements, including those of the *Miami Herald*, *St. Petersburg Times*, *Daytona Beach News-Journal*, and *Tampa Tribune*.[38]

Johns's loudest supporter was the *Orlando Sentinel*. Publisher Martin Andersen, a tireless booster for Orlando and Central Florida, had propositioned Johns bluntly when the acting governor came to visit: "What are you going to give me?" Johns promised more roads for the region and specifically the one Andersen wanted most, a shortcut from State Road 50 east of Orlando to the fast-developing Cocoa area south of Titusville, which would save eight congested miles of travel for the *Sentinel*'s circulation trucks. Johns had it under construction by May.[39] "It is one thing to believe in ideals in politics," said one of Andersen's editorials. "It is quite another to get results. Charley Johns is a result-getter, and the proven road-building friend of Orange County and Central Florida."[40] Johns eventually won the *Fort Lauderdale News*. He also had the *Palm Beach Post-Times*, the *Jacksonville Journal*, the *Pensacola News Journal*, and the eighteen other daily and weekly papers belonging to Perry Publications, a New York–based chain.

Collins accused Johns of promising too many roads. He loved to tell stories and anecdotes and had a favorite that he applied to Johns. It concerned a farmer who boasted of owning a bull that could outrun a freight train. When friends came to check, the farmer's hired hand said he had left that morning for Atlanta, New Orleans, San Francisco, Alaska, Chicago, New York, and Miami and would return that night. When the friends asked how that was possible in a single day, the hired man said, "Why, he's riding that fast bull." Collins said Johns was "riding a fast bull all over the state, promising roads he can't build." Collins also made an issue of Johns's support for the 1935 slot machine bill.[41]

Sectionalism became a strong factor. When a Dade County legislator announced that Collins and Odham had endorsed reapportionment of the rural-dominated Legislature, Johns committed himself only to "considerable study."[42] At Miami and in other urban areas, the Collins campaign relentlessly attacked Johns for his opposition to the anti-Klan bill. Trying to explain that vote to the Orlando Junior Chamber of Commerce, Johns said cryptically that his "first loyalty" had to be to "the people that sent me to the Legislature" and that he had worried that the antimask bill might be used against any secret society such as one to which he said he belonged. Responding to another persistent line of attack from Collins, Johns said he had opposed the

Minimum Foundation Program only because it required school superinten-
dents to have college degrees, which would "disenfranchise 98 percent of my
people from being county school superintendent."[43] (The Florida Supreme
Court eventually ruled the requirement unconstitutional. It also struck down
the anti- Klan act as overbroad.)

A month before the primary, Allen Morris forecast what few other journalists were willing to predict: a Johns-Collins runoff. He said Odham's campaign had become as dispirited as Collins's had been earlier.[44]

The campaign marked a transition from old-style Florida politics, when
candidates barnstormed the state with sound trucks, to a media and mass-
market strategy. Collins chartered an airplane.[45] One of the best ideas of the
campaign, which Bob Fokes, a Tallahassee lawyer, managed for Collins, was
to print its letterhead stationery with Collins's portrait occupying the reverse
side so that it could double as a campaign poster.[46]

Politicians from the rural, northern regions had long feared the possibility
of Dade County uniting behind a candidate.[47] On May 4, 1954, they saw it
begin to happen. Johns ran a pallid third in Dade, polling only 31,023 votes—
24 percent—compared to 54,661 for Collins and 43,345 for Odham. Statewide, Johns carried forty-eight of the sixty-seven counties, to only sixteen for
Collins and three for Odham, but he had majorities in only twenty-eight, all
of them small and rural. His cumulative vote of 255,787 was just 38.4 percent
of the total. Collins was close behind with 33.4 percent. Though Collins carried only two counties north of the Suwannee River, his own and neighboring Jefferson, he had pluralities in six of the ten largest counties. Johns led in
Hillsborough, Orange (home of the *Sentinel*), Escambia, and Duval.[48]

The count was still incomplete at 10:30 p.m., when Odham conceded that
he was eliminated, publicly endorsed Collins, and surprised him with a telephone call offering warmly to do "everything I can to get you elected." Collins
was elated. "My spirits are high, my hopes and confidence great," he said.[49]

Andersen's *Orlando Sentinel*, Johns's most indefatigable supporter, tried
to gloss over the situation with an erroneous claim that no first-primary leader ever had lost a subsequent gubernatorial runoff.[50] Johns was actually in
deep trouble: More than 400,000 people had voted against an incumbent
governor. Both finalists were North Florida natives, but one was now the
huge favorite of populous South Florida, and the other had only a precarious
lead.[51]

The rhetoric intensified. Johns belabored the tax commission issue to the point that one newspaper said it "apparently has become the principal issue" of the runoff.[52] Collins charged that notorious Tampa gambling racketeers were supporting Johns. He hit repeatedly at Johns's "political machine," and at allegations of payroll padding and overspending.[53]

Before the primary, Johns had refused to share a stage with Collins or Odham, heeding advice that he was neither man's match in debate. He disregarded the warnings when Miami television station WTVJ invited him and Collins to a live debate that would be broadcast over a statewide radio hookup. It turned into a disaster for Johns and the defining incident of the campaign.[54]

The Johns campaign scheduled a two-column advertisement in the *Miami Herald* edition of the day following the debate to boast that he had won it: "Well, Senator Collins . . . You asked for it on television last night—AND YOU GOT IT. You didn't look so good, Senator. Did you?"[55] Whoever placed the ad apparently did not know that the *Herald* would have an early edition on the streets before the debate began. During supper, Collins was alerted by telephone by someone at the newspaper.[56] Collins confronted Johns on camera. His voice was sharp but a smile played on his lips as he held up the newspaper and read from the ad in which "I find that I'm already convicted." Johns, flustered, said he hadn't known anything about the ad, which others had arranged. "The citizens of Florida know that's not Charley Johns," he pleaded.[57]

Collins kept up the attack. He compared the ad to the mass dismissal of McCarty's appointees: "Perhaps that's your nature to judge before any hearing or any opportunity to anybody else to be heard on this subject."[58] Collins kept Johns on the defensive throughout the debate, forcing him to concede that "I made a mistake" in voting against the anti-Klan bill. Collins also hectored Johns for the Mathews "so-called white supremacy bill that would have denied the right of the colored people to vote."[59]

Despite those issues, Johns won the endorsement of the *Pittsburgh Courier*, an influential Negro newspaper, which credited him for apologizing and for having appointed three blacks as barber or beauty parlor inspectors. In some black neighborhoods where the numbers racket was popular, it did not hurt Johns to be called soft on gambling. By one analysis, the black vote split closely, with an edge to Johns.[60]

It would be a long time before another Florida campaign in which segregation was not an issue. But when the Supreme Court's monumental decision in *Brown v. Board of Education* broke just four days after the debate, it was essentially a one-day story. Attorney General Richard Ervin and Thomas D. Bailey, the state school superintendent, issued a joint statement citing the delay in implementation, and the chairman of the Southern Governors Conference turned down a Johns proposal for a meeting to discuss the ruling. "As a political explosive in the Florida Governor's race," the *Tampa Tribune's* Tallahassee correspondent wrote at week's end, "it looked a dud."[61]

The candidates returned to their slugfest, both predicting victory. Collins mockingly identified Edward Ball, the duPont financier, as one of the "little people" whose support Johns claimed. Collins, closing his campaign with a statewide radio broadcast from Tallahassee, sought to make character an issue. "Our governor," he said, "is the person who more than any other sets the pace and charts the course of government. His character, his leadership for good or bad goes all through our whole fabric of government. . . . I mention these things tonight because I so want to make you and your children and my own a good governor."[62]

Collins specified his personal goals: "Clean, efficient, economical government at all levels," constitutional revision, "fairer" reapportionment, and consolidation of agencies for efficiency. Then he turned to a slashing attack on Johns: "You can look around you in your own city and in your own county. Find the racketeers, or the nearest thing that you have to racketeers in your county, and you will find them solidly behind the acting governor. . . . It is a matter of common talk, that if the acting governor is elected, those operating outside the law and within the outer fringe of the law all expect to have things easy." He concluded with "One final pledge: LeRoy Collins will never let you down."[63]

The polls opened in good weather and, atypically, to a larger voter turnout for the runoff than for the primary. Johns carried forty-four counties, more than half of them by landslide proportions of greater than 60 percent. From Orlando north, only four counties—Volusia, Seminole, Leon, and Jefferson—went for Collins. But Collins nearly carried Orange County despite the *Sentinel's* almost daily attacks and won twenty-three others, including the vote-rich prizes of Pinellas, Hillsborough, Palm Beach, Broward, and Dade. He had 380,323 votes to 314,198 for Johns, a 66,125-vote, 54 percent margin for which Dade alone nearly accounted. At that moment, Florida was two distinct states.[64]

In Tallahassee, exuberant supporters overflowed Collins's storefront headquarters. He thanked them, expressed special gratitude to Odham, telephoned his son—now a midshipman at the United States Naval Academy—and led his family and some friends to the nearby St. John's Episcopal Church, where the rector celebrated a special service for the next governor of Florida.[65]

"God's will be done," Johns told his supporters. "God's will was that we lose." He wired Collins his congratulations on a "splendid victory," saying, "Despite the bitterness of the campaign I extend my hand to you in friendship for the good of all Florida and offer to you all the help and cooperation my office and I can give you in the difficult period of transition when you take over as governor in 1955." It was an unsubtle reminder that Johns would be acting governor for seven more months.[66]

Chapter 10

Interregnum

The unanimity of the Supreme Court's school desegregation decision owed to the political skills of the new chief justice, Earl Warren, California's former attorney general and governor. Several justices hesitated to repudiate precedent, and one, Kentuckian Stanley Reed, intended to dissent on the merits until Warren won him over at almost the last minute. Warren's draftsmanship was the key to the consensus.[1] Unlike many other historic decisions, *Brown v. Board of Education* was masterfully understated. It did not criticize the sophistry and racism of *Plessy v. Ferguson*, the 1896 decision holding that segregation connoted inferiority "solely because the colored race chooses to put that construction upon it."[2] Warren wrote simply that much had changed since then, particularly in the understanding of how children respond to discrimination. It came down to one question, and one answer:

> Does segregation of children in public schools solely on the basis of race, even though the physical facilities and other "tangible" factors may be equal, deprive the children of the minority group of equal educational opportunities? We believe that it does. . . .

> To separate them from others of similar age and qualifications solely because of their race generates a feeling of inferiority as to their status in the community that may affect their hearts and minds in a way unlikely ever to be undone. . . .

> We conclude that, in the field of public education, the doctrine of "separate but equal" has no place. Separate educational facilities are inherently unequal.[3]

To lessen the shock to the South, the Court acknowledged that it needed advice on the manner of compliance and invited all segregationist states to submit briefs and arguments.[4] Some were defiant and refused to cooperate; Georgia's incoming governor, Marvin Griffin, vowed that the races "will not be mixed, come hell or high water." Florida's voices spoke moderation. Attorney General Richard Ervin was thankful that the schedule promised "a considerable period of delay." The state school superintendent, Thomas D. Bailey, called for "careful thinking together with planning untainted by hysteria." The issue all but vanished from the daily press.[5]

Florida's relative tranquility was partly because people were "stunned," as Collins later described himself. Many refused to believe that the Court meant it. "In the first place," Collins said, "people just didn't think it was true. . . . They first thought it was some quirk that the Supreme Court would try to correct itself. Then they got to thinking there would be other means for overturning it."[6]

It was a moment when strong leadership could have desegregated schools in some parts of Florida. By year's end, desegregation, though often only token, had begun in nine other states and the District of Columbia. The governors of Maryland, Kentucky, Tennessee, West Virginia, Arkansas (before Orval Faubus), and even Alabama (before George Wallace) had pointedly refused to sign a defiant statement proposed by Johns, whose solicitude for black voters did not outlast the campaign. Collins declined to sign the Johns statement on the grounds that he was too busy to be "diverted to a newspaper discussion on subjects which breed discord, disharmony and demagoguery."[7]

But Florida had a leadership vacuum under its 1885 constitution, which allowed the governor only a single term and diffused executive power in an elected Cabinet. The Board of Education consisted of the superintendent of public instruction, attorney general, treasurer, secretary of state, and the governor, who was chairman by custom.[8] An activist governor could take the initiative, but for seven months in 1954 Florida was effectively between governors, and Florida's course under *Brown* was charted before Collins's inauguration. It was the attorney general who set it; Ervin thought himself duty-bound to defend the segregationist constitution and laws as long as possible.

His personal instincts were moderate, but he submitted an obstructionist brief to the court. Richard Kluger, whose *Simple Justice* is the definitive history of the desegregation cases, wrote that "Of the six segregating states that chose to join the final *Brown* argument—Arkansas, Florida, Maryland, North Carolina, Oklahoma and Texas—Florida submitted the most extensive and spirited brief and offered some wrinkles that seemed to have been beneath Virginia's dignity."[9] Ervin recommended, among other things, that the federal courts rule individually on the application of each black child with the judges having broad discretion to say no. In his 243-page brief, filed on October 1, Ervin contended that immediate desegregation would provoke violent resistance. (That day, a jeering mob of some four hundred white youths and adults demonstrated outside a desegregated Baltimore high school.)[10]

Ervin cited the findings of a study financed by the Board of Education and conducted by Lewis M. Killian, a Georgia-born sociologist at Florida State University. It was intended not only to estimate the degrees of resistance or cooperation in various communities but also, through the device of a figurehead advisory committee, "to reassure the citizens of Florida that their state government was doing something . . . not just standing idly by while the floodwaters of desegregation rolled over the school system."[11] Killian polled not what the public thought about desegregation but rather how law enforcement authorities, educators, editors, elected officials, clergy, and other opinion leaders would react to it. About 30 percent of white leaders opposed *Brown* so strongly that they would either refuse to cooperate with desegregation or actively oppose it. A clear majority, however, would accept whatever the courts and school officials required. Although most people did not expect serious violence, the fear of it was highest among peace officers, elected school officials, and legislators. The most worrisome finding was a lack of confidence in the ability of the police to contain disorder, and this was "especially true of the peace officers themselves except in Dade County." Killian doubted the police would act forcefully. Legislators were problematic also. Of the seventy-nine who replied, thirty-two wanted to preserve segregation indefinitely "by whatever means possible." Only four wanted to permit voluntary compliance.[12]

In some communities, Killian said, "desegregation could be undertaken now if local leaders so decided." In others, "widespread social disorder would result" from desegregating too quickly. "It may be concluded," Killian warned, "that the absence of a firm, enthusiastic public policy of making desegregation effective would create the type of situation in which attitudes would be most likely to be translated into action."[13] But there would be no such leadership. Ervin was under pressure from segregationists in the Bar, the public, the media, and even his own staff to defy the Court rather than appear to cooperate. Killian believed that Florida missed its opportunity in 1954.[14]

Appearing before the Supreme Court in the *Brown II* hearings, Ervin relied on the Killian study to argue that Florida needed time to comply. "If you will allow us the opportunity to work under this decision, not against some deadline, we feel eventually we will bring about full integration," he said.[15] "Eventually" would turn out to be some seventeen years.

Interviewed in August 1954, Sen. Spessard Holland, Florida's most respected politician at the time, said that the *Brown* decision "is the law and we should accept it. It is no longer a question of having what we want. The Supreme Court has decided that question." He noted that three Southern justices had participated in the ruling.[16] Less than two years later, however, Holland and all but one other member of Florida's delegation signed a document known as the Southern Manifesto accusing the court of a "clear abuse of judicial power."[17] Rep. D. R. "Billy" Matthews of Gainesville called the decision as "terrible a thing as World War I, World War II, or the emergence of communism."[18]

Returning from a meeting of Southern governors, Johns said he would ask the Cabinet to rescind Ervin's funding and cancel the Killian study, but Ervin and Bailey had more influence with their colleagues than he did. Ervin warned that the second ruling could go worse for Florida if the state did not participate in the *Brown II* arguments.[19]

After blocking a pay increase for the vacant University of Florida presidency, forcing the chosen candidate to withdraw, Johns sabotaged the next nominee, University of Louisville president Philip G. Davidson—whom the Board of Education had approved over Johns's dissent—by saying he would refuse to sign Davidson's salary warrant until he had a chance to interview him. Davidson withdrew the same day. Johns said later that he understood that Louisville had desegregated its student body and had experienced "a definite infiltration of communism." Killian remembers Johns asking at a Cabinet meeting, "He's not a nigger, is he?"[20]

Johns was stalling so that the July 1 expiration of two of the seven terms on the Board of Control might help him pack the university's administration with people who would owe their jobs to him instead of to Collins.[21] In December, Johns met secretly with J. Wayne Reitz, the provost of agriculture, to offer him the presidency on the condition he agree to replace John Allen, the executive vice president and acting president, with Kenneth Williams, a Floridian then working at the University of Georgia. Reitz refused, only to hear the offer repeated from a member of the Board of Control a week later. "I would no more think of doing that than I would fly," he said.[22]

At nearly the same time, during his last weeks as acting governor, Johns called on the Board of Control to pick a president immediately. The board declined, claiming inability to muster a quorum on short notice. Collins said Johns should "take his grasping political hands" off of the board and "the future of our Florida boys and girls." A governor should not involve himself in selecting a president, Collins said, before the Board of Control recommended a candidate to the Board of Education.[23]

Collins did not wait for his inauguration to hold the hearings he had promised to the suspended McCarty officials, who said they would resign once he had cleared them. He called for resignations from two McCarty men whom Johns had kept. He also decried what the gubernatorial primary had cost—$331,892 for him, $376,748 for Johns, and $147,509 for Odham—and said he would try to do something about election spending. "To raise funds without getting your hands tied raises a real problem," Collins said.[24]

Reacting to urban South Florida's decisive role in Collins's victory, rural legislators revived the notion of a county unit voting system like Georgia's and threatened a special session to enact it in time for Johns to sign it into law. Johns flirted with the idea until strong opposition from the Florida Democratic Executive Committee and among legislators themselves convinced him that it would be hard to pass. The Supreme Court disposed of the Georgia system in a 1963 decision famously defining proper representation as "one man, one vote."[25]

Johns spent the months after his defeat building more roads than Collins thought there was money to pay for; firing several state employees suspected of having backed Collins, along with two members of the game commission that had cost him an insurance commission; accelerating construction of the new Florida Turnpike, which Collins tried to block; and spending $218,000 for road maps and other public documents bearing his name and photograph.[26] Johns's Road Board also prepared to begin construction on a controversial North Florida road project that would benefit Ball and the duPont forest lands. Collins's Road Board stopped the project but eventually let it go through.[27]

Almost unnoticed, there had been a Republican Party primary with two candidates for governor. The winner, with 24,429 votes, was J. Tom Watson, a former Democratic attorney general and an unsuccessful candidate for governor in 1932 and 1948. Collins acted as if Watson was irrelevant. He withdrew from his law firm to plan his administration and visit state institutions. He refused to debate Watson or engage in any visible campaign, and reported spending only $174 on the November election.[28]

Watson, a strong segregationist and labor-baiter who fathered the 1944 "right-to-work" amendment to Florida's constitution, suffered a stroke and his campaign faltered. There were rumors of a right-wing plot to persuade Watson to step aside in favor of a retired National Guard general, Sumter Lowry, who had been on the banquet circuit making ultranationalistic speeches against communism and the United Nations. Republican Party leaders wanted to dump Watson in favor of someone else, but nothing came of either intrigue because the nearly invalid Watson refused to quit. At his penultimate appearance, he haltingly told a small, primarily black audience at St. Petersburg that "God Almighty segregated the races" and left the platform in tears. Watson, sixty-eight years old, died six days later, on October 24. Ignoring suggestions to name Johns as his successor, the Republican state committee nominated no one and asked, for technical election law reasons, that Watson's name remain on the ballots. On November 2, Collins won with 287,769 votes—fewer than half as many as in the runoff—to 69,852 for Watson, who had polled nearly 20 percent from the grave. There was no other statewide race to inspire a larger turnout by Democrats.[29]

Though Collins feared nothing from Watson or Watson's ghost, he recognized the Republican Party as an emerging threat to Democrats. On election eve, he campaigned with Sens. Holland and George Smathers at a rally in St. Petersburg, the largest city in the first Republican county, to plug for the reelection of all seven Democratic U.S. House members who had opposition. Six won, most of them easily, but William C. Cramer of St. Petersburg, who had narrowly lost in 1952, became Florida's first Republican member of Congress since Reconstruction.[30] It was the first step toward the present-day Republican domination of Florida.

Chapter 11

"So Much to Be Done. So Little Time"

In late November, LeRoy and Mary Call and a group of friends toured three Latin American countries, partly as a vacation but also to promote a proposed Inter-American Cultural and Trade Center (Interama) at Miami. (Never built, Interama eventually became the site of a branch campus of Florida International University.)[1] Collins invited their hosts and diplomats from many other countries to his inauguration and was surprised when twenty-one people from seven nations accepted.[2]

Returning to Tallahassee, Collins worked on staffing his administration and culling those on the payroll who had campaigned for the acting governor. The Road Department lost 114 positions. There were also mass purges at the Beverage Department and at the Motor Vehicle Commission, where a list sent to Collins named fifty-eight Johns supporters. When the commission's chief clerk, an employee for twenty years, publicized a letter from Collins advising him to resign, Collins was unapologetic. "I called on every state worker actively working for Johns to stop and made it clear that I didn't want any of them campaigning on my behalf either," Collins said. The agency, which recorded all automobile titles and issued more than 1.5 million license plates annually, had the reputation, as Collins put it, "of being a political dumping ground for campaign friends who didn't seem to fit anywhere else." To demonstrate his intent to reform it and to show "that a good woman could handle this job as well as a good man," Collins asked Bailey to recommend an experienced female school administrator to head the agency. Ina Hester Thompson of DeFuniak Springs became the first woman to head a "Little Cabinet" department. A sister-in-law of Collins's Senate friend Ernest Graham, she was surprised at her appointment because she had done nothing to help elect Collins beyond voting for him.[3]

Tallahassee was unusually festive for his inauguration, the first of a native son since 1897. "Coming into the city was like entering a carnival city," reporter Lowell Brandle wrote, noting that the Florida state flag seemed to be flying wherever the national flag did. But the inauguration was clouded by news the night before of the assassination of Panamanian President José Antonio Remón, who had hosted the Collinses during their trip the month before, and whose wife was en route to the inauguration when he was slain.[4]

The social events taxed Tallahassee's resources. Friends lent silver and china to Mary Call and helped her serve eighty dinner guests at the Grove. The governor-elect having decided that he should honor Leon County's pretensions to be dry, cocktails were served only at parties elsewhere. Many of these pre-dinner festivities lasted too long, leaving some of the guests unable to appreciate the unfamiliar Southern cooking.[5]

Collins was sworn in at noon January 4, 1955, by Justice Glenn Terrell, who had inspired him to study law. Fair weather and bright sunshine favored the inaugural party and thousands of spectators filling a small public park between the west front of the Capitol and the Supreme Court building.[6]

"I leave with malice toward none," Johns said in a short farewell address that must have tested his self-restraint because of what he had seen in an advance text of Collins's speech.[7]

The voters who voted for him, Collins said, did so not "to get a job or to get a road" but because "you sought in me leadership for something clean and good and wholesome."

> You wanted a government you could be proud of, a government to which you would be willing to entrust your state's future, and your children's future. . . . I so anxiously want the people of Florida to understand that progress in business, industry, and human welfare can only go so far with a ward-heeling, back-scratching, self-promoting political system. . . . I pledge to the people of Florida that, insofar as the strength within me lies, government by trade, barter, and sale will be out for the next two years."[8]

Collins quoted from the Bible, as he would often do, to elaborate on the theme that "man cannot live by bread alone." Government, he said, "cannot live by taxes alone. Or by jobs alone. Or even by roads alone. Government, too, must have qualities of the spirit. Truth and justice and fairness and un-selfish service are some of these."

Collins reiterated constitutional revision and his other campaign goals, promised to see that "wrong does not go unpunished at any level," and voiced soaring visions for Florida, "a young state, a growing state," facing unlimited opportunity. "I want to make it crystal clear," he said,

> That the emphasis of this administration will be on the positive. To achieve our goal of building a greater state we must move forward bold-ly, and with an adventuresome spirit. We must not, and we will not, be deterred from our course by those of different purpose, or by those of lesser faith. We must not procrastinate, we must not vacillate, we must not hesitate. So much to be done. So little time.[9]

Walter Edge, who had urged Collins not to procrastinate, vacillate, or hes-itate in declaring his candidacy, was seated nearby. They exchanged glances and smiled.[10]

Collins referred only obliquely to the slumbering desegregation crisis. "There is no place under our sun for the demagogue. We must discard the false prophets who would array little counties against big counties, section against section, and class against class," he said.[11]

"Anxiously" was one of Collins's favorite words; its frequent use in the speech reflected the anxiety he brought to his new office. "So much to do, so little time" was not idle phrasemaking. He was still a young man in a hurry.

Close friends, one newspaper reported, had tried to persuade him to delete the language disparaging Johns. He was said to be angry over a month-old al-legation by Johns that Collins was trying to secure the University of Florida presidency for a Spessard Holland law partner, William McRae. Johns said little if anything after the speech, but he nursed a grudge until Collins left office six years later. In a letter timed to arrive on Collins's last day, Johns wrote that "your insinuations and innuendoes against my administration made your closest friends hang their heads in shame."[12] Brailey Odham was ecstatic over Collins's "fighting speech," but Allen Morris, who had excellent sources among legislators, wrote that many felt Collins had insulted them too.[13]

As his family gathered in his new offices for sandwiches before the inau-gural parade, Collins asked his mother what she thought of his address and the ceremony. "Well," she said, "everything was very nice, but I still think you would have made a better Methodist bishop."[14]

For the inaugural ball that night, held at Florida State University, Mary Call wore an imported Dior original gown described as "egg-shell silk and tulle, strapless," and a necklace of seed pearl medallions that had been Richard Keith Call's gift to her grandmother. Many admiring words were written about the youth and vitality of the Collins family, especially four-year-old Darby.[15]

In his first official act, Collins formally reinstated seventeen suspended McCarty officials. As prearranged, most offered their resignations. He kept roughly half, including Richard Simpson, a former legislator who had chaired the McCarty Road Board. He also accepted the resignation of James E. "Nick" Connor, a senator and friend of Johns, whom the acting governor had appointed public-relations officer for an agency.[16]

The Road Board occasioned many problems for Collins over the ensuing six years. Wilbur Jones, a Miami estate planner who had met Collins during the campaign, was his first chairman; Collins eventually replaced him with someone he considered a more forceful administrator but who stepped down himself on the verge of a Senate investigation. Al Rogero, a Clearwater real estate and insurance broker whom Collins appointed to a part-time district road board seat, involved the administration in an extremely controversial bridge and causeway project in Pinellas County, invested in property whose value could be affected by road projects, and faced income tax evasion charges, of which he was acquitted, after leaving office.

As a veteran observer, Allen Morris considered it noteworthy that five of Collins's seven full-time department heads—the "Little Cabinet"—had never held public offices. They were Jones; Mrs. Thompson; John R. Ring, secretary of the Racing Commission; Richard Edgerton, a professional hotelier from Mount Dora who was the hotel and restaurant commissioner; and J. D. Williamson, a Collins boyhood friend and neighbor who headed the Beverage Department, one of the most sensitive positions. The only political veterans in the Little Cabinet were James T. Vocelle, Industrial Commission chairman since McCarty, and Ernest Mitts, a former legislator from Fort Myers who became conservation director.[17]

The governor's office was thinly staffed by comparison to the present day. His de facto chief of staff, officially an administrative assistant, was Joe Grotegut, a Daytona Beach newspaperman who had worked in his campaign. Fokes, a former aide to Claude Pepper, was the other administrative assistant. The secretary was Erin Shelley, who had worked for Holland. The receptionist, Betty McCord, had been Collins's secretary in the 1953 legislative session. His driver was Lieutenant Joe Cook of the Florida Highway Patrol, who had been McCarty's driver. There were two part-time administrative assistants. Collins had the Legislature authorize a traffic safety coordinator, Roger Collar, who came on loan from the Highway Patrol. It was seven months before Collins appointed a full-time press secretary, officially another administrative assistant. The job went to John Perry, the *St. Petersburg Times* reporter whose precampaign profile had lauded Collins as "the statesman" in the governor's race. A fourth full-time administrative assistant, J. Edwin Gay, a former assistant United States attorney from Jacksonville, joined the staff at about the same time. The appointments secretary was Sunny Van Brunt. Collins appointed temporary lobbyists for his first legislative session. Responsible for the House was John Germany, a young Tampa lawyer Collins had tried to hire full-time. Richard Gardner handled the Senate.[18]

Collins relied heavily on volunteer advisers, naming more than thirty citizens' committees to work on constitutional revision, tourist development, tax reform, agriculture, and other issues. In 1955, the Legislature gave official status to one of them, the Florida Constitution Advisory Committee. James W. Prothro, a Florida State University political science professor who was a neighbor of Charles Ausley, gave Collins private advice. He and Perry were considered the liberal influences in Collins's inner circle.[19]

The First Family moved into the governor's mansion knowing that it probably would not be for long. Two weeks after his inauguration Collins told the Cabinet he preferred that the new mansion, for which the 1953 Legislature had appropriated $250,000, be built on the site of the old, where it would be more accessible to the public than the previously selected location. The Cabinet concurred with one dissent. The Grove made a convenient and adequate temporary executive mansion while the official governor's residence was demolished and replaced. Collins installed an office in the basement of the Grove so that he could work long and irregular hours. "I am constitutionally incapable of working by the clock," he said.[20]

The mansion came with a small domestic staff headed by Martin Tanner, the sixty-two-year-old butler who had been a prison trusty and would now be serving his eleventh governor. He had watched Mary Call Darby roller-skating on the mansion's circular sidewalk. A month after the inauguration, a telephone call interrupted Collins at dinner with the "awful" news, as he put it, that a police vice raid had caught Tanner that afternoon walking in the door of a nearby residence with a bolita ticket in one hand and $2.60 in the other. W. Dexter Douglass, a brand-new lawyer trying his first case for Millard Caldwell's firm, convinced a city judge to rule the raid an illegal search and dismiss the gambling charge against Tanner. Though Collins detested the numbers racket, he did not fire Tanner, who avoided further trouble. It took time, however, for Mary Call to persuade Tanner to run the mansion her way; "He had his idea where things should be, and I had mine."[21]

Though Collins had good relations with most members of the Capitol press corps, he was unwilling to trust his public image entirely to them. He undertook monthly radio broadcasts to the people, as Holland had done, and filmed them for television.[22]

The University of Florida presidency remained undecided. Collins and Ervin, responding to a complaint from Capitol reporters, publicly urged the Board of Control, which often closed its meetings, to hold them all in public. The board declined; its chairman said the press had to be excluded from some meetings because *Tampa Tribune* correspondent Jim Powell refused to promise to keep certain things confidential. "I would feel as if I were a party to some conspiracy," said Powell.

Meeting in secret in regard to the fifteen-month-old presidential vacancy, the board split bitterly between John Allen, the acting president whom Johns had wanted purged, and Kenneth Williams. When four of the seven members voted for Williams, Chairman Hollis Rinehart put in a desperate telephone call to Collins, who surely knew by then that Williams was Johns's choice. Collins objected so strongly that the board, still meeting in secret, compromised on Reitz, the agriculture provost who had insisted for months that he didn't want the presidency. This time, he took it. It was a controversial choice because of academic tension between Reitz's agricultural institute and the liberal arts faculties at the university.

When one of Williams's supporters made a public issue of Collins's intervention, the governor said he had "not, at any time, suggested that the Board of Control nominate anyone." He admitted, however, that he had "expressed shock and surprise" over Williams and said that he had lost confidence in the board over its secret meetings. Johns attacked Collins in a letter released to the press. "I want to borrow your exact words because the events of the last few days prove that they fit you: 'Keep your greedy, grasping, political hands off the Board of Control.'" The Board of Education approved Reitz's appointment four votes to one, with Bailey dissenting. The school superintendent said that the control board had promised to consider only "outstanding educators from out of state" and that he had "sincere doubts that decisions were reached in a climate conducive to mature judgment."[23]

Johns had lost the battle for the University of Florida. Allen, who survived it, would soon become president of a new state university at Tampa. But Johns would return to haunt both institutions as instigator and chairman of a legislative committee investigating homosexuality in the public schools and colleges.[24] Williams eventually became president of another new state school, Florida Atlantic University.[25]

Comptroller (and banking commissioner) C. M. Gay's decision to retire gave the new governor the opportunity to appoint a replacement to the Cabinet position. In choosing Gay's assistant, Ray Green, Collins neglected to secure his commitment to support a tax consolidation bill that Collins wanted. The bill would erode the comptroller's individual authority, and Green's opposition dealt Collins one of his most severe early legislative defeats. Mallory Horne, a freshman House member from Tallahassee who supported Collins on the issue, found the pressure so intense that he and another member hid out in Thomasville, Georgia, the night before a key committee vote. Although the bill would have meant more power for the Cabinet collectively, most of its members took Green's side, Horne recalled, "because they all wondered who would be next."[26]

It was a powerful reminder to Collins where real power lay in Tallahassee. Cabinet members were eligible to be reelected without limit, which made them the dominant and enduring force in the executive branch. In 1955, Collins shared the Cabinet table with a secretary of state and a treasurer who had each been in office twenty-five years, a commissioner of agriculture who had served twenty-one, and an attorney general and a superintendent of education who had each preceded him by six years. Three of the Cabinet officers were old enough to have been his father.[27]

Chapter 12

"Whew!"

Enough floral displays for a hundred funerals overflow the Florida Senate and House chambers when the Legislature convenes. A reporter once claimed to overhear a drowsy visitor mumbling "My, doesn't he look natural?"[1] Few people were nodding off on April 5, 1955, as they awaited Collins's first State of the State address, but it was not as fiery as the inaugural.[2]

A "great and modern" state, he said, needed most of all a "great and modern" constitution providing for fair legislative representation rather than the "grossly unsound and unfair" apportionment of the day. Florida was by far the worst among the states because a Senate majority could be elected by merely 12 percent of the people, and 18.8 percent could elect a majority of the House. Collins reminded the Legislature of their constitutional duty to reapportion themselves that year.[3] But the constitutional formula itself made fairness impossible. It guaranteed each county a House seat and allowed no county more than three, meaning that a member from Dade inevitably represented a hundred times more people than his colleague from Liberty. The constitution required Senate districts to be as nearly equal as "practicable," but no district could have more than one senator, and no county could be split. The six largest counties with more than half the population elected less than one-sixth of the Senate.[4]

Collins also urged a new constitution for the sake of executive branch and judicial efficiency, prison reform, home rule for cities and counties, and a lieutenant governor. Nothing less than a complete revision would do. To get there, Collins wanted an amendment establishing a constitution revision commission with the power to recommend an entire new constitution to the voters as soon as possible.[5]

There had been ninety-four amendments to the 1885 constitution—voters having rejected another fifty—because the Legislature lacked authority to undertake an overall revision.[6] Assuming that it would not care for the independent commission he proposed, Collins said he would accept an alternative process—which came to pass a decade later—allowing the Legislature itself to propose a comprehensive revision. In that event, an appointed commission would advise the Legislature.[7]

He had only warmed up. He wanted many other things, among them a development commission to consolidate Florida's industrial and tourist promotion efforts; a budget department responsible to the governor rather than to the Cabinet; an auditor independent of either; a department of finance for all state revenue, purchasing, and investment; a merit system protecting all twenty-five thousand state employees; extensive administrative reforms at the Road Department; and authorization to extend the so-called bobtail turnpike, on which construction was just beginning from Miami to Fort Pierce, all the way to Georgia, following an inland route that the *Orlando Sentinel* stridently demanded.[8]

He asked for more troopers for the Highway Patrol and for a law allowing the use of "modern enforcement devices, such as radar." Six years after ridding its highways of cows, Florida still had no fixed statewide speed limits; Collins asked for rural speed limits of 60 mph by day and 50 at night and a 30 mph limit in any business or residential district not otherwise posted. He wanted driver education to be taught in all schools, financed by traffic fines or an increase in the driver's license fee. It had taken until 1939 to establish a state highway patrol over the opposition of Florida's elected sheriffs, and there was still no state police force to fight organized crime. Now the Florida Sheriffs' Association and the attorney general proposed the creation of a Florida Sheriffs' Bureau, staffed with well-trained investigators and directed by a board comprising the governor, attorney general, and five sheriffs. Collins endorsed this but objected that the bureau could act only when asked by a sheriff. He wanted also to abolish the fee system that compensated sheriffs' departments based on how many arrests they made and court papers they served, which he said was "totally out of place" in twentieth-century Florida. Differing with civil libertarians on the meaning of the Fourth Amendment, he wanted to legalize the use of improperly seized evidence.[9]

Collins wanted to repeal Florida's "quickie" divorce law, which, much like Nevada's, allowed a spouse to sue after only ninety days' residence in the state.

"[W]hat we lose in income, we shall gain in integrity," he said. He asked for more money for public health, mental illness, and indigent health care. He recommended a $200 raise for teachers, less than they were asking, and proposed that school boards help pay for it by pressuring their tax assessors to value property realistically.[10]

His major proposal for education was to expand the junior college system as "our most effective answer" to an "impending tidal wave of high school graduates." Though he endorsed a study being done by the Board of Control, he did not recommend any new universities. Believing nuclear energy to be the South's economic salvation, Collins asked for a $500,000 appropriation to the University of Florida to undertake nuclear research.[11]

He alluded to school segregation only in a two-paragraph passage reiterating his promise to use all his "lawful power . . . to preserve this custom and law" and warning that legislation enacted before the Supreme Court ruled on implementation would likely "inflame the passions of our people unnecessarily and develop an emotional atmosphere which will make the proper solution of our problems even more difficult."[12]

Though he remarked that "no state has a greater stake" in protecting natural resources, Collins had no recommendation to restrict the dredging and filling of estuaries, already a hotly controversial subject in Pinellas and some other coastal counties whose shorelines were being exploited by real estate developers. In that regard, he asked only for the creation of a water resources study commission. Reflecting the influence of Edge and other plantation owners, he urged the Legislature to buy additional public preserves rather than try to stop private owners from keeping other hunters out. For the moment, he wanted higher taxes only on dog tracks. He asked for a permanent Citizens Tax Council to study inequities in sales and property taxation, for longer and higher unemployment compensation benefits, more money for agricultural research and livestock diseases, and an end to the Milk Commission's powers to set minimum prices for anyone but the farmer.[13]

He proposed what it would take twelve more years to achieve: open meetings of all state or local boards or commissions with legislative or administrative powers. "[T]he people," he said, "have yielded to us no right to decide what is good for them to know or what is bad for them to know." Last on his enormous list was what some might consider a "little thing," but he was "very anxious"—that word again—to see the state flag flying over every school and public building. The Legislature should repeal an old law restricting its use.[14]

The text of his speech filled twenty-four single-spaced pages. "Whew!" remarked the *Tampa Tribune*'s editorial. The *St. Petersburg Times* called it the "most progressive and far-reaching program" of any governor but criticized the evidence proposal, which would be defeated by a House committee.[15]

The Legislature did not share the media's rapture. Eight of the thirteen members of the Senate Rules Committee had supported Johns for governor. Johns himself made nine, and the press ranked three more as "doubtful" for Collins, leaving him with just one advocate on the panel that would control the Senate's debate calendar late in the session. The Senate promptly voted to continue allowing closed committee meetings, defying Collins's request to ban them. "At this writing, the Senate to all intents and purposes is lost to the governor," reported the *Miami Herald*. Johns filed bills designed to provoke Collins, including one for a segregationist pupil assignment law.[16]

Within three weeks, a Senate committee killed both Collins's independent constitution revision commission and his alternative. Saying he was "sick deep inside," the governor pledged to continue the fight "everywhere honorable men and women can fight for law reform and for a better state." Sen. Russell O. Morrow of Palm Beach County resigned from the committee in protest.[17] Collins appeared to win a significant victory, his first, when the Senate voted thirty-three to three to require a year's residence for divorce-seekers, but a House committee composed entirely of lawyers killed the bill by a vote of 8 to 2. The divorce trade would just go elsewhere, "taking that much money out of the pockets of us poor country lawyers," said Rep. Marion B. "Bart" Knight of Calhoun County.[18] The House did come through for Collins, 60 votes to 30, on the turnpike extension, and the Senate passed it 30 votes to 8, surprising Collins aides who had expected a defeat.[19]

Collins's remaining hope for constitutional revision rested upon a watered-down plan, eventually approved, that created a committee to recommend article-by-article revisions to the 1957 session, when legislators thought there would be a new governor. Legislators would hold eighteen of the thirty-seven positions on the committee. Collins accepted this as preferable to a proposed study by the Legislative Council, composed entirely of legislators. "We can't get a good new constitution through the efforts of people who do not believe we need a new constitution," Collins said.[20] (It would take thirteen years to achieve a new constitution, which voters ratified in the same election that put an end to Collins's political career.) The dog track tax was raised at the price of allowing the $2 million in new money to be shared equally among the counties. This was a foretaste of the reapportionment struggles to come.[21]

Only two segregation measures passed. One was a meaningless memorial, not subject to veto, calling on the Congress to preserve school segregation. It expressed a sexual paranoia that infused white attitudes on the issue. School integration, it said, "would tend to encourage the reprehensible, unnatural, abominable, abhorrent, execrable and revolting practice of miscegenation . . . leaving us a mongrel breed devoid of culture, tradition, background and inherent character."[22] The other was Johns's pupil assignment bill, which some school officials said simply affirmed their existing authority. But there were signs of worse to come. Rep. Prentice Pruitt of Jefferson County, one of the only two Florida counties with more black residents than white, won a House majority for a constitutional amendment to replace public schools with private schools, but by four votes too few to overturn a committee vote against it. The Legislature finally made national Memorial Day a Florida holiday, but Confederate Memorial Day remained on the statute books.[23]

Collins's own scorecard for the session listed twenty-eight successes, including constitutional revision—a dubious claim—and twelve defeats. The successes included the state flag, Sheriffs' Bureau, junior college expansion, his traffic safety and industrial promotion initiatives, and an expanded merit system into which he immediately placed the Motor Vehicle Commission, the Road Department, and another three agencies he controlled. The major defeats that he acknowledged included tax consolidation, the evidence bill, milk pricing, budgeting reforms, the fee system, quickie divorces, open government, mental health programs for public schools, and the speed limits. Though he had not asked for it, he praised the passage of a proposed constitutional amendment to relieve the Supreme Court's workload by establishing three intermediate appeals courts.[24] Journalist Bob Delaney wrote that the session resembled Collins's 1954 campaign: "slow start and strong finish."[25]

Collins was so proud of his civil service reform that he spoke about it to the Southern Governors' Conference. No other Southern state had gone so far to immunize government workers from politics, and at least one did not want to. After Collins finished, Alabama governor Jim Folsom, whose nickname was "Kissin' Jim," remarked that "in Alabama we have a merit system that I am sure works better than his would. It is simply this: My friends have got the merit, and I've got the system."[26]

In his June radio broadcast, Collins said that the 1955 Legislature left a budget deficit that he and the Cabinet would have to control by spending less than authorized.[27] His official scorecard conspicuously omitted reapportionment, which failed on the last day of the regular session when the Senate refused to create a South Florida district that might elect a Republican.[28] The constitution obliged Collins to call a special session. He neglected to mention another defeat: a Johns bill to build a new tuberculosis hospital in rural Union County that was authorized over his veto. (It was never built.)[29]

Johns was also the unlikely sponsor of a new law prohibiting hotels from advertising that they discriminated on the basis of religion. It was apparently his reward to his one liberal staff member, but as Johns himself explained, it was very limited. "It merely provides that no one can advertise that Jewish people are kept out of the hotel." Hotels could continue to be "restricted"—a euphemism meaning they were closed to Jews—so long as they did not talk about it.[30] Collins may have had Johns's ambitions in mind when he vetoed legislation giving legislators immunity from libel or slander suits resulting from committee or floor debate. The House sustained the veto.[31]

What proved to be one of the session's most historic accomplishments narrowly avoided Collins's veto. It authorized the boards of control and education to plan for a new state university somewhere in the Tampa vicinity. It would become the University of South Florida, the nation's first entirely new state university since the 1800s. Legislators from Palm Beach, Broward, and Escambia counties amended the bill to start the process for what would become Florida Atlantic University at Boca Raton and the University of West Florida at Pensacola. (There are now eleven institutions in the State University System of Florida, compared to three in 1955.) Collins strongly preferred expanding the junior college system—there were only five junior colleges enrolling fewer than sixteen thousand students—to the costlier construction of new universities. With Florida State University and the University of Florida having put aside their rivalry to lobby jointly against new competition, the odds had seemed to be against Tampa. Moreover, FSU president Doak S. Campbell was a close friend of Collins, who was also surrounded by ardent University of Florida alumni including John Ausley, one of his former law partners. Tampa's champion in the House, second-term representative Sam Gibbons, believed the bill would have died in the Senate but for his father's personal friendship with Shands, the Gainesville senator who usually asserted the University of Florida's interests.[32]

Collins's veto was a definite threat, but to Tampa's good fortune Mary

Call Collins went to Europe, and John Germany's wife and child returned to Tampa after the regular session. The governor invited his young lobbyist to keep him company at the mansion during the extraordinary session on reapportionment. Germany, a Harvard law graduate who had earned his baccalaureate at the University of Florida, took the opportunity to lobby Collins for a university at Tampa to serve young working people in an urban setting. Collins finally yielded, but he signed the bill without a picture-taking ceremony for Tampa's legislators and said that it was still his "firm conviction" that no new university was yet necessary. Collins spoke like a proud father, however, at the university's opening convocation five years later. "No other state in this generation has built a new university plant from the sandspurs up, as we have," he said.[33]

Collins used his first session as governor to develop a lobbying technique that Horne, the only person ever to preside over both the House (1963–64) and Senate (1973–74), regarded as matched only by Collins's successor Farris Bryant. Collins relied on his few friends in the Senate, among them Pope and Doyle Carlton Jr. of Wauchula, to vigorously debate bills they knew they could not defeat in their own chamber. The purpose was to set them up to be stopped in the House, where Collins had more support. His tactical advisers later included Sen. Ed H. Price Jr., who had become one of Collins's closest friends during the 1954 campaign and was elected a senator in 1958. "We had some horrible legislation that would pass the Senate," Price explained, but in those days "you had a lot more debate on the floor."[34]

Part of the strategy would be to have team members situated at desks throughout the House chamber, so that what they said would seem to be reflecting statewide consensus. There were usually about twelve House members on Collins's team. One of the most prominent was Gibbons, a World War II veteran and lawyer from Tampa who later served thirty-four years in Congress. Robert T. Mann Jr., also from Tampa and a famously outspoken iconoclast, joined this group after his election in 1956.

Collins, who excelled at personal diplomacy, "talked to everybody who would listen to him or had moments with him," Horne recalled. The governor used even his limousine to advantage, inviting legislators to join him on the long car trips he favored over Tallahassee's rudimentary commercial airline service. "I drove to Miami with him several times," said Horne. "It was like a sermon, constant sermons, ten hours." Horne remembers Collins lecturing him over reapportionment: "You cannot make a constitutional decision, or a right or wrong decision, based on your friendship or respect for anybody." That, said Horne, "was the defining difference between him and anybody else I knew."[35]

Collins gave Mann a ride to Tallahassee after his election along with gubernatorial advice on how a freshman legislator should dress. "You're going to be seated on platforms, and the white leg shows. Wear over-the-calf socks," Collins advised.[36]

Florida elected its Supreme Court, but in practice most justices were appointed to vacancies created by death or resignation. Collins had the rare opportunity to appoint two during his first year. On April 30, John E. Mathews died of an intestinal hemorrhage. Four days later, Collins appointed Campbell Thornal, an Orlando lawyer and friend for twenty years then serving on his Road Board. Three months later, Justice H. L. Sebring's departure for a law school deanship enabled Collins to recruit another friend and campaign supporter, Stephen O'Connell of Broward County, whom he persuaded to give up a new house and a law practice paying him $100,000 a year to support a wife and four children on a justice's salary of $15,000. When O'Connell resisted, Collins visited their home to plead his case directly to Rita O'Connell, who weakened, saying, "Well, maybe later." O'Connell called Collins the next day to say they would come. Thornal and O'Connell were strongly conservative, perhaps more so than Collins himself. He said that he chose them because he was confident in their integrity.[37]

Between the regular and special sessions, Collins took some thirty businessmen on the first of several northern tours to promote Florida industry and tourism. He visited *Time*, where a private interview with publisher Henry Luce paid off in a flattering cover story on Collins. He also visited *Forbes* magazine, saw the governors of New York and Massachusetts, took in a Boston Red Sox game—noting in his diary that he "met Ted Williams"—and visited two brokerage houses. In New York, he threw caution to the winds and went to the theater with John Germany to see *Damn Yankees*. Gwen Verdon's sensuous performance as the Devil's assistant embarrassed Florida's straight-laced governor. As she turned up the heat in "Whatever Lola Wants," Germany noticed Collins slouching lower and lower in his front-row seat, as if trying to avoid being seen.[38]

Chapter 13

The Pork Chop Gang

With the prospects for constitutional reform and reapportionment looking hopeless in the spring of 1955, Rep. Fred C. Petersen of Pinellas County said the larger counties should consider seceding from the state. It was only a one-day story because Petersen rarely was taken seriously; his Capitol nickname was "Meathead," and he was, moreover, a Republican. Before long, however, even serious thinkers began to agree with him. Collins would leave office six years later considering reapportionment his greatest failure. The constitution required Collins, like Caldwell ten years before, to call the Legislature into "extraordinary" session if it failed to redistrict itself, but Collins was the first to insist on a semblance of fairness. The lawmakers returned on June 6 and met sporadically and fruitlessly for a total of seventy-four days before declaring a final recess until after the 1956 election. Technically, they remained in that special session for seventeen months.[1]

The Senate established its defiance late in the regular session with a plan that preserved Clarke's Jefferson County district with a population of 9,964 but failed to split the district comprising Sarasota, Manatee, and Charlotte counties, where nearly 87,000 people were represented by one senator. The Senate also proposed a constitutional amendment with a senator for each of the sixty-seven counties. As amended by the House and sent to the 1956 ballot, it also added 40 seats to the House, in which half of the new total of 135 districts would be apportioned by population. Each county, however, would still be guaranteed one seat, meaning that less than 30 percent of the population would elect a majority of the House while a mere 8 percent would soon dominate the Senate. The referendum was a cynical stratagem. It gave the rural bloc a pretext not to carry out the existing constitutional provision, and if voters approved the amendment, the smallest counties would own the Senate indefinitely.[2]

The amendment would also be immune to veto. Collins continued to insist on a better short-term Senate redistricting. House reapportionment was essentially automatic: three seats for the five largest counties, two seats to each of the next eighteen most-populous counties, and one seat to each of the remaining forty-four counties. The Senate, however, was required only to have districts "as nearly equal in population as practicable," which meant it could do whatever the majority pleased. Collins threatened to call a second special session if the Senate did not approve a reapportionment that he could accept. That implied that he believed he could veto a reapportionment resolution, which no predecessor had attempted.[3]

Collins and the Senate had accepted a proposed deal during the regular session only to see it rejected in the House because Jefferson County, smaller than forty-six others, would continue to have a senator of its own. The Senate was protecting not Jefferson County but the county's senator, the grand old man of the senatorial ruling clique. Scott Dilworth "Dil" Clarke, who had first gone to Tallahassee as a House member in the 1907 and 1909 sessions, had been in the Senate since the 1930 election, and would retire in 1966 with the all-time Senate record of thirty-six years. In 1955, the banker from Monticello was one of the most powerful members, cementing his influence with frequent loans from his own pocket to other legislators. Johns in particular enjoyed a generous line of credit with Clarke, who lent him a cumulative $71,181 over twenty years. Johns, who was in debt to Clarke while acting governor and during the 1955 reapportionment struggle, once said that Clarke "has been like a daddy to me." What Daddy wanted from the Senate he usually got, typically after a one-line speech saying, "This is a good bill," or "This is a bad bill." When the Senate grudgingly added the smaller counties of Wakulla and Liberty to his district, Clarke objected that he would have to travel too far to visit constituents. "If you give me Liberty," he said, "you give me death." His real fear was that one of the House members from Liberty or Wakulla might have designs on his Senate seat. By tradition, not always honored, there were private agreements to rotate Senate seats among the counties in multicounty districts.[4]

In the rare event that personal loyalties weakened, the clique had other ways to enforce discipline. Hearing that Collins had co-opted Sen. Irlo Bronson of Kissimmee during a fishing trip, the Senate leadership showed Bronson a new map that eliminated his district. He did not need a second look.[5]

Collins addressed a joint session during the fourth week, not long after Senate president W. Turner Davis of Madison had described the special session as "completely useless." It was the first of two Collins speeches some legislators considered insulting and would be slow to forgive. It was a tense moment for the governor, who strode directly to the House Speaker's rostrum without pausing for the customary handshaking and small talk. He agreed that the session had been useless in accomplishments, "but not in purpose." The uselessness, he said, "can be laid at your own door and it is due to your own failure to act as required by the Constitution."[6]

Collins insisted, among other things, that Bay, Monroe, and Manatee should constitute districts of their own. He knew that likely would result in Sarasota electing the Senate's second Republican senator—Pinellas had the first—which meant he was asking for a harder bargain than he had been willing to accept earlier, and he threatened explicitly to veto a less satisfactory measure the Senate was preparing to pass. He appealed for "open minds—fair minds—minds not surrounded by tight barbed wire fences charged with the evil current of sectionalism, minds not dulled to the perception of duty by personal affection or attachments."[7]

The veto threat was rash as well as provocative because Collins did not know whether he had the authority to veto a reapportionment resolution. The speech won him no friends in the Senate and sharpened some enmities. "We have an obligation under the constitution the same as the governor," said Sen. Dewey M. Johnson of Gadsden County, "and we have as much brains in the Legislature as he has in the governor's office." The House defied the threat by passing the bill 39 votes to 37. In the Senate, Johns accused the administration of offering roads, jobs for friends of senators, and insurance and construction contracts as "bribes" for votes against the bill, which Collins denied. Johns even resorted to race-baiting, shouting that "[Y]our governor will have them going to school with Negroes if you don't watch out." The Senate sent Collins the bill by a vote of 17 to 9. Banking on a veto, even Clarke voted for it "in the interest of harmony," although it added Liberty County to his district. Collins said he was "sick about it" and asked the Supreme Court for an advisory opinion on his veto power.[8]

He had told the justices to expect the request, and they replied with unusual speed the next day, voting 4 to 1 as he had hoped. Roberts, the dissenter, said the majority opinion offended the principle of separation of powers. Collins vetoed the redistricting act less than half an hour after receiving the court's opinion, and the House sustained the veto. He vetoed a similar Senate bill a month later; the Pork Chop majority was far short of the two-thirds needed to override. A decade later, Roberts helped draft a new constitution that eliminated the governor's veto over reapportionment; the Supreme Court thereafter would review legislative districting plans. Although that too eroded the separation of powers, Roberts and others contended that it would keep federal courts from intervening in redistricting. They were wrong.[9]

Hoping to influence what the court would say, *Tampa Tribune* associate editor James Clendenin wrote the most memorable of all Florida newspaper editorials, coining the phrase "Pork Chop Gang" for the Senate's ruling bloc. Clendenin, who later became editor of his editorial page, meant it as a reference to political spoils, but to the press and public "Pork Chop Gang" was a brilliant metaphor for the Senate's rural governance. It became a staple of Florida political dialogue relished even by some of those it had been meant to insult. Sen. L. K. Edwards Jr. of Marion County, the longest-lasting Pork Chopper—he retired in 1968—said they had been "proud of the name and why shouldn't we be?" Edwards, a short, rotund man who favored white linen suits and prodigious quantities of steaks and raw oysters, explained that "The thing we had in common was our country background. A boy brought up on a farm learns early the value of things. . . . That was the philosophy we tried to live by in developing Florida."[10]

The Legislature settled into a state of siege, in and out of recess. The two sides fought through the media, with the Pork Choppers contending that Collins's designs would jeopardize the rural counties' shares of South Florida's race track revenue. That was a "a bugaboo pure and simple," Collins replied, because even in a fairly redistricted Senate most members' counties would lose more than gain by reallocating the gambling taxes.[11]

As the special session passed the two-month mark, Collins said in a broadcast that Senate malapportionment was "the equivalent of allowing some people to stuff the ballot box" and that it was "as fundamental as the issue which brought on our war of independence in 1776." He was expressing a messianic instinct that would assert itself again over segregation. Another statewide broadcast voiced a sense of mission as Collins explained why he refused to let the redistricting bill become law: "The defeat or victory, whichever may be achieved in this fight for reapportionment, is not for me, LeRoy

Collins, but for the people of Florida—all the people of Florida. . . . Right is still right and wrong is still wrong and wrong cannot be made into right."[12]

On Labor Day, with the Legislature in a month-long recess, Collins delivered two exceptionally provocative speeches. To an outdoor audience at Dunnellon, he said the twenty "selfish and greedy" senators opposing him spoke for barely 660,000 people, while the eighteen supporting him represented more than two million. Collins said he was resisting advice to punish the opposition senators by withholding projects or firing their constituents from state jobs because "I must live with myself and my conscience." But he implied that he would try to turn the senators out of office. Perspiring in a jacket and tie, Collins declared that "I shall expect to meet them as political foes whenever and wherever our paths may cross."[13]

At Dunnellon and again in his monthly statewide broadcast that night, Collins also began exhorting voters to defeat the 67-senator, 135-House member amendment. He denounced it as "about the worst suggestion that has ever come out of the Florida Legislature," a formula for perpetual stalemate between large counties in the House and small ones in the Senate.[14] The Dunnellon audience included two of the Pork Choppers: Edwards, the local senator, and Connor, who represented an adjacent district. Some of their colleagues contended for a long time that Collins had insulted them.[15]

There was no compromise on the table when legislators returned from a second long recess. If anything, positions had hardened. Small-county legislators in both houses said they would agree only to a special early election on the 67-senator, 135-representative plan they had already sent to the November 1956 ballot. Collins had already said what he thought of that. The climax came in the last week of September, involving a combative speech by Collins and a white paper, which he reportedly helped draft, signed by twenty-nine representatives and published in the House *Journal.* Of the twenty-nine, only five were from North Florida: Bryant of Marion County, C. Fred Arrington of Gadsden, J. B. Hopkins of Escambia, and Horne and Kenneth Ballinger of Leon. The white paper contended that the issue was not sectionalism but rather "the refusal of some members of the Senate to give up their personal political control over state, city and county government, and their personal political control over laws affecting large segments of the business interests of the state."[16]

That was the truth. Though the twenty-two Pork Chop senators owed their strength to malapportionment, they owed their allegiance to the business lobbies. In 1960, at the height of their power, Martin Waldron of the *Tampa Tribune* documented extensive financial ties to influential business lobbies that benefited from how they cast or withheld their votes. "Members vote together more regularly on special interest bills than they do on reapportionment, although in this latter field the record is nearly unanimous," Waldron wrote. The Pork Chop Gang's favorite hideaway was a fishing camp owned by a former senator lobbying for the small-loan industry. Johnson, the Senate president in 1959, represented the duPont estate's St. Joe Paper Company, and he borrowed liberally from the estate's Florida National banks. Journalist Robert Sherrill wrote that the Pork Chop Gang filled a leadership void that Edward Ball left when he withdrew about 1950 from active politicking in Tallahassee. As the duPont estate's million acres of timber were spread over twelve of the Pork Chop counties, Ball was the Gang's largest and most influential constituent.[17]

The Pork Chop Gang also counted on the votes of certain urban senators when commercial interests were at stake. The business lobbies were their "true constituency," wrote Frank Trippett, a *St. Petersburg Times* bureau chief; "to its services the entire structure of the Senate was dedicated."[18]

On the day his allies published their white paper, Collins spoke defiantly to a joint session. Acknowledging failure—he alluded to "the ruins of this fight"—Collins asked the Legislature for a new constitutional amendment he knew they would not approve. If they would not pass it, he said, "surely you should not stay here and continue a useless expense. If you are to violate the constitution, it is far better that you do it on your own time."[19]

The challenge was rhetorical, for public consumption. He was declaring a war he said he would fight in the spring primaries: "I predict the organization throughout Florida of citizens groups crusading for fair representation. Candidates for all elective offices, statewide and local, will be required to take an open stand for fair representation or for the status quo. It matters not whether I am a candidate for governor. I will, God willing, *be* governor, and the full weight and force and influence I possess and can honorably use will be thrown into this fight for fair play for all the people of Florida."[20]

That was Collins at his best as an orator but his worst as a practical politician. There was no reason for the Pork Chop senators to fear the threat. They had cosseted their voters with money for local projects and jobs for supporters, and they were popular in their districts for refusing to cede power to urban South Florida.[21] If Collins "has his eye on returning, which he has, then he had better start fighting for his own hide in our county. . . . Our Senator Randolph Hodges is safe," said one rural weekly.[22] Some of the legislators welcomed a fight with Collins. "I challenge the governor to come to Walton County and speak against me in the next campaign," said Rep. Tom Beasley. The only advice that the Legislature accepted from Collins was to go home; it recessed until June 4, 1956, a date subsequent to the spring primaries.[23]

Collins or someone on his staff had prepared an even more confrontational version of the speech challenging recalcitrant legislators to "take your party affiliation elsewhere, if they will have you." It went to the archives, prudently unused.[24]

What he did say was too much for Farris Bryant, his erstwhile ally, who intended to run for governor in 1956 and suspected that Collins meant to run also. Bryant, a Harvard-educated lawyer with a facial resemblance to President Dwight D. Eisenhower, issued a three-page statement charging angrily that Collins, not the Legislature, was to blame for the failure of reapportionment. He said Collins had sent mixed signals, vacillated among proposals, encouraged an untimely recess, and "raised an emotional and political barrier" in the Labor Day speech. "The battle for reapportionment was lost, in the last analysis, by the deliberate and calculated refusal of the governor to use that influence and prestige entrusted to him by the sovereign people of this state," Bryant said.[25]

His statement was in effect the opening battle of the 1956 campaign. Collins, however, said it reflected favorably on his refusal to use patronage as a weapon. "Is he suggesting that I should stop the state's road construction program in his own county of Marion because his own senator will not vote for fair reapportionment?" Collins asked. "Is he suggesting that I penalize our universities because the senators from the counties where they are located have been opposing us? Is he suggesting that I should have bargained for Senate votes with the appointment of a judge? Some would have done this, but I would not and will not."[26]

One Pork Chop supporter saw it the same way. Accusing Bryant of "poor sportsmanship," Beasley praised Collins for refusing to follow Al Rogero's public advice to use roads for leverage. Collins, he said, "was too big a man to go along with that and I congratulate him for it."[27]

There was controversy over whether Collins had improperly lobbied the Supreme Court. A Pork Chop senator, Shands of Gainesville, disclosed what he called "an ugly rumor" that Collins had met secretly with four members of the court as they decided whether he could veto reapportionment bills. Collins admitted that he had visited the court but only to tell the justices that he would be asking for an opinion. He denied that he had tried to suggest how they ought to vote. Moreover, he believed that his constitutional power to seek advisory opinions entitled him to do so "orally," and that he thought other governors had done so. Terrell, the acting chief justice, supported Collins's version of the events, which Terrell rationalized as "merely an informal meeting." Neither statement noted, however, that the court had not given an equivalent audience to legislators or anyone else who might dispute a governor's authority to veto reapportionment legislation.[28] The incident would be prohibited today by stricter ethics standards at the court and a provision of the 1968 constitution—another legacy of the Collins era—requiring that the court hear interested persons before issuing an advisory opinion.[29]

Collins was soon in another pitched battle, this one with the Cabinet, over constitutional revision. Addressing the new advisory commission at Tampa in late October, Collins singled out the "entire so-called Cabinet system" for review. He conceded that it "has an advantage in that it protects our people and the stability of their government against weak governors." He believed, however, that "surely we should be able to assume that Florida will elect good governors and not be required to sacrifice efficiency for this kind of protection." It was an angry Cabinet that confronted Collins at their next meeting a few days later. R. A. Gray, the normally soft-spoken secretary of state, alluded to "dictatorship" as a worse evil than inefficiency. Collins protested the inference but said in a press release that he was "delighted that my remarks have stimulated interest in our Cabinet system" and insisted that "I said nothing which in any way reflected upon any Cabinet member." He argued that the system was basically sound but that the time for changes had arrived. He cited the prison system as an example of a program that would work better with one person rather than a committee in charge. "I don't blame the Cabinet members," he said.[30]

As with reapportionment, Collins had planted more seeds that would be slow to sprout. He would secure a measure of prison reform during his term, but it would be 1969 before the governor's powers were enlarged at the Cabinet's expense, and it would take until 2002 to reduce the elected Cabinet seats from six to three.

Chapter 14

Massive Resistance

Desegregation of the public schools was still only an abstract threat to white Floridians when Collins was inaugurated. But some other potentially explosive racial issues were ripening. Virgil Hawkins's lawsuit to desegregate the University of Florida College of Law was in what should have been its final phase. Even sooner, Collins would have to decide whether to spare Walter Lee Irvin, a black man condemned to the electric chair for the rape of a white woman. The Irvin case was internationally notorious for the shooting deaths of two other defendants, for a riot that had terrorized their hometown of Groveland, and for convictions based on fabricated evidence.

Collins persuaded the Pardon Board to commute the sentence to life in prison. "In all respects my conscience told me that this was a bad case, badly handled, badly tried, and now on this bad performance I was asked to take a man's life. My conscience would not let me do it," Collins said later.[1]

Early on the morning of July 16, 1949, Norma Padgett, a seventeen-year-old farm housewife in Lake County, said she had been abducted and raped by four Negro men. Walter Irvin and Sammy Shepherd, both twenty-two, were arrested that day. Charlie Greenlee, sixteen, was already in jail on an unrelated charge. The fourth suspect, Ernest Thomas, was shot dead ten days later by a posse led by Lake County sheriff Willis McCall. McCall had hidden the other defendants from a lynch mob, but the press report of his claim that they had confessed set off rioting by whites that destroyed Shepherd's home and two others at Groveland, forced the town's 350 black residents to seek refuge at Orlando, and required the National Guard to be called out. The *Orlando Sentinel* published a front-page editorial cartoon showing four electric chairs and the caption "No Compromise."[2]

The United States Supreme Court reversed the Shepherd and Irvin sentences in an unsigned order based on exclusion of Negroes from the jury. Justices Richard Jackson and Felix Frankfurter denounced the entire trial as "one of the best examples of one of the worst menaces to American justice."[3]

Groveland became an international cause celebre because of Harry T. Moore, executive secretary of the Florida Conference of the National Association for the Advancement of Colored People, whose lawyers established that the defendants had been tortured; their confessions were so questionable that the prosecution could not use them at trial. Yet all three defendants were convicted. The jury voted to spare only Greenlee's life, making death sentences mandatory for Irvin and Shepherd, who appealed. When the Florida Supreme Court upheld the convictions, Governor Fuller Warren wired prosecutor J. R. Hunter that "As soon then as I can legally issue death warrants will do so."[4]

In November 1951, McCall shot Shepherd to death and gravely wounded Irvin while taking them from the state prison to a Lake County hearing on a motion to move the retrial. He said the manacled prisoners had attacked him. Irvin claimed the shootings were unprovoked. A coroner's jury absolved McCall.[5]

Thurgood Marshall, the NAACP's chief counsel, defended Irvin at the retrial in neighboring Marion County. Warren, who had become sensitive to the notoriety of the case, tried to have Irvin plead guilty in exchange for a life sentence, but Irvin refused even when Marshall advised him to accept it. In the retrial, an expert defense witness testified that plaster casts purported to be of Irvin's footprints at the abduction scene had been made when the shoes were empty, yet Irvin was convicted and condemned a second time. He lost his appeals.[6]

Collins inherited the case under heavy pressure from both sides, especially from the *St. Petersburg Times*, which had exposed the weakness of the case in 1950.[7] After hearing witnesses, including a former *Times* reporter, the Pardon Board agreed with Collins to postpone Irvin's clemency hearing for more investigation. When the attorney general suggested a poll, Collins said that public opinion was irrelevant.[8]

Collins was most impressed by what he heard from Hunter. The prosecutor had talked to Irvin the morning after McCall shot him, and though Irvin thought he might be dying, he still refused to admit guilt even in confidence.[9]

Collins requested advice, as he would often do, from his former law firm.[10] William C. Harris, a young associate, told Collins there was no evidence to support a conviction other than eyewitness testimony by the victim and her husband. The scant forensic evidence was flawed. Among other things, the plaster casts that purported to be of Irvin's shoes at the abduction scene matched a pair found at his home after he had been arrested with a different pair on his feet, and at that were "palpably false," having been made "by a shoe without anybody in it." The state's rape case consisted largely of evidence that was "crude," "third-rate," and "speculative." Harris could not decide whether McCall had shot Irvin and Shepherd without provocation.[11]

Collins spoke at least once with McCall, apparently at the request of the sheriff, who wrote him that clemency for Irvin would be a "gross miscarriage of justice . . . a victory for [the] NAACP who [*sic*] has set out to destroy the authority of our courts." It would mean "one thing," McCall added: "That all a negro criminal would need to do would be pick out some innocent helpless white woman as a target to satisfy his ravishing sexual desires, keep his mouth shut, proclain [*sic*] his innocence and let NAACP furnish the money and lawyers and beat the rap."[12]

The white sexual paranoia McCall expressed was beginning to concern Collins almost as much as the question of Irvin's guilt. Over the previous twenty years, Collins determined, Florida had executed twenty-three black men but no whites for rape. The racism shook the governor's confidence in segregation. "If race interfered with justice at the basic level of preserving life itself," he wrote in an unpublished autobiography, "what about the role of race in all other aspects of life?" Collins still professed that "separate but equal" was fair, "but in those lonely moments when I had to decide to take or spare the life of a man, there began a serious process of self-examination."[13]

From 1924 through 1964, Florida electrocuted forty-two men for rape, the last nine on warrants Collins signed. All the victims were white.[14] Collins commuted ten death sentences, nearly one in every four that came to him during his six years in office, but only Irvin's was controversial.[15]

The constitution required a favorable clemency recommendation from the governor and agreement by at least two of the four Cabinet members on the Pardon Board. On December 15, 1955, the board voted unanimously to commute Irvin's sentence to life in prison. In a sop to white sentiment,

Collins also criticized the NAACP for protests "prompted by the bare fact that the defendant is a colored man rather than by a careful evaluation of the circumstances of his guilt or innocence."[16]

That was unfair. Guilt aside, race was plainly responsible for Irvin having been on death row. But for the NAACP, Irvin would already have been as dead as the man most responsible for saving him. Moore, Florida's first civil rights activist, was murdered twenty-three days after urging Gov. Fuller Warren to suspend McCall for the Irvin-Shepherd shootings.[17] Moore and his wife, Harriette, died of injuries from the bombing of their home near Mims, in Brevard County, on Christmas night of 1951. The FBI conducted a vigorous investigation at the Brevard sheriff's request; it implicated several Ku Klux Klansmen, one of whom killed himself after questioning, but no murder charges resulted. Six Klan suspects who were indicted for perjury before a federal grand jury went free when a judge ruled that the Moore murders, Klan floggings, synagogue bombings, and other crimes under investigation violated no federal laws. Florida never filed charges.[18]

There was surprisingly little public reaction to the Irvin commutation, which the *Tampa Tribune* questioned as "dubious" and persuasive only "from a humanitarian viewpoint."[19] Some blacks thought Collins should have freed Irvin, but Gilbert L. Porter, executive secretary of the Florida State Teachers Association, said Collins had done all he could. "In view of all the circumstances here in Florida, the action of the Pardon Board should really be considered as a victory," he wrote to the NAACP's national office. "For the first time, to my knowledge, the Negro has a true friend in the Governor at Tallahassee."[20]

Collins was indecisive, however, in another racial controversy centering on McCall. Three days after his inauguration, he received a poignant complaint from Allen Platt, a fruit picker living with his wife and five children at Mount Dora. McCall, the county's most powerful politician and a recently appointed director of the National Association for the Advancement of White People, had barred Platt's children from the local white schools on the presumption that they were black. Platt, who had documentary proof from South Carolina of the family's Native American and Irish descent, had written unavailingly to Johns. Now he sought the new governor's help.[21]

"Being thrown out of school is not the most important thing," Platt told Collins. "To have my family branded as niggers is far worse." Though Collins's investigator substantially supported Platt, the governor merely advised Platt to "seek relief in our courts."[22]

Remarkably, however, Collins also told Platt that the real problem "goes much deeper than the law. . . . You are getting a look at prejudice, perhaps the most tenacious and blinding of all the human emotions." Prejudice, wrote Collins, "dethrones reason and justice, and prospers in the atmosphere of fear which it spawns. Prejudice is a disease of the heart and mind. It cannot be corrected by law or by the edict of a court or by the executive order of an official even if such is within his power to issue. The correction must also come from within." Collins cautioned Platt to think carefully how his children might be treated by their peers at a white school.[23]

That letter, which Collins knew would be published widely, is the earliest reflection of his internal conflicts over segregation. Though he understood racial prejudice to be wrong, he could not imagine the government doing anything about it. Yet he wanted Floridians to know "that I did not condone the kind of prejudice which had been exhibited in the Platt case."[24]

There was one more pathetic letter from Platt, saying he rejected advice to sue in federal courts because he did not want to upset Florida's segregation laws.[25] In October, a state circuit judge, Truman Futch, ruled that the children were entitled to attend any white school. The next day, shotgun blasts broke up a citrus workers' union meeting in Lake County. When the union requested his suspension, McCall said his detractors were "communists and their political sympathizers."[26]

Two weeks after Futch's final order, the Platts' home was firebombed with minimal damage. To complaints that he should have protected them, McCall responded: "I'll be just as good to them as any other niggers I know of. I can't baby-sit with them." Collins declared to the press: "These outbreaks in Lake County have just got to stop. Not only are the individual rights involved but the good name and reputation of this fine county and our state have become involved." A decade later, Collins expressed regret that he had not done more to protect the Platts, who moved to Orange County after shotgun blasts damaged their home. Their children remained in a Mount Dora private school, where church groups were paying their tuition.[27]

The Virgil Hawkins case was escalating simultaneously. One of his attorneys would write that it was Florida, not Virginia, that originated "massive resistance" to desegregation.[28] Florida still insisted that Hawkins should enroll in a hastily established, segregated law school at Florida A&M University.

The state's position flouted a landmark 1950 U.S. Supreme Court decision disallowing an identical Texas scheme. Two months after the Texas decision, the Florida Supreme Court told Hawkins he could attend the University of Florida only so long as it took to open the school at A&M. Hawkins refused to settle for that or accept a subsidy to study out of state. Once again, the state court turned him down but delayed its final decree to stall his federal appeal. Four more years had elapsed when the U.S. Supreme Court, a week after the *Brown* decision, sent his and similar cases back to their respective state courts "for consideration in light of the Segregation Cases decided May 17, 1954 . . . and conditions that now prevail."[29]

Though the precedents were unmistakable, the Florida Supreme Court was unmoved. It kept Hawkins in suspense until after the *Brown II* decision declaring that desegregation of public schools should proceed with "all deliberate speed," which the Florida court interpreted as license to stall Hawkins yet again. Conceding "our inescapable duty" to order Hawkins admitted, B. K. Roberts's majority opinion detailed how Florida would evade it. The high court's orders, Roberts wrote, did not impose "a clear legal duty" to admit Hawkins "*immediately*, or at any particular time in the future." Because the Board of Control objected that his enrollment would cause "public mischief" at the university, the court appointed Circuit Judge A. H. Murphree of Alachua County to take testimony on how students, parents, and alumni would react. Terrell, the friend and mentor who had inspired Collins to study law and had sworn him in as governor, wrote a separate concurring opinion extolling segregation, which said in part that "[S]egregation is not a new philosophy generated by the states that practice it. It is and has always been the unvarying law of the animal kingdom. . . . [A]nd when God created man, he allotted each race to his own continent according to color, Europe to the white man, Asia to the yellow man, Africa to the black man, and America to the red man, but we are now advised that God's plan was in error and must be reversed."[30]

There were dissents this time. Justices Elwyn Thomas and H. L. Sebring said Hawkins should be admitted "on the same basis as any white student."[31]

Hawkins refused to participate in Murphree's hearings and petitioned the U.S. Supreme Court yet again. He was now forty-eight years old. His four coplaintiffs had long since quit under various threats and job-related pressures. Hawkins himself had been fired by a black-owned life insurance company but was now safely employed as public relations director of the black

Bethune-Cookman College at Daytona Beach.[32] He had dreamed of being a lawyer since he was six years old, when he had seen black defendants accused of playing penny-ante poker brought to court without lawyers and sentenced to a chain gang where they would earn money for the sheriff.[33]

His wife's job as a Lake County teacher was in jeopardy so the couple pretended to be divorced. Mrs. Hawkins often drove by night to Daytona Beach, a 160-mile round trip, to spend a few hours with her husband before teaching the next day. A teenaged niece rode along to make sure she stayed awake.[34]

In Washington, the Supreme Court's patience ran out. Disdaining any more argument from Florida, it declared: "As this case involves the admission of a Negro to a graduate professional school, there is no reason for delay. He is entitled to prompt admission under the rules and regulations applicable to other qualified candidates."[35] That seemingly final decision, issued on March 12, 1956, came six days after Collins had filed for reelection in a Democratic primary that was degenerating into a contest with a single issue: segregation. Collins panicked. He said he would take the matter before the Cabinet, that Florida would "continue to wage this fight by all legal and peaceful means" and would not surrender "in our battle to protect our state's customs and traditions." Collins said he would appear in person before the U.S. Supreme Court if it would let him. Attorney General Richard Ervin, facing his own re-election campaign against an arch-segregationist state legislator, accused the Supreme Court of having acted in a "precipitous, unreasonable and arbitrary manner"—seven years and the Texas precedent notwithstanding.[36]

Though they were playing to a political gallery, there were some plausible concerns. A white riot at the University of Alabama the month before had intimidated its trustees into expelling their first black student, Autherine Lucy. Could Gainesville erupt the same way? Reitz said publicly that he anticipated no trouble at his university, but Collins and Ervin ignored that. Asking the U.S. Supreme Court to reconsider, Ervin cited a Board of Control study purporting that some 41 percent of parents wanted no integration at the university "under any circumstances" and that nearly 33 percent would withdraw their sons and daughters. (Student responses were notably less hostile; nearly 23 percent favored immediate integration, and only 21 percent opposed it under any circumstances.) But the court refused without comment to hear either Ervin or Collins.[37]

The Florida Supreme Court took another year to respond to that presumably final decree. For a fifth time, it denied Hawkins and for a second time directly defied the nation's highest court. "[W]e cannot assume," Roberts wrote, "that the Supreme Court intended to deprive the highest court of an independent sovereign state of one of its traditional powers . . . the right to exercise a sound judicial discretion as to the date of the issuance of its process in order to prevent a serious public mischief." Dismissing Hawkins as someone who "does not, in fact, have a genuine interest in obtaining a legal education," Roberts invoked the state's survey and Murphree's findings to predict that integration would "seriously impair" student and state support for the white universities. Four justices concurred, Collins's two appointees among them.[38]

The majority based its five-to-two decision on a selective reading of Murphree's report, which was uncertain of violence and implied that whites might object only to rooming with Negroes.[39]

Terrell wrote another separate concurring opinion that remains notorious for saying that "segregation is as old as the hills. The Egyptians practiced it on the Israelites; the Greeks did likewise for the barbarians; the Romans segregated the Syrians; the Chinese segregated all foreigners; segregation is said to have produced the caste system in India and Hitler practiced it in his Germany, but no one ever discovered that it was a violation of due process until recently."[40]

"It seems to me," dissented Justice Elwyn Thomas, "that if this court expects obedience to its mandates, it must be prepared immediately to obey mandates from a higher court."[41]

"The technique is to wait so long that I will get discouraged," Hawkins said. "After 10 years of delaying tactics, they talk about gradualism and patience. How patient can we be? I wish I were nine years younger." He appealed again; the U.S. Supreme Court, unwilling to risk a third act of defiance by the Florida Supreme Court, suggested he apply to a federal district court that presumably would be more likely to obey the law. But by the time Hawkins could get U.S. District Judge Dozier DeVane to rule on his class-action lawsuit—an appeals court had to order DeVane to hear it—Florida had implemented admission standards, including an aptitude test, that the aging Hawkins could not satisfy. At his lawyers' suggestion, Hawkins withdrew his application to the university. DeVane then ordered Florida's white graduate schools to admit qualified blacks. The result was a legal paradox: The named plaintiff in a class-action suit won for the class and lost on behalf of himself.[42]

A year or so earlier, Collins had privately told the Board of Control, still dominated by Johns and McCarty holdovers, that Florida should desegregate the universities, but the board refused to do it in the absence of a court order. It could have been accomplished five years earlier, one member said, but now the public had been inflamed. Now there was a court order that Collins called on Floridians to accept. "In this respect," he noted laconically, "Florida now joins the great majority of Southern states." Indeed, there were already desegregated colleges and universities in eleven of the sixteen states, including Louisiana and Virginia, notable hotbeds of resistance to the desegregation of elementary and secondary schools.[43]

The University of Florida was finally desegregated in September 1958, when Morehouse College graduate George H. Starke Jr., twenty-seven years old, enrolled without incident in the College of Law. Nothing appeared out of the ordinary except for two state troopers in mufti, apparently sent by Collins, who accompanied Starke through registration. Gainesville police kept special watch for a while, but by Thanksgiving that was seen to be unnecessary. There was no white flight.[44]

Chapter 15

Backlash

Southern politicians of his generation believed in segregation or said that they did. *How* they said it distinguished moderates from hardliners. Collins's lack of passion contrasted with the rhetoric from states such as Georgia, which had amended its constitution to authorize public financing of private schools; South Carolina, which had repealed its compulsory assignment law; and Virginia, where Gov. Harry Byrd incited the legislature to "massive resistance" that included the closing of any school integrated by a court. Virginia was the first of eight states to adopt a resolution of "interposition," a doctrine originating in the antifederalism of Thomas Jefferson and James Madison that claimed states could nullify decisions by Congress and the federal judiciary. Many Southern politicians understood, however, that interposition was propaganda. Gov. James Folsom of Alabama likened it to "a hound dog baying at the moon and claiming it's got the moon treed."[1]

White Southerners indulged in a massive self-deception typified by an *Orlando Sentinel* front-page editorial cartoon on May 18, 1954, that attributed the *Brown* decision to "liver lipped Commie agitation" and depicted the "majority of our colored folks" as content with segregation. Collins recalled that at first, "People just didn't think it was true" and came to believe that the Court would change its mind. "Resistance to the court decree is stiffening throughout the region," wrote Charleston newspaper editor Thomas R. Waring in a January 1956 *Harper's* article that elaborated stereotypical prejudices against schooling white children with blacks. Many Floridians, "apparently the majority," reported the *Tampa Tribune*, "have an abiding faith that the state government—the political and economic leaders—will find a way to maintain the color line."[2]

Ralph McGill wrote that the first *Brown* decision was followed briefly by "a period of silence and hope. . . . But much of the silence was sullen. And hope was soon to be rebuffed by defiance and demagoguery at high-decibel levels."[3]

In March 1956, nineteen of the twenty-two Southern senators and seventy-seven representatives declared that the *Brown* decisions were "a clear abuse of judicial power" that was "destroying the amicable relations between the white and Negro races." The document commended states that were resisting "by any lawful means." Only one of Florida's representatives, Dante Fascell of Miami, refused to sign it.[4]

Between the two *Brown* decisions, wrote historian Nunan V. Bartley, the Border States made "constructive preparations for compliance." The Deep South "entrenched itself yet further."[5]

Collins hoped to devote his 1956 campaign to constitutional revision and other issues the 1955 session left unfinished. In January, not yet a declared candidate, he used his monthly broadcast to warn against racial politics: "While at the helm of our ship of state, I am constantly on watch for rocks and shoals, which could wreck our progress. We are not out of the narrows yet, and the course we sail in the next few years will determine whether our children and their children will avoid the storms of dissension and strife on one side and the becalmed waters of apathy and mediocrity on the other." He quoted a prayer written by a clergyman friend: "May we have courage to face the social evils of our time and to rebuke injustice and oppression wherever it may be."[6]

In January, refusing to join some other Southern governors at a meeting to promote interposition and organize resistance, he said Florida so far had "avoided furor and hysteria and at the same time [had] effectively supported our traditions."[7]

Collins, not saying whether he wanted to run again, did not want to appear too eager and hoped that someone else would contest his eligibility. A Palm Beach County constable named Peaslee Streets, thought to be a stalking horse for Fuller Warren, declared his own candidacy and sued to bar Collins, but a circuit judge refused to decide the question until after Collins declared in December that he would run if he could. Upon being ruled eligible, Collins said he hoped the Supreme Court would decide the appeal swiftly.[8]

The judge's ruling came with Collins in California on a secretive mission that his new press secretary, John Perry, described only as of "vital importance in connection with Florida's industrial expansion." In fact, Collins had been invited by Howard Hughes, the idiosyncratic industrialist, aviator, film producer, and playboy. Collins understood from an intermediary, developer Del Webb, that Hughes intended to build a major medical research center somewhere in South Florida. At a private dinner at Los Angeles, Hughes outlined a plan that impressed Collins as the "finest research capability ever assembled." Collins was less pleased when Hughes put him in the copilot's seat of a small plane and flew him to Palm Springs for lunch and then back to Los Angeles at night. "I knew he was a capable pilot, but I was uneasy with fear," Collins said. The two issued a vague announcement of a forthcoming Florida project, and Collins returned on a commercial flight to Tallahassee. There was already public speculation on the medical institute; the formal announcement would come three months later, at an opportune moment for the Collins campaign.[9]

The governor's industrial promotion tours, including a trip to the Midwest just before the 1956 campaign, were effective politics. To the dismay of Bryant and other prospective opponents, Collins made the cover of the December 19, 1955, issue of *Time*, which described him as "one of the most interesting and effective governors in the U.S. today."[10] Florida—and Collins—also reaped valuable publicity in *Fortune*, *Collier's*, *Saturday Evening Post*, *Kiplinger's Changing Times*, *Holiday*, *Look*, and *U.S. News and World Report*, which published a six-page interview with Collins less than a month before the primary. The *U.S. News* interview, its second article on Collins, did not allude even indirectly to segregation, which had become the dominant issue of the campaign.[11]

The candidate who made it so was Sumter Lowry, a Tampa businessman and retired general in the Army National Guard, who had no other plank in his platform. Despite being a novice candidate, Lowry quickly overtook Fuller Warren and Farris Bryant, the political veterans who were assumed to be Collins's principal rivals. Lowry, a remarried widower aged sixty-two, was connected through blood or marriage to many prominent old-line Tampa families. Nominally a Democrat, Lowry openly supported Republican Dwight D. Eisenhower for president in 1952. In the National Guard, he had served on the Mexican border in 1916, where he court-martialed a private for publishing letters in a Tampa newspaper; in France in World War I; and in the South Pacific during World War II. Lowry's peacetime battles had been fought on the banquet circuit, against communism, the United Nations, any public figures he suspected of disloyalty, and a political science textbook at the University of Florida. He had attacked even the American Legion as insufficiently patriotic.[12]

Lowry previewed his segregation campaign with a speech to the Duval County Democratic Executive Committee at Jacksonville denouncing the NAACP and desegregation as inventions of international communism for the purposes of destroying Christianity, the white race, and the United States through "mongrelization." The speech propelled Lowry's candidacy as well as his resignation from the board of an insurance company with many African-American policyholders.[13]

Bryant became the first announced candidate with a statement attacking Collins for "deplorable leadership." Bryant, a forty-one-year-old Harvard law graduate whose hometown newspaper described him as having "made statecraft a life study," did not mention segregation. Martin Andersen's *Orlando Sentinel* praised Bryant as "one of the best-qualified men in Florida" but said Orange County would support Collins this time because of roads and other favors.[14]

Collins did not intend to share a platform with Bryant or any other rival and declined his challenge to debate. The press credited him, however, with civil service reforms so stringent that state employees could not campaign for him even on their own time. The attorney general held that it applied even to students holding part-time campus jobs.[15]

Bryant was the first to recognize Lowry's potential, replying in racist terms to a question concerning segregation. "In the homes of Negroes," Bryant said, "we find different intellectual levels, and moral and sanitary standards. . . . Negroes have come very far in these past one hundred years, but not as far as they will go in the next one hundred."[16]

The interposition movement concerned Collins more than he cared to reveal. He sought advice not from the attorney general, who might have a conflicting political agenda, but from Ben C. Willis, his attorney in the eligibility litigation whom Collins would eventually appoint to a circuit judgeship. Willis advised Collins that though the Civil War seemingly had put interposition to rest, the doctrine "does have a considerable moral appeal" that might discourage aggressive federal desegregation efforts. He warned that Florida's public mood was hardening: "I sense a demand that state officials in every legal and honorable way possible resist to the utmost." Willis wrote again three weeks later, saying he feared violence in the absence of moderate leadership and that school desegregation should be postponed until Florida was ready to accept it, which he did not expect to happen in "the foreseeable future."[17]

Willis's apprehension was shared by Collins and many other moderates. The governor profoundly feared disorder, and he considered the NAACP extreme for advocating desegregation in the face of white hostility. It was what Collins did *not* say, however, that distinguished him from his rivals and even many of his supporters. He did not voice any version of the Southern white paranoia that black men were sexually obsessed with white women, never used the catchphrase "race-mixing," and said nothing that implied that blacks were inferior or that segregation was natural or divine law.[18]

Lowry formally declared his candidacy with a promise that "there will be no mixing of the races in the schools." He accused Bryant and Warren of being either weak or silent on segregation and said of Collins: "The few evasive remarks he has uttered on this vital subject indicate he either favors race-mixing or that he has not yet decided what is the politically expedient course for him to follow."[19]

Collins retorted in a prepared statement that aggressive resistance could actually hasten desegregation. He extolled moderation without defining it or explaining precisely what he intended to do. That no integration had occurred in Florida, he said, meant that "our leadership has been far more effective than has been the case in many other states in which a great deal more noise and confusion have been generated." Collins emphasized that "I am against defiance of constituted authority. I am against any effort to make political capital out of segregation. I am for the orderly and effective assertion of our rights under authority of law." Should Florida stray from its course, he said, "I fear we will actually lose ground in our efforts to maintain segregation and to carry Florida forward."[20]

Writing to a professor who had urged gradual desegregation immediately, Collins said it "would be far more dangerous to all our people than the continuance of segregation." The end of segregation, he asserted, "can only come when there is a basic change in the hearts and minds of our people."[21]

Collins was rationalizing, as much to himself as to the public. He said in retrospect that there had been no single moment, no "on the road to Damascus" epiphany, that changed his beliefs on segregation. Rather, it came to him gradually "as an acceptance of the responsibility that I had as governor."[22] In 1956, he was still not ready to confess that segregation was inherently wrong, but he could no longer deny it to himself.

At some point that year, Collins or some staff person drafted a remarkable statement. "I do not contend," it said, "that segregation in public schools, or at public meetings, or on public conveyances is consistent as a matter of principle with Christianity or the basic American ideal of equality before the law. . . . But the end of segregation, if and when it comes . . . can only come when its acceptance is developed in the hearts and minds of the people and, in spite of the [Supreme] Court's great power, these hearts and minds are beyond its reach and control." The document also said that the South should be "ashamed" of not having done more for black health, education, and economic opportunity. But the archival copy bears a notion in pencil, doubly underlined, "not issued."[23]

Within four years, Collins would no longer be keeping such thoughts to himself. To have said them aloud in 1956 likely would have elected Lowry. Twenty years later, Collins suggested to biographer Tom Wagy that "political realities" had influenced his public statements. Two men who befriended Collins when they were young Episcopal priests have told this author of conversations in which Collins expressed internal conflict between his conscience and his politics.[24]

What Collins did say aloud contrasted so starkly with the demagoguery in neighboring Georgia that Ralph McGill remarked in an *Atlanta Constitution* editorial: "Florida has not integrated its public schools but neither has it destroyed them. Other states might well study the example being set by Governor Collins and the others connected with his state government."[25]

Still waiting for the Supreme Court to say whether he could run, Collins delivered what sounded like a campaign kickoff in Tampa in early February. He touched on many issues, including the reapportionment failure that he called a "great deficiency in the very heart of our democratic way of life." However, segregation led the news reports even though he had put that topic off until the fourteenth page, where he warned against racial issues that would discourage prospective Florida investors. "It is high time he quits pleading the cause of the NAACP," Lowry said.[26]

What Collins feared was evident in Alabama that week: the expulsion of the University of Alabama's first black students in response to rioting by whites. Bryant, speaking elsewhere, said he wished segregation was not an issue in the campaign "because it is an issue that gives itself to passionate rather than reasonable treatment."[27]

Less than a week later, Truman G. Futch, the circuit judge who had sentenced Irvin to death, summoned the Lake County grand jury to investigate Irvin's commutation. He acted on a petition signed by 121 citizens including Irvin's accuser and members of her family. The petition insinuated that the lawyers who had advised Collins belonged to the NAACP. Political motives were apparent. McCall had just declared his candidacy for reelection. In a Rotary Club address, Futch denounced the U.S. Supreme Court and described desegregation as a foreign Communist plot "to reduce the South to an amalgamated mongrel section of people." Futch also campaigned for Warren until a newspaper reported that it was judicially unethical.[28]

There was no precedent for a judicial investigation of clemency for any grounds other than bribery. Collins said he would not appear before the grand jury "unless I am required to do so," which the attorney general said he was not. Collins offered, however, to answer questions from the judge, the state attorney, or the foreman of the grand jury provided they met in the Capitol's Cabinet Room "with the press table fully occupied." The offer was not accepted. "There is nothing to investigate except LeRoy Collins' judgment and conscience," Collins said. "Both are beyond the control or coercion of a grand jury." Alluding to the racism involved, Collins declared that "[H]uman life is just as sacred whether it is clothed in a dark skin or a light one. No person stands before the Governor of Florida with his life or liberty jeopardized because of his race, color, or creed."[29]

Collins and other Pardon Board members declined invitations from the grand jury. The governor insisted, however, on making scheduled speeches in Lake County, where a trap awaited him at the Washington's Day parade in Eustis. Norma Padgett, escorted by some of McCall's deputies, approached the open convertible where Collins was seated, identified herself as the rape victim, and asked the governor, "How would you feel if your wife or daughter were raped by four Negroes?" Collins answered uncomfortably, telling her that Irvin would not be paroled any time soon. The incident troubled him for years.[30]

The governor's opponents relished the confrontation. A Fuller Warren newspaper advertisement asked, "Will LeRoy Collins ever explain to the citizens of Florida his shame and why he excused this Negro to the shame of every decent white woman of our state?" Streets, Warren's suspected front man, filmed an interview with the woman and broadcast it on a Miami television station. The public impact of the issue compelled Collins to prepare a form letter explaining that the constitutional responsibilities of the governor and Pardon Board were not the same as those of the courts.[31]

Collins's opponents also exploited his appointment of Florida's first black assistant state attorney, Henry H. Arrington, a former trial attorney for the U.S. Department of Justice. George Brautigam, the elected state attorney for Dade County, had asked the governor for a black lawyer for "the investigation and prosecution of colored capital crime cases and only that." But Arrington said in an incautious radio interview, which was tape-recorded and distributed statewide, that he was not restricted to black cases and that Brautigam had told the white secretaries to take his dictation or "pick up their checks." At Collins's request, Brautigam subpoenaed a copy of the tape, confirmed the remarks, and frantically urged Collins to suspend Arrington, which he did. Brautigam was defeated in a campaign dominated by other local issues.[32]

Four former governors had tried to return; only one had succeeded, in 1896. Hoping to be the second, Warren promised to preserve segregation, double the homestead exemption, and amend the constitution to preclude taxation of groceries, medicine, and inexpensive clothing. Lowry, who had discovered Warren's veto of the 1951 segregation proviso, told voters to beware "of this Judas kiss from the former governor." Bryant, who shared Collins's devotion to education, attacked Warren's homestead plank as "the most diabolical, demagogic, dangerous device ever designed to buy public favor." Said Collins: "I don't see how the citizens of Florida could possibly follow that road again."[33]

Collins's nonchalance toward Warren reflected a private poll in Dade County, where he knew he would need another huge vote surplus that he feared Warren, now practicing law in Miami, might erode. The poll turned out almost too good to be true. Researcher Ross Beiler of the University of Miami said Collins's local popularity "exceeds anything I have ever seen in politics anywhere. Frankly, it is so unique and phenomenal that there is only one way it can go and that is down." Warren, moreover, was overwhelmingly unpopular. But Beiler warned that Collins's popularity had a "distorting effect"; those who were not for him were shy about saying so.[34]

The Supreme Court waited until March 5, the eve of the filing deadline, before ruling that Collins was eligible to run for a full term; the prohibition, Glenn Terrell's opinion said, applied only to someone who had already served a full elected term. Roberts disqualified himself, having prejudged the question in 1954.[35]

Collins acknowledged his candidacy in a brief statement saying that the campaign "[W]ill be almost as simple as this: Will Florida want to go backward for a re-run of the era of bombast, privilege, plunder, and apology, or does our state want to continue forward on the firm foundation we have thus far effectively advanced?" He did not mention segregation. "All that the governor has to do now," editorialized the *Lakeland Ledger*, "is to defeat former Gov. Fuller Warren."[36]

Bryant, in the unprecedented role of running against both a former governor and a sitting governor, devoted his campaign kickoff speech to a scathing attack on both of them. He accused Warren of a shameful administration and Collins of a "record of unperformed promises, seldom, if ever, equaled." For the moment, he saw no need to mention Lowry.[37]

But only for a moment. The U.S. Supreme Court decision ordering—ineffectively—Virgil Hawkins's admission to the law school dominated the following day's headlines. Collins had already recorded for release that night a broadcast boasting, "[T]he manner in which we have handled this segregation program has been effective. We have obtained results and there has been no integration in Florida." The Hawkins decision made that ring hollow. That night, there was a cross-burning, the signature act of the Ku Klux Klan, in front of the University of Florida administration building. Within a week, the Board of Control ordered Florida State University and the University of Florida to tighten their graduate school admission standards. Collins called an emergency conference of the Cabinet and other concerned officials.[38]

Ervin abandoned moderation under pressure from a last-minute opponent, Rep. Prentice Pruitt of Jefferson County, a radical segregationist who accused Ervin of having "surrendered to the forces who advocate integration by degrees." Ervin responded by endorsing a proposed constitutional amendment (and a special session to put it on the ballot) empowering the governor to assign students to their appropriate schools and universities. "The governor is not subject to coercion or control by Federal process," Ervin said.[39]

He was dead wrong about that, as Gov. Claude R. Kirk Jr. learned in 1970 when a federal judge fined him $10,000 a day for seizing control of the Manatee County schools in a vain attempt to thwart desegregation.[40] During the panic of 1956, however, Ervin's theory was plausible to those who wanted to believe it. But he agreed with Collins that the Legislature should not be recalled until after the primary elections; to do it sooner, Collins warned, would risk having Florida portrayed as a "seething caldron of hate and fear and tension." Bryant took that as his cue to urge an immediate special session to adopt an interposition resolution and other extreme measures.[41]

Convening the emergency conference, Collins admitted that the Hawkins ruling had been a political shock. He complained that segregation as a campaign issue was causing "a dangerous deterioration in our racial relations generally." He expressed a Pollyannaish view of the "mutual respect and confidence" between the races, professed that blacks were comfortable with segregation, and warned that "all this progress" could be lost "as the extremists and radicals on both sides wage their irresponsible war." Among reports that had alarmed him: Whites no longer attended the Florida A&M choir's Sunday afternoon vesper services. In his mind, no matter what might be wrong about segregation, the consequences of fighting it were worse.[42]

The conference agreed that Collins and Ervin should appoint a committee of judges and lawyers to draft legislation to submit to a postprimary special session. Florida would also petition the U.S. Supreme Court to reconsider, the Board of Education would begin to oversee university admission policies, and Florida would ask President Eisenhower to meet with Southern governors. The first point had consequences, but the Eisenhower appeal was campaign propaganda.[43]

Collins was not the only moderate still in denial. A *Tampa Tribune* editorial, for example, said the state should "continue building adequate Negro schools in Negro communities, so that the natural boundaries of residential segregation and the Negro's knowledge that he is getting equal facilities will gradually smother the issue."[44]

The president, meanwhile, wanted as little as possible to do with desegregation. Although his Justice Department had supported civil rights legislation and the *Brown* plaintiffs, Eisenhower never expressed a personal view on the decision. Rejecting Florida's request, he wrote ambiguously to Collins, "[T]he progress already made in certain regions of the South before and since this decision is a clear indication that we can look forward to even greater progress if we can look to moderate and responsible leadership supported by a spirit of patience on the part of all of our people." That leadership would have to come from somewhere other than the White House.[45]

There was an ironic response from Virginia. Though the state was preparing to close public schools, the governor's office told Collins that there had long been desegregated graduate programs at the University of Virginia and blacks were enrolling in several other colleges.[46]

Lowry mocked the Collins strategy. "My opponents in this campaign claim that they favor maintaining segregation so long as it can be done in a nice, quiet way without alienating the pinks and fellow travelers," he said. Florida needed a governor "strong enough and determined enough to tell the federal government to stay out."[47]

The governor's first formal campaign speech, a paid broadcast on thirteen television stations, claimed that "we have had no integration in Florida" thanks to a policy of "resisting within lawful and peaceful means." Collins stressed his efforts for constitutional revision, industrial development, reapportionment, road-building, and the Sheriffs' Bureau. He returned to the race issue only once, and only by inference, in a statement that seemed aimed more at Warren than Lowry. "There are some who would take us back to that era of bombast and privilege and apology that we remember so well," Collins said. "There is no place under the Florida sun for the demagogue."[48]

Warren's retort charged Collins with having profited on land sold to Florida State University in 1952, while he was a state senator. Collins did not answer the allegation, which was truthful but short-lived as an issue.[49]

Lowry claimed but could not prove to be interested in nonsegregation issues. In a campaign television broadcast, Collins gleefully recited what he said were Lowry's answers at a news conference: Reapportionment was "for the legislature to decide." He had "no position" on the 67-senator amendment. Constitutional revision? "When I get to be governor, I'll go into that thoroughly." A lieutenant governor? "I'll think about it." Tax agency consolidation? "I'd rather give that careful thought before answering." His position on homestead exemption? "I have none." In the event Florida needed new revenue, "I'll make a study of it at that time."[50]

Lowry, who claimed the U.S. Supreme Court had "always honored" interposition resolutions, was not counting on sophisticated voters. Jack Peeples, a University of Florida law student who volunteered to speak for Collins in some rural counties, encountered a Gilchrist County voter who asked him why Collins had not "vetoed that Supreme Court decision." Playing it safe, Peeples replied, "That's one of the few things I don't understand." He shared a platform that night with Warren, Bryant, and Lowry, whom he accused of having a single-issue platform. "He's right," Lowry replied. "I've got one plank: Segregation, it's a four by four, it's a mile long, and there's room for every cracker in the state of Florida to get on it right now." Collins ran a distant fourth in Gilchrist.[51] In rural counties, Lowry distributed pictures of Collins shaking hands with black teachers. "I cannot imagine any governor doing otherwise," Collins said.[52]

By early April, the press was speculating that it would be Lowry, not Warren, in a runoff with Collins, who could see for himself that Lowry was his main rival. Collins devoted an entire paid broadcast on ten television stations to attacking Lowry's fixation with segregation and reiterating that Florida was one of only three states where there had been no integration.[53] He stepped up his appeals to urban voters, and to women in particular, in anticipation of a poor showing in rural Florida. At the peak of the campaign, he had no campaign chairmen in seventeen counties.[54]

Collins staged an elaborate press conference, a month before the primary, to reveal Howard Hughes's grand promises for Florida. Typically, Hughes was not present; in a statement read by a publicist he said he would establish an aircraft manufacturing plant in addition to a medical institute on an island off Miami. Hughes credited both to "my talks with Governor Collins—who is, in my opinion, just about the best salesman any state ever had." Warren smelled a hoax. Lowry remarked that Chief Justice Earl Warren, author of the *Brown* decision, was from California also. The Collins campaign capitalized on the announcement in a campaign jingle that said, "Floridians, here's a governor we must choose, Or we'll lose that project with Howard Hughes," but that turned out to be very nearly the last that Florida heard of Hughes. Though the Howard Hughes Medical Institute did establish a modest presence near the University of Miami, Hughes had created it as a tax dodge, and it did not become a significant biomedical charity—headquartered elsewhere—until long after his death in 1976. Nothing would ever come of the aircraft factory, but the campaign was history before that became obvious.[55]

With less than a month until the primary, Dilworth Clark acknowledged Lowry's inroads into Warren's Pork Chop territory. "If Fuller loses out, I'm for Sumter in the runoff," he said.[56] Lowry, meanwhile, was trying to revive the world federalism issue that had not worked for Johns against Collins in 1954. Bryant's panic surfaced in a statement saying Collins should have suspended Hollis Rinehart, the most liberal member of the Board of Control, for endorsing desegregation. Collins's major speech that day was on nuclear energy. His strategy, he said, "was to work hard all through the campaign at being governor and to stay away from Sumter Lowry."[57]

His attempts to deemphasize the segregation issue concerned some of his supporters. After touring West Florida, Charles Ausley warned Collins that he might lose the election if he did not give the segregationists more of what they were hearing from his rivals and other Southern governors. John Perry, a witness to the meeting, described Collins pacing around his office, which he often did under stress or when trying to concentrate. Collins paused at a window overlooking the Supreme Court building. "I don't have to get re-elected," he said at last, "but I do have to live with myself."[58]

Collins was the overwhelming favorite of the newspapers. Of Florida's forty dailies, twenty-one recommended him. Several, notably the *Tampa Tribune*, repeatedly denounced Lowry, Warren, and Bryant. "They are too busy throwing bricks to lay any," the *Tribune* said. The *St. Petersburg Times*, a liberal paper that regarded even Collins as "too extreme" on segregation, wrote that in all other respects Collins "offers Florida Democrats about everything they could hope for and dream of in a candidate for governor." Only his hometown *Star Banner* endorsed Bryant. The rest recommended no one.[59]

Bryant brought out that Claude Pepper's nemesis Edward Ball, whom George Smathers considered "the most conservative man I ever knew," was backing Lowry. In particular, Dan Crisp, a duPont lobbyist who had helped George Smathers defeat Pepper, was Lowry's public relations adviser."[60]

Johns openly supported Lowry, whom he said he preferred to Warren because the 1951 veto showed how the former governor "feels about segregation."[61]

There were two ways to read voter sentiment on segregation. Grotegut told Collins of a confidential poll showing that in all but five counties—Dade, Broward, Pinellas, Sarasota, and Charlotte—majorities opposed integration under any circumstances. "The same figures, however, can be taken to mean that in these same five counties segregation would not now be an hysterical issue, and I think this confirms our own findings," Grotegut wrote. Collins handily carried all five.[62]

In a paid telecast late in the campaign, Collins attacked what he called the "dirty, filthy misrepresentations, lies, and insinuations" in a Lowry pamphlet that he tore into shreds on camera. "If you want a governor who is going to seek to have white people hating colored people and colored people hating white people, then you do not want LeRoy Collins," he said.[63]

Four days before the primary, the Lake County grand jury conceded the legality of the Irvin commutation but recommended that the Legislature investigate the governor's motives. The presentment denounced the *St. Petersburg Times* for its persistent coverage of the case.[64]

Lowry concluded his campaign by harping on the news that blacks attending an African Methodist Episcopal Church convention at Miami's Dinner Key auditorium were being housed at white hotels, normally open only in winter, and were being served by white waitresses. "These 3,500 Negroes are using our beaches and being served by white girls," Lowry railed, "and this man Collins does nothing about it." Collins said he was "shocked," but that the attorney general had advised him there was no law against it and nothing he could do.[65]

Collins raised more money than any of his rivals, spending $291,183 to $194,682 by Warren, $115,216 by Lowry, and $63,048 by Bryant.[66] Collins's treasury was the inflation-adjusted equivalent of some $2 million today. That would not go far in Florida now, but Collins made good use of it in 1956, particularly in television, seizing that potential sooner and better than any of his opponents. Collins's election-eve campaign broadcast, which ran for a half hour on thirteen stations, featured his family at the Grove. Only his son was absent, which was an opportunity to remind the audience that LeRoy Junior was a Naval Academy cadet. Six-year-old Darby sang a song in Spanish that she had learned at kindergarten, an early instance of bilingual politicking in a state where it is now routine. Collins stressed his support of education. There were final blasts at Lowry, the "one man . . . who has sought to incite hate and furor and violence"; at Warren, for "that four-year period of buffoonery and demagoguery and pop-offs and apologies and the corruption and crime that went with that regime"; and at Bryant, who "challenges my leadership and yet the facts don't bear him out and the record doesn't bear him out."[67]

If the 1956 campaign was not quite Florida's ugliest—the 1950 Smathers-Pepper race holds that distinction—it was not for lack of someone trying. The most egregious fouls were by Warren in campaign material referring to Collins as the "curly-haired boy" of communists and the NAACP—a snide suggestion of black ancestry—and to the NAACP as the National Association for the Advancement of Collins Politics.[68]

On election day, May 8, conventional wisdom still held that Collins would be short of a majority and would have to face a rival, most likely Lowry, in a runoff. But as only the *Miami Herald*'s political editor had dared to predict, Collins made history by winning the Democratic nomination outright with 51.7 percent of the total vote. At his storefront campaign headquarters in Tallahassee, Collins claimed victory shortly after midnight, thanked his supporters, and praised the press for its "unprecedented support." Many of his supporters wanted to party, but Collins said, "No, I think what we need to do is go say our prayers." As he had done after winning the runoff in 1954, he crossed the street to St. John's Episcopal Church for an impromptu service led by his close friend the Rev. Harry Douglas. "I'd like to have each and every one of you come with us," he told the exuberant crowd.[69]

Warren lost more than his last campaign that night. He arrived at his Miami Beach law office early the next morning to find that his partners had removed his name from the door and changed the locks.[70]

In postelection interviews, Collins talked more about resuming the reapportionment fight than about the Republican opponent he would face (and swamp, with 73.7 percent of the vote) in November.[71] But the Pork Choppers sent word that the election had changed nothing and that they were standing firmly behind the 67-senator amendment, which remained on the November ballot.[72]

The official canvas recorded 434,274 votes for Collins to 179,019 for Lowry; 110,469 for Bryant; 107,990 for Warren; and 8,331 for two minor candidates. Collins won on the strength of epic landslides in Southeast Florida and the Tampa Bay area. Dade, where he won 72 percent of the vote, gave him a 69,239-vote edge over all the others. He carried Broward with 78 percent and a 17,116-vote majority. Collins also scored above 60 percent in Martin, Pinellas, Sarasota, Monroe, Palm Beach, Volusia, and St. Lucie counties, and had at least a majority of the votes in Brevard, Leon, Highlands, Hillsborough (Lowry's home), Manatee, Orange, Collier, Charlotte, Indian River, and Lee counties. He led the field, but with less than half the vote, in another fourteen counties, including Lake.

But that left thirty-four counties where the incumbent governor did not finish first. Lowry, the neophyte single-issue candidate, led the field in twenty-seven, with majorities in seven. A map of the counties that Collins did not carry depicted the constituencies of the Pork Chop Gang. In thirteen small counties, he received less than one in every five votes. Among them was Liberty County, one of the few places in Florida where it was still not safe for blacks to vote, and where twelve had taken their names off the rolls after being threatened, an event to which Collins seemed indifferent. Liberty's white voters gave a majority of their votes to Lowry and only 9 percent to the incumbent governor.[73]

The *Tampa Tribune* hailed Collins's victory as "Thunder from the Polls" that showed the nation "that at least one Southern state is grown-up enough to meet the segregation problem with reason rather than emotion." The *Washington Post* said that Florida voters "in the main, rewarded the moderates."[74] Outwardly, those were reasonable interpretations. Florida's black voters had come to the same conclusion about Collins despite his defensive rhetoric and had given him all but a handful of their votes.[75]

But there was another way to look at it. A sitting governor who was the overwhelming favorite of the major newspapers and who enjoyed a sizable advantage in campaign contributions had avoided a runoff against a single-minded racist who was conspicuously unprepared to be governor by only 14,232 votes out of the 840,083 that had been cast. "I'm particularly glad I didn't have to run the next three weeks against that man Lowry," Collins said.[76]

"As irrational as Lowry could appear, on one point he exposed a dark truth most Floridians, including the governor and his admirers in the press, seemed unwilling to admit publicly," wrote Kevin Klein, a scholar of the period. "Preserving segregation by 'lawful' and 'peaceful' means was oxymoronic. . . . Lowry's success at coming from obscurity to second place testified to the power of racial antipathy in Florida."[77]

Considering how else it might have come out, the 1956 campaign was, in the long term, a victory for moderation, as Collins demonstrated through subsequent actions and speeches. But he had committed himself to a special session that delayed public school desegregation and spawned a legislative investigating committee that had serious consequences for many people and for the university system. Moreover, the 1956 campaign established a political marketplace for Bryant's reactionary victory four years later.

Chapter 16

Pressure

The primary election did not dissipate the segregationist momentum. Ervin called for repeal of Florida's compulsory attendance law, tuition grants to segregated private schools, an interposition resolution, local-option school closings, and a stronger pupil-assignment statute. Collins was astounded by Ervin's radicalism in the aftermath of what had become an easy election victory for him. The press speculated that Ervin considered integration inevitable and wanted the record to show that he had done all he could to prevent it.[1]

Tallahassee was now the scene of the nation's second bus boycott, provoking the segregationists and worrying Collins. The boycott was prompted by the May 26 arrests of Florida A&M students Wilhelmina Jakes and Carrie Patterson for refusing to give up their seats next to a white woman on a Cities Transit bus. Two dimes might have prevented what followed; the students offered to leave the bus if their fares were refunded, but the money was already in the coin box, and the driver was either unable or unwilling to pay it himself. Events escalated swiftly; a cross was burned outside the home where the young women boarded, other FAMU students blocked a bus from passing through the campus, and the adult black community took up the boycott under the aegis of the black Ministerial Alliance and its charismatic leader, the Rev. C. K. Steele.[2]

Unlike the landmark bus boycott in Montgomery, Alabama, which established the national reputation of the Rev. Dr. Martin Luther King Jr., Tallahassee's was unprepared, spontaneous, and a surprise to the NAACP, which had considered Florida blacks too docile for such action. Fearful of a test case, the city dropped the charges against the students, but the black community, modeling its organization on Montgomery's, presented demands including first-come, first-served seating, courteous treatment by white drivers, and the hiring of black drivers for predominantly black routes. The bus company might have agreed, but its franchise stipulated segregation, and city officials refused to yield.

Collins tried to stay above it. When journalists insisted on the governor's comments, they were in writing, brief, and noncommittal, expressing nothing stronger than "disappointment" that the boycott organization, the Inter-Civic Council (ICC), had refused to settle on terms perpetuating separate seating. "It is a local problem, however, and should be solved on that basis," Collins said.[3]

The city commission remained uncompromising despite the news on June 5 that a three-judge federal court had declared Montgomery's bus segregation ordinance unconstitutional. As in the Hawkins case, it was if the entire Southern way of life were at stake.[4] The beleaguered bus company shut down July 1. So did Collins's patience. He denounced the NAACP, which was supporting the boycott, for a "miscarriage of ambition." He said it should concern itself "with other conditions of far more importance than where people sit on buses."[5] When Cities Transit resumed service on altered routes two weeks later, the city foreclosed further negotiations and stepped up police harassment of drivers in the ICC's car pools.[6]

Tallahassee's intransigence had statewide consequences. Police investigator Remus J. Strickland spied on Steele and other ICC leaders, investigated their backgrounds, infiltrated their organization, and sent the governor's office a thirty-three-page confidential report naming FAMU faculty and staff members who were allegedly "rabid for integration."[7] The boycott contributed to the Legislature's decision to investigate the NAACP; Strickland was hired to lead the probe. Mark Hawes, a Tampa lawyer the city had hired to prosecute the ICC, became the chief counsel to the investigating committee, whose futile search for communists in the NAACP metamorphosed into a purge of suspected homosexuals in the schools and universities.[8]

Collins determined that the special session would be about more than segregation. Among other things, he wanted money to improve prison conditions, a riot having freshly demonstrated the need for "basic and far-reaching reform," and to defend the citrus industry against a fruit fly infestation. Prompted by a *Miami Herald* exposé, Collins prepared legislation to regulate the mail-order sale of swampland to unsuspecting Northerners.[9]

The Legislature was still technically in a special session limited to reapportionment. It returned in June for a week, accomplished nothing, and recessed again until the expiration of its term in November. Though eleven senators would be leaving, five by choice, five by defeat, and one by death, the Pork Choppers kept firm control. Only one of them would be replaced by a Collins supporter. In a tough campaign of his own, Collins had not tried to unseat any of them. There was nothing he could do about reapportionment but wait for the November referendum on the 67-senator amendment, which if ratified would vest Senate control in counties with 8 percent of the population.[10]

When the Supreme Court said he could call lawmakers out of recess for a session on other issues, Collins summoned them for twenty days beginning June 23. The main agenda was to act on the report of an advisory commission chaired by L. L. Fabisinski, a retired circuit judge from Pensacola.[11]

The commission's report was moderate by comparison to Virginian or Georgian rhetoric. Though it denounced the Supreme Court for a "usurpation of power" that endangered "the entire American system of government," it did not advocate interposition and opposed any school closings. Instead, it recommended legislation authorizing school boards to assign pupils "on the basis of individual needs and abilities" with no mention of race or segregation. Appeals to the Cabinet and then to the courts were calculated to yield delays of two years or more. The Fabisinski recommendations provided also for the governor to close any public facility in order to "preserve the peace . . . and prevent domestic violence."[12]

As enacted, the pupil-assignment bill called for students to be tested and placed according to "such sociological, psychological and like intangible social scientific factors as will prevent, as nearly as practicable, any condition of socio-economic class consciousness among the pupils." Politicians who had criticized the Supreme Court for citing sociology to outlaw segregation were now invoking sociology to perpetuate segregation. They appeared blind to the irony.[13]

The commission presented the report to Collins, the Cabinet, and two legislative committees at a day-long session that was barred to the press for more than three hours despite the governor's open-government policy. He won enough secret commitments to assure him that the session would not enact Ervin's more extreme proposals or a bill by Pruitt to outlaw the NAACP. Excluding the press was intended also to keep federal judges from reading that the pupil-assignment law was crafted to maintain segregation, but the reporters said so nonetheless. "It is avoidance by legal means, not evasion by subterfuge," Collins insisted. To anyone paying strict attention, however, the underlying message was about delay rather than defiance. Desegregation, said Fabisinski, was "the law of the land and we are going to have to live with it whether we like or not." In another irony, there were no recommendations dealing specifically with Hawkins, whose case was the proximate reason for the commission and the special session.[14]

Collins worried about how to keep the radicals in check. "It seems that my troubles and work pile higher and higher every day. We will have a special session of the Legislature week after next and that really will be messy," he wrote to Bootsie at summer camp. "Oh well, I sure asked for it, didn't I?"[15]

Collins cautioned in a speech to a joint session that unwanted stronger legislation "might well weaken the legal efficacy" of the Fabisinski recommendations. The Florida conference of the NAACP called the proposals a "disgrace before God and Man."[16]

The Senate passed the program unanimously within two and a half hours of receiving it. In the House, there was scattered resistance to the emergency measures, which Bryant and Gibbons managed to limit to five years. Collins said he did not oppose the legislation that would let him close schools "because I knew I wasn't going to close one unless it had to be closed, but I wouldn't trust the county school boards."[17]

Only one legislator voted against the pupil-assignment bill. He was Rep. John B. Orr Jr. of Miami, who had just acknowledged membership in the NAACP. Orr, a thirty-eight-year-old lawyer completing his first term, took the floor to tell the House that he had opposed the Fabisinski program because he favored gradual desegregation. "[H]ad we devoted as much energy, time, and talent to discovering means to live under the law instead of in defiance of it," he said, "we could have discovered a way."[18]

Orr, scion of a prominent Miami family, had uncommonly good personal relations with North Florida legislators, in part because he could drink moonshine whisky with the toughest of them. They listened silently, if not in shock, as Orr continued. "I believe segregation is morally wrong," he said. "The fact that the custom is one of long-standing makes it no less wrong. Surely not many of you would argue today that slavery was morally justifiable and yet this was a custom of long-standing."[19]

The House was as silent as a sepulcher during his eight-minute speech and when he sat down. Some members complimented him privately on his courage, but none dared to agree with him. Sensing anger in the crowded galleries, several colleagues made sure he did not leave the chamber alone. A Miami segregationist group tried to get Orr expelled from the House, and his family received telephone threats. When classes resumed in the fall, Orr's son, Tom, wondered why his father's campaign manager was driving him to and from school.[20]

Orr was reelected in November; his only remaining ballot opponent was a Republican, and a write-in opponent failed. He was defeated in the 1958 Democratic primary in a campaign that dwelled on his vote and his speech two years before. It was regarded as a loss for Collins even though the governor had said nothing in Orr's support.[21]

Collins had a sympathetic House Speaker in Ted David, whose rules committee blocked proposed bills to reinforce university segregation, but the committee approved several other unwanted measures including Pruitt's interposition resolution. Bryant was on the verge of passing interposition in the House when Collins invoked a never-used constitutional provision to declare the Legislature adjourned. He gave only momentary warning to the presiding officers. Bryant took it in stride. "I have no feeling on it at all. He's the governor," he said on his way to Collins's office for a final handshake.[22] "The session deserves as much credit for what it didn't do, as for what it did do," Collins said. "It steadfastly refused to be stampeded into taking irrational and damaging actions."[23]

The Senate leadership was undismayed by the adjournment, having won something much more potent than an interposition resolution. Its prize was the creation of a joint committee to investigate "organizations advocating violence or a course of conduct which would constitute a violation of the laws of Florida." The panel, officially the Florida Legislative Investigation Committee, was eventually known as the Johns Committee for its cofounder and occasional chairman. Though Collins as a senator had opposed just such a "snake committee," he let this one become law without his signature. The lone Republican, Frank Houghton of St. Petersburg, was the only senator who fought it to the end this time. *Tampa Tribune* columnist Jim Powell implied that Collins had agreed to it if the Senate would pass no segregation legislation stronger than the Fabisinski recommendations.[24]

The undisguised purpose of the investigating committee was to harass the NAACP; or, as a House member said in debating another measure, "these

New York nigger lawyers" who would be suing school boards over segregation. The law created a committee of three senators and four House members with a budget of $50,000, supposedly to be discharged after a report to the 1957 session. The committee survived, however, until the 1965 session refused to continue financing it. Collins rationalized that investigations were a legislative prerogative and that the committee could investigate the Ku Klux Klan as well as the NAACP—as if they were moral equals. He expressed confidence, which turned out to be misplaced, that the committee would not "abuse the broad powers granted them."[25]

Frustrated by successful appeals of its attempts to identify the NAACP's members and supporters, the Johns Committee turned to searching for homosexuals in the schools and universities. It would have little influence on desegregation, but its sexual obsession and assaults on academic freedom ruined scores of careers and reputations and nearly strangled the University of South Florida at its birth. Florida legislators were not unique in the belief that the civil rights movement was inspired by communism and other unwelcome influences; at least four other Southern states established similar investigating committees. But only Florida's went so far beyond politics. The committee met its end after publishing a lurid and widely derided booklet, *Homosexuality and Citizenship in Florida*, that newly elected governor Haydon Burns—a former supporter—called "a disgrace to this state and most especially to any person who had any part in its printing."[26]

The 1956 session gave Collins most of what he wanted for prisons, mental health, highway safety, and the fruit fly infestation. Collins also obtained a law to penalize misleading advertisements for Florida real estate, but it was ineffective compared to later legislation.[27]

The pupil-assignment law was effective, though ultimately short-lived. It was no sooner enacted than Tallahassee lawyer John Wigginton, a member of the Fabisinski commission, warned that some integration, by some "exceptional Negro child," was inevitable. Collins predicted that Florida's method would forestall integration more effectively than Virginia's "massive resistance," and time proved him right.[28]

Collins attended the Democratic National Convention as an alternate delegate for Adlai Stevenson, the ultimate nominee, who was becoming a close friend and who believed he was a very distant cousin of Mary Call Collins. Though the Florida delegation unanimously endorsed Collins for vice president, the governor said he was not a candidate and remained uninvolved when the convention, left to its own by Stevenson, chose Senator Estes Kefauver of Tennessee.[29]

As if to atone for the Fabisinski legislation, for which black organizations had severely criticized him, Collins began to speak in tones unfamiliar to Southern ears. "We must improve the welfare of our Negro citizens," he said at a Miami-area Chamber of Commerce banquet. "Too many are still living in crime and disease-producing slums; too many do not receive adequate medical care; too many do not receive adequate educational opportunities. We must not let our desire to maintain our traditions of segregation blind us to our responsibilities to aid their improvement and advancement."[30]

Collins's staff had quietly assembled state agency data documenting many inequities. One was that despite spending more since 1951 to build black schools than white schools, Florida's current expenses still favored the white children by 13 percent. The Department of Education attributed the difference to higher salaries for more experienced white teachers and to the fact that a "few counties" still paid black teachers less.[31]

As schools opened that summer and fall, some measure of desegregation was reported from 723 districts in Southern and Border states, but none in Florida, Alabama, Georgia, Louisiana, Mississippi, North Carolina, South Carolina, or Virginia. The only desegregation in Florida was at U.S. Defense Department schools on two military reservations.[32]

The fury of racism in rural Florida fell on a white public health physician who broke one of the strongest taboos. Dr. Deborah Coggins lost her new job as public health officer for Madison, Jefferson, and Taylor counties for having had a business lunch with a black nurse in the private dining room of a Madison hotel restaurant whose employees had consented. The news prompted vile sexual rumors and petitions to have her fired from the $675-a-month position. One after another, the three county commissions complied. When Coggins demanded a reason, Jefferson's board chairman was candid: "The only cause we heard is that you took darkies in there and had lunch with them." When the Madison board similarly refused to give her a valid reason, Coggins told them: "You're all fools, fools! And I'm going to be in Madison and you're going to have to look at me for a long time." Collins said that he was "sick" about "an evil act" that "cannot be squared with right and justice and conscience," but that there was nothing he could do. He said Coggins had become a scapegoat for "the passion aroused by efforts to coerce integration of the races against the will of the people."[33]

Coggins, a thirty-two-year-old Florida native who had graduated from the Duke University medical school, remained in Madison, where her husband, also a physician, had been born. The governor invited them to Tallahassee for a private meeting where, she recalled, "he was very gracious and said he wished he could have done more." The *Tampa Tribune* said that he should have. It analogized the county commissions' actions to "saying a sheriff has no choice but to unlock the jail door when a lynch mob approaches."[34]

In Tallahassee, meanwhile, the city began arresting black car pool drivers for failing to have motor carrier permits. Steele appealed in vain to Collins to intervene.[35] But Collins acted firmly in response to a near-lynching. The victim, Jesse Woods, was kidnapped in late October from the jail in Wildwood, in rural Sumter County northwest of Tampa, where he was held on drunkenness and disorderly conduct charges after supposedly speaking flirtatiously to a white woman at a grocery. It was assumed that Woods would be murdered, the notorious fate of fifteen-year-old Emmett Till for a similar allegation in Mississippi the year before. But Woods turned up in Alabama a week later, saying he had been beaten and left for dead by a gang of whites before relatives spirited him out of Florida, hidden in a rolled-up blanket. Collins strongly denounced the kidnapping, put the new Sheriffs' Bureau on the case, and assured Woods's family that he would be protected if they surrendered him. The Sheriffs' Bureau produced seven suspects, but, as in the Mississippi case, none was convicted. The charges were dismissed after the witnesses changed their stories.[36]

There was still an election to be held; Collins did not take Republican nominee William Washburne entirely for granted. The seldom-heard Washburne was beginning to sound like Lowry, denouncing Collins for foiling the interposition resolution and implying that Collins opposed segregation. Collins won with 747,753 votes, nearly 74 percent, to 266,980 for Washburne. In Florida's first election with a million-vote turnout, Collins outpolled even President Eisenhower, who carried the state over Stevenson. "My opponent got more votes than he should have," Collins wrote to his son, "but we still won with a very substantial margin."[37]

To Collins's immense relief, the Pork Chop Gang's 67-senator amendment was decisively defeated, 288,575 votes to 187,662, in a torrent of "no" votes from all the larger counties except Duval. Fewer than half the people who had voted for governor and president troubled themselves to vote on reapportionment.[38]

The year's end brought little relaxation for Collins, who had to deal with a dispute over where to build what would become the University of South Florida, and with worsening tension in the bus boycott at Tallahassee. The university dispute pit two of his strongest constituencies, Hillsborough and Pinellas counties, and two of his most supportive newspapers, the *Tampa Tribune* and *St. Petersburg Times*, against each other. Hillsborough had a lock on the Democratic Legislature because Pinellas lawmakers were Republicans, but Pinellas refused to accept the reality. Its civic leaders derided Tampa as a city of "gambling and houses of ill fame." The *Times*, referring to a planned brewery near a possible Hillsborough site, sarcastically named the university "Bottlecap U." Gibbons, who considered the *Times'* editor his friend, heard that the newspaper's reporters were combing Hillsborough court records in a fruitless search for land that Gibbons might own near any of the sites.[39]

The Board of Control eventually voted 5 to 2 for a site northeast of Tampa, but Collins said he was not prepared to accept it and wanted to hear more about another that faced open water. He still doubted, moreover, that a new university should take precedence over expansion of the junior college system and the existing universities. That was stunning news at Tampa, which still feared losing the university to Pinellas. But if Collins really wanted a waterfront site, he would get one; a friend of Gibbons had clients who would donate acreage bordering both the chosen site and the Hillsborough River. Gibbons left the negotiations to a county commissioner, Ellsworth Simmons, who reported success but admonished Gibbons, "Don't ask me how I did it." The price, it turned out, was his promise to build a road past the donors' remaining property, immensely increasing its value. For a long time, it was known as the "Road to Nowhere." Collins relented. On December 18, the Board of Education voted unanimously to establish the university on the primary site, to open in the fall of 1960.[40]

In Tallahassee that winter, the bus situation was deteriorating. City officials refused to desegregate despite a U.S. Supreme Court decision against Alabama's similar bus segregation ordinances. The Inter-Civic Council, its car pools crippled by the city's legal tactics, decided to test the Alabama ruling by ending the boycott and asking blacks to sit where they pleased on the buses. The company was willing, but the city was not; it arrested the manager and nine drivers and suspended the company's franchise. A federal judge issued a temporary injunction allowing the buses to run while the city and company sued each other in state court. Violence would ensue.[41]

Yet Collins seemed to face the new year with much lighter shoulders. Allen Morris, the veteran observer, wrote in his December 30 column that after two rugged campaigns in three years and a "Legislature that wouldn't go home," the governor now seemed "more buoyant, more self-possessed, and with more time to be thoughtful of others than he has since the 1954 campaign. He is more the Roy Collins that the home folks knew—a fellow who occasionally might unseeingly pass you on the sidewalk because of being intensely engrossed with some problem, but whose hearty 'Hello, there!' was convincing the rest of the time."[42]

Figure 1. Official portrait of LeRoy Collins. Courtesy of the Florida State Archives.

Figure 2. LeRoy and Mary Call Collins, early in their marriage. Courtesy of the Collins family collection.

Figure 3. Collins easily won in 1950 despite Julius Parker's attacks. The propaganda is primitive compared to contemporary styles. Courtesy of the University of South Florida.

Figure 4. Acting Gov. Charley Johns and LeRoy Collins on their way to Collins's inauguration on January 4, 1955. Sarah Darby Collins is with her father. Courtesy of the *Orlando Sentinel* and the Collins family collection.

Figure 5. Florida's new, lively First Family leading the grand march at the 1955 inaugural ball. From left: Jane Collins (Aurell), LeRoy Collins Jr., Mary Call Collins, the new governor, Darby Collins, and Mary Call "Bootsie" Collins (Proctor) with unidentified escorts. Courtesy of the Department of Commerce Collection, Florida State Archives.

Figure 6. Collins, shown here with friend Rainey Cawthon, was an avid fisherman. Courtesy of the Florida State Archives.

ADOPTED by the Senate on _____April 18, 1957_____

_____
PRESIDENT OF THE SENATE.

_____
SECRETARY OF THE SENATE AND
EX-OFFICIO ENROLLING CLERK.

This concurrent resolution of "Interposition" crosses the Governors desk as a matter of routine. I have no authority to veto it. I take this means however to advise the student of government who may examine this document in the archives of the State in the years to come, that the Governor of Florida expressed open and vigorous opposition thereto. I feel that the U.S. Supreme Court has improperly usurped powers reserved to the states under the Constitution. I have joined in protesting such and in seeking legal means of avoidance. But if this resolution declaring decisions of the court to be "null and void"

APPROVED this _____ day of _____, 19___

is to be taken seriously, it is anarchy and rebellion against the nation which must remain "indivisible, under God "if it is to survive. Not only will I not condone "Interposition" as so many have sought me to do, I decry it as an evil thing, whipped up by the demagogues and carried on the hot and erratic winds of passion, prejudice, and hysteria. If history judges me right this day, I want it known that I did my best to avert this blot. If I am judged wrong then here in my own handwriting and over my signature is the proof of guilt to support my conviction.

LeRoy Collins
Governor

GOVERNOR.

FILED in Office of Secretary of State on _____May 2, 1957_____

igure 7. Though the "interposition" resolution was immune to veto, Collins declared in his
wn hand what he thought of it. Courtesy of the Florida State Archives.

gure 8. Collins became a media star as chair of the raucous 1960 Democratic convention. At final
ssion, *from left*: Collins, John F. Kennedy, Lyndon B. Johnson, Sam Rayburn, James Roosevelt, Hubert
. Humphrey, Adlai Stevenson, Stuart Symington, Edward G. Robinson. Courtesy of the Florida State
rchives.

Figure 9. "Gentlemen, This Here Town Is Due For Some Changes."
—from *Straight Herblock* (Simon & Schuster, 1964).

Figure 10. The photograph that doomed Collins's career. Near the conclusion of the Selma to Montgomery march, he is talking with Andrew Young. Martin Luther King Jr., Coretta Scott King, and Ralph Abernathy are visible to his left. Reproduced by permission of AP/Wide World Photos.

Figure 11. President Lyndon Johnson presents Collins with a pen he has used to sign the 1965 Voting Rights Act. U.S. government photo, courtesy of the University of South Florida.

Figure 12. Congressman Edward J. Gurney, pictured at the inauguration of Gov. Claude R. Kirk Jr. in 1967, looked much younger than Collins though they were only four years apart. Courtesy of the Florida State Archives.

Figure 13. Collins lived to see Florida led again by like-minded governors Bob Graham (1979–87) and Reubin Askew (1971–79). Courtesy of Donn Dughi Photos.

Figure 14. Collins told photographer Donn Dughi that this was his favorite portrait. It dates to his service on the Constitution Revision Commission, 1977–78. Courtesy of Donn Dughi Photos.

Figure 15. Collins in 1990 at his cherished Dog Island retreat. He was fighting cancer when this picture was taken. Reproduced by permission of www.availablelightphoto.com.

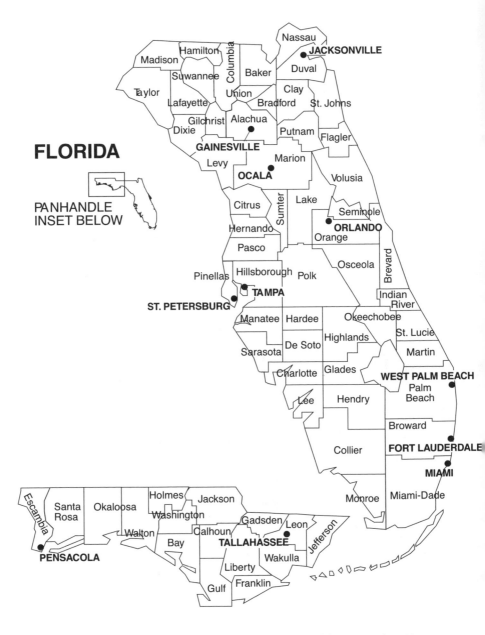

Map 1. Florida by counties, with major cities noted. Courtesy of the *St. Petersburg Times*.

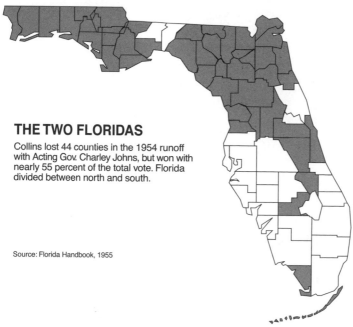

THE TWO FLORIDAS

Collins lost 44 counties in the 1954 runoff
with Acting Gov. Charley Johns, but won with
nearly 55 percent of the total vote. Florida
divided between north and south.

Source: Florida Handbook, 1955

Map 2. The two Floridas. Courtesy of the *St. Petersburg Times.*

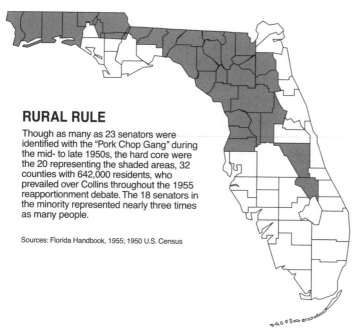

RURAL RULE

Though as many as 23 senators were
identified with the "Pork Chop Gang" during
the mid- to late 1950s, the hard core were
the 20 representing the shaded areas, 32
counties with 642,000 residents, who
prevailed over Collins throughout the 1955
reapportionment debate. The 18 senators in
the minority represented nearly three times
as many people.

Sources: Florida Handbook, 1955; 1950 U.S. Census

Map 3. Counties represented by the Pork Chop Gang. Courtesy of the
St. Petersburg Times.

Chapter 17

Turning Point

On December 27, an armed mob of some two hundred whites confronted the Rev. C. K. Steele and his demonstrators at a bus stop, forcing them to cancel a scheduled ride. On New Year's Eve, shotgun blasts damaged a grocery store owned by cousins of another boycott leader; bricks were thrown onto Steele's porch and rocks through his windows. Collins declared a state of emergency the next morning and ordered the capital's bus service suspended. His aides said the order responded to the violence rather than to a White Citizens Council request that the buses be idled. Nonetheless, Collins appeared to be giving the segregationists what they wanted, and there was no suggestion of protecting the buses and their riders instead. His proclamation decried "inflammatory statements" by whites and Negroes, and in denouncing the violence he also called the demonstrators irresponsible for forcing an issue that he did not believe mattered to most blacks.[1]

Two days later, a federal judge ruled that Miami's bus segregation ordinance—and any comparable state laws—were unconstitutional. Tallahassee quickly amended its bus franchise ordinance to replace the segregation clause with a subterfuge, inspired by the new pupil-assignment law, requiring drivers to tell passengers where to sit for their safety. Refusal would cost up to $500 and sixty days in jail. To preclude any court ruling that would upset this, the company and the city withdrew their pending litigation. That week, in an apparent rebuke to Collins, the Southern Regional Council contrasted his emergency declaration with peaceful bus desegregation that had taken place elsewhere.[2]

The New Year's Day proclamation had quieted the city but not the governor's conscience. He set to work on an inaugural address that would become a turning point in the politics of race. The night before the ceremony, he invited an old friend, businessman Frank Moore, to the Grove to hear what would become the historic passages in his speech. Moore warned Collins that he would be criticized, but Collins changed nothing.[3]

The inaugural audience, an estimated four thousand people enjoying a sunny day with temperatures in the sixties, did not suspect what was coming. Nobody had leaked to the press what Collins would say, and his cheerful demeanor gave no clue. Even so, Florida State University's band director, Manley Whitcomb, told his musicians to pay attention to a man who was going to lead Florida "out of Dixie and into mainstream America."[4]

Collins opened with an anecdote about a physician who, stumped by a patient's skin disorder, asked whether he had had it before. Yes, said the patient. "You've got it again," said the doctor. Florida, Collins said, had it again.[5]

The speech seemed at first to be a conventional laundry list of accomplishments and of goals, most of all a new constitution. Then it became a sermon. It was not enough, Collins said, that Florida was growing by five hundred people a day; the question was whether Floridians were growing "in spirit, in moral concepts, in selflessness, in knowledge, in strength of character?" It was time to talk about the school desegregation decisions. Like it or not, they had happened, and it would do "no good whatever to defy the United States Supreme Court." The idea that a state could resist its decisions was "little short of rebellion and anarchy." Violence and disorder could never be the answer. "Above all," he said, "hate is not the answer. One may be hated and still retain his human dignity, but one who hates suffers a shrinking of soul. We can never find the answer by destroying the human spirit. Indeed, through hate, we magnify our bewilderment and fortify our fears.

"It is not easy to say," he continued, "but it is nevertheless true and I feel I should stand up and say it. The Supreme Court decisions are the law of the land. And this nation's strength and Florida's strength are bottomed upon the basic reverse premise that ours is a land of the law."[6]

He was confident, however, that the Fabisinski laws would forestall public school integration "as long as such is not wise in the light of the social, economic and health facts of life as they exist in the various localities of the state." He expected school segregation to prevail "for the foreseeable future" and promised to do everything possible to enforce the new laws.[7]

What he did *not* say was the most significant. There was no promise to prolong segregation in higher education. Then he got to the point that must have most alarmed Moore: "I am convinced," he said, ". . . that the average white citizen does not object to non-segregated seating in buses, any more than he objects to riding the same elevators with Negroes or patronizing the same stores. He does resent some of the methods being used to achieve certain ends. . . . We can find wise solutions, I believe, if the white citizens will face up to the fact that the Negro does not now have equal opportunities; that he is morally and legally entitled to progress more rapidly, and that a full good-faith effort should be made forthwith to help him move forward in the improvement of all his standards." Collins also cautioned the black community, in patronizing terms, that they should "strive to be wanted . . . to avoid being resented." He still did not think that the majority's hearts and minds could be changed through judicial decrees.[8]

Collins that day became the first governor south of Tennessee or Maryland to instruct his white constituents to change how they thought. He was also the first to endorse nonsegregated seating on public transportation.

Then he quoted from a hymn, "Once to Every Man and Nation," that he had asked his friend Harry Douglas to read at a prayer breakfast that morning.[9] The stanzas he quoted said in part:

Once to every man and nation
Comes the moment to decide,
In the strife of truth with falsehood,
For the Good or Evil side;

. . . .

Then it is the brave man chooses,
While the coward stands aside.

James Russell Lowell, The Present Crisis[10]

As Collins knew, author James Russell Lowell was a leading abolitionist. Slavery's progeny, segregation, was the issue now.

"As I see it," Collins concluded, "we must side with truth even though now we may share her wretched crust. History requires that we not stand aside, coward-like, waiting for the multitude to make virtue of our position. . . . Those who say we are incapable of this do not know the Southerners I know nor the South I love. . . . We have a state to build, a South to save, a nation to convince, and a God to serve."[11]

One report said there was only polite applause; perhaps poor amplification and airplane noises kept the audience from hearing much of it. But the reporters had the text, and their coverage emphasized the point he most wanted heard: Supreme Court rulings must be obeyed. *Time* credited Collins for "specifics that went remarkably far for a Southern governor." Responded Georgia Attorney General Eugene Cook: "He's giving in. He should know better than that."[12] Eleanor Roosevelt, the widow of the late president and a liberal icon, said Collins had been courageous and agreed that "you simply cannot change the mores of thousands of persons overnight." The *St. Petersburg Times*, one of only three liberal dailies in Florida, complimented Collins's "personal courage and soul-searching" but warned that delays breed delays, and "next year becomes a generation."[13]

Some of Florida's black leaders praised the speech without reservation. So did John B. Orr. Robert T. Mann, the newly elected House member from Tampa, congratulated Collins on a "magnificent" speech, "forthright and candid." William S. Shands, the incoming Senate president, remarked that it was "a very frank speech, and I agree with most of what he said." Sen. Harry O. Stratton of Callahan better reflected the Pork Chop consensus: "I don't admit that the Supreme Court segregation decisions are the law of the land."[14]

Though the Tallahassee City Commission did nothing in response, Collins rescinded the suspension order three days later, saying that he did not think the new seating ordinance would solve anything and that he would suspend the buses again if need be.[15] Collins wrote to Luther Hodges, the governor of North Carolina, that he "didn't feel happy at all" about having invoked his emergency powers but thought that he had to.[16]

By January 1957, the Southern Regional Council recorded twenty-one cities in Arkansas, North Carolina, Virginia, Texas, and Tennessee that had voluntarily repealed bus segregation ordinances.[17] Tallahassee held firm. Though the demonstrators had declared an end to the boycott, few blacks rode the buses. Hoodlums continued to harass ICC leaders. Under pressure from Collins, police chief Frank Stoutamire rounded up and lectured eight white youths—pranksters, he called them—but did not charge them. When black and white students from FAMU and FSU tried to ride the buses together, two of the blacks and one white were arrested, grilled by the Legislative Investigating Committee, and sentenced by a city judge who called them "fly-by-night martyrs" to serve sixty days in jail and pay $500 fines. The state and U.S. Supreme Courts denied their appeals, and the two from FAMU served fifteen days before the city commission granted them clemency. The FSU student fled.[18]

White Tallahassee was aghast that white students had joined a black cause. It particularly concerned FSU president Doak Campbell, whom Collins had appointed to a biracial advisory commission chaired by Fabisinski. Campbell, who had already expelled a graduate student for inviting three FAMU students to a FSU Christmas party, told the commission in late January that he might have silenced his student newspaper, the *Florida Flambeau*, over its pro-integration editorials but for the fact that there were informers on its staff. Commission members worried groundlessly that the prohibited off-campus social gatherings of black and white students would result in fights over women.[19]

Collins used the new Fabisinski commission for coordination with agencies that had potential roles in desegregation, and most important, for influencing the city through back channels to let the bus seating ordinance die by neglect. Blacks eventually returned to the buses, though not as many as had ridden them before the boycott. Collins's commission quietly established a biracial statewide network of consultants to deal with local crises. The commission also put pressure on the health department and the Hotel and Restaurant Commission to insist on the same standards for black facilities as for whites, and called for more black dentists and nurses.[20]

The commission employed two lawyers, J. Lewis Hall and John Wigginton, members of the previous commission who maintained that some integration was inevitable. Collins intended the commission to facilitate desegregation at opportune moments and to help defeat the radical legislation that Ervin and many legislators were still promoting. Ervin's opinion on interposition "was read with much derisive comment, particularly on the part of the legal minds present," the minutes said.[21]

In late January, Collins presided over the dedication of the Florida Turnpike, formally the Sunshine State Parkway, which began at Miami and ended temporarily at Ft. Pierce. The road had been finished too quickly, and within weeks there was extensive rain damage along an eleven-mile section that would cost $400,000 ($2.6 million today) to repair. Collins instructed his staff to let the Turnpike Authority chairman handle the public explanations. The buck was to stop there.[22]

Intending to ask the Legislature for substantial prison reform, Collins obtained the Cabinet's consent to recruit Richard Culver, a Federal Bureau of Prisons administrator, to take control of the major prisons at Raiford, Belle Glade, Chattahoochee, and (for women) Lowell. Each was run by a superintendent directly responsible to the Cabinet. The forthcoming law would create a new Division of Corrections incorporating the Road Department's network of prison camps. "It is just impossible to describe conditions in some of our institutions, other than to say they are ghastly," Collins said. "Overcrowding, filth, poor administration with badly limited personnel, inadequate supervision, and little emphasis on returning a good citizen to society, are commonplace."[23]

Collins would have to balance the prison crisis against a depressing revenue forecast and the problem of teachers who were threatening to walk off the job while the Legislature considered the Florida Education Association's demand for a $1,000-a-year pay raise. Collins said the state could not afford so much and demanded a merit rating system. He contended also that county school boards ought to contribute more to teacher salaries. Eighty teachers made public a letter to him contrasting the $3,600 salaries he was asking for his cook and housekeeper with the average beginning teacher's income of less than $3,000.[24]

School budgets were suffering. Collins knew that thirty-six of the sixty-seven school boards had already raised their tax rates to the constitutional limit. This strengthened both his determination to create a state tax commission and the will of the tax assessors and their friends in the Legislature to resist it. Johns, for one, publicly assured the assessors in his two counties that the Senate would reinstate them if Collins suspended them for undervaluing property. In the 1957 session, Collins's tax equalization bill was fated to die in a House committee amidst "great gales of laughter," as a reporter described the deliberations.[25]

Chapter 18

The Right to Be Loved

It was routine for a governor to extradite fugitives sought by other states. But as Collins prepared for another difficult legislative session, he also came under public pressure in an extradition case that was far from ordinary. Massachusetts was demanding the return of Melvin Ellis, forty-five years old, and his wife, Frances, thirty-seven, who had fled their home at Brookline rather than surrender the child, Hildy McCoy, whom they had arranged to adopt upon her birth in February 1951. The childless couple prearranged the adoption and paid Marjorie McCoy's doctor bills. But on learning six weeks after the birth that the Ellises were Jewish, Miss McCoy, an unmarried Roman Catholic student nurse, revoked her consent and demanded that Hildy be given to an agency for adoption by a Catholic couple. The Roman Catholic Church and the government of Massachusetts took the birth mother's side, citing a new state law that "where practical," children should be adopted by persons "of the same religious faith as that of the child."[1]

Hildy was four years old when the Massachusetts Supreme Court ruled against the Ellises despite their desperate offer to raise Hildy as a Catholic. Having sold their home and dry cleaning business, they escaped late one night with Hildy wrapped in a blanket, to live as fugitives in several states before settling in Miami Beach, where Ellis became a salesman for New York clothing manufacturers. Massachusetts traced them and had them arrested on kidnapping charges three weeks after Hildy's sixth birthday. Released to the custody of their lawyer, they refused to waive extradition and appealed to Collins to deny the Massachusetts request.[2]

The United States Constitution provides that fugitives "shall on demand" be returned to the state seeking them.[3] However, governors in Collins's time had discretion under an 1861 Supreme Court decision that refused to compel Ohio to extradite a free Negro who had helped a Kentucky slave escape.[4] Collins agonized over to which side he owed the greater moral obligation. His office was inundated with letters, telegrams, and editorials; the governor of Massachusetts telephoned him personally. Mary Call thought nothing but the Irvin death sentence ever burdened him so heavily.[5]

It was the only occasion that Harry Douglas could remember when Collins sought his spiritual advice on how to govern Florida. Douglas could not find a helpful precedent in the Bible apart from the inapplicable example of Solomon. "Finally," he said, "I just based it on the New Testament best ethic of love. These people [the Ellises] had given that life of love."[6]

Public pressure intensified through April and May. There was a war of words between South Florida's secular press and the *Florida Catholic* newspaper, which emphasized that the Ellises had previously been married to other people and referred to it as "The Miami Beach Kidnapping Case."[7] The governor's mail was at least as heavy with letters and petitions from Massachusetts as from Florida, especially in the pro-Ellis category. There was open anti-Catholicism and anti-Semitism. "The Catholics demand a sort of 'divine right' to take away all the rights of children born with a Protestant parent," wrote a Michigan woman, reacting to a report that Hildy's natural father was Protestant. "You should think of the fact that the child will be brought up Jewish. Never to know and believe in our Lord and Savior Jesus. . . . [I]t would break my heart and I'm sure yours too if one of my little girls or your Darby should have to be brought up a Jew," a Miami woman wrote.[8]

Collins scheduled a hearing for the Ellises in Tallahassee. Normally, one of the lawyers on his staff would conduct it. This time he would.[9] Hildy remained with a neighbor in Miami, knowing only that something unusual was happening. She became aware that she had been adopted "before I knew what the word meant," and her parents had told her that there were some people who wanted them to go back to Massachusetts, but she did not know that their lives together were at stake in Tallahassee on May 23, 1957.[10]

The hearing room was filled to capacity. Fighting back tears, Frances Ellis told Collins that if Hildy were taken, "I don't like to say it because it sounds dramatic but I don't think she would survive." An assistant district attorney from Massachusetts conceded that "there would no doubt be severe hardship" but argued that the wishes of Hildy's natural mother, who had since married, should prevail. He asserted that the Ellises "cannot complain unless they have clean hands," and that the issue was not whether the law was fair but whether it would be obeyed.[11]

The two-hour hearing was over by noon. Collins must have decided beforehand what he would say unless he heard something to change his mind. He did not go home for lunch that day. He wrote out a statement and returned to the crowded conference room to announce his decision. Citing a technicality, the governor asserted that the Massachusetts indictments did not properly charge an offense and could not support extradition.[12]

Collins could have left it at that, but it would have invited Massachusetts to file new charges. So he went on to make it clear that no matter what, the Ellises were safe in Florida. Calling the criminal cases "synthetic," he said it was clear to him that "No crime of kidnapping in a proper sense is involved." The real issue was who would have the child, "and I think simple right and justice require that Hildy McCoy's present home life should not be disturbed."[13] It had been argued, he continued,

> [T]hat the natural mother has the right to have Hildy reared in the environment of her own faith. This is a right I respect, but it must yield to more fundamental rights. The great and good God of all of us, regardless of faith, granted to every child to be born first the right to be wanted, and second the right to be loved. Hildy's mother has denied both of these rights to her. . . . The mother claims that she now loves the child, but this cannot be true in a real sense. She may want to love the child, but love can only result from the giving of one's self to another. This she has never done, although she may have a genuine desire now to do so.
>
> It was the Ellises in truth and in fact who have been the persons through whom God has assured these first two rights as one of His children. It was the Ellises who wanted Hildy to be born. It was they who anxiously awaited her birth with tender emotions of excitement, anticipating fulfillment of the joys and obligations of parenthood. It was the Ellises also who have given of themselves to Hildy, as only parents can understand, thereby fulfilling Hildy's right to be loved.
>
> With no feeling against the natural mother, except that of pity and compassion; with no antagonism toward our great sister state of Massachusetts; I further deny this application based upon the equities in-

volved. . . . I sincerely hope that this child can now be allowed to continue to grow and develop in the only home, and with the only mother
and father, she has ever known.[14]

The audience applauded wildly. Reporters wrote that there were few dry
eyes in the room. Ellis wept for several minutes before he could compose
himself to answer questions from the media.[15]

The Ellises flew home that evening to find a throng of journalists waiting.
It was 10 p.m., past Hildy's bedtime, when they went to the neighbor's house
to awaken her and take her home. "Mommy and Daddy are back from their
'vacation,'" Ellis whispered to the drowsy child. The photograph of Ellis hug-
ging his daughter ran on the front page of the next day's *Miami Herald* under
a double-banner headline.[16]

The governor's decision was also front-page news at the *New York Times*
and worldwide. Letters, postcards, telephone calls, and news clippings continued to inundate his office, eventually filling twelve boxes of the Collins
archives at the University of South Florida. Of the eight reserved for letters,
all but one were marked "favorable." Collins recalled that there had been nine
thousand communications of all kinds, more than any other issue of his administration. He personally answered a selected few. Months later, a carload
of tourists from Michigan recognized Collins while his car was stopped in
traffic and thanked him for the Ellis decision.[17]

On July 10, a circuit judge at Miami rejected Massachusetts' persistent
objections and granted the Ellises' petition to formally adopt Hildy. The saga
was over.[18]

Thirty years after Collins gave sanctuary to the Ellises, the U.S. Supreme
Court unanimously reversed its 1861 precedent and ordered the governor of
Iowa to extradite a man wanted for vehicular homicide in Puerto Rico. The
Court's opinion was written by Justice Thurgood Marshall, who as counsel
for the NAACP Legal Defense Fund had often relied upon the 1861 precedent in urging northern governors to refuse to extradite blacks to Southern
states where the courts might be biased against them.[19]

Chapter 19

"An Evil Thing"

Previous governors had asked for little and expected less from their second sessions, but Collins was not a lame duck and challenged the 1957 Legislature with a program that one newspaper labeled "gargantuan." He did so despite having lost much of his influence in the House, where Doyle Conner of rural Bradford County had succeeded urban liberal Ted David of Broward in the Speaker's chair and only one of Collins's allies would hold a major chairmanship this time.

Nonetheless, Collins asked for new taxes—on "nearly everybody," as one newspaper put it—and for substantially more spending. He wanted a new constitution so desperately that he would settle for a reapportionment formula sacrificing reform of the Senate for more equitable representation in the House. He asked again for legislation that had failed before, including the divorce and speed limit bills, central purchasing, and the tax commission. He wanted a chancellor to run the university system, a commission to develop public television, and urban renewal powers for local governments. He requested money to buy primary highway rights of way (a burden on local government at the time), to build six new junior colleges, the new university in Hillsborough County, to raise schoolteacher pay by up to $700 subject to a merit system, and to help build the new classroom Florida needed every five hours. Collins recommended extending the sales tax to automobiles, alcoholic beverages, and clothing costing less than $10. To help school boards do their part, he proposed local-option motor vehicle taxes. Collins wanted to abolish the Milk Commission and the controversial practice of naturopathic medicine.[1]

He sought also to restrict the dredging and filling of submerged land, which the state had encouraged by selling bay bottoms as casually and cheaply as it once sold off its swamps. One sale before he became governor created an immense development in Boca Ciega Bay between St. Petersburg and barrier islands that caused intense, endless controversy for Collins and his Road Board. Collins and Ervin were suing—unsuccessfully—to rescind the sale; he asked for a law to help, and to encourage counties to limit such developments.[2]

He spoke carefully on race, minimizing the issue within the middle part of his speech. He cautioned that tampering with the pupil-assignment law might provoke the federal courts to overturn it. He asked for money to finance further studies by the Fabisinski commission, which he said had already determined that Florida's black citizens were "woefully lacking" in health, education, employment, and housing.[3]

Collins wrote to his son, the Navy cadet, that he had given legislators "a real broadside."[4] They answered in kind. Two days later, the House adopted the interposition resolution, declaring the U.S. Supreme Court's desegregation decisions and other controversial rulings to be null and void. Despite the governor's announced opposition, his staff did not attempt to lobby against it, rationalizing that it would be "foolish to burn up all our energy on that right at the start of the session."[5] Only Verle Pope and Doyle Carlton Jr. voted against it at a Senate committee meeting where Sumter Lowry and Ervin were the principal advocates. Ervin, who later compiled a liberal record on the Florida Supreme Court, said in retirement that interposition was "a bum error on my part."[6]

The Senate voted 20 to 18 against delaying the resolution and promptly adopted it by voice vote. The press reported that Edward Ball's lobbyists helped to pass it.[7] Rebutting Ervin's statement that interposition could have moral force as an expression of the people's wishes, Collins said: "The resolution is on its face a lie. I cannot attribute any moral value to a lie. Nor can I attribute any moral value to defiance of this nature."[8]

Protocol required Collins to forward copies of the resolution to President Eisenhower and other officials specified by the Legislature. He said in his cover letter that he would have vetoed it if he could.[9] Without announcing it at the time, Collins also wrote and signed a scathing opinion across the last page of the original document (see page 141):

> This concurrent resolution of "interposition" crosses my desk as a matter of routine. I have no authority to veto it. I take this means however to advise the student of government, who may examine this document

in the archives of the State in the years to come, that the governor of Florida expressed open and vigorous opposition thereto. I feel that the U.S. Supreme Court has improperly usurped powers reserved to the states under the constitution. I have joined in protesting such and in seeking legal means of avoidance. But if this resolution declaring decisions of the court to be "null and void" is to be taken seriously, it is anarchy and rebellion against the nation which must remain "indivisible, under God" if it is to survive. Not only will I not condone "interposition" as so many have sought me to do, I decry it as an evil thing, whipped up by the demagogues and carried on the hot and erratic winds of passion, prejudice, and hysteria. If history judges me right this day, I want it known that I did my best to avert this blot. If I am judged wrong, then here in my own handwriting and over my signature is the proof of guilt to support my conviction.[10]

Interposition exemplified how malapportionment distorted Florida's public policy. In procedural votes, the twenty-nine-member House minority that opposed interposition represented nearly 55 percent of Florida's population; the eighteen anti-interposition senators represented nearly 70 percent. Racism was a significant factor in the Pork Chop Gang's objections to fair apportionment. They and many of their constituents believed that urban legislators would accept desegregation.[11]

Interposition did not sate the rage of the arch-segregationists, who continued to fill committee dockets with bills having such potent consequences as the dismissal of pro-integration students and "nigger schoolteachers," as one legislator put it. That bill was entombed in a House subcommittee. "Even a justice of the peace court would hold this unconstitutional," said Gibbons.[12]

But there was no stopping Ervin's so-called last resort bill, which provided for communities to vote to close their schools to prevent desegregation. Collins warned that he would "never approve any attempt to abolish any public school anywhere." In a memorable House debate, Rep. Ralph Turlington of Alachua County contended that the bill would *encourage* desegregation. His tongue-in-cheek theory was that the NAACP would target schools where parents would be less likely to vote to close them. He cited Joel Chandler Harris's well-known fable of Brer Rabbit, who escapes a fox's clutches by feigning desperate fear of being thrown into a briar patch. The bill might even have been conceived "in the heart of Harlem," Turlington declared, "with the hope that some good Southern sucker would pick it up and pass it for 'em." Turlington no more believed what he was saying than most of his colleagues did, but some welcomed it as a plausible pretext for voting against the bill. They gave him a nickname: "Br'er Rabbit."[13]

The toils of the two-house system disposed of most of the rest of the radical segregation agenda, including several of the Legislative Investigating Committee's attempts to suppress the NAACP. The committee succeeded only in extending itself for two years. Once again, Collins withheld his veto, allowing Johns to become chairman when a more temperate House member resigned.[14]

Collins's first big victory of the session established a six-month residency requirement to put an end to "quickie" divorces. The junior college bill, more than doubling the number of two-year schools, soon followed. The naturopathy bill passed with broad exemptions that led to it being ruled unconstitutional. One of Collins's priorities was defeated when the House killed a bill to require public meetings by all boards and agencies. That would take ten more years to pass.[15]

Collins reluctantly accepted legislation doubling the small-loan limit to $600 and raising interest rates. The small-loan lobbyist was one of the most influential: Raeburn Horne, the former senator who hosted Pork Chop caucuses at his isolated fishing camp. Sitting in the House gallery, Horne was seen making hand signals to instruct his supporters how to vote on the bills. He was a first cousin of Rep. Mallory Horne, whose father angrily rebuked him for voting against "family." It came out later that twenty-four of the ninety-five House members owned small-loan stock. Despite the odor, Collins rationalized that the comptroller needed the legislation.[16]

Another lobbying controversy involved Collins's unsalaried confidante, Charles Ausley, and Ausley's client Charles Rosenberg, whose Rose Printing Company printed all the Legislature's documents and an estimated half of all state business. A *St. Petersburg Times* article implied that Ausley had helped Rosenberg keep printing out of the governor's purchasing bill.[17]

The Legislature compromised on raising teacher pay by as much as $900 a year depending on experience, with a minimum $4,000 for tenured teachers. It also authorized incentive raises based on merit; however, seniority soon became the singular criterion for merit. Collins welcomed the bill but threatened to veto the sales tax on food and medicine by which some lawmakers proposed to pay for it.[18]

With a week remaining, *Miami Herald* veteran reporter Steve Trumbull wrote that it was the worst session in ten years. He said Collins's program had been "cut up, mangled and fed to the meat grinder" without any sign of help from him for legislators who were fighting bad bills. Collins lost his temper over the implication that he was weak, which could encourage legislators to treat him that way, and complained to the publisher that it was a "grossly slanted and prejudiced" article.[19]

Though property tax equalization was a bitter defeat, Collins managed to arrange a study comparing assessment ratios among the counties. The data armed him for a stern speech to the assessors that fall; it showed that three counties valued property at only 20 percent of actual value and that only four assessed as high as 80 percent.[20]

There were successes, including a formula to redistribute primary highway funds according to need rather than equally to each road district—a rare defeat for the small-county bloc—but the much-amended purchasing bill exempted printing and protected the Cabinet members' patronage in the customary way: another Cabinet commission, this one for purchasing.[21]

With a week to go, there was no agreement for tax increases or constitutional revision, which was still snagged on reapportionment. House and Senate committees insisted on a formula allowing geography and "community of interest" as factors in Senate districting. When Collins denounced that as a step backward and threatened to call a special session, the Senate promptly passed the amendment by the bare minimum of 23 votes to 14. There were renewed complaints from Collins supporters that timely lobbying or veto threats from his office could have turned at least one vote.[22]

The legislators voted to extend the session rather than allow the governor to call them back later, a tactic intended to make it harder for him to successfully veto the school-closing bill. The Senate then passed it by a vote of 26 to 11, enough to override a veto. Collins said he expected the extended session to be rough. By then, however, he had already achieved all or part of his remaining major goals. But he had lost bills to abolish the Milk Commission and Tuberculosis Board, authorize urban renewal, and provide for more troopers, driver reexamination, and a saltwater fishing license.[23]

Collins's much-amended submerged land bill was enacted during the extension over strenuous opposition from the prodevelopment Pinellas County delegation. "If we study this bill all summer," asked a legislator from nearby Bradenton, "isn't it possible Manatee County bays will end up as bad as Pinellas County bays?" The heavily amended bill was a tentative reform that proved ineffective. "When and where is that local board down there going to draw the line against further filling of Boca Ciega Bay?" Collins complained a year later. The law left so much discretion to the counties that Pasco drew its line two miles out in the Gulf of Mexico. The plunder was not stopped until 1967, when developers finally were confronted with strict environmental-impact standards.[24]

Collins called the Senate's latest reapportionment scheme "the most unsound, unacceptable and abominable" constitutional proposal he had ever seen and said he would campaign against any proposed constitution that contained it. Taking him at his word, the House decided to shelve the constitution. Nobody accused Collins of inaction this time. John Crews of Baker County, a widely respected member, alleged pressure over appropriations and roads and gestured toward Wilbur Jones, the Road Board chairman, in the House gallery. Constitutional revision was put off for a special session that Collins would call in the fall.[25]

Taxes could not wait; the Legislature compromised on $120 million in new revenue, mostly from retail sales, for the ensuing two years. In relative terms, it more than doubled the original sales tax package of 1949. Groceries remained exempt, but the sales tax was extended to all clothing, beer and mixed drinks served at bars and restaurants, cigarettes (in addition to the existing excise tax), oil and grease, and (at 1 percent) automobiles and heavy machinery. The Legislature also lowered the collection threshold to ten-cent purchases—at that level, a tax rate of 10 percent. Higher taxes on bank deposits, stocks and bonds, and documentary stamps accounted for the balance. For all that, legislators conceded they had raised substantially less than they had voted to spend, which meant the Cabinet budget commission would be burdened with spending cuts. Florida's fisc was already falling behind population growth; by November, 115 schools would be on double sessions, an increase of 63 percent over the year before, and statewide enrollment was more than ninety thousand students above declared capacity. But Collins wanted no more new taxes for the rest of his term.[26]

He vetoed the "last resort" school-closing bill. In a lengthy explanation, Collins objected that the legislation would be a "come on to the professional agitators and extremists and on many issues other than integration could result in a community being torn asunder under a siege of hysteria emanating from mere suspicion and propaganda." He contended also that it was unnecessary, would be impossible to administer, and would jeopardize the pupil-assignment law. He wrote that the bill "pours across the face of a great State the highly combustible fuel of racial hatred and beckons to firebrands and the irresponsible to come and ignite the flames.

"When men harbor hatred in their hearts for their fellow-men, it is a regrettable thing," he said. "But when government is used as an instrument for translating racial hatred into a force to destroy the very institutions which nurture and sustain it, then such is an even more serious wrong, and I condemn it.[27]

If the veto were to be upheld, it would have to be the House that did it. The governor and his allies worked desperately that night and the next day to shore up the thirty-six representatives who had voted against the bill on May 14. He had to keep at least thirty-two on his side. Of particular concern was Dempsey Barron, a rangy, red-headed freshman from Bay County, a Panhandle constituency where Collins's arch-segregationist rivals had held the governor to 35 percent of the Democratic primary vote. Collins telephoned Barron, who had survived the sinking of his torpedoed ship in the Pacific, with what one witness recalled as an urgent appeal "to his manhood, his love of the state, his patriotic fervor." Johns, Clarke, and at least seven other Pork Chop senators were seen lobbying on the House floor during the debate. Collins did not lose a vote and gained six members who had initially supported the bill. The veto was upheld on a roll call of 48 votes yes, 42 no. The votes to override represented only 19 percent of the people of Florida.[28]

Five North Florida lawmakers—Beasley, Barron, Crews, C. Fred Arrington of Gadsden County, and J. B. Hopkins of Escambia—voted to sustain the veto. In 1958, voters reelected all but Hopkins, who ran against an incumbent senator who later tried to make it a felony to teach in an integrated school. Reubin Askew, a future liberal governor, succeeded Hopkins in the House.[29]

Legislatures habitually complete most of their work at or near the last minute. Florida's 1957 session, no exception, left a heavy workload of bills on Collins's desk. He vetoed thirty-four, including a liquor price-fixing bill on which he and Johns were on the same side for once. He also vetoed three submerged-land giveaways that he said were "in sharp conflict with my understanding of a public duty to protect a public trust." Another was of a patently racist bill to disallow welfare payments to seventeen-year-olds not making passing grades in school. The 1959 session upheld most of the 1957 vetoes.[30]

Collins extensively remade his staff that spring and summer to replace Bob Fokes, his chief political aide, and several others who left for private practice or judgeships. The replacements included two young lawyers who would be greatly influential: William Killian of Miami, whose duties included advising Collins and the Fabisinski commission on racial strategy, and who would become Road Board chairman in 1960; and William L. Durden of Jacksonville, who as a circuit court judge years later would implement by decree the full-value property tax assessment that Collins had been unable to get from the Legislature. To replace beverage director J. L. Williamson, who was returning to private business, Collins named H. G. Cochran Jr., a businessman from Lake City who had been one of Collins's few supporters in Pork Chop country in the 1956 campaign.[31]

For the third time, the Collins family packed up and moved across the street, on this occasion from the Grove to Florida's newly completed executive residence, where the younger daughters used the dumbwaiter as an elevator until their parents caught on. The family decided to return the rent the Legislature had appropriated for using the Grove as a governor's mansion.[32]

Mary Call borrowed five paintings for the mansion from storage at the state-owned Ringling Museum, provoking a successful lawsuit by U.S. Rep. James A. Haley, the late donor's brother-in-law, who contended that his will did not allow any of the art to leave Sarasota. The 1959 session passed a law to overturn the court decision. When the bill seemed to be in trouble, Collins called Sen. Ed Price to his office. "For goodness' sake, get Mary Call's bill passed or I'm not going to be able to go home," the governor said.[33]

The Duke and Duchess of Windsor were guests at one of the quail plantations that year. Collins welcomed them to the new mansion and Capitol and seemed to be vastly amused when Betty McCord fumbled protocol in introducing them to the staff. Collins was laughing as much at himself as at her; as she learned later, he had introduced United Press reporter Barbara Frye as "Barbara Stanwyck," the actor.[34]

In the fall, Grotegut notified the capital press corps that Collins would hold regular weekly news conferences if they would limit their requests for exclusive interviews and their telephone calls to the mansion, which the governor or First Lady usually answered personally. Transcripts of the conferences were mailed to news editors and editorial boards so that they could read for themselves what Collins was saying.[35]

Collins used the first conference to warn that he would suspend tax assessors for undervaluing their rolls. At another, he acknowledged that Mary Call had vetoed the idea of a state airplane for the governor because she was "rather strongly opposed to having me ride in airplanes any more than is necessary." Speaking for herself, she said she feared that a state pilot would fly where a commercial airline would not. "A pilot employed by the state isn't going to stand up to the governor," she said.[36]

On Christmas Eve 1957, Willis McCall precipitated another Lake County race crisis by arresting Virgil Hawkins's nephew, Melvin Hawkins Jr., on suspicion of raping a prominent white woman. McCall released him after Collins sent his own investigators to the county in response to a midnight telephone call from the NAACP. McCall then framed a mentally retarded white youth, Jesse Daniels, whom an obliging judge sent to the state mental hospital at Chattahoochee to avoid a trial that would expose the flimsiness of the case. When his mother complained, Collins told the press he was confident the boy would be well defended. In fact, Daniels did not have a vigorous defense until new lawyers successfully appealed pro bono for his release fourteen years later. The Legislature eventually voted money to Daniels and his mother for wrongful imprisonment.[37]

Collins's travels, more frequent than when he was a legislator, troubled his family. He often recounted a conversation in which Darby, six years old when he began his second term, asked him why people were talking about a lieutenant governor. Collins explained that a lieutenant governor fills in when a governor is away. "Gosh, I sure wish I had a lieutenant daddy," Darby said.[38]

Fifteen-year-old Mary Call wrote in a school essay her teacher sent to the governor that his travels were making the whole family somewhat unhappy with politics. Nonetheless, she said, he was still available for good advice. "The main trait which I admire him the most for is, he has always had the courage to stand up for what he thinks is right, no matter what anyone else says or thinks." But he was not perfect; "at times he may become hot tempered and also absent minded." Once when she and her mother drove him to the airport, he flew off with the car keys. "He is a wonderful father and I could never do without him," she concluded.[39]

Chapter 20

Little Rock

Preparing for the 1957 meeting of the Southern Governors' Conference at Sea Island, Georgia, chairman Luther H. Hodges of North Carolina asked Collins to speak on the topic "Why Can't a Southerner Be Elected President of the United States?" Collins rephrased the title: "Can a Southerner Be Elected President?" Recent experience had persuaded many Southerners that the answer had to be no, that the vice presidency was their glass ceiling. Gov. Marvin S. Griffin of Georgia, no fan of Collins, said before hearing the speech that a Southerner could not become president "without knifing his own people."[1]

A desegregation crisis was developing at Little Rock. Like Collins, Arkansas Gov. Orval Faubus had moderate instincts; his state, unlike Florida, had placidly desegregated several school districts, the University of Arkansas, and six of seven state colleges. Like Collins, Faubus won a 1956 first primary victory over strident segregationists by running as a moderate.[2] But opinion polls convinced him he could win another two-year term in 1958 only as a racial demagogue. Assuming the same indifference from the Eisenhower administration as during the University of Alabama riots, Faubus called out the Arkansas National Guard to keep nine Negro students from attending Little Rock's Central High School as ordered by a federal court. The soldiers also barred the school's black cafeteria workers and janitors. For the first time since Appomattox, American troops were defying the United States government. Yet Eisenhower did nothing for more than three weeks but talk to Faubus and appeal ineffectively for the court orders to be obeyed.[3]

Collins, meanwhile, prepared his speech and previewed it with a friend, this time *Tallahassee Democrat* editor Malcolm Johnson, who warned that it was too liberal for his constituency. Once again, Collins changed nothing. He recorded and filmed portions for the Florida media before leaving for the conference.[4]

Collins, Faubus, and some of the other governors stopping in Atlanta for a meeting of the Southern Regional Education Board were invited to a Saturday night football game between the University of Georgia and the University of Texas. The crowd was largely indifferent to the introductions until Faubus's name was called; it set off an ovation so tumultuous that Collins feared the stadium might collapse. Raucous fans swarmed around Faubus. After the game, they marched through the streets chanting his name. Collins and John Perry, his press aide, found themselves recalling the newsreels of Adolf Hitler's nighttime rallies in Nuremberg.[5]

Before leaving Arkansas, Faubus had responded to a federal district court contempt citation by agreeing, or so he said, to admit the black students. But on Monday, September 23, Faubus double-crossed the court by withdrawing the National Guard entirely, abandoning to the mercies of a mob the eight black children who tried to attend school that day. Segregationists rampaged for three hours, damaging the school and beating up black and white reporters. Little Rock police rushed the children to safety.[6]

Collins did not revise the text for his speech that afternoon, in which he said a Southerner could be elected president provided he had the right qualities of style and substance. That candidate, he said, "must have a compelling and persuasive presence on the television screen, for it is here that future campaigns will be won and lost." But issues would dominate; there were things the South would have to do if a Southerner were to be electable. States' rights, he said, could no longer serve as a "shoddy excuse for the states to do nothing, or as a stimulus for disunity and discord." No longer could Southern states continue to default their responsibilities to the federal government. Here, Collins asserted a political philosophy that he would reiterate for the rest of his career: America should spend more on domestic needs and less on the military, the arms race, and the Cold War. That would necessitate a new foreign policy, a new sense of leadership "for the progress of the whole world." The first test, he made clear, would be in how a presidential candidate approached American racial issues that Collins considered not regional but national in scope. "Negroes throughout the nation," he said, "are still badly in need of better homes, better health, better schools, better employment opportunities." That was more important than immediate desegregation, and "these improvements simply cannot be brought about in an atmosphere of racial furor."[7]

Collins had a message for the Northern public also. Northern politicians could easily make rousing speeches about civil rights, he said, but "It is something else for a Southern leader to work effectively for the brotherhood of mankind, and the dignity of law, in areas alive with emotions deeply rooted in the past, and still have his people with him."

Effective leadership, Collins continued, "requires more than the vision to see and the courage to act, although both these qualities are essential. A leader also must have the discretion and judgment required to raise a standard out front, but not so far that it is beyond the horizon of the people and, therefore, cannot be seen and understood and followed by them. If one gets beyond this view, even if only a little way beyond, he becomes lost from view. . . . [H]e makes himself impotent and his efforts are futile."[8]

Collins was plainly rationalizing his own actions. But he followed with a broader admonition. "I am convinced that the prevailing sentiment in this nation is not radical," he said. "It is realistic and understanding. It does not condone arrogance and the irresponsible forcing of issues. It believes that the decisions of the United States Supreme Court are the law of the land and insists that ours be a land of the law. It does not sanction violence, defiance and disorder. Above all, it abhors hate. The Southern leader who understands and accepts these facts will find himself not opposed to national sentiment but in harmony with it. He who does not might as well stay home."[9]

Collins also asserted, with barely any mention in the press, that Congress should involve itself in desegregation. He concluded that "Yes, a Southerner can be elected President now," but only if he were an "uncommon man with a common touch," a man who, among other things, "must know injustice not because he can place the blame for wrong, but because he has righted it."[10]

The *Washington Post* reported that Collins received "long, loud applause from all but a gubernatorial fringe." The *Tampa Tribune* headlined the "forcing of issues" quotation. The *Atlanta Constitution*'s reporter emphasized his "law of the land" remark. Ralph McGill's editorial said it was an "eloquent testimonial of faith" that "almost certainly will become a classic of textbooks in the field of political science and technology."[11]

But it was Faubus who was surrounded by a cluster of reporters most of the day, and Little Rock kept Collins's remarks off the front pages except in Florida.[12] Eisenhower, his patience exhausted, said he was prepared to use federal force and was reported to be meeting with the secretary of the army, which put even the moderate Southern governors on the defensive.[13] Assuming that Eisenhower meant to federalize the Arkansas National Guard, Collins said he wanted to hear more from the president before agreeing that it was justified. "The whole mess out there is sickening," he said. It seemed to him, he said in a subsequent statement, that a long-range solution would have to contemplate desegregation in some places but not others.[14]

On Tuesday morning, the mob formed again outside Central High School. At Sea Island, the Southern governors, desperate to forestall the use of troops, wanted to send a committee to discuss other solutions with Eisenhower. But the president who had waited too long would wait no longer. He put the National Guard under federal command to keep Faubus from using it and after a second day of mob rule sent one thousand riot-trained Regular Army troops of the 101st Airborne Division to Little Rock. On Wednesday, with a cordon of paratroopers around the school, the children were admitted. Not since Reconstruction had federal troops enforced civil rights in the South.[15]

As that was happening, the Southern governors were meeting in executive session—without Faubus, who had flown home—to elect a new chairman. With Hodges's help, Collins made and won a last-minute campaign against Griffin, who had been the choice of a nominating committee dominated by unyielding segregationists. With the vote pending, Perry took a telephone call for Collins from *Washington Post* publisher Philip Graham, whom Perry understood to be an intermediary for the White House. Perry said he kept the phone line open, feeding periodic reports to Graham, who, after hearing that Collins had won, said that the president wanted Collins to know that "this day he has saved the Union."[16]

Much of the South reacted to Eisenhower's action as if it had been an invasion. Convening for a special session on constitutional revision, the Florida Legislature adopted a memorial to Congress accusing the president and the 101st Division's commanding general of "fascism and military arrogance." Only five legislators opposed it.[17]

Eisenhower agreed to meet with the Southern governors' committee. Hodges appointed himself, Frank Clement of Tennessee, Collins, Theodore McKeldin of Maryland, and Griffin. Griffin, the only arch-segregationist, withdrew on hearing that Eisenhower might try to talk about other desegregation issues in addition to the Little Rock crisis. Collins wired Griffin that he was disappointed. "You place the other members of our committee in an awkward position," he said. "These are dangerous and critical times. If we close the barriers to discussion we just make our position more difficult."[18]

On October 1, the committee consulted with Faubus by telephone before an afternoon meeting at the White House with Eisenhower and two presidential aides. They negotiated a communiqué to which Faubus agreed, but it was another double-cross. In the draft statement, Faubus was to say that if the troops were withdrawn, "the orders of the federal courts will not be obstructed." As actually issued in Little Rock, the statement said that "the orders of the federal courts will not be obstructed *by me*" (emphasis added). It implied that once again Faubus would allow the mob to obstruct them. Eisenhower said it left him no recourse but to keep the troops at Little Rock. "I am terribly disappointed," Collins said. "We went over every word of every statement with Governor Faubus and it was my understanding that he specifically agreed to everything verbatim just as the president did."[19]

The episode left Collins nearly as disillusioned with Eisenhower as with Faubus. The president took Collins aside during the negotiations to confide that he regretted the necessity of sending troops, that he did it only to enforce a court order, that he "understood how you folks feel in the South" and would not have regretted a Supreme Court decision upholding segregation. Collins, shocked, could say only "Thank you, Mr. President." He wished later that he had told Eisenhower that the South was not so single-minded as he seemed to think.[20]

In a speech to the National Municipal League, Collins lamented that Little Rock had "destroyed" the position of Southern moderates. The federal troops were long gone when Faubus was renominated in 1958 with nearly 70 percent of the vote in a primary election that also turned out Arkansas' moderate congressman, Brooks Hays. Armed with a new state law, Faubus closed all four Little Rock high schools. The schools reopened a year later, peacefully desegregated, after voters elected an anti-Faubus majority to the school board and a federal district judge declared his legislation unconstitutional. In November 1960, Arkansas voters emphatically rejected a constitutional amendment providing, like the legislation Collins had vetoed, for local-option school closures. Faubus voluntarily left office after the 1966 election. He attempted unsuccessfully to return to the governor's office in 1970, 1974, and 1986; his last loss was to a future president, Bill Clinton.[21]

Chapter 21

Failure?

Collins had promised to call a special session on constitutional revision if legislative leaders compromised on a reapportionment formula acceptable to him. Caucusing secretly in early September 1957 at Raeburn Horne's Aucilla River fishing camp, the Pork Chop Gang proposed seven new Senate seats. Four, including a separate Sarasota County district, were intended for South Florida. The concession was too slight, however, to threaten rural domination, and the addition of "pertinent factors" other than population made it a step backward that could ensure Pork Chop rule forever. But Collins said he would accept it with a sizeable increase in House membership. A House caucus proposed adding nineteen seats to the existing ninety-five and Collins called a special session to begin September 30.[1]

It was perilous timing in light of the news from Little Rock. Many members were eager to reintroduce the last resort bill or something worse. This time, however, Ervin counseled caution, saying they could muddle the governors' meeting with Eisenhower.[2] Collins counted on there not being the two-thirds majority necessary to act on subjects he did not specify.

In his welcoming speech, he admitted that he was not completely satisfied with the proposed constitution but said that overall, it was "generally the result of honorable compromise, the essence of all constitutions," and would furnish "a tree, trim yet sturdy upon which fruits of good government will grow." Some others, however, suspected that his yearning for a new constitution had overwhelmed his principles. Under the proposed reapportionment formula, the thirty-four smallest counties would still have one House seat each, confirming rural control despite additional seats for some larger counties. Senate redistricting would regress, with the ten largest counties sustaining a net loss in proportional influence.[3] Some of Collins's strongest supporters refused to follow. Ralph Turlington said Collins had been "brainwashed" by a "group of Philistines." Sam Gibbons called it a "sorry spectacle."[4]

Collins left at that point for Washington, returning two days later to a full-blown struggle over a reintroduced school-closing bill similar to the one he had vetoed. The Senate passed it 31 votes to 5, with even Verle Pope supporting it, but in the House it fell four votes short of the two-thirds needed to consider it.[5] When the ten-day session ended, however, only one racial bill had reached the governor's desk. Sponsored by a Collins loyalist, Rep. James S. Moody of Hillsborough County, it made Florida the first state to provide for the instant closure of any school occupied by federal troops. A newspaper reported that some senators whiled away the final minutes of the session singing Negro spirituals. With the session over, Collins, in Miami for a speech, felt safe in saying at a press conference that "Someday, somewhere, somehow we are going to have integration of our schools in Florida." Johns remarked, "He is running for president, you know."[6]

Collins said he considered the Moody bill unnecessary but would sign it because it was "almost ridiculous to assume that any sound educating could be carried on under the pressure of armed guards." A week later, he announced that, as expected, he would appoint Moody to a newly created circuit judgeship.[7]

The Legislature proposed a new constitution, including a potentially troublesome clause allowing "emergency" assistance to private schools, packaged in the form of fourteen separate amendments. Each provided that if the voters disapproved any of them, none would take effect. The linkage was calculated, as Sen. Dewey Johnson admitted, to force Collins and like-minded voters to accept rural rule indefinitely as the price of an elected lieutenant governor and a few other constitutional improvements. Legislators informally named the package the "daisy chain." Gibbons and other opponents had votes enough only to prevent a special referendum in November 1957, which won them more than a year to campaign against ratification.[8]

The League of Women Voters and many of the governor's other customary allies did not share his enthusiasm for the compromise. "I am not willing to see South Florida grant political domination to North Florida for all the foreseeable future for a little clarified language and a few improvements," the publisher of the *Fort Pierce News-Tribune* wrote personally to Collins. Reply-ing to Rep. Beth Johnson of Orlando, Collins said their disagreement "gives me an uncomfortable feeling, like wearing something that doesn't fit right." Martin Andersen, the *Orlando Sentinel* publisher, berated him so severely at a social function that Andersen wrote afterward to apologize for his tone. "I just believe that this new constitution has far more good in it than bad," Collins replied, "and I think the state will lose if we let our antagonism about the shortcomings cause us to send the overall good down the drain." The *Tampa Tribune*'s criticism was so fierce that Collins wrote to the publisher, "I am quite worried about the head-on collision between the *Tribune* and me." Replied the publisher, "not only am I worried, but grieved."[9]

Taking his case to the people, Collins admitted in his monthly broadcast that the proposed constitution fell far short of what he had hoped. In a guest column he sent to the *Miami Herald*, Collins wrote that nothing in twenty years of public service had hurt him more than a television interviewer's sug-gestion that he had sold out. But when a reporter asked whether he would vote for the reapportionment plan if it stood alone on the ballot, Collins paused long before answering: "I'm certainly not satisfied with that appor-tionment plan, but I come back to the position that that plan is better than what we have now." His fear, he said in a subsequent speech, was that the daisy chain was the last opportunity for a generation or two, and its defeat would "usher in an era of sectional strife for our state which can be devastating to all Florida's progress."[10]

The passionate debate turned out to be premature. Four months before the referendum date, the Florida Supreme Court ruled unanimously that the daisy chain linkage was an improper attempt to do what only an elected con-vention could. Collins, conceding that the daisy chain would have failed at the polls, said he would ask the 1959 session for unlinked amendments.[11]

But by 1959, the lame-duck syndrome was in full force and the Legislature had no interest in a new constitution. As Johns and other Pork Choppers saw it, they needed to adopt only a new reapportionment article. Collins thought he had no choice but to work with them. Few people thought that the fed-eral courts ever would intervene in state apportionment, and even Collins said they would have no "proper business" doing so. What the session sub-mitted to the voters was as obvious a sham as the daisy chain provision had been. House membership would increase from 95 seats to 103, and the Senate would be expanded from 38 seats to 44, but while South Florida would have more legislators speaking for it, their votes would carry no more weight. Tiny Jefferson County would still boast its own senator, apportionment would be frozen for twelve years, and the Senate formula would forever allow "geographic area and economic affinity" to negate population equality. Thomas Beasley, the House Speaker, boasted to a North Florida audience that the so-called compromise would perpetuate small-county control of both houses.[12]

Some South Florida newspapers and legislators agreed with Collins in 1959 that it was time to take what they could get. Rep. Wilbur H. Boyd of Manatee, eager to see Republican-leaning Sarasota County carved out of the Senate district he aspired to represent, rationalized that "this helps Manatee, because we are in for a senator.... If you are hungry, why hold out for a steak? Go ahead and eat humburger" [*sic*]. But Price, the new senator from the existing district, refused to "buy this at the expense of other populous areas of Florida."[13]

There were enough votes this time to set a special election for November. Collins bitterly attributed selfish motives to some of the urban legislators who opposed the amendment; he accused them of not wanting to share with new colleagues their influence over local legislation and patronage. Collins also complained that some urban business interests preferred to work with rural legislators.[14]

Gibbons, the League of Women Voters, and the *Tampa Tribune* were on Collins's side this time. So was the *Miami Herald*, which called the amendment "odious in principle" but the best that could be had. The Jacksonville, Pensacola, and Ocala newspapers endorsed it also, but the dailies in St. Petersburg, Fort Lauderdale, Palm Beach, Daytona Beach, and Fort Pierce fought it strongly. Collins was particularly hurt; "They hadn't been up here knowing how hard it was to get that half a loaf," he said. Leading opponents included two of Collins's former close allies who were now running for governor, ex-Speaker Ted David and John McCarty, whom he had appointed a circuit judge.[15]

Fearing defeat in a light turnout, Collins made a final appeal on the eve of the referendum. "People of Florida, understand what you have at stake," he said. "You can get fourteen additional legislators to fight your fight.... I anxiously want to see my successor have a better fighting chance to obtain a solution of this issue than I have had. We have struggled through five sessions. I can see no hope without reinforcements."[16]

The turnout was light—less than a fourth of the registered voters—and the plan was rejected, 177,955 votes no, 146,601 yes. Forty-three counties, including Hillsborough and Orange, favored the amendment but could not overcome the enormous opposition in Broward, Dade, Palm Beach, and Pinellas. Collins expressed disappointment and defeat; he said he would not ask the Legislature to try again. It was the only time that he had lost the support of so many large newspapers. But twenty-five years later, in a speech honoring the late Nelson Poynter, editor and president of the *St. Petersburg Times*, Collins confessed that "I had no heart for that campaign and deep down doubted my own judgment to compromise."[17]

Collins left office believing that reapportionment was his greatest failure. When he said so at a Washington dinner party several years later, one of the guests told him that he had not failed. The guest was a Supreme Court justice who explained that the Court had considered Collins's unavailing five-year struggle while debating in 1962 whether to reverse precedent and intervene in legislative districting. After deciding that it would enter that "political thicket," the Court ordered Florida to reapportion on the basis of population, and in 1967 a federal district court drew new districts statewide.

It is uncertain who the talkative justice was. Collins said in 1975 that it was William O. Douglas but wrote in 1988 that it was Hugo Black. Circumstantial evidence points to Douglas, with whom Collins was already acquainted, the justice having been a guest at the governor's mansion. According to Hugo Black Jr., Douglas was a more frequent partygoer and talked more to outsiders about the Court's business than his father did.[18]

Chapter 22

Spotlight

In 1957, the national media began to speak of Collins as a unique South-ern politician who would be a plausible candidate for president or vice president. A *New York Times* profile described him as "the personal possessor of one of the most mellifluous old Southern accents below Mason and Dixon's line" and as a six-footer "elegant in dress." His staff encouraged the political speculation and subscribed to a national clip-ping service for all editorials mentioning him. Interviewed in May 1958 on NBC's *Meet the Press*, he admitted that he would be receptive to a presidential draft or an offer to be someone's running mate. "I don't think anybody would be intellectually honest to say that he would turn down a call to serve in a capacity of that kind," he said, "but I am honest in saying to you that I am not seeking that honor and have no intention of seeking it."[1]

The spotlight also brought increasing criticism that Collins's mod-eration was more talk than action. After hearing Collins decry the "dis-ease of racial intolerance" in a speech to newspaper publishers, *Charles-ton News & Courier* editor T. R. Waring, an outspoken segregationist, wondered acidly why Collins had not called on Miami's resort hotels to desegregate. *Time*, which had been so complimentary in 1956, observed that "LeRoy Collins' moderation has begun to look more and more like the protective coloring of a good politician who has discovered the magic combination for winning friends in the North and offending precious few in the South." William L. Rivers, a University of Miami professor, wrote in the *Nation* that Collins "doesn't sit on the fence; he *runs* on it. . . . Instead of playing both ends against the middle, he's playing the middle against both ends." Collins, who ordinarily left press rebuttals to Perry, complained in a personal letter to Rivers that he deserved credit for opposing interposition and vetoing the last resort bill. Rivers replied that leadership should consist of "positive action" as well as vetoes. At about the same time, Collins declined to attend a conference on civil rights for which the Dade Council on Human Relations believed it had his verbal commitment. Collins wrote that he would not have the time, but he confided the truth to Grotegut: "It is not the right time for this—whatever I would say would be misapplied."[2]

Only four months later, Collins acknowledged the accuracy of Rivers's characterization. "I am convinced that unless we reinforce the middle ground, it will become a no-man's land across which the extremists will fight," Collins wrote under his byline in *Look* magazine. The article promoted a plan Collins was devising for transferring desegregation jurisdiction from the federal district courts to civil rights commissions that Congress would establish in each state, their members jointly appointed by the president and the respective governors. Their role, he said, should be "to guard against improvident integration as well as to facilitate integration where feasible." He said he feared rioting in "countless" Southern communities if it were left to the NAACP to decide "where and when to desegregate."[3]

He made the same point in a milder way in a widely publicized, well-received Jefferson-Jackson Day dinner speech to the North Carolina Democratic Party at Raleigh. "The tragedy of our plight today," he said, "is that the reformers, and I mean the well-intending as well as those with other motives, often destroy our power to make progress toward the goals they themselves espouse." But he also declared that "universal brotherhood must be our goal. It is our Christian obligation as well as our legal obligation to accommodate our hearts and minds to it. We must abandon the defiant attitude of 'never.'" Justice, he said, "can never walk hand in hand with legally coerced racial discrimination in any part of our land."[4]

That went far beyond his remarks on segregated bus seating in the 1957 inaugural address. But the more he talked in that fashion, the more the media demanded to know what he was going to do about it. The *Meet the Press* interview, on the occasion of his election as chairman of the National Governors Association, pressed him relentlessly on Florida's lack of apparent progress. Responding to panelist Bill Baggs, a friend who edited the *Miami News*, Collins said there were probably some Florida communities, "not many at the present time," where desegregation could be undertaken safely. Reminded of his remarks at Raleigh, Collins conceded that justice was being delayed in Florida. There were times, he said, "when wisdom has to restrain the unfettered pace of justice until it can catch up and walk hand in hand."[5]

Justice was being held to a snail's pace in 1958. The University of Florida College of Law was finally desegregated with the admission of one student, but all forty-six Negro children who applied to white schools at Miami were turned down.[6]

Collins tirelessly promoted his congressional action proposal for more than two years. He pitched it personally to Senate Majority Leader Lyndon B. Johnson over a Sunday breakfast at Johnson's home in Washington and thought Johnson had been receptive. But Johnson had been evasive. Perry recalls Johnson taking him aside, poking him in the chest, and saying, "You get me the votes in the Senate for that plan, and I'll champion it." Collins was unable to get even a hearing in Congress or an endorsement from his own National Governors Association.[7]

Not to his surprise, the idea met keen suspicions on both sides. Liberals were unwilling to sideline the federal judiciary or accept the dubious premise that the threat of violence justified deferring a moral right. "We do not need an act of Congress," said Gov. Theodore McKeldin of Maryland, "to spell out for us what the decision of the Supreme Court has made so clear—that a citizen is a citizen." Marvin Griffin said that he was "not interested in implementing any plan of desegregation anywhere."[8]

Race was rarely absent from Florida headlines. In March 1958, Sheriff Roy Baden of Manatee County infuriated Collins by leading a Ku Klux Klan motorcade through black neighborhoods in Bradenton. Collins said Baden should have banned any demonstration "which could reasonably be calculated to produce disorder and incidents of violence."[9] Within the month, Klan culpability was suspected but not proved in dynamite blasts that damaged a Jacksonville school for Negroes and Jewish temples in Miami and Jacksonville.[10] Collins rebuked Baden again after his deputies raided homes occupied by Hispanic migrant workers and ordered their "white" wives to leave the county, but the governor resisted calls for the sheriff's suspension.[11]

He would not pass up the next opportunity. Baden apparently did not take seriously the governor's warning in a speech to sheriffs in June 1958 that he would suspend any of them who were indifferent to illegal gambling. In December 1959, raids by the local state attorney's office and agents from Collins's state beverage department, planned without Baden's knowledge, exposed widespread bolita and moonshine whisky operations in Manatee. Collins swiftly suspended Baden, accusing him of neglect of duty and incompetence, and appointed a replacement. Baden was popular in Manatee and the suspension was not, but Price sustained the action in the 1961 Senate.[12]

Though most previous governors had suspended officials only in response to indictments, Collins acted on his own instincts; Baden's was his twenty-seventh suspension, and the Senate normally upheld them. Another was of Sheriff Al Cahill of Duval, the second-largest county, whom Collins suspended after Cahill refused to testify before a grand jury investigating gambling and prostitution. Collins said the grand jury report revealed Cahill to be incompetent. But a few months later, Suwannee County sheriff Hugh Lewis kept his job despite refusing to testify to the Johns Committee concerning a black man who had been kidnapped and flogged by the Ku Klux Klan. Collins's staff could cite no legal grounds to remove Lewis.[13]

One of Collins's most controversial suspensions did not succeed. Seminole County Democrats renominated tax assessor Mary Walker after Collins had suspended her—partly as an example to other assessors—for valuing property at only 40 percent of its value. Collins restored her to office after the primary, satisfied that his interim assessor had reformed the rolls.[14]

The first major shakeup of Collins's administration came in June 1958, when he replaced Road Board chairman Wilbur Jones with Grotegut. Not saying why, he gave Jones a new job administering Florida's interstate highway program.[15] Soon after, Collins grudgingly yielded to what he called a "campaign of distortion" from the *St. Petersburg Times* and overruled Road Board member Al Rogero's plan to refinance the Sunshine Skyway from Tampa Bay from Pinellas to Manatee to help pay for new road projects in the district.[16] These would not be the last of his troubles with the Road Department.

Collins's prison reform was causing political complications. R. O. Culver, the retired U.S. Bureau of Prisons official he had recruited, quickly got on the wrong side of Charley Johns, who regarded the Raiford prison as a personal fiefdom and its correctional officers as core constituents. Johns complained that Culver was recruiting supervisors from other states. Culver replied that he could not find qualified local people for what he could pay, but it was more likely that he could not find any he would trust. At first, Collins stoutly defended Culver. Before long, however, Collins said reported brutality at the Raiford prison showed that it was not yet "a tight ship" and criticized Culver for announcing dismissals in the press before notifying the Cabinet. Soon after, Culver issued a backhanded apology for insulting Johns during an argument at Raiford that left his own staff aghast at Culver's belligerence.[17]

The 1959 session of the Legislature had barely begun when Collins abruptly demanded Culver's resignation. Refusing to explain, Collins called Culver a "nice man" and denied his charge that he was fired to appease the Legislature. Culver's subordinates understood, however, that Johns had threatened to abolish the two-year-old Division of Corrections if Culver remained. In a letter that Culver made public, Johns threatened another prison official that he would be "hard to live with" if a friend of his—a man whom Culver considered illiterate—was not hired as a prison guard. Collins and the Cabinet having learned their lesson, Culver's successor would be a native North Floridian, Collins's beverage director H. G. Cochran Jr., who knew how to coddle state senators. The law needed to be changed to waive Cochran's lack of experience in corrections, and Johns passed the bill over the objections of other Pork Chop senators who resented Cochran's tough administration of the beverage laws. "God knows we don't want another Culver," Johns said.[18]

Chapter 23

The Last Session

The parents and sister of Willie Horne Jr. came to the governor's office to beg for his life. Collins heard them personally, as he always did when the weeping families of men awaiting execution appeared unexpectedly at the Capitol or telephoned his home. It was the worst part of being governor. After one late telephone call, Mary Call said, "neither of us slept any more that night."[1]

Collins once told his staff that he thought he had a moral obligation to witness one of the executions he was commanding other people to perform. Aides talked him out of it. "It's just not the kind of thing that a governor should see," said one who had. Collins dreaded death warrants so intensely that he trembled when he could no longer delay signing the black-bordered parchment waiting on his desk. "He would think of everything else to do that day rather than take a look at it," said John Perry. Collins endured what he called this "soul-wrenching" experience twenty-nine times, second only to the thirty-five executions during Spessard Holland's wartime administration.[2]

Collins also commuted ten death sentences, a record shared with Gov. Fred Cone (1937–41),[3] but Horne would not be one of those spared. The twenty-five-year-old Jacksonville man died in January 1959 for a rape in which the victim's escort was beaten unconscious with a tire iron. The Florida Supreme Court said it had seen few cases "in which the evidence so overwhelmingly sustains the charge."[4]

Face to face with the governor, Dessie Horne Williams, a Miami schoolteacher, asked a question that pierced his soul: "Do you think that my brother is going to die because he is black?" No, Collins said, it was because he had committed a very bad crime; his race, the governor tried to assure her, made no difference. But the governor's conscience was more troubled than he let on. He knew the statistics: Had the victim been black, or both parties white, a majority of the jury almost certainly would have voted for mercy.[5]

Collins heard again from Mrs. Williams in July 1964 after a widely publicized confrontation with Sen. Strom Thurmond of South Carolina, who tried to block his appointment to head the federal Community Relations Service. Ever since the meeting in his office, Mrs. Williams wrote, "we have always thought of you as a kind, understanding man, who feels compassion for human suffering no matter what color the skin of the sufferer might be." The Thurmond incident inspired her to write what she had been thinking since 1959.

"To me and the many Negroes who live, work, and play in Florida," she wrote, "you are the kind of man so many Southern men think themselves to be, and are not; you're the kind of man the Negro thinks of when he thinks of the South that he loves—that South with the sweetness, the warmth, and that deep-down good feeling on a sunny morning that makes total strangers—even white strangers—pass a friendly, glad-to-be alive smile; you, Governor Collins, are a *true* Southern gentleman. May God keep you through the coming trials."[6]

In January 1959, Horne was one of three men facing imminent execution in the three-legged wooden electric chair that Raiford inmates had built. Collins decided at that time to try to repeal the death penalty. His fundamental objections were religious and moral, but when Killian brought him a sheaf of pertinent quotations from great philosophers, Collins smiled and said that it would not work. He thought that the Legislature would respond, if at all, only to practical persuasion that the death penalty was not a deterrent to crime.[7]

Collins dared not mention the racial disparity to legislators already febrile over desegregation. They were particularly alarmed by federal and state court decisions in January 1959 that said Virginia could not selectively close only desegregated schools. Twenty-one black children were admitted without incident to schools that the governor had shuttered in Norfolk and Arlington, but Prince Edward County, a defendant in the original *Brown* case, observed the rulings by keeping all of its public schools closed until 1964.[8] To Collins, the Virginia cases signified that Florida would have to desegregate some of its schools, but to some legislators they meant that Florida should close them all, and they were indignant when Dade County integrated two schools.

Collins, Fabisinski, Ervin, and Bailey had met in mid-December at the governor's mansion with school officials from Dade and four other large counties. None volunteered to be the first to desegregate, and Collins said he thought the climate throughout the South had worsened since his optimistic comments on *Meet the Press*. Dade, however, soon announced that it was considering experimental desegregation at Orchard Villa Elementary, an underutilized school in a neighborhood that was changing from white to black. Orchard Villa held the potential of upsetting the pupil assignment law because black children living nearby had been rejected, as the superintendent acknowledged under oath, only because of race.[9]

It was a time when Collins felt acutely alone. "There has been some fine editorial support, such as your own," he wrote to a friendly publisher. "But the truth is we have had a paucity of local and state officials willing to tell the people the simple truth. Fear of political reprisals seems to be in control."[10] He knew that the 1959 legislative session would be inflamed by campaign politics. Speaker Tom Beasley and Bryant were assumed candidates for governor in 1960. Millard Caldwell, the former governor, was stirring up the banquet circuit with speeches defining moderate politicians as "spineless" people who stood for "things not acceptable to the South."[11] Fred Kent, another potential candidate, whom Collins had refused to reappoint to the Board of Control, told the Tallahassee Rotary Club that Collins had "committed political suicide" by allowing the University of Florida and Orchard Villa to be desegregated. Nobody but Thurgood Marshall would attract fewer votes in the South, Kent said. Collins declined the Rotary Club's invitation to reply. "You can't suppress bad speeches without suppressing good ones," Collins wrote to the club president, "and all this points up the necessity for public education if our democratic system is to survive."[12]

Collins confronted the racial hysteria in a major speech in Daytona Beach, a relatively liberal community, defending public education as "the bedrock upon which our progress as a free people has been founded." It was tragic, he said, that "there are those—some emotionally upset, some timid, some crass and indifferent, some scheming for political advantage—who are willing to abolish that system. . . . This is not an issue that will be resolved by big voices and little minds." In several speeches, Collins stressed his opinion that if Florida did not voluntarily desegregate schools of its own choosing, the NAACP would select them. Still, even the token desegregation he was advocating was too much for many legislators. Beasley, who had been instrumental in defeating the last-resort bill, accused him of lending comfort to "the enemies of our way of life" and warned him to expect "slim" success with his 1959 legislative program. When Collins proposed to close FAMU's expensive graduate schools because the white universities would be desegregating theirs, Beasley remarked that Floridians would pay "whatever is necessary to maintain segregation."[13]

On February 19, the Dade County School Board voted unanimously to assign four Negro children to the Orchard Villa school. Collins, forewarned by two of the board members, said their decision would strengthen the pupil assignment law and forestall mass desegregation. Nonetheless, some legislators sounded hysterical. Beasley threatened to vote for the last-resort legislation he had opposed "if no other solution presents itself." Dewey Johnson, the incoming Senate president, said token integration was like a "small bite by a rattlesnake." Johnson and at least seven other senators called for closing all of Florida's public schools. Allen Morris wrote that "the hidden depth of legislative feeling against Collins because of the segregation dispute is almost unbelievable" and that "many legislators do not want to risk being identified with the governor on any proposal regardless of its merit."[14]

Collins had been saying for months that he would confront the Legislature with another ambitious program, little of which would be enacted. Having appointed John Germany to a judgeship, Collins found a new House lobbyist at his old law firm: Jack Peeples, the surrogate who had debated Lowry.[15]

"The people of Florida want to open schools, not close them," Collins told the Legislature in his session-opening State of the State address. "I urge you never, never, never set up any plan or device by which our public schools can be closed. When you put a padlock on a school you padlock minds, the minds of children. Our children are in a very real sense a part of us. But more than this they are the whole hope of our future."[16]

For the first and last time, a Florida governor asked the Legislature to abolish the death penalty. Collins suggested life in prison as the alternative, with no possibility of parole or clemency for twenty-five years except on proof of innocence. He said that execution was not a deterrent, which would be the "only possible justification" for it. "We should take Florida out of this barbaric business of state killing," he said. "Only God can give human life. Man should not take it away."[17]

The death penalty bill never got out of committee despite the personal sponsorship of Beasley, who had been the defense attorney for a man executed two months earlier.[18] A House committee rationalized that lynchings would resume if the death penalty were repealed. Price's Senate version died at a hearing held solely by the chairman, his pocket full of proxies that he voted against the bill. The Legislature created a study commission that opposed abolishing capital punishment.[19]

Some legislators said they considered it an inopportune time to abolish the death penalty because four young white men from Tallahassee were facing trial for their lives for the armed kidnapping and rape of a young black FAMU student and there was nationwide interest in the case. The prosecution was vigorous, and the four were convicted swiftly, but the jury gave them life sentences, prompting an unavailing demand from the NAACP that Florida never again execute a black man for rape.[20]

Surprising many, the Legislature also buried most of the thirty-three segregation bills that were introduced, some of which outdid Virginia's "massive resistance" in their ferocity. The seven it did pass were relatively innocuous, including one, never implemented, to allow schools to be segregated by sex. The Legislature also voted to spend $500,000 in concert with other Southern states on prosegregation propaganda in northern advertising media. Collins told Ralph McGill that he was tempted to accept it, since he would choose the Florida members of the board that would spend the money. The *Atlanta Constitution* editor agreed that it would be like "throwing bones out of the kitchen back door to quiet the dogs down." But after thinking overnight, Collins vetoed the bill.[21]

Despite his presession tub-thumping, Beasley was instrumental in thwarting the arch-segregationist agenda. The House Speaker, whose wife was a schoolteacher, sent all segregation bills to a new special committee and established a rule requiring a two-thirds vote on the floor to withdraw bills the committee would not hear. These devices worked as intended to trap the Senate's last-resort bills as well as radical constitutional amendments that Collins could not have vetoed. Collins praised Beasley as "Horatius at the bridge" for doing that and for blocking a session extension that would have exposed many of his vetoes to immediate overrides. Collins said the session's best work was defined by what did not pass.[22]

Late in 1960, Collins appointed Beasley to a circuit judgeship. It was understood that during the 1959 session Peeples, Collins's impetuous young lobbyist, had engaged Beasley in a dialogue about judicial appointments. As Peeples told the story: "The governor asked me point-blank, 'Did you promise him a judgeship?,' and I said, "No, sir, I discussed how you felt about judges and how you didn't decide on a political basis; you decided upon the kind of records you thought they had.' And he said, 'I think you appointed a judge.'"[23]

Less fortunate for Collins was the creation of a joint legislative committee to investigate the Road Department. That worried Grotegut, who arranged for Beasley to clear most of his appointees with the administration, but there was no point in trying to influence the Senate president's choices.[24]

To replace Cochran as beverage director, Collins promoted Peeples, who lacked administrative experience but had the legal background that the governor had decided the job required.[25]

Collins led a delegation of governors on an official tour of the Soviet Union in late June and July. The announced purpose of the foundation-funded trip was to study equivalent state-government functions in the USSR, but Collins's primary interest was to alleviate Cold War tensions.[26] The distance and duration of his absence from the state would be unprecedented, and Collins took the precaution of obtaining a Supreme Court advisory opinion that Senate president Dewey Johnson could not declare himself acting governor. Johnson said he was "shocked and hurt" that the governor doubted his integrity. Collins left after signing twenty-seven veto messages and participating in his son's June 10 wedding to Tampa debutante Carol Jane Sisson, a Florida State University graduate and a commercial artist whom he had met in Tallahassee on leave from the Naval Academy.[27]

The governors stopped by the White House for experienced diplomatic advice. In dealing with the Soviets, President Eisenhower told them, they should "try to stay in good humor and don't get too mad."[28] Eisenhower said he hoped they could encourage American-Soviet reciprocal visits.

In letters home, Collins lavishly praised Russia's art museums, his free medical treatment for a bad cold, and an evening at the Bolshoi Ballet that was "beautiful beyond description." He found the Soviet people to be regimented but still warm and friendly. "I don't have any doubt," he wrote, "that there is more anti-Russian feeling among our rank and file than anti-American feeling among their rank and file."[29]

The highlight of the trip was a visit to a Baptist church on the outskirts of Moscow, where the singing of the congregation, comprising mostly elderly women, "lived up fully to the tradition of good Baptist churches." Through an interpreter, Collins praised the Soviet people's sacrifices in World War II. He said that he was inspired to find them worshipping in a liturgy not dissimilar from his own under a banner that said "God Is Love." He remarked that it was a universal thought under which all people could march for peace everywhere.

"From the audience there was a spontaneous chorus of 'Da! Da!'" Collins wrote to his wife. Then they all sang "God Be with You till We Meet Again"—each group in its own language. "As they sang," he wrote, "each person held high a handkerchief, waved, and I had to fight back tears. As I looked out in that great group I couldn't see a dry eye anywhere. Church going is not too easy for these people. They have to have a very deep faith."[30]

The governors had an opportunity to apply Eisenhower's advice in an interview with the famously combative Soviet prime minister, Nikita Khrushchev. Their requests for an audience with him were still unanswered when Averill Harriman, the former governor of New York and a wartime ambassador to the USSR, stopped by Collins's hotel room. Projecting his voice at a ceiling light fixture that he assumed hid a listening device, Harriman said Khrushchev's unavailability meant either that he was seriously ill or perhaps on the verge of being overthrown. Less than an hour later, Collins's Intourist guide knocked on the door. An automobile was waiting; Khrushchev would see them right away.[31]

Khrushchev was truculent at times during the interview, but so were some of the governors. Each side was suspicious of the other's motives; the Soviet leader, in a notably faulty prediction, said it would be "impossible" for the Soviet people to be persuaded to abandon communism for capitalism. "We respect the right of every people to have the kind of government they want," Collins responded. "We would no more expect to convert your people than you would to convert the Americans who visit here to socialism." For his part, Khrushchev could not understand why the U.S. State Department was discouraging trade in nonstrategic products. "People who want to live in peace, trade," he said.[32]

Collins wrote home that Khrushchev had put him on the defensive by being better informed than he had expected. "He makes your blood boil and then just as you are about ready to throw a chair at him he shifts to some highly humorous observation that releases the tension," Collins said. "He doesn't expect you to take what he dishes out without fighting back. And actually if you get in some good solid blows he seems to respect and admire you for it."[33]

A month later, LeRoy Collins Jr. and Coyle E. Moore Jr., a boyhood friend who had been a groomsman at his wedding, were joy-riding in a private plane when the engine failed and it crashed in a field near Tallahassee, seriously injuring them. At the hospital that night, Harry Douglas, whom Collins in 1956 had appointed official chaplain to the Cabinet, waited with the governor and Mary Call while their son underwent facial surgery. Mary Call could not compose herself and remained in another room while the governor and the clergyman visited LeRoy Jr. after the operation. "Roy," Collins said to the heavily bandaged patient, "your Daddy and Harry Douglas are here."

"Is it *that* bad?" the younger Collins responded. It was not, and he returned to navy duty after additional surgery and treatment at the Bethesda Naval Hospital.[34]

He was home on convalescent leave in December 1959 when Cochran brought the twenty-one-member chorus from the women's prison to sing at a press party at the governor's mansion. The governor had invited them to the dismay of his wife, who feared for the mansion's silver. The women, several of whom had postponed their paroles to sing for the governor, behaved impeccably.[35]

Chapter 24

"Moral, Simple Justice"

In 1960, young African Americans who had lost patience with the glacial progress of school desegregation began direct action against discrimination. They targeted Southern department stores that welcomed their money for merchandise but refused to serve them food. Their protest tactic was the lunch-counter sit-in. For the civil rights movement and for the governor of Florida, it was a watershed year.[1]

Token desegregation had come peacefully to Florida public schools in Miami on September 8, 1959. Four black children registered with eight whites at Orchard Villa Elementary, a school with a capacity of 420 in a formerly all-white neighborhood that would soon be virtually all black. With police on guard, only two segregationist protestors appeared. No one seemed to notice the more significant desegregation of a Dade County school known as Air Base Elementary, where all the pupils were dependents of personnel at Homestead Air Force Base. Twenty-one black children went to school with 732 whites that day, an event that the Miami area media had intentionally underplayed, usually "below the fold, where readers were likely to miss it." That was done, said Philip Meyer, the *Miami Herald* education writer, "because the danger to children was very real."[2]

"Dade County school authorities have acted responsibly. They have preserved the right of local decision for their own county, and indirectly for every other county in the state," Collins said. Yet he remained conflicted over civil rights. Though he conceded that blacks were being bullied out of registering to vote in five Florida counties cited by the U.S. Civil Rights Commission, he objected strongly to the proposed appointment of federal voting registrars. In a speech to the New England Weekly Press Association, Collins said the South was entitled to resent coercion by Northern politicians who "do not practice what they preach."[3]

The first sign of a more activist civil rights movement was in Miami in the summer of 1959, when the Congress of Racial Equality (CORE), which had developed sit-ins and other direct nonviolent action tactics against discrimination in the North, targeted a large department store that promptly closed its lunch counter. Ervin issued an attorney general's opinion that an outwardly race-neutral 1957 Florida law, barely noticed when enacted, allowed retail management to bar any customer considered potentially "detrimental."[4]

At least one Miami area establishment, a Wolfie's delicatessen with a large Jewish clientele, desegregated swiftly. But when Miami's city manager ordered the community's parks, playgrounds, and swimming pools desegregated, the city commission held a special meeting to unanimously overrule him.[5]

Two FAMU students from Belle Glade, sisters Patricia and Priscilla Stevens, organized a Tallahassee CORE chapter in October 1959. They were still gingerly testing Tallahassee's rigid segregation practices, avoiding confrontation, when on February 1, 1960, an event hundreds of miles away put an end to restraint. It took place at Greensboro, North Carolina, where four black college freshmen decided on the spur of the moment to request service at a Woolworth's lunch counter. They sat there all day, waiting. Nineteen more students joined them the next day, and eighty-five on the third day. Similar demonstrations had failed, with little notice, in at least sixteen other cities. This one inspired others throughout the South.[6]

Ten students from Tallahassee CORE staged their own Woolworth's sit-in without incident on February 13, a Saturday. The management closed the lunch counter, and they left. Seventeen sat in a week later; this time, eleven who refused the mayor's order to leave were arrested, among them the Stephens sisters and Henry and Charles Steele, the two sons of bus boycott leader C. K. Steele. Another group sat in at the McCrory's lunch counter early in March. When the Woolworth's and McCrory's managers refused to negotiate, CORE scheduled sit-ins at both stores for March 12. The dozen arrests that day included white students whom Tallahassee police denounced as "you white niggers." White civilians armed with knives, baseball bats, and ax handles, unmolested by the police, blocked access to the Woolworth's, and some one thousand FAMU students led by Patricia Stephens marched in protest from their campus. A phalanx of local police, sheriff's deputies, and state troopers barred the students and dispersed them with tear gas. Apparently recognizing her as a leader, one of the policemen told Stephens, "I want you," and shot tear gas into her eyes, permanently injuring them.[7]

There were mass arrests, including the white editor and three reporters from Florida State University's *Florida Flambeau*, who were put in the same cell with six black students despite the state's jail segregation law. Only the journalists were released without charges. The FSU administration ordered its students to take no part in the demonstrations, and the Board of Student Publications censored the *Flambeau's* next edition. By then the sit-ins had spread to DeLand, Sarasota, Miami, St. Petersburg, and Tampa, where high school senior Arthenia Joyner, a future Florida legislator, helped to shut down a lunch counter.[8]

Collins strongly disapproved, saying at his March 3 press conference that the tactic was unlawful and dangerous. He said that he understood how the black students felt but that the merchants had the law on their side.[9]

The lunch-counter discrimination manifested the same powerful Southern taboo that had cost Deborah Coggins her job. To share meals, even at separate tables, implied social equality in ways that banking at the same teller's window did not. CORE targeted national chains it considered sensitive to their black patronage outside the South, but the manager of the Tallahassee Woolworth's, S. T. Davidson, told Lewis Killian his orders were still to respect local customs. "I'll consider desegregating my lunch counter when you people at the university do more about desegregating it," he said.[10]

After the events of March 12, Collins recommended that Florida A&M confine its students to campus "as effectively as possible." (It wasn't possible.) Other ways must be found, Collins said, "for the airing of grievances and the resolving of racial antagonisms." But the city and the Tallahassee Chamber of Commerce emphatically rejected his suggestion that they appoint a local biracial committee. Beasley, meanwhile, urged Collins and the Board of Education to expel the sit-in demonstrators and threatened to have the Legislature call itself into session.[11]

Beasley meant *all* student demonstrators. Tallahassee's white citizens and North Florida politicians were horrified at the involvement of whites from FSU. The townspeople assumed that professors had put them up to it and began to refer to the Chapel of the Resurrection, the Episcopal church serving primarily FSU students and faculty, as the "Chapel of the Insurrection." There was particular suspicion of Killian, a member and close friend of the liberal pastor, and there were efforts to get him fired. The city commission formally called on Collins to see that offending faculty be "properly dealt with." The university's new president, Robert M. Strozier, an urbane humanist who had succeeded Doak Campbell in 1957, resisted the intense political pressure to purge his faculty and student body but suffered a fatal heart attack soon after and was mourned as a martyr for civil rights.[12]

Tension increased with the approach of the March 17 trial of the eleven Woolworth's defendants. City judge John Rudd was openly hostile to them, ruling that racial discrimination was irrelevant to the case. The Stephens sisters, Henry Steele, and five other students chose to begin serving sixty days in jail rather than pay $300 fines.[13]

There was violence against demonstrators in St. Augustine that week, and Tallahassee feared similar trouble on the weekend. CORE agreed, however, to suspend demonstrations while Collins prepared a speech on the issue. What he would say, they didn't know. Neither did Killian and Charles Grigg, a fellow FSU sociologist, who had asked CORE for the moratorium after Collins had called them to his office on Sunday afternoon.[14]

The invitation to meet with Collins, apparently prompted by Perry, was the governor's first overture to Tallahassee liberals who were not old friends. He knew Killian only by reputation as "pretty radical," or so he told Prothro when the professor suggested he read a Killian paper titled "The Subtle Hypocrisy of Delay." But on this tension-filled Sunday afternoon in March, Collins wanted to hear all sides and from more voices than just his own staff members, who disagreed sharply among themselves. The professors said that there was more at stake than simply keeping the peace. As Killian remembers it, "We said to him that he appeared to have denied any moral basis to the actions of the demonstrators and to have treated the whole issue as one of law and order at a time when the laws involved were appearing more and more at odds with the changing national morality."[15]

Killian and Grigg left with the impression that Collins would say something helpful if CORE gave him breathing room. The governor's next speech, at the diamond jubilee of Florida Southern College at Lakeland, was outwardly ambiguous but subtly sympathetic to the demonstrators. "If the leaders in the Kremlin had worked up a plan to weaken us throughout the world," he said, "I can think of none which would be more effective than the script we are now following." It made America appear to be "incapable of dealing justly with one another in a spirit of mutual respect and brotherhood." At last, Collins was saying there *was* more to it than simply keeping the peace.[16]

Speaking two days later at FSU, he insisted that "a demonstration under all these circumstances is a dare for trouble" and should be stopped by "the full proper force of the law . . . when this becomes necessary." But he went on say that "We cannot pretend that somehow racial problems will just go away. We cannot ignore the problems any more than they will ignore us." Noting that it was the Lenten season, he said that politicians who ignored racial problems reminded him of Pontius Pilate, the Roman administrator, attempting to wash his hands of responsibility for the execution of Jesus.[17]

Collins arranged a statewide broadcast from Jacksonville for Sunday night, March 20. There would be an unprecedented network of thirteen television stations in six major markets, and a number of radio stations would broadcast the speech. Collins appealed to Floridians to tune in. He would appear to be speaking extemporaneously, but he spent much of Saturday drafting and memorizing most of it. Though Perry and others wrote many of his speeches, he edited them heavily in pen and blue ink until the syntax and vocabulary were his. He rewrote and rehearsed them so thoroughly that his delivery rarely strayed from the printed text that had been issued to the press.[18] Collins needed no primitive teleprompter and could maintain eye contact with his audience.

The advance text barely hinted at the remarks that would make the March 20 speech the most memorable of his career. No one else knew what was coming, though some of his friends had been so apprehensive that they tried to talk him out of saying anything.[19]

Viewers saw him sitting behind a low table lined with books, speaking what he had largely memorized, gesturing frequently, consulting a text only to read from the Bible. Collins began by talking about his duty as governor to "represent every man, woman, and child in this state . . . whether that person is black or white . . . rich or poor . . . influential or not influential." He remarked that the City of Tallahassee "took a rather rigid and punitive position" that made things worse. It concerned him that the "wildest rumors imaginable" were circulating in his city. There was supposedly a busload of Negro students who had come to Florida A&M with "a lot of baseball bats . . . to put on some sort of demonstration," but they turned out to be a baseball team that had come to play a scheduled game.[20]

Collins reiterated that "We are going to have law and order in this state" respecting a merchant's legal right "to select the patrons he serves." But there were also moral rights involved.

"And so far as I am personally concerned," he said, "I don't mind saying that I think that if a man has a department store and he invites the public generally to come into his department store and trade, I think then it is unfair and morally wrong to single out one department though and say he does not want or will not allow Negroes to patronize that one department. Now he has a legal right to do that, but I still don't think that he can square that right with moral, simple justice."

Someone had remarked to him, he said, how "'all this could be eliminated if the colored people would just stay in their place.' Now friends, that's not a Christian point of view. That's not a democratic point of view. That's not a realistic point of view. We can never stop Americans from struggling to be free. We can never stop Americans from hoping and praying that some day in some way this ideal that is embedded in our Declaration of Independence is one of these truths that are inevitable, that all men are created equal, that that somehow will be a reality and not just an illusory distant goal."

No Southern governor had spoken in such a way. But what Collins could do was less dramatic than what he could say. He could not suspend the law; to ask the Legislature to change it would be an act of folly. He announced that he would appoint a new biracial commission, chaired by Tampa lawyer Cody Fowler, to succeed the one led by Fabisinski, who had died of a heart attack in January. Moreover, Collins recommended that every community in Florida create such a committee to attempt "honestly and sincerely" to resolve racial grievances.

Again, he told the story of Pontius Pilate capitulating to a mob. "Friends," Collins said, "we've got mobs beginning to form now. . . . We cannot let this matter and these issues be decided by the mob. . . . Where are the people in the middle? Why aren't they talking? They must start working."[21]

Aides who had helped him prepare and rehearse the speech were astonished by his additions. A two-page extract released just before the speech contained the words "simple, moral justice," but not the passages relating Christianity to equality. Few Southerners had heard even the clergy address the conflict between religion and racism.[22]

Long afterward, Collins said that he had been influenced by the Lenten service he attended that morning. "I kind of actually believed something from the church service that day," he said.[23]

Collins had suspected that many Floridians would disagree. Confirming this, the television crew that had greeted him cheerfully when he arrived gave him only cold stares after the speech, saying nothing. As the governor and his party left to inspect flood damage in Orlando and Tampa, a journey that would take them through much of North Florida before their return to Tallahassee, Collins remarked wryly to the driver, "Now lieutenant, be sure not to get lost."[24]

The speech permanently affected Collins's relations with Malcolm Johnson, the Tallahassee editor he had taken to be a friend. The newspaper never editorialized on what Collins had said, but Johnson's silence spoke volumes. Those newspapers that did comment tended to do so favorably.[25]

The speech profoundly upset Tallahassee's white society and the Collinses were ostracized by some of their supposed friends. "There weren't forty people in the old Tallahassee set that would even speak to Roy," said Duby Ausley, the son and nephew of the governor's former law partners. To avoid confrontations, his mother, a Collins loyalist, declined social invitations.[26]

The Legislature's presiding officers threatened again to call a special session. "He is a strict integrationist and will sell his soul to prove it for the benefit of his national political ambitions," groused Senate president Dewey Johnson. Jacksonville mayor Haydon Burns, one of ten Democrats running for governor, said he thought merchants owed blacks nothing more than "separate but equal" dining and restroom facilities and refused to appoint a biracial committee. (There was rioting in Jacksonville by both blacks and whites five months later.) Farris Bryant, another contender, said it would be reckless for any candidate to comment on what Collins had said but emphasized that his own segregationist credentials were "clearly established." The only candidate who fully agreed with Collins, former Speaker Ted David, would run a poor sixth.[27]

Black leaders were impressed despite their disagreement with Collins over the sit-in tactic. "Coming from a Southern governor, it's a speech to be admired," said Dr. John O. Brown, head of the Miami CORE. The Rev. T. R. Gibson, a Miami NAACP leader who was risking jail by resisting the Johns Committee, declared that "With that speech, Governor Collins became to me one of the greatest statesmen Florida has ever known."[28]

The public's reaction was massive and, as measured by the correspondence, mostly favorable. Supportive letters, telegrams, and postcards filled seven file boxes; hostile comments took up only one. "Every decent American citizen is proud of you today, Sir," wrote a man from New York. It was "the finest sermon on Christian duty I have ever heard. I was moved to tears," wrote an Orlando woman who said she was a Republican who would like to see Collins elected president. Many people asked for transcripts, which Collins sent with a note apologizing for his ad lib "grammatical irregularities."[29] A *Washington Post* editorial hailed his "heartening reminder that there are still rational and moderate men in the South who cherish ideals of justice and morality." The *U.S. News & World Report* reprinted much of the speech under a headline, "By a Southern governor—LUNCH-COUNTER SEGREGATION; 'LEGALLY RIGHT, MORALLY WRONG.'"[30]

The hostile correspondence, slower to arrive, ranged from letters simply accusing him of changing his views for political reasons to virulent racism. A Fort Myers man wrote that he had fired his black maids and yard man because of the demonstrations and that "personally I would like to see every one sent back to Africa." Collins's standard response said in part, "I hope you will at least approve my candor in speaking."[31]

At a press conference eleven days after the speech, Collins said he was "extremely happy" that there had been no more demonstrations and that he was pleased with the quality as well as the volume of the public's favorable comments. But what he was hearing privately from some Tallahasseans he had considered friends distressed him so much that he asked Harry Douglas to walk with him so that they could discuss it without distractions. Collins remarked in an interview that while he thought many Floridians agreed with him, he wished that they were "more articulate than they are."[32]

Four Miami lunch counters were desegregated without advance notice or incident at almost the same time as Jacksonville's riots. There were no more sit-ins at Tallahassee, likely due to the Fowler Commission's intercession with CORE, but it would take until January 1963 and the economic pressure of a black boycott to desegregate the capital's lunch counters, a development coinciding with the beginning of mass demonstrations (and mass arrests) to desegregate the city's movie theaters.[33]

Fifteen years after his speech, Collins was still struck by the intensity of the criticism, even though he had expected that some friends would not understand. He spoke of letters that were "harsh and cruel," of a burning cross he and Mary Call found on the mansion lawn one night, and of eggs thrown at their door. The hardest for some people to take, he believed, was his classification of discrimination as morally wrong; "It was as if I had just burned the Bible, or something." But, he said, "I felt "that time and history would prove me to be correct all along."[34]

Chapter 25

"Reaction, Retreat, and Regret"

The 1960 gubernatorial campaign was significant to Collins even though he was not a candidate. It became in effect a referendum on his racial moderation and ended with the gubernatorial victory of an unconverted segregationist, C. Farris Bryant, the Harvard-educated apostle of interposition, over moderate state senator Doyle E. Carlton Jr., who was seen as Collins's surrogate.[1]

Collins professed the customary neutrality of an outgoing governor until four days before the runoff, when Millard Caldwell's fiery endorsement of Bryant provoked him into endorsing Carlton, who was already far behind Bryant, a more polished and physically attractive candidate who benefited from having run statewide before.[2]

Six serious candidates contested the Democratic nomination. Three had claims to Collins's loyalties: Carlton, former House Speaker Ted David, and John M. McCarty, the late governor's brother, who had grudgingly deferred to Collins in 1954. The other major candidates were Haydon Burns, the strongly segregationist mayor of Jacksonville; Sen. Fred O. Dickinson Jr., of West Palm Beach; and Bryant. Beasley stayed out. Caldwell changed his mind on the day he had planned to announce his candidacy, saying instead that to be governor again "would be like eating yesterday morning's poached egg." Caldwell would carry the segregationist banner on Bryant's behalf and satisfy his resentment of the credit Collins had taken for the 1947 Minimum Foundation Program. Collins urged Ed Price, his closest friend in politics, to run for governor, but the freshman senator demurred for personal reasons and strongly endorsed Carlton.[3]

Bryant and Carlton finished first and second in the May 3 primary, nearly tied with 40 percent of the vote between them. Burns, McCarty, and Dickinson followed with David, the only perceived liberal, running sixth with 8 percent of the vote. David had little organization or money outside South Florida; moreover, he had endorsed the lunch-counter speech.[4]

The segregation issue once again dominated an ugly runoff campaign. Carlton called Bryant a "race-baiter"; Bryant accused him of siding with "northern demagogues." Unlike Lowry, however, Bryant had articulate positions, informed by experience, on reapportionment, education, roads, and other issues.[5]

"He stands for moderate integration. I am a firm believer in segregation," Bryant said, and made an issue of Carlton's enormous first primary support in Jacksonville black precincts. Carlton retorted that Bryant had shared a meal with some of those same voters. Bryant acknowledged that he had stopped by the gathering to ask for votes but insisted he had eaten nothing.[6]

They agreed only that they would not close integrated schools, although Bryant stressed that he "would use every honorable and lawful means to see that the order was not effected. I would appeal and appeal." Asked at their final televised debate whether they would send their children to an integrated school, Bryant said he would choose a segregated private school, but Carlton said that his children would attend the public school. "What is good enough for one of us is good enough for all of us," Carlton said. Decades later, Floridians remembered that as a defining moment in the campaign, and it was cited as a mark of courage in a Senate resolution following his death in 2003.[7]

Caldwell endorsed Bryant in a statewide television address that was intended to provoke Collins into publicly supporting Carlton. "The battle against the compromisers, the pinks, the NAACP, and the do-gooders is a battle which can be won by determined resistance, guided by able counsel, supported by a courageous governor. There must be no surrender, no voluntary submissions such as took place at Miami," Caldwell said. Confirming that he favored Carlton, Collins revealed what he had written on the 1957 interposition resolution. Bryant accused Collins of trying to establish a dynasty and mocked the Carlton endorsement as a "desperation attempt to salvage the crown prince." Collins retorted in a statewide television broadcast on election eve that Bryant's election would signify "reaction, retreat, and regret."[8]

The election returns were even more starkly sectional than those of 1956. Bryant carried fifty-five counties, including even Collins's own, with 55.2 percent of the vote. Carlton attracted nearly two-thirds of the votes in Broward and in Dade, where he polled virtually as many as Collins had in 1956, but not by the gross numbers he needed to counter Bryant's statewide lead of 96,705 votes. Of the other large counties, Carlton won only Hillsborough and Pinellas—just barely—and despite a deliberately crafted "country boy" campaign style, the rancher from rural Hardee carried no small counties except for the four he represented as a senator. Bryant's majorities topped 70 percent in thirty-two of the sixty-seven counties.[9]

Bryant had made much better use of television, which Carlton could not exploit as Collins had. "I loved to talk with him, he's got that old Cracker drawl and he tells you a lot of funny stories and everything else," Ed Price said, "but he didn't come along with—what's that overused word?—charisma."[10]

The rout extended to two Cabinet seats that were opened—a rare event —by retirements. Tom Adams, a Pork Chop senator from Orange Park, was nominated for secretary of state over Jess Yarborough, a Dade School Board member who had voted to desegregate the two elementary schools, and Doyle Conner, House Speaker during the turbulent 1957 session, was elected commissioner of agriculture. Adams, Bryant, and Conner were so closely linked that their nickname was "the ABC Ticket." Collins, who had gone fishing to relax on election day, said he was disappointed but did not regret having tried to help Carlton. Caldwell exulted that the vote "takes Florida out of the category of the pinks and the NAACP." Expecting Caldwell to have enormous influence over the next governor, Collins and Carlton supporters began referring to the forthcoming inauguration of "C. Farris Caldwell." Caldwell collected his reward in February 1962, when Bryant appointed him to the Supreme Court upon Justice T. Frank Hobson's retirement.[11]

On runoff day, the Democratic National Committee formally confirmed that Collins would chair its 1960 national convention at Los Angeles, but he would have preferred to be the keynote speaker. This episode is the subject of the next chapter.

Collins's last year was complicated by problems at the Road Department. Pork Chop resentment at his policy of giving priority to areas of greatest need, especially the urban segments of the nascent interstate highway system, contributed to the formation of Sen. Scott Kelly's joint legislative investigating committee, which a Collins supporter on the panel called a "witch hunt."[12] But, in fact, there were examples of misfeasance that resulted in a congressional investigation of how Florida applied federal aid. As the state probe intensified in January 1960, Grotegut found it timely to resign as Road Board chairman to become general manager of the well-connected Rose Printing Co. and its affiliates. It soon came out that Grotegut was outspending his revenue much like the Johns administration had done. Collins appointed William Killian, his young legal assistant, to replace Grotegut for the administration's last year, promising him a free hand and admonishing him to "simply do the right thing." Killian subsequently barred three influential contracting companies from bidding on new projects and fired fourteen state engineers for transgressions including under-the-table payments from road-builders they supervised. All the contractors and twelve of the state employees were reinstated during the next administration.

The Kelly committee's particular target was Road Board member Al Rogero of Clearwater, a campaign supporter whom Collins had appointed against Mary Call's advice. He confirmed her suspicions by speculating in real estate near highway projects and defying intense local opposition to route a complex toll bridge and causeway system known as the Pinellas Bayway over the same private dredge-and-fill project that Collins had tried to stop. The Bayway controversy waxed so fierce that the governor's office tried to distance itself, ordering that public comment come only from Rogero or Killian. Collins said years later that he wished he had heeded his wife's instinct but did not explain why he had put up with Rogero for six years.[13]

Collins wanted to begin construction on the authorized turnpike extension north of Fort Pierce but was unwilling to refinance the existing debt as financial advisers recommended. He reluctantly left the project to Bryant after the governor-elect refused to endorse his plan to borrow only for the new construction. Collins objected that Bryant's refinancing plan could cost as much as $23.5 million in extra premiums and higher interest. That became the principal scandal of Bryant's term.[14]

Cody Fowler's biracial commission took its mission seriously, warning in a report to Collins of forthcoming sit-ins, wade-ins, and other direct demonstrations by better-educated blacks "seeking an end to the stigma of inferiority." Unlike the primarily legalistic approach of Fabisinski's commissions, Fowler's took a sociological perspective; its staff attorney, Saul Silverman, was also a part-time instructor at the Florida State University School of Social Work. But the commission was crying in a wilderness. Among the hundreds of municipalities it urged to appoint local commissions, only nine replied that they had done so, some twenty others said they were thinking about it, and the rest were silent.[15]

Jacksonville was among the silent, and only a few months later became the only Florida city where lunch-counter demonstrations led to prolonged rioting. The demographics were particularly volatile; so many white residents were from the neighboring state that it was known as "the second-largest city in Georgia," and it had the largest black population of any Florida city. Many of the blacks, Collins noted, lived in notoriously bad slums. Mayor Haydon Burns, who was also the police commissioner, had instantly rejected the governor's suggestion to appoint a biracial committee and soon after was running a segregationist campaign for governor, laying the foundation for his election in 1964. Not quite four months after the 1960 primary, police stood by as a riot broke out between black sit-in demonstrators and white hecklers. The rioting spread over twenty blocks the next day and recurred for three nights with fire-bombings, shootings, many injuries, and one death. Even then, Burns refused to appoint a biracial commission or to cooperate with one that the ministerial association said it would establish privately. Collins criticized him to no effect. By December, however, the Fowler commission reported that Miami and eleven other cities had openly ended lunch-counter segregation and ten more had done so tacitly without formal announcements.[16]

Barely a week after the riots, Florida sustained the worst hurricane in many years. After surveying widespread property damage, Collins called for a tough statewide building code.[17] It took years to adopt one, and another devastating hurricane to prove that it was not strict enough.

The number of circuit judges depended on the most recent census figures. Ervin told Collins that he could appoint new judges as soon as the U.S. government officially certified the 1960 census rather than leave them to Bryant, who enlisted Caldwell's law firm in an unsuccessful lawsuit. The outcome was in suspense until December 19, two weeks before Collins left office, when the Supreme Court ruled in a split decision that Collins could make twenty appointments. Among those to whom Collins offered judgeships were Beasley and Durden, who accepted; Killian, who did not; and Peeples, who had to remind Collins that he had not been a member of the Bar for the required ten years.[18]

As his time in office was running out, Collins busied himself with a campaign-style schedule of speeches, sometimes two or three a day, dedicating junior colleges, highways, prisons, and other new facilities. At the University of South Florida's first convocation, he boasted that "No other state in this generation has built a new university plant from the sandspurs up, as we have."[19]

For the first time since Florida was a territory, an incumbent governor gave his daughter in marriage. On October 1, Jane Brevard Collins wed John Aurell, a recent Washington and Lee graduate whom she had met on a blind date. They had a glittering but alcohol-free reception at the new governor's mansion. A *Life* photo spread, "Darby's Day at Sister's Wedding," featured ten-year-old Darby in six of the seven pictures. To an editor who apologized for the magazine having ignored the governor and slighted the bride, Collins wrote back good-naturedly: "The fact that Darby stole a show that was not really hers is nothing new in this family. In fact, at the age of four everybody in Florida agreed that she stole her father's inauguration ceremony." Darby had also been the one to break the ice when Jane introduced her fiancé to the family. Darby slapped Aurell on the back and said, "Welcome, brother!"[20]

Bryant, meanwhile, coasted to an inexorable victory in the November 1960 election, but not by quite the usual Democratic landslide. Republican George C. Petersen polled 569,936 votes, more than twice as many as Washburne against Collins in 1956, and carried ten counties. The GOP's 40.2 percent was its best showing since Reconstruction. Though Petersen owed many of his votes to moderate and liberal Democratic dissatisfaction with Bryant, Collins agreed with the state Republican chairman that the two-party system had arrived.[21]

Collins spent his last week in office hunting pheasants, recording a final radio address, and traveling to Orlando to receive a portrait that friends had commissioned. At his last press conference, Collins announced that his office was publishing a 400-page book, *Florida Across the Threshhold*, documenting the six years of his administration. He did not mention that he had hastily enlisted Allen Morris, the "Cracker Politics" columnist and editor of the biennial *Florida Handbook*, to compile it. Morris did not want that known; one reason was that it might bias Bryant against him.[22]

The book's extensive section on race relations left out a candid summary Silverman had submitted in which he asserted that the Collins administration had "found a middle ground, i.e., it prevented integration where it could not be handled and encouraged it where it could." Silverman thought the

Collins example would make it "difficult, if not impossible" for Florida to experience riots such as had occurred in New Orleans and Little Rock.[23]

Collins told his last news conference that he was leaving with a deep sense of regret. Despite some very heavy burdens, he said, "I want the record clear that I have thoroughly enjoyed this work." Future governors, he said, should be allowed to succeed themselves. He bade farewell by saying he was "deeply grateful" for the journalists' coverage. He had not always liked what they wrote, but Collins knew and appreciated that they had been invaluable in his struggles against Pork Chop politics and racism. Some had become casual friends and occasional fishing partners as well, a relationship Collins had cultivated with at least one overnight fishing retreat for the press.[24] Most editors would frown upon or forbid such camaraderie today.

"On behalf of myself and anyone else who would like to join me," said the *Orlando Sentinel*'s Bob Delaney, "I would like to say this. We may have differed on the relative merits of bream and bass fishing, but during the past six years there has never been a day when I wasn't proud that you were governor of this state."

"I'm not allowed to make flattering statements like that," said the *Tampa Tribune*'s Martin Waldron, a large man often described as Falstaffian, "but my wife asked me to convey the same regards." The Associated Press reported that as Collins thanked them and rose from the table, "his voice wavered and a couple of tears came."[25]

On Christmas Eve, the Collins family left the governor's mansion for the last time, to spend the holiday at the Grove.[26]

Bryant's inauguration day was cold—forty degrees—overcast, and blustery, and there were many empty seats. The bands from Florida State University and the University of Florida, Bryant's alma mater, repeatedly played "Dixie."[27]

The master of ceremonies was Millard Caldwell, all smiles, who introduced Collins as "our neighbor and our friend." Collins spoke for only six minutes. "The pomp and ceremony, the motorcycle escorts, the long black Cadillac, the outer trappings of being governor, are in the past for me," he said. "But deep in my conscience will always be the inner satisfaction that I have kept faith with the people, that I have served them well." In phrases aimed at his successor, he said that a governor's job "requires constant dedication to the simple proposition that a governor's obligations extend to every citizen—every man, woman, and child in his state, of whatever race, color or creed, whether rich or poor, influential or defenseless, whether a person of deep faith, or a wandering lost soul."[28]

Charley Johns, sitting silently among the dignitaries, would have the last word. Timing his letter to arrive on Collins's final day in office, he poured out an anger that had seethed since Collins's first inaugural address. "Your insinuations and innuendoes against my administration made your closest friends hang their heads in shame," Johns wrote, adding that Bryant was "too big a man to make such a speech against your administration as you did against mine." The letter was released to the press, but Collins's staff said he had left the office without seeing it.[29]

Chapter 26

"A Big, Loud, Noisy Show"

During most of his last year in office, Collins did not know what he would do next. He did not want to return to his old law firm, and he declined interest in the vacant Florida State University presidency, citing his "very strong feeling . . . that a man should not serve as the head of a university in his own home town." He would change his mind about that.[1]

He was hoping for something much greater: a place on the 1960 Democratic national ticket or a post in the next president's Cabinet. Some of his staff thought that was the reason for John Perry's return after a four-month absence. Perry was his liaison with the national press, which was already interested in the man the *New York Times* described as "a one-man bridge between the Northern and Southern factions of his party."[2]

But his segregationist enemies at home were trying to undermine him. Caldwell did not wait for the convention delegation to be selected before asserting that it should be chaired either by Holland, the senior senator, or Rep. Robert L. F. Sikes, the dean of the congressional delegation and no friend of Collins.[3] Collins had already conceded the "favorite son" role to Smathers, though both of them came to regret it; it meant that none of the serious presidential candidates would campaign in Florida, depriving Collins of national media exposure. Collins was also uncomfortable honoring Smathers, whom he thought deficient in idealism. From Smathers's perspective, being a favorite son severely limited what he could do to help any of the three friends who were serious candidates for the nomination: Lyndon B. Johnson of Texas, Stuart Symington of Missouri, and John F. Kennedy of Massachusetts.[4]

Collins craved the role of keynote speaker at the convention in Los Angeles and cultivated the support of former President Harry S. Truman during a visit to Key West.[5] The national party chairman, Paul M. Butler, wanted Collins to preside over the convention instead. House Speaker Sam Rayburn, the permanent convention chairman, needed to be free to help Johnson, his fellow Texan. Collins understood that Butler preferred a chairman who was not a senator like all the declared candidates or a Roman Catholic like Kennedy, Butler himself, and Rayburn's close friend Rep. Hale Boggs of Louisiana, who coveted the gavel. Collins's moderate record on race and especially his lunch-counter speech worked in his favor at a closed-door debate of the arrangements committee, where Boggs was criticized for having signed the Southern manifesto.[6]

Collins's personal favorite for the presidency was Adlai Stevenson, the former Illinois governor who had been the nominee against Eisenhower in 1952 and 1956. But Stevenson was waiting for a draft. "You are the best; the nation needs the best. Don't close the doors too tightly," Collins wrote to him in 1959. That friendship concerned Kennedy, who believed that irregular vote switching had cost him the vice-presidential nomination in 1956 and wanted assurances it would not happen again. Collins met individually with all the candidates to promise that he would be impartial. However, he and Perry interrupted their train trip to Los Angeles to spend a night at Stevenson's home in Illinois.[7]

Collins was deeply disappointed at losing the choice keynote assignment to Sen. Frank Church of Idaho, and he thought the neutrality expected of the convention chairman would chill his vice-presidential prospects. Asserting that he should not even cast a vote, he resigned as a member of the Florida delegation. His mood improved, however, when Butler told him that he would be welcome to make a speech.[8]

With providential timing, the formal announcement came on the day of the runoff primary that dealt him what the *New York Times* correctly reported as a "rude political defeat." Though the primary made Collins less attractive as a running mate by implying that he could not carry his own state, the convention chairmanship would put his speaking skills and personality on display to the entire country.[9]

He would also be demonstrating them to a prospective private sector employer. Collins was a candidate, though few others knew it, for the vacant presidency of the National Association of Broadcasters, whose selection committee put him on its list not long after the lunch-counter speech. Glenn Marshall, general manager of the *Washington Post* television station WJXT in Jacksonville, advised that Collins was interested but unwilling to decide before midsummer.[10] Collins was keeping his political options open.

Convention politics were tumultuous when Collins arrived in Los Angeles. Southern delegations were incensed by a strong civil rights plank in the proposed party platform that referred to the lunch-counter sit-ins as "peaceful demonstrations for first-class citizenship." The Florida delegation was also in a stew over Butler's efforts to limit tickets and prevent time-wasting demonstrations for favorite sons. Nine days before the convention, Truman, who favored fellow Missourian Symington, resigned as a delegate and charged that the proceedings were being rigged in Kennedy's favor. But as Kennedy already had 600 of the 761 delegate votes he needed, it was very late for a "Stop Kennedy" campaign by Truman or anyone else. The only possible strategy was to prevent Kennedy from clinching the nomination during the first roll call. This heightened his concern over vote-switching.[11]

Collins, resenting Truman's insinuation, said in an NBC *Meet the Press* interview that he would insist on a fair and orderly procedure and that if the Rules Committee did not regulate vote changes, he might do so himself. But when the convention began, the Florida caucus embarrassed Collins by voting to ask Truman to come to Los Angeles to help "unrig the riggers." That was Caldwell's doing, and although other Floridians managed to suppress the provocative language, it was apparent that Collins could scarcely command his own delegation's respect. The eventual compromise was to have Collins appeal from the rostrum for Truman to change his mind and attend the convention. Truman remained in Missouri.[12]

The convention was out of control long before the scripted moment for Collins to take the gavel. Cheering, chanting demonstrators for the "Draft Stevenson" movement encircled the Los Angeles Sports Arena and infiltrated the hall. Under the best of circumstances, a national political convention is a bedlam of unceasing noise and jam-packed aisles. When it was time for Collins to deliver the speech he had been preparing for months, to his largest audience, the galleries were more than half empty and the delegates on the convention floor were paying no attention.[13]

In substance, it was the keynote speech he had hoped to make, an opportunity to declare his philosophy on foreign as well as domestic policy. He had barely begun speaking, however, when the previous tumult seemed tame. A frenzied ovation greeted Eleanor Roosevelt's ill-timed entrance into the gallery, where Mary Call Collins had to hastily vacate the seat she had not known was reserved for the party's most iconic figure. The governor, meanwhile, had been entirely upstaged. "For those of you who cannot see," Collins announced, "I understand that our distinguished First Lady of the World, Mrs. Franklin D. Roosevelt, has just come into the chamber." The official transcript records what followed: "Standing Ovation. Stops Proceedings. Applause, Gavel, Horns."[14]

It took strenuous effort for Collins to end the ovation, and the audience remained so noisy and inattentive that he was about to cut his speech short when Butler sent him a handwritten note saying that it was playing well on television. Two weeks later, he received a letter of apology from Mrs. Roosevelt, who had been hearing from Floridians who were unhappy with her. Collins replied that they ought to know she had not done it deliberately. "I cannot think of a nicer person to cause the interruption than yourself," he wrote.[15]

Collins had barely finished his speech and was preparing to bring up the controversial platform report when the galleries erupted in another massive demonstration. This one was for Stevenson, arriving to take his seat as an Illinois delegate. After thirteen minutes and several futile whacks with the gavel, Collins called Stevenson to the rostrum to acknowledge the cheers. Referring to the chaos at the headquarters hotel and in the convention hall, Stevenson quipped to the delegates that he already knew who would be nominated: "The last survivor."[16]

Ten Southern delegations, not including Johnson's Texans, sponsored a minority report on civil rights. Holland was booed when he said the majority plank would "drive the Southland out of the house of our fathers, out of the Democratic Party in November." The Southerners appeared to get the better of a desultory voice vote but did not appeal Collins's ruling against them because they knew they would lose a recorded vote.[17]

Collins shattered three pounding boards trying to control the raucous convention. At the start of the nominating session on the third day, he warned the delegates and news media to "give better attention and maintain better decorum" because they were alienating voters. Kennedy was already on the brink of victory; the question was whether he would clinch it on the first ballot. If Collins allowed states to switch to Kennedy before he announced the official results, there might be no need for a second ballot and no opportunity for Kennedy support to erode. But the Rules Committee still had not stipulated a procedure, so Collins announced his own policy: After all delegations had voted, any that wanted to change their votes would be recognized in alphabetical order. It seemed simple enough, but it was a promise he would not keep.[18]

Then came six hours of nominating and seconding speeches and scripted "spontaneous" demonstrations for Johnson, Kennedy, Smathers, Symington, and Stevenson; and for favorite son governors from Iowa and Kansas, who withdrew, and from New Jersey and Mississippi, who stayed in. To enforce a ten-minute limit on demonstrations, Collins threatened to order seconding speeches to begin in competition with the marching, shouting, sign-waving, and horn-blowing. As he was trying to say so, he accidentally activated the podium elevator and within seconds found himself towering over the microphone before someone managed to bring him down and end the surreal moment.[19]

The tedium was broken by one of the memorable theatric moments in American politics, Sen. Eugene McCarthy's impassioned nominating speech for Stevenson. "Do not reject this man who made us all proud to be called Democrats," he pleaded. "Do not, I say to you, do not leave this prophet without honor in his own party." That was the signal for what political historian Theodore H. White described as "the greatest and most authentic demonstration of emotion" since the chants of "We want Wilkie!" that overwhelmed the Republican convention of 1940. This time, however, emotion would not prevail. Stevenson's chances had evaporated four hours earlier when, having decided at last that he wanted the nomination, he heard Mayor Richard Daley, the shrewd and cynical political boss of Chicago, tell him bluntly that his own state's delegation was for Kennedy.[20]

Stevenson's last hurrah came mainly from the galleries, not from delegates. Even so, the demonstration used up twenty-five minutes and what remained of Collins's patience. "Nobody can be nominated president of the United States if we are going to conduct ourselves like a bunch of hoodlums," he declared.[21]

There was booing at that, but it turned to applause when Collins said that delegates themselves were appealing for order and that "if Governor Stevenson were here on this stand he would be one of the first to ask that you stop." At the podium for a Stevenson seconding speech, Mrs. Roosevelt urged the delegates to "clear the aisles of this convention and allow the work to go on." Collins said he was tempted to ask her to take over the chair.[22]

Kennedy won before the end of the first roll call. Wyoming put him over the top to the dismay of the Minnesota and New Jersey favorite-son delegations that had hoped to do it with vote switches. Kennedy finished with 806 to 409—mostly from the South—for Johnson; 86 for Symington; 79½ for Stevenson; and 137½ for all the others. Moments later, Missouri's chairman moved to make the nomination unanimous. Collins, forgetting or ignoring his promise to allow states to change their votes individually, put the motion to an immediate voice vote that approved it overwhelmingly. That kept Florida and other favorite-son states from climbing aboard the Kennedy bandwagon or from switching to Johnson as Mississippi had planned to do. Collins rationalized that Missouri's motion mooted the necessity for state-by-state changes, but that did not appease Mississippi's senators, James O. Eastland and John C. Stennis, who argued intensely with him at the rostrum. Eastland bore a grudge for years.[23]

The only remaining suspense was Kennedy's choice for the vice presidency, which dismayed some key supporters, including his brother Robert, when he offered it to Johnson, the Texan who had been his strongest opponent. To the surprise of both Kennedys, Collins, and many others, Johnson accepted. It supposedly was the occasion of former vice president John Nance Garner's legendary if imprecisely quoted advice that the job "isn't worth a pitcher of warm spit." Aware that labor leaders strongly opposed him, Johnson insisted by one account that John Kennedy reaffirm his offer. According to Collins's notes of a subsequent private conversation with Johnson, Robert Kennedy had gone behind Johnson's back to Rayburn to try to get Johnson to back out. But the deal was firm by the time delegates reconvened, and no other name was placed in nomination.[24] In interviews twelve and fifteen years later, Collins said Robert Kennedy and others talked to him at the convention about making him the running mate. Collins thought it might have been possible but for the obvious lack of support for him within his own delegation. Texas, moreover, had more electoral votes.[25]

The convention marked time on Thursday with a stack of resolutions, one of which commended the news media. Speaking from the podium, Collins complimented the broadcast industry's gavel-to-gavel coverage, which he called "an outstanding contribution to good government and to the progress of our nation." *Broadcasting*, the trade magazine whose publisher almost certainly knew that Collins was in consideration for the association presidency, reported his remarks without noting that they might be self-serving.[26]

Collins had become a media celebrity. Lunching at the Brown Derby, he was flattered when Jack Benny and George Burns asked to join him. Newspaper columns and editorial pages, the *New York Times* among them, praised his presence on the convention's center stage.[27]

Collins, his wife, their two younger daughters, and their driver left Los Angeles by car for what they expected to be an uneventful trip to Tallahassee. They had settled into an Austin, Texas, motel one night and had begun dinner when Johnson telephoned to insist they spend the night at his ranch near Johnson City. He sent an airplane for them. Collins told his reluctant spouse, not for the last time, that "You can't tell Lyndon Johnson no." Describing the visit to Harry Douglas, Collins marveled that everything on the ranch seemed to bear the initials "LBJ."[28]

Returning to Tallahassee, Collins told a press conference that the convention "was beyond the possibility of orderly management," and he thought nondelegates should be banned from demonstrating inside the hall. But despite the tumult that had made the convention "a big, loud, noisy show," he did not favor a national primary. "After returning to my duties here, I had a glimpse of heaven one night in a dream," he wrote to a friend, "and in a great auditorium there—imagine it!—the aisles were completely clear."[29]

Collins's immediate political concern was a segregationist scheme to make the Democratic electors of Florida and other Southern states "independent" of the national party. He threatened to make the Legislature deal with reapportionment if it called itself into session, which it did not do.[30] But he came to one of his press conferences leaning on a cane and quacking a distress call on a hunter's duck caller, a lame-duck joke reflecting the serious reality that Collins, on poor terms with his successor and holding no reins over his state party, was powerless to help the Kennedy-Johnson campaign in Florida. Bryant and most other top Florida Democrats made it clear they would vote for the national ticket without enthusiasm and do nothing more. Smathers, the exception, became Southern campaign manager for the ticket. One of the strongest endorsements that Kennedy received from a Florida politician came from Charley Johns, who was offended by an evangelist's attack on Kennedy's Catholicism. "I never thought I'd live to see the day that hatred and venom against a fellow man would be the subject of a sermon in my church," Johns said.[31]

Hoiland's prediction of a Republican Southern sweep did not come true in 1960, although it would later. Among the former Confederate states, the Kennedy-Johnson ticket lost only Florida, Tennessee, Virginia, and Mississippi, where unpledged electors won. The 46,776-vote margin in Florida for Richard Nixon and Henry Cabot Lodge was barely a fourth of the Eisenhower-Nixon plurality four years before.[32]

Chapter 27

Dog Eat Dog

The National Association of Broadcasters (NAB) needed a new image as well as a new president. It feared a crackdown by Congress and the Federal Communications Commission (FCC) in response to the exposures of rigged quiz shows and of record company payoffs to disc jockeys and program directors. To succeed their deceased chief executive, the broadcasters were interested in hiring some public figure whose reputation might enhance theirs. An early Collins rival was United Nations ambassador Henry Cabot Lodge, who become the Republican vice-presidential candidate.[1]

Collins grew keenly interested and contacted *Washington Post* publisher Philip Graham, whose father had served with him in the Florida Senate. Soon after, John S. Hayes, head of the *Post*'s broadcast division and a member of the NAB selection committee, visited the governor's mansion overnight and reported that Collins was "most impressive, articulate, well educated, intelligent and, I would judge, decisive." Hayes noted that Collins did not strike him as someone "who could be pushed around or take instructions unless he himself has had some part in arriving at those instructions."[2]

The NAB presidency was far more lucrative than any political possibility; the $75,000 salary was more than three times Collins's governor's pay of $22,500 and came with generous benefits and allowances for housing and entertainment. With two daughters still in school and little cash on hand, Collins needed a good income. He had not put the power of the governor's office to any personal use. Louis E. Wolfson, the Jacksonville financier whose subsidy led to the 1969 resignation of Supreme Court justice Abe Fortas, named Collins as one of only five public officials who had refused his offers of financial assistance. Though Collins's net worth in 1960 was the equivalent of more than $3.5 million today, very little was liquid; nearly all of it represented the Grove, the beach home, and investment real estate. With embarrassment, citing "some personal economic struggles," Collins accepted a doctor's offer to reduce his fee for surgery on his son's injured ear. A commercial venture to open the Grove as a tourist attraction had lost money and left the family with some $3,000 in unpaid bills.[3]

Graham lobbied for Collins and wrote him that he had found Sol Taishoff, the influential publisher of *Broadcasting*, "quite enthusiastic." The selection committee, he said, "will want to decide whether they want a man of ability and stature or whether they merely want someone 'safe.' If they want the latter you surely don't want the job anyway."[4]

Collins did not intend to be a "safe" front man. He believed that he could fend off excessive government regulation by persuading the industry to police itself. To anyone reading his speeches, which the selection committee evidently did not, it would have been clear that he thought self-policing was urgently in order. In his 1959 State of the State address, Collins objected that a proposal to curtail summer school would leave children at the mercy of "a steady diet of television programs which keep our children under continuing instruction in every conceivable technique of crime, and brings to them sordid influences for decadence and moral degeneracy." Speaking at a child welfare workshop six months later, he accused television, motion pictures, and other popular media of desensitizing children to "killings, crime, and violence." Less than a month after Marshall's overture, Collins returned to the attack during an address to his daughter Jane's graduating class at Randolph-Macon College: "The producer of a television program has no moral license to concern himself only with what will attract the largest audience. He has an obligation to consider whether he is elevating or debasing the sensibilities of the millions to whose homes he has access. The gratification of a viewer's desire for violence and sadism in television programming is no more defensible morally than the gratification of base desires through forms of vice."[5]

The selection committee's impression was reflected in *Broadcasting's* headline, "NAB PICKS A POLITICAL CHARMER." That would be the high point of his relationship with the dominant trade publication. "If the broadcasting industry has a conscience," Frank Trippett wrote in the *St. Petersburg Times*, "it can expect to have it needled by the leader it has just chosen." Collins said he saw broadcasting as another opportunity for public service.[6]

Washington, where the family settled into a historic Georgetown home, was a new and not entirely brave world for the Collins family. Darby noticed nervously that her father continued his lifelong habit of greeting passing strangers, something that even a ten-year-old knew simply was not done in the capital that John F. Kennedy famously described as a "city of Southern efficiency and Northern charm." The curriculum at the exclusive National Cathedral School for girls was much harder than that of the Florida State University School back home. True culture shock awaited at a sixth-grade class party hosted by the ambassador from Liberia, the first occasion she had been in a black person's home. "It was a wonderful house on Embassy Row, but what struck me," she said, "was that their help were all white."[7]

Collins took a personal vanity to Washington. He used a sun lamp on the premise that anyone from Florida would be expected to have a tan.[8]

A new Federal Communications Commission chairman, Newton Minow, arrived in Washington at the same time. He was a thirty-five-year-old law partner of Adlai Stevenson. Collins already knew him casually, and they became friends despite disagreement on the extent to which the government should regulate broadcasting. They thought so much alike about the industry's deficiencies that *Washington Post* cartoonist Herbert Block portrayed them as Western heroes facing down black-hatted ruffians (see fig. 9). *Broadcasting* took instant alarm, warning Collins, after only a week on the job, to "not be deluded by the sweet talk about harmony between the regulators and the regulated."[9]

Florida politics at its worst had not prepared Collins for a special-interest constituency with its own aggressively protective press that would repeatedly attack him during the ensuing three and a half years. He confided to his daughter Mary Call that his first year was very difficult; he "simply felt that I didn't know what it was all about. I couldn't even talk the basics of the broadcast language much less understand it well enough to feel that I could assert effective leadership."[10]

Broadcasting criticized his first testimony to a Senate committee, where he urged repeal of equal-time requirements that inhibited the broadcasting of political debates but also spoke favorably of the so-called fairness doctrine. The magazine said that "fairness is impossible to define with precision."[11]

There was more controversy following a speech, five weeks on the job, to the NAB's board of directors at Palm Springs, California, where he offended some of his employers by releasing to the press what he had said in executive session. (John Perry, still his speechwriter, said later that he had publicized the text to keep the board from suppressing it.) Warning that he would irritate them from time to time, Collins told the directors that pressure from Congress and the FCC reflected the public's "dangerously low" opinion of the industry, which he said "simply cannot afford to become identified with what is cheap and degrading." Collins also said that it was courting trouble to rely on audience rating services that broadcasters did not supervise.[12]

In a series of speeches, Collins called for more quality programming and decried "violence for the sake of violence." There was favorable coverage in the national press but consternation at *Broadcasting*, which said, "The paradox of an FCC chairman and an NAB president who see to eye on programming defies all precedent."[13]

At the NAB convention that May, Minow expressed his memorable characterization of American television as "a vast wasteland," warned the broadcasters that public service was the price for using the airwaves, and said that license renewals would no longer be automatic. Collins again criticized the rating services and told the broadcasters that more of them should editorialize on the air if they wanted to be as respected as the print media. "If you want someone gently to paddle NAB's boat into the stagnant pockets of still water," he said, "then you do not want me—nor I, you." *Variety*, under the headline "HOT NEW ACT; MINOW & COLLINS," said their speeches left broadcasters "more stunned than appreciative." *Broadcasting*'s editorial warned of possible resignations from the NAB "on the premise that broadcasters deserve something better than a scolding from their president." Collins had been their president for barely four months.[14]

By August, *Broadcasting* had apparently dedicated itself to being Collins's nemesis and was harping on idle rumors that he was using the NAB as a stepping-stone to run for the U.S. Senate. Collins did nothing to prepare to oppose Smathers in 1962 or Holland in 1964, although he confided to an old friend that he thought Florida was poorly represented in Congress. With his NAB contract due to be renegotiated, he ruled out running for governor again in 1964.[15]

To Minow's applause, Collins worked intensively at strengthening the NAB's voluntary "codes of good practices" on issues such as the frequency of commercials, violence and sex in program content, and advertising to children. During a round of speeches at the NAB's fall regional conferences, Collins criticized "some trade press editors"—meaning Taishoff—for frightening broadcasters into believing that Minow and the FCC intended to control their programming, an eventuality that Collins would oppose. He said also that Minow had "overstated his cause" in the "vast wasteland" speech. *Broadcasting* declared a temporary truce, conceding that Collins "needs and deserves the help of every NAB member." A year into his term, *Broadcasting* was still apprehensive but kept itself under control after Collins sternly criticized the FCC for holding hearings on the quality of programming by Chicago stations whose licenses were not due for renewal.[16]

But the stresses of his new job were obvious to his friends and family. Robert T. Mann, the Florida legislator, remembered a conversation in Collins's office sometime in 1961. When Mann mentioned having seen *A Man for All Seasons*, Robert Bolt's play about the martyrdom of Sir Thomas More, Collins asked whether he had seen Henrik Ibsen's *An Enemy of the People*, concerning a conscientious health officer whose warnings make him a pariah. For Darby Collins, it meant being nervous when her father came home from work; "the least little thing might set him off." He often described his day as "Dog eat dog!" Anticipating a tense meeting with directors, he wrote his middle daughter that while he thought he would weather the storm, "I wish they would stop making my life so miserable at times." He said they wanted him to present an "image I don't like and won't take." He wrote to his eldest daughter on another occasion, "Sometimes I feel that I couldn't have a better job, and then . . . some of these characters will make me want to never see a broadcaster again."[17]

More of them felt the same way about him after a sensational speech at Portland, Oregon, in November 1962, calling on the industry to restrict tobacco advertising that appealed to children. "A sense of moral responsibility demands it," he said. That part, added late to his speech after the pages had already been numbered, acknowledged "the mounting evidence that tobacco provides a serious hazard to health" and contended that advertising aimed at children was enticing more of them to smoke. If the tobacco companies would not clean up the advertising, Collins said, the broadcasters should."[18]

The Portland speech, reported in apocalyptic headlines by the trade press, was the moral equivalent of asking Southern stores to voluntarily desegregate their lunch counters. "Collins Aims at $134-Million Customer," screamed the headline on *Broadcasting*'s news story. Its editorial, entitled "Collins Crisis," implied that he ought to be fired. Collins remarked that he would not want the job if he could not be a leader.[19] There was some doubt that he would keep it. The terms of his three-year contract required renegotiation at the end of the second year, which meant right then. Surprisingly, the NAB's directors in January gave him a two-year extension, through 1964. The syndicated columnist Drew Pearson speculated that Collins was not fired only because the directors assumed it would be a public relations disaster.[20]

Collins placated his industry critics through most of 1963 by sharpening his opposition to various FCC regulatory initiatives. But on November 30, he set them off again by denouncing the American Tobacco Company for a commercial claiming that its Lucky Strike cigarettes "separate the men from the boys, but not from the girls." Collins accused the company of consciously exploiting every boy's desires for manhood and sex. "I resent this advertisement deeply, and I feel that I should say so," he said. The point of the ad, the company replied, was that only adults should smoke.[21]

His next speech, to a Chamber of Commerce banquet in Columbia, South Carolina, was the most controversial of his career. It came eleven days after the assassination of President Kennedy and the wounding of Texas Gov. John Connolly in Dallas, which Collins saw in a larger context of verbal and physical violence including the deaths of four children in the bombing of a Birmingham church and the assassination of Mississippi NAACP leader Medgar Evers. Collins wanted to say that no matter who the actual murderers were, many others shared the blame. "For too long," he said,

[W]e have permitted the South's own worst enemies to speak for it. We have allowed the extremists to speak for the South. . . . They have done it in speeches on the floor of Congress which have sounded like anti-American diatribes from some hostile foreign country. They have done it in the national press and on the national radio and on television to such an extent that citizens outside the South would be entitled to wonder if they might not need visas to pass through our region.

And all the while, too many of the rest of us have remained cravenly silent or lamely defensive while Dixie battle cries have been employed to incite sick souls to violence, egged on by the rabble-rousers' call to "stand up and fight!"

. . . And I ask you tonight, how long are the majority of Southerners going to allow themselves to be caricatured before the nation by these Claghorns? How many Sunday school children have to be dynamited to death? How many Negro leaders have to be shot in the back? How many governors have to be shot in the chest? How many Presidents have to be assassinated?

All these evil happenings have been the products of environments where hatred has been preached and lawlessness extolled—environments which you and I know are foreign to the South for which we care deeply and are repugnant to most Southerners.

It is time the decent people in the South, with all their might and strength, told the bloody-shirt-wavers to climb down off the buckboards of bigotry.[22]

Collins did not intend to blame the South for Kennedy's death, but that is how the Associated Press reported it. Many newspapers carried this AP dispatch: "Former Gov. LeRoy Collins of Florida said Tuesday the assassination of President Kennedy was fostered by 'Dixie battle cries which incite sick souls to violence.'" The *New York Times*, not relying on the wire services, led its story with the "buckboards of bigotry" quotation and mentioned the assassination only in passing. The Associated Press eventually corrected its account, but too late to spare Collins lasting political damage.[23]

Some Southern editors praised the speech. "These are good words, and they were said by a good Southerner. Read them well, think of them well, put them on your conscience and on your hearts," commented the *Raleigh Times*. Typical of another side was the *Greenville (S.C.) Piedmont*, which said that but for Southern politeness and good manners, his audience "would have walked out long before he finished his unfounded diatribe."[24]

Former South Carolina governor James F. Byrnes canceled a breakfast with Collins at which he had intended to give him a copy of his autobiography, *Speaking Frankly*. A radio station in Florence, South Carolina, said it was quitting the NAB until it got "a more responsible president." *Broadcasting* insinuated again that Collins was running for the Senate, said there was "considerable doubt that he has the necessary interest" to be a good president of the NAB, and called in effect for him to be fired at a directors' meeting in late January.[25]

Some broadcasters defended Collins. But his job was definitely in jeopardy when the NAB directors met in Sarasota on January 28, 1964. In yet another editorial, occupying a full page, *Broadcasting* declared that "No one can be called a leader if he marches down the street by himself."[26]

Collins refused a buyout offer and kept his job by a vote of 25 to 18 after publicly denouncing the magazine's "bitter vendetta" and delivering in private a speech that was one of the finest, if least reported, of his career. If they wanted only a good front man, he told the directors, "then you have certainly misled me." No one would listen to such a man who, "after a while . . . I suspect, would even stop listening to himself." But it was a Pyrrhic victory because the vote in his favor was less than the two-thirds that would be necessary to renew his contract.[27]

Unknown to his employers, Collins had declined an offer from Kennedy in 1962 to be ambassador to Canada. He was unwilling to take a much lower salary for only a noncabinet post and he suspected that Smathers might be pulling strings to send a potential opponent out of the country.[28] Other events, however, would result in his taking leave of the NAB before Taishoff's claque could fire him.

The Birmingham and Mississippi murders came in the course of an increasingly intense civil rights movement that saw the nation shocked by mass arrests and police brutality in Birmingham and uplifted by the peaceful March on Washington, where Dr. Martin Luther King Jr. delivered his immortal "I have a dream" speech. Collins, as he wrote later, had been "a tiny speck, just one person in a throng of 200,000" on the mall when King spoke. Kennedy responded by asking Congress for strong legislation to protect voting rights, desegregate lunch counters and all other public accommodations, and desegregate schools by requiring federal aid to be spent without racial discrimination. The bill was still pending when Kennedy died. In his first address to Congress, the new president, Lyndon Johnson, asked for its passage as a tribute to Kennedy.[29]

Much of the impetus for the bill, as it turned out, came from Collins's home state: violent local resistance to desegregation demonstrations at St. Augustine, which had been targeted because it was preparing to celebrate its four-hundredth anniversary, and where the new governor, Farris Bryant, was conspicuously reluctant to do anything helpful. The seventy-two-year-old mother of Massachusetts governor Endicott Peabody was one of the demonstrators who volunteered for arrest. Bryant, who had let Collins's biracial committee lapse into disuse and ignored the U.S. Civil Rights Commission when it tried to warn him of trouble brewing at St. Augustine, did nothing but ban night marches—a federal judge overruled him—and belatedly send state troopers to try to keep the peace. On June 10, the day after acid was poured into a swimming pool where blacks were trying to swim, the Senate for the first time broke an organized Southern filibuster against civil rights legislation.[30]

It would be the strongest since Reconstruction. One of the provisions established a Community Relations Service to help localities peaceably resolve their civil rights issues. Johnson persuaded Collins to become the first director.[31]

Collins accepted despite a severe reduction in income and other misgivings; he had had enough of the broadcasters, whose directors were happy to let him out of his contract and eased his way with a $60,000 settlement and the Cadillac and color television set that he had been using. *Broadcasting* editorialized that it was worth the money to be rid of him and that firing him would have cost more.[32]

Chapter 28

Selma

Although Lyndon Baines Johnson had hewed to the segregationist line in Congress, his elevation to Senate majority leader and his presidential ambitions altered his perspective. In 1957, Johnson was instrumental in passing the first civil rights act since Reconstruction, though it was so extensively compromised to placate Southern senators that the great black labor leader A. Philip Randolph denounced it as "worse than no bill at all."[1]

In 1964, however, there was no mistaking the strength of the legislation that the new president was impatient to sign or his commitment to enforcing it. But he feared violent resistance to the enforced desegregation of restaurants, hotels, theaters, barber shops, and other public accommodations. That informed the urgency of his search for a director of the Community Relations Service (CRS). The ideal person would command the respect of the Southern governors and be someone "that the Negroes will have confidence in and won't say that I've fixed them."[2]

Few obvious candidates had such dual qualifications, and Johnson's list kept getting shorter. His first choice, accomplished labor mediator George Taylor, declined. So did liberal Atlanta mayor Ivan Allen Jr. Johnson was unenthusiastic when Secretary of Commerce Luther Hodges, whose department would house the conciliation service, suggested Collins. But as Allen was adamant, Johnson agreed to let Hodges clear Collins with the Florida senators. The president remarked that Smathers might even be eager to see a potential rival in a job that "is not going to be any place to win any popularity contests." Hodges said he thought Collins "would sacrifice anything in the world for the principle of doing a job for his country." Collins would never know that he had not been the president's first or even second choice.[3]

James Eastland objected strenuously, however, during a conversation with the president about the disappearance of three civil rights workers in Mississippi. (It would turn out that the Ku Klux Klan had murdered them, but Eastland dismissed it at the time as a publicity stunt.) Unaware that Johnson taped his telephone calls, Eastland exploded at the mention of Collins's name: "He's a damned cheap double-crosser and a liar and he's strictly dishonest. Now he agreed at the convention to recognize us to vote for you and he went back on his word. I called him a goddamned, lying son of a bitch out there."[4]

"Well, we don't want him then, do we?" the president replied. "Hell, no!" said Eastland.[5] But Hodges refused to give up on Collins and reported on June 25 that Collins would make the sacrifice if Johnson could persuade the NAB to let him go. Johnson saw Collins that afternoon and called in the NAB's executive committee the next day. He also lobbied the NAB through Graham at the *Washington Post*.[6]

Johnson told Collins that "you are the one we all want to take on this job." Collins accepted only tentatively; he worried about subsisting in Washington on a sharply reduced salary of $20,000, and he and Mary Call foresaw that the post would be a liability in any future campaign. But Johnson framed it as a patriotic duty, and Collins committed to serving for one year. "There was never any doubt in my mind, really, but I kept repeating over and over to myself, 'Why me, Lord?' and the answer I kept getting back was something like, 'This is no time for questions like that,'" Collins said.[7]

Johnson signed the Civil Rights Act and formally announced the Collins appointment during a televised ceremony on July 2. The president appealed to the nation: "Let us close the springs of racial poison. Let us pray for wise and understanding hearts." In a private remark that became famous, Johnson told his assistant Bill Moyers that he feared the Civil Rights Act had "handed the South to the Republicans for our lifetimes."[8]

Within the month, blacks were served without incident at restaurants, motels, and public golf courses across the South, but there were also many reports of flagrant resistance and overt violence. Atlanta restaurant owner Lester Maddox, a failed candidate for mayor, armed white supporters with ax handles to drive away blacks testing the day-old law. Maddox closed the restaurant after losing an appeal and a year later was chosen governor of Georgia. In St. Augustine, the Ku Klux Klan frustrated compliance until a federal judge ordered merchants to obey the law. Governor Bryant had remarked, "I don't propose to collect taxes and I don't propose to enforce civil rights."[9]

Eastland was not the only Southern senator spoiling to make trouble for Collins. Strom Thurmond of South Carolina, who held the Senate individual filibuster record for holding out twenty-four hours and eighteen minutes against the 1957 civil rights bill, wanted retribution for the speech at Columbia. He turned what should have been a half-hour confirmation hearing by the Senate Commerce Committee into a three-hour-and-fifty-minute ordeal.[10] Collins accused Thurmond of being "grossly unfair" in implying that he disliked the South. "I could give you my hopes and aspirations that I feel about the South and they would be different from yours, but don't you challenge my deep feelings about the South," he said.[10]

Thurmond suggested Collins was hypocritical in his changing viewpoints on segregation. (That was brazen of Thurmond, for it was an open secret in South Carolina, acknowledged as true after his death, that he had fathered and supported a daughter by his parents' black maid.) "There are some inconsistencies," Collins conceded. "We all agree that we all change. We all adjust to new circumstances." Thurmond retorted: "So you have grown since you have been on the national scene?"

"I hope I have grown since I left my mother's knee and I hope I continue to grow," Collins replied. "And I hope as long as the good Lord lets me live on this earth I will continue to grow and to recognize changes and to meet the new responsibility as changes require."[11]

Having twice invoked the absence of a quorum to keep the committee from approving Collins, Thurmond resorted on the third day to physical force to bar Sen. Ralph W. Yarborough of Texas from the committee room. The two sixty-one-year-old senators were wrestling on the corridor floor, sweating and panting, when Chairman Warren Magnuson emerged to put a stop to it. Magnuson had made certain of having enough votes this time, and Collins was approved, 16 to 1. Thurmond continued to oppose him on the Senate floor, where Collins's nomination was confirmed by a vote of 53 to 8, with 39 absent.[12]

On a subsequent visit to Tallahassee, Collins had an unpleasant encounter with his long-time barber, Isaac R. "Shorty" Meloy, who was refusing black customers in defiance of the Civil Rights Act. When Collins called for an appointment, the barber refused, saying he was so upset that he might hurt

Collins by accident. Collins's feelings were wounded, but Meloy eventually got over it and cut his hair again.[13]

Collins's new job occasioned his second appearance on *Meet the Press*, where he was questioned again about how his racial views had changed. His son, house-hunting in Charleston, South Carolina, called that night to say he had seen the program at a prospective landlord's home. "Are you using your real name?" his father asked.[14]

Collins had to build an agency without any precedent. Within the first month, he visited the governors of twenty-six states. Though Johnson had worried chiefly about violence in the South, Collins understood from the outset that there were racial issues nationwide. Two days before his confirmation, a white police officer in Harlem fatally shot a fifteen-year-old black and rioting resulted. Collins said on *Meet the Press* that such disorders were symptoms of poor housing, education, and other "very deeply entrenched" circumstances. The South, he said, might resolve its problems sooner than the North.[15]

The agency established that race-related discontent did not stop at the Mason-Dixon Line. In its first nine months, the CRS responded to 213 complaints or requests for assistance from 120 communities in 28 states. One of the unsung successes was an agreement to desegregate "School Days" at the Florida State Fair. Nearly a third of the cases were from outside the South. In an episode that Collins loved to retell, the mayor of Moultrie, Georgia, awarded a key to the city to Abe Venable, a black CRS conciliator from Philadelphia, for mediating a school boycott that had led to hundreds of arrests, but the mayor took pains to present it out of sight of the local public and press.[16]

The CRS could not publicize its successes because Congress had stipulated that its casework be confidential. So it could not alert the press when in 1965 it found omens of violence in eleven Northern and Western cities. Collins invited the eleven mayors to Washington for private conferences. Nine took him seriously, but Richard Daley of Chicago refused to come and Richard Yorty of Los Angeles rejected the agency's principal recommendation to accelerate the delivery of federal antipoverty assistance. Both cities later sustained serious riots.[17]

The agency's interest in urban intelligence owed largely to the advocacy of Roger Wilkins, a thirty-two-year-old black lawyer and nephew of NAACP leader Roy Wilkins, whom Collins had hired at Perry's urging. Wilkins described his meeting with Collins, over lunch in the Department of Commerce executive dining room, as "the damndest employment interview I ever had." Collins spent much of it telling political anecdotes and rarely looked at Wilkins, who sensed that his prospective employer was uncomfortable. He was surprised when a high-salaried job offer ensued. Collins acknowledged in an interview eleven years later that he had been ill at ease when he began working with black people in Washington but was proud to have overcome it.[18]

Collins's discomfiture over a business lunch reflected the deep imprint of certain Southern taboos and stereotypes. When Wilkins was recommended to him, Collins said that it would not do for Southern politicians to hear a "Negro voice" on the agency's telephone. In fact, Wilkins sounded like any other well-educated person who had been raised in New York and Michigan.[19]

Collins kept a busy calendar; since the agency's deeds could not speak for it, he would. However he might still be wrestling with private anxieties, he was now publicly committed to equality. "[T]this whole matter of civil rights—of human dignity, of individual freedom by whatever name you prefer to call it—is the big test of our time," he said. Barely ten years since he had campaigned for governor as a segregationist, he now declared civil rights to be "the most important moral issue of our time." Collins repudiated his own old argument that morality could not be legislated. "Laws do not make people moral but they certainly can and do prevent people from doing immoral things," he said. He embraced the principle of the *Brown* decision that inequality had a "crushing impact on the minds and spirits" of black children. The man who once deplored bus boycotts and other confrontational tactics would no longer presume to tell Negro leadership how to protest, "for the very good reason that I am not a Negro."[20]

He was forthcoming about having changed his views. "Yes," he said, "I am the first to admit that over the span of my life I have been quite inconsistent in positions I have taken, both public and private, concerning civil rights and the place of the Negro in our American society." He acknowledged the "sting" of Thurmond's criticism. "What sustained me throughout all of this . . . is the sure conviction in my own heart that my determination to do what was 'right' had not changed. What had changed was my own understanding and comprehension of what was right." Collins admitted that he had looked at segregation "through the eyes of a man who was raised from a boy on the

privileged side of a racially segregated social system." He had even rationalized "that Negroes actually preferred it that way."[21]

On that occasion, speaking in Birmingham on January 30, 1965, Collins
told the story, described in chapter 2, of the old black man who ate lard and
syrup for lunch. "My sense of injustice went no further than stopping the hole
in his paper tray," he confessed. But now he knew that "Wherever poverty is
at its worst, there you also find that both the greater percentage of the poor
and the poorest of the poor, are Negroes.

"And this, friends, is no accident. No heartless God so willed it. We did
it, we white Americans. It was we who installed the institution of slavery on
this continent . . . who perpetuated it as long as we could . . . who found more
subtle substitutions for slavery when it was ended. . . . Now, thank God, all of
that is doomed to pass away in America."[22]

In Selma, Alabama, the Macon County seat, ninety-seven miles away from
where Collins spoke that weekend, a two-year-old civil rights confrontation
was building to a historic climax. Despite massive protests and hundreds of
arrests, only 335 of the county's 15,000 voting-age blacks were on the voter
rolls. Selma exemplified the need for a stronger voting rights act, but Johnson
was ambivalent. Though he had lost only six states in 1964—his 61 percent
popular vote landslide is still the record—Johnson was keenly aware that
Georgia, Mississippi, Alabama, Louisiana, and South Carolina had defected
to Republican Sen. Barry Goldwater, an opponent of the 1964 act. Nonetheless, Johnson implied in his January 4 State of the Union message that a voting rights bill would be forthcoming to remove "every remaining obstacle to
the right and the opportunity to vote."[23]

Dr. Martin Luther King Jr. and his Southern Christian Leadership Conference (SCLC), unwilling to wait, targeted Selma as "a symbol of bitter-end
resistance" and took charge of the demonstrations from the Student Nonviolent Coordinating Committee (SNCC). Negroes would "march by the
thousands" to the courthouse to demand to be registered, King said. If that
failed, there would be another massive march on Washington.[24]

Events did not quite follow the script. Sheriff James G. Clark ordered
mass arrests, often accompanied by brutality vividly reported in the national
media. Following the death of Jimmie Lee Jackson, a twenty-six-year-old
army veteran who was shot by a state trooper at a sympathy demonstration
in a neighboring county, movement leaders called for a protest march to the
state capitol in Montgomery, fifty-four miles away. This would result in the

most influential day of the civil rights revolution, an event memorialized as "Bloody Sunday."[25]

As pressure built within Congress for new legislation and as the White House and Justice Department tried to work out the terms, Alabama governor George Wallace determined to block the march. King, who had tried to postpone it by a day, was not in Selma when some six hundred people, having marched only a few blocks to the middle of the Edmund Pettus Bridge on U.S. Highway 80, came upon ranks of helmeted state troopers backed up by Clark's civilian posse on horseback. Shouting through a bullhorn, an officer gave demonstrators two minutes to turn back and disperse. Believing it impossible to turn so large a crowd, SNCC leader John Lewis passed the word to kneel and pray. Without waiting the two minutes, the troopers and posse attacked the marchers with clubs, horses, whips, and tear gas, driving them all the way through Selma to Brown's Chapel, the church where they had organized. Some ninety marchers needed medical care; seventeen were hospitalized, including Lewis, a future member of Congress, who suffered a fractured skull. Television and still photographers had recorded the savagery for the nightly newscasts and the next day's front-page headlines. King called for another march on Tuesday. This time he would lead it, and by telegram he asked hundreds of religious leaders from around the nation to join him.[26]

The SCLC petitioned Frank Johnson, one of the few sympathetic Southern federal district judges, for an order to protect the marchers, but he insisted on holding a hearing first and wanted there to be no more marches in the meantime. The president, desperate to avert another bloody event, ordered Collins to Selma to try to talk King into waiting. Arriving before dawn Tuesday, aboard a twin-engine air force jet at the nearby Craig Air Force base, Collins and an aide spent what was left of a sleepless night and all of the morning in shuttle diplomacy, but King said the demonstrators were so emotionally committed that he could not stop them if he tried and that if he did not lead them, they would march on their own. "I knew," said Collins, that "he was dead right."[27]

Collins's memoirs differ on points of timing but not in substance with David Garrow's detailed account in *Protest at Selma: Martin Luther King, Jr., and the Voting Rights Act of 1965*. According to Collins, it was during that first meeting that he outlined a compromise that would save face for both sides. The march would proceed only as far as the bridge; there would be a short prayer service, and the demonstrators would return to Brown's Chapel.

If Collins could sell that to Clark and Al Lingo, the Alabama state public safety director, would King agree? King was skeptical that Clark, Lingo, or his own followers would accept it, but he told Collins to see what he could do. Garrow's history suggests, however, that Collins first articulated the plan during his subsequent meeting with Clark and Lingo.[28]

Collins found Clark and Lingo at a makeshift command post in a vacant auto dealership near the bridge. He knew by then that the judge had signed a restraining order and it had been served on several of the leaders, but the crowd of more than two thousand persons, many of them white—among them, the wife of U.S. Sen. Paul H. Douglas of Illinois—was in no mood to obey it. At one point, Lingo asked Collins to wait outside the office; Collins assumed it was so he could contact Wallace by telephone. Clark then drew a map, handed it to Collins, and told him that if the marchers would stop where the map indicated, spend no more than twenty minutes singing or praying, and then turn back, his men would not attack them. Otherwise, he said, he would "do what it takes to force them back."[29]

According to Garrow's account, Collins made two trips between the opposing headquarters. Collins recalled only one, but the stories converge on the essential point: The march had begun, with King in the lead, when Collins arrived and handed him a piece of paper. King asked whether he could guarantee that Alabama would honor the arrangement; Collins said he would personally seize the first trooper who advanced. "I really couldn't have physically held any of those troops," he wrote much later, "but so help me, I would have tried."[30]

The marchers, few of whom carried bedrolls or other gear sufficient for a four-day journey, reached the bridge shortly after 3 p.m. They paused to hear a U.S. marshal read the judge's order. The marshal then stepped aside, allowing King to lead the head of the column across the bridge to a point just fifty feet from the front line of some one hundred Alabama state troopers. There King stopped, called for prayers from four different people and for the singing of "We Shall Overcome," and turned back toward Brown's Chapel. At that moment, in a move likely ordered by Wallace to embarrass King, the troopers withdrew to the side of the road, ostensibly clearing the way to Montgomery. King did not take the bait and continued the reverse march. The demonstrators were surprised and shocked, and many were irate. But they followed, grateful to be alive and unhurt. "Tears were left on the bridge that day," Collins wrote, "but no blood." Congratulating Collins privately, the president said that but for him "the ditches would have been knee-deep in blood."[31]

There was blood still to be shed in Selma. That night, club-wielding whites fatally injured James M. Reeb, a Unitarian minister from Boston, one of the 450 white clergymen in Selma at King's request. Fearing mass violence, the White House telephoned Collins in Gainesville, where he was scheduled to speak at the University of Florida, and another air force jet took him back to Selma. The press there had uncovered his supposedly confidential role, and he confirmed to reporters that he had helped to arrange the compromise at the Pettus Bridge. Testifying in Frank Johnson's court, where the Justice Department intervened in support of the demonstrators, King put the negotiations on record.[32]

On one of Collins's missions, he went to Brown's Chapel on a cold, rainy night to find it surrounded by a cordon of police whose weapons were pointed toward the nonviolent demonstrators huddled around a fire, rather than at an encircling white mob that was the source of rock-throwing and random gunshots. Collins challenged one of the troopers to protect the demonstrators. "Now listen, fed," the man replied, "I'm doing my job like I was told to do it. Why don't you go back to Washington and do yours?" Collins saw a young black woman with a bloodstained face carried into the church. A nearly spent bullet had pierced her upper lip and knocked out a tooth. Another white volunteer, Viola Gregg Liuzzo, a Detroit housewife, was shot to death by Ku Klux Klansmen on a highway near Selma after the march had ended.[33]

Collins discovered that segregation still prevailed at Craig Air Force Base and other Selma-area federal facilities in flagrant violation of government regulations. He reported that to Johnson, who called the press into a cabinet meeting to witness him ordering an immediate end to it.[34]

Reeb's death intensified the public and political pressure that the White House had felt since Bloody Sunday. Wallace flew to Washington on Saturday to complain to an unsympathetic president that the demonstrators, not the state, were the problem. Johnson took him before the press corps for a public rebuke and an announcement that he would send a voting rights bill to Congress within the week.[35]

On March 15, Collins was back in Washington to witness the president's forty-five-minute appeal to a joint session of Congress. He and Mary Call dined with the Johnsons at the White House and accompanied them to the Capitol to hear the most stirring speech of Johnson's career.[36]

"I speak tonight for the dignity of man and the destiny of democracy," the president began. To deny voting rights because of race, he said, "is not only to do injustice, it is to deny America and to dishonor the dead who gave their lives for American freedom." Yet, Johnson said, "every device of which human ingenuity is capable has been used" to thwart Negroes from voting.

> The Negro citizen may go to register only to be told that the day is wrong, or the hour is late, or the official in charge is absent. And if he persists . . . he may be disqualified because he did not spell out his middle name or because he abbreviated a word on the application.
>
> And if he manages to fill out an application he is given a test. The registrar is the sole judge of whether he passes this test. He may be asked to recite the entire Constitution, or explain the most complex provisions of state law. And even a college degree cannot be used to prove that he can read and write. For the fact is, that the only way to pass these barriers is to show a white skin.[37]

"What happened in Selma," Johnson said, "is part of a far larger movement . . . the effort of American Negroes to secure for themselves the full blessings of American life. Their cause must be our cause too, because it is not just Negroes, but really it is all of us, who must overcome the crippling legacy of bigotry and injustice.

"And we *shall* overcome."[38]

The Southern president's invocation of the civil rights movement's signature anthem was a moment to be cherished forever by those who heard it. Listening at Selma, Martin Luther King wiped away a tear.[39]

Johnson signed the Voting Rights Act on August 6 and gave Collins one of the pens he had used in the ceremony (see fig. 11). Strong and comprehensive, the act provided, among other things, for suspending literacy tests. In the 1968 election, 52 percent of Selma's Negroes voted.[40]

There remained another Alabama mission for Collins, a fateful one. Frank Johnson having granted an injunction on behalf of the demonstrators, the Selma to Montgomery march was rescheduled for March 21 under detailed plans approved by the judge. The president called 1,800 Alabama National Guardsmen into federal service to protect the marchers and sent Collins to Montgomery to arrange an orderly reception. Once again, it was necessary for him to take plans to the leaders of the march and obtain their agreement.[41]

The march was in its second day. Collins parked his car beside U.S. 80, found King and his associates at the head of the column, and walked with them while they discussed the details. With some apprehension, Collins noted a truckload of photographers taking pictures. The Associated Press photograph, as printed by his hometown newspaper and many others on March 23, showed Collins talking with the Rev. Andrew Young, with Dr. King, Mrs. King, and the Rev. Ralph Abernathy walking alongside them (see fig. 10). The caption reported that Collins "joined civil rights demonstrators staging a 54-mile protest march from Selma, Ala., to the state capitol at Montgomery." Though the text identified him as "President Johnson's representative on racial problems" and said that he walked only "about a mile" with the marchers, the absence of a full explanation made it appear that he had joined them by choice.[42]

Mary Call had returned to Tallahassee for the expected birth of a grandchild. She warned Collins by telephone of an intensely hostile community reaction to the photograph. Arriving at the Tallahassee airport late that night, Collins found no taxi and called the Grove to ask his wife to pick him up. No, she said, she was alone with sleeping grandchildren.

"How am I going to get home?" he asked. "Well," she said sharply, "you might *march*."[43]

Chapter 29

Watts

In a letter to his sister Sue Evans, Collins mused on his affinity for controversy. "I seem to be specially adept at heading into such of it [as] is nearby and if there is none to head into I seem to be able to create it, don't I?" he wrote. Having had enough at the Community Relations Service, he was preparing to ask the president for another job. If Johnson had nothing suitable, "then we will be ready to pack up and go back to Florida."[1]

Johnson had considered Collins before appointing John T. Connor to replace Hodges, a Kennedy holdover who left at the start of Johnson's full term. Three months after Selma, he nominated Collins to be Connor's undersecretary of commerce. The job was less prone to controversy and would ease Collins's transition back to private life or elective politics. He was sworn in at a White House ceremony where Johnson lavished praise on his record at the Community Relations Service. But Johnson had no successor in mind for the CRS, where Collins's assistant Calvin Kytle, a Georgia-born journalist, became acting director. So Collins had to continue to oversee the agency.[2]

In his last speech as CRS director, on July 1, Collins tried to warn a Los Angeles audience of the peril that Yorty had ignored. They were "dead wrong," he said, "if you think the Los Angeles metropolitan area has relatively few human relations problems, or that this is a place where minority groups, such as Negroes, have not suffered deprivation as they have in other urban centers, or that the twin evils of discrimination and poverty, which walk hand-in-hand in other major cities, are strangers here." But the law did not allow him to say what Los Angeles needed most to know: Its mayor had sloughed off an explicit warning.[3]

The Watts riot began forty-one days later. The arrest of a black motorist on drunken driving charges was the spark for six days of turmoil that encompassed more than forty-five square miles, took thirty-four lives, injured more than a thousand persons, saw more than four thousand arrests, damaged or destroyed hundreds of buildings at a cost estimated at more than $200 million, and required the mobilization of some fifteen thousand soldiers of the California National Guard.[4]

Initially, the CRS itself was not involved beyond leaking to the *Washington Star* and the *New York Times* that Yorty, who was blaming the federal government for the riot, had been warned and had refused the agency's help. The *Times* effectively identified Kytle as its source, which numbered his days in Johnson's administration. Johnson then sent Collins to Los Angeles as his personal representative to unleash federal antipoverty funds that were being held up by turf-guarding city, state, and federal officials. The antagonists included Yorty himself and Rep. James Roosevelt, who had run against him for mayor that spring. Collins's assignment was to fashion a community action agency in the face of bureaucratic resistance from Yorty and almost everyone else. "Every politician had a knife out," Wilkins wrote in his autobiography, "and every politician was protecting his own back." Collins somehow got the job done; the *New York Times* described his achievement as a "psychological coup in the effort to smooth community relations." But the agreement that satisfied the politicians enraged community activists who felt they had been excluded. Their fury surfaced during a meeting at a church where Collins was exposed for the first time to such "raw expressions of black rage," as Wilkins described it, that he turned pale.[5]

The negotiations took a personal toll on Collins. Toward the end, he told Wilkins and Perry, whom he had taken to Los Angeles despite Johnson's order to go alone, to wait in Perry's hotel room while he met privately with California's Democratic boss, Jesse Unruh. Doing as they were told, the aides watched a televised baseball game. When they next heard from Collins, he was enraged, irrationally accusing them of not being available when he needed them. The men surmised that one of the California politicians had cut a deal behind Collins's back.[6]

Calming down, Collins told them to go out for dinner and enjoy themselves. As they were driving back to their hotel, they experienced firsthand why the city had been primed to explode. Two white police officers pulled them over, ordered them at gunpoint to come out of the car with their hands up, and subjected the two business-suited federal officers to a rough, spread-eagled search. The one frisking Wilkins called him "nigger." Unimpressed by Wilkins's two federal government identification cards, the policeman demanded his driver's license. "I wasn't driving and I'm not going to show you another goddamn thing," Wilkins said. The officer was menacing Wilkins with his firearm when his partner, having seen Perry's identification, warned, "We've made a hell of a mistake."[7]

Wilkins and Perry did not believe the police when they said they had been looking for robbers who fit their description. As they saw it, the officers had acted out of bigotry. They complained unavailingly to the police chief but did not publicize the incident because of Johnson's order to keep the mission confidential. Wilkins learned later that the gun-waving policeman had previously shot and killed a Hispanic youth for looting a pair of sneakers.[8]

Two days or so later, Collins called them to his room to watch Johnson announce on television that James Roosevelt would resign from Congress to become a member of the diplomatic mission to the United Nations under Arthur Goldberg, who was resigning from the Supreme Court to become the ambassador. As this eliminated a rival to Yorty, Wilkins and Perry took it to be Yorty's price for agreeing to the community action agency and the subject of Collins's unpleasant meeting with Unruh.[9]

The community action agency was announced that afternoon. The next day's *New York Times* credited the deal to Collins, quoting him extensively. Johnson ordered Collins back to Washington within hours after the article appeared and sent Deputy Attorney General Ramsey Clark to Los Angeles to finish the work he had started.[10]

Three days later, however, the president gave Collins an extremely high-profile assignment, naming him and Sen. Wayne Morse, D-Ore., as special emissaries to avert an impending steel strike. He told them to make clear to labor and management, which had suspended negotiations, that the president wanted a settlement, and to either get the two sides talking again or bring recommendations to Johnson. They went by a presidential helicopter to Andrews Air Force Base, where another executive jet was waiting to take them to Pittsburgh. No agreement ensued, and they returned to Washington the next night, a Sunday, to recommend that Johnson intervene personally. A White House breakfast the next morning left Collins with an indelible impression of Johnson's table manners. The president, having taken no rolls for himself, was helping himself to the ones on Collins's plate. Johnson called the steel negotiators to Washington, where he successfully pressured them to agree on a contract and avert the strike.[11]

There was an amusing incident about this time—entertaining, that is, to everyone but Collins himself—aboard the nuclear submarine USS *James Madison*, where his son was the weapons officer. Startled awake by the noise of a surfacing maneuver, the undersecretary of commerce struck his head on the bunk above him and staggered out of the compartment to seek help because he thought he was bleeding. He was unhurt; he saw red because it was the vessel's normal nighttime illumination.[12]

Collins was giving thought to whether he should run for governor in 1966 or for Smathers's Senate seat in 1968. Alarmed by the Republicans' 1960 showing, Florida Democrats had amended the constitution to elect the governor and Cabinet in nonpresidential years. Haydon Burns, who had won the two-year transitional governor's term in 1964, was eligible to seek the succeeding full term but was a vulnerable incumbent following the special referendum defeat of his top-priority $300-million road bond issue. A subsequent newspaper poll indicated that Collins could defeat him; so did a poll that Collins commissioned himself, and he gave the impression to some friends that he would run. But he announced in December 1965 that he would not. His real interest was in running for the Senate.[13]

Collins liked Washington, especially the intellectually charged Georgetown dinner party circuit, and Mary Call had found a niche "hobnobbing with the antique-loving ladies" at Mount Vernon, as he referred to the volunteers at George Washington's estate. Moreover, Miami mayor Robert King High, a man with similar principles who had lost the 1964 runoff to Burns, was already in the 1966 governor's race. A third likely reason was to wait for the Selma furor to die down. "I cannot support a man who would stoop so low as to march with that bunch of hoodlums" read a typical letter he received on that topic.[14]

Collins may also have been tipped off that the Senate seat would be open in 1968. Four weeks after Collins declined the governor's race, Smathers announced that he would retire from the Senate when his term ended. He said he had a "serious, complex, but not incurable" physical condition. Skeptics suggested that his real ailments consisted of persistently critical journalists; the impending indictment of Bobby Baker, a close friend and sometime business associate who was secretary to the Senate Democratic majority; and the prospect of having a serious opponent—Collins—for the first time since he defeated Pepper in 1950. "George says he's got a bad stomach, but I think he's just got a thin skin," Holland said at the time. Many years later, Smathers confessed that there had been no health problem and that he left the Senate because he could go no higher in the leadership, missed departed friends, was bored with Congress, and needed to earn more money.[15]

Johnson, meanwhile, moved the Community Relations Service to the Justice Department, which Collins thought unwise. On hearing rumors, Collins protested to Vice President Hubert Humphrey that the mediation service would be less effective as an arm of a law enforcement agency. Collins was called two days later to the White House, where Joseph A. Califano Jr., a special assistant to the president, told him that Humphrey was about to make the reorganization announcement. Moreover, Collins was expected to tell the press that he supported it. He refused, agreeing only to give a pep talk to the CRS staff, some of whom wept. Collins told members of Congress who tried to override Johnson's executive order that he would not volunteer to testify against it.[16]

In early May, Collins announced that he had opened an "unofficial" Senate campaign office. In Florida's Democratic runoff primary later that month, High defeated Burns for the gubernatorial nomination, and Charley Johns—the last of the original Pork Choppers—was defeated in a four-seat, twenty-four-county senatorial district that the Legislature created in an unsuccessful attempt to satisfy the U.S. Supreme Court.[17]

A month later, Collins announced that he was resigning to run for the U.S. Senate seat. Cody Fowler, who had chaired Collins's last biracial commission, made a place for Collins in his Tampa law firm. Collins left the Commerce Department on October 1 with a presidential letter of gratitude that specifically extolled his mediation at Selma. Collins may have asked Johnson for that to counter the impression that he had been "marching" there.[18]

Collins's "unofficial" campaign office accompanied him to Tampa, with Joe Grotegut, recalled from private enterprise, in charge. Collins's arrangement with the law firm allowed intensive speechmaking. "I am doing considerable legal work, though few really believe this, I am sure," he wrote to a skeptical journalist in November 1967.[19]

Darby remained in Washington to complete her senior year as a boarding student at the prestigious Madeira School. LeRoy Jr. decided against his father's advice to leave the Navy to begin a business career, spend more time with his wife and three children, and assist in the next campaign. He disappointed Democratic Party officials in Brevard County, where he had been stationed at Port Canaveral, who wanted him to run against the two-term local congressman, Republican Edward J. Gurney.[20]

Chapter 30

The Last Campaign

Collins gave two years' notice that he would run for the Senate in 1968. He meant that to discourage other potential candidates. Smathers, for one, was letting it be known that his health had improved. Collins was also concerned about Farris Bryant, U.S. Rep. Charles Bennett of Jacksonville, and Claude Pepper, who had returned to Congress in 1963 as a House member from Miami and was sounding out people who might help him reclaim the seat he had lost to Smathers. Though he would write later that "I was not tempted," Pepper complained to a mutual friend in August 1966 that Collins made his decision "before consulting with me."[1]

Collins had been alerted to watch out for Florida attorney general Earl Faircloth, who as a one-term state House member from Miami had narrowly upset incumbent attorney general James Kynes in 1964. After a three-month tour of the state, Collins's field coordinator, Radford Bishop, reported in August 1966 that when Faircloth's name came up he did not hear people say that they would support him. Bishop assessed Collins's chances as "almost too good to be true," warned against "a danger of complacency on the part of some," and remarked that the Selma photograph remained on the minds of voters for whom race was an issue. He predicted "many 'Republicans for Collins.'"[2]

Though Florida had voted Republican in three of the previous four presidential elections, the GOP had not mounted a serious threat in any other statewide race since Reconstruction. Republican Claude R. Kirk Jr., a Jacksonville insurance executive, had managed only 36 percent of the vote against Holland in 1964. Registered Democrats still outnumbered Republicans by more than four to one. But three months after Bishop's report, Kirk defeated High for the governor's office with 55 percent of the vote. High's runoff victory over Burns had been another sectional confrontation, which Kirk easily converted into an issue of the Miami mayor's alleged "ultraliberalism." To many voters, that was about race, not economics. Kirk carried all but nine of the sixty-seven counties. Of the urban counties, High won only Dade, his own, and Hillsborough.[3]

The potency of the "liberal" label was fresh in his mind when Collins was shocked to read in the *Miami News* that Smathers was reconsidering his retirement for fear that Collins, a "known liberal," would be unable to defeat Edward J. Gurney, the likely Republican nominee. Collins wrote plaintively to the paper's political editor, Charles F. Hesser: "Charlie—I know you did not intend to hurt me in this but it did hurt and I wanted to explain why— the term "liberal" is being construed to apply to everything people don't like. So you might have well as characterized me as a 'known criminal' so far as public impact was concerned." He concluded, "What can I do about this, good friend? Actually, I am most encouraged about our progress to date and confidently believe we can win."[4]

Hesser's source could have been Smathers himself. At about the same time, Smathers telephoned Charles Ausley to ask that he persuade his former law partner to abandon the race. "Tell him yourself," said Ausley. Smathers continued to feed rumors that he would run if Collins backed out.[5]

At qualifying, Collins and Faircloth were the only significant candidates for the Democratic nomination. There were two minor contestants. Gurney and St. Petersburg mayor Herman W. Goldner had the Republican primary to themselves.

Collins would face a vastly larger and much less familiar electorate than that of his last campaign. Since 1956, Florida had registered 1,158,566 more voters, a 72 percent increase. That depreciated his greatest asset, his reputation as governor. He would have to introduce himself to nearly half the electorate. "To a lot of voters, Collins is going to *look* a lot older than they remember him," warned his national campaign consultant, Joe Napolitan. Though Collins at fifty-nine was only four years older than Gurney, he looked much older, and he was ten years older than Faircloth. Gurney, almost totally unknown outside his district, started the campaign with a blank slate.[6]

What many supporters regarded as Collins's great strategic mistake was evident fourteen months before the primary, when the *Tampa Times* remarked that "Collins is already going to some lengths to recast himself as less liberal and more conservative" than his reputation as governor. Collins confided to some supporters at the time that "if everybody that was a Republican [in Florida] registered as a Republican, Democrats would be in a huge minority."[7] He would pitch his Democratic primary campaign to those closet Republicans.

For the first time, Collins relied heavily on polling. Early reports reflected keen public concern over the Vietnam War, which Johnson had escalated, but Collins's initial position was to stay the course with "this frustrating, difficult—but nonetheless necessary—war in Vietnam." He opposed both abrupt withdrawal, which would "abandon freedom and abandon our national commitments," and a "reckless escalation," which would "threaten immediate and long-range consequences quite the opposite of the peace we seek." So from the beginning Collins was untenably in the middle of the issue that was to bitterly divide his own party. Gurney, on the other hand, said the United States should either fight to win or get out. Collins's pollster had warned privately that many Floridians felt the same way.[8]

Collins greatly underestimated the Faircloth threat. Long before their formal campaign declarations, the Democratic state chairman, Pat Thomas, urged both Democrats to avoid replicating the High-Burns bloodbath that had elected Kirk. Only Collins tried to comply. Collins relied on a poll showing him defeating Faircloth everywhere but in North Florida, where the Pensacola newspaper had long since put the Selma photograph to use against him. But as Napolitan noted, "one-third of the Democratic primary vote is located there." Napolitan remarked on Collins's "tendency to ramble" when he was uncertain of facts or his position and said he needed to adopt more definitive policies on Vietnam and other issues. Warning that Faircloth "will make a major effort to make this a liberal-conservative contest," Napolitan advised Collins to criticize Johnson's controversial antipoverty program and "avoid public links with organized labor." That suited Grotegut's instincts, and Collins largely complied, anguishing his liberal advisers. Jay Janis, a Miamian who had worked for Collins at the Community Relations Service and Commerce Department, complained later to researcher Ruth Espey that "Joe's idea of the campaign was that Collins had moved way too far over to the left," and that Grotegut persuaded Collins to avoid talking about race, Democratic politics, or Johnson's domestic programs.[9]

Faircloth took the initiative on racial issues, exploiting them relentlessly. Urban riots, including seven in Florida in 1967, and the rise of a militant

"Black Power" movement contributed to a powerful backlash and to the potency of "law and order" as racist code words. Faircloth made the most of them, beginning with an interview in October 1967 in which he materially misrepresented what Collins had said in the March 1960 speech on lunch-counter segregation.[10]

The federal civil rights legislation of 1964 and 1965 did not address discrimination in the sale or rental of housing. Collins was not ready to cross that last, most sensitive frontier, and he dismayed Florida liberals, including the Miami television commentator and newspaper columnist Larry King, by opposing the "Fair Housing" legislation that Johnson would sign into law in April, a week after the assassination of Martin Luther King Jr. in Memphis. Collins said it would have been inconsistent for him to oppose private property rights. King replied that open housing was "too great a *moral* issue to be politically skirted."[11] Though Collins and Faircloth essentially agreed on that issue, it did not help Collins with conservatives and it hurt him with liberals.

A dilemma vexed Collins throughout the campaign: How to display some independence from Johnson without sounding disloyal. "I don't think Collins can win because he's tied too closely with Lyndon Johnson," said Rep. Syd Herlong, a conservative Democratic from Leesburg. When Collins defined himself as an "independent Democrat," Faircloth retorted that he had "supped well" at the president's table. Intensifying his attacks as the primary neared, Faircloth called Collins an "aging ultra-liberal" and a "political chameleon."[12]

Money was another problem that Collins could not master. He disliked asking for campaign contributions and tried to leave that to others. "He didn't want to be in the room when talk about money came up," recalled son-in-law John Aurell, who was practicing law in Miami. Some former contributors told Aurell they would give him no money because their previous gifts had earned them no favors. "Finances appears to be the real weak spot in the campaign and I am by no means certain that everything that can be done is being done," Napolitan warned four months before the primary.[13]

Faircloth's formal announcement was a barrage of "law and order" themes. One appealed to racism by asking whether America should "continue along a jungle course, with all that it implies, riots and looting, crime in our streets, destruction of property rights, legislative and judicial excesses, fiscal irresponsibility and the apparent belief that progress is achieved by civil disobedience."

He condemned a "misguided leadership . . . motivated more by hatred for the South than compassion for the Negro" that had "led inevitably from Selma, through Watts, to Detroit—looting, burning, sniping, and hatred."[14]

The hate mail accumulating in Collins's files included a tabloid-sized flyer of uncertain origin showing the Selma march photograph with a caption accusing Collins of having arranged and taken part in it "along with numerous reds, pinks and degenerates." The Florida Coalition of Patriotic Societies convention featured the Selma sheriff and Lester Maddox.[15]

Collins printed a platform card declaring "Seven Vital Goals for America!" of which the first was to "Restore law and order in this land!" The others, in order, were to "guarantee justice and opportunity for all citizens. End the war in Vietnam. Make the dollar worth a dollar. Provide fairness in taxation. Help cities meet vital needs. Protect our land, air and water from pollution and blight." His formal announcement speech, at a $100-a-person fund-raiser at a Cuban restaurant in Tampa, sounded mostly positive notes. Law and order "will require more than fierce-sounding slogans and dramatic gesturing and picture taking," Collins said. He intended to run on his record because "I anxiously want the people of Florida to be *for* me in this race."[16]

Collins tried in vain to avoid race-related issues. The riots that broke out in more than sixty cities after King's murder, a month before the primary, hurt him and helped Faircloth, who published a leaflet asking "Why is Collins afraid of a photograph?" and said in a campaign newsletter that Collins "seems to believe that anyone's mention of Selma . . . or riots, looting, burning, sniping and hate for 'whitey' is a personal reference to him."[17]

Despite his desperate finances, Collins personally vetoed a Tallahassee public relations firm's proposal to film a faux "news interview" subsidized by advertisers. But everyone around him sensed that he knew the campaign was not going well. He was taken aback by the unexpected difficulty. In a March 14 "eyes only" memorandum, Grotegut told him: "My only real concern (and in this I am joined by people whose identity and numbers might surprise you) centers around the fact that you do not seem to be happy with the way the campaign is going. In fact, you seem to be too frequently irritated, upset and downright demoralized." Though Collins was having second thoughts about Vietnam, Grotegut told him not to flinch and to "happily expect a big victory" in his campaign.[18]

Only two weeks later, however, another "eyes only" memorandum acknowledged that the campaign was $40,000 in the red and was fortunate that its telephones had not been disconnected. Five weeks before the primary, Collins had to abandon much of his planned billboard, radio, and newspaper supplement advertising to save what money he had for half-hour television specials like those that had worked well in 1956. "There is nothing wrong with this campaign that money wouldn't solve," Collins said. He still owed the Columbia Restaurant $963 for his kickoff luncheon three months earlier, and Grotegut had to defer part of his salary. Faircloth, meanwhile, had enough money to schedule hundreds of television spots as well as thirty-five half-hour broadcasts for the final weekend.[19]

As in 1956, Collins refused to debate a Democratic opponent. He had all the urban newspaper endorsements except for the *Palm Beach Post*, the *Pensacola News-Journal*, and the *Orlando Sentinel*, which was for Gurney, its local congressman, from the beginning and recommended no Democrat in the primary.[20]

The May 7 primary was a defeat for Collins disguised as a victory. He led with 426,096 votes to 397,642 for Faircloth, but fell 4,186 votes short of a majority. Enough votes had been cast for the two minor candidates—Sam Foor, publisher of a Tallahassee newsletter that politicians considered little more than a shakedown racket, and Richard Lafferty, a segregationist from Jacksonville—to require a three-week runoff campaign in which Faircloth would have the momentum and Collins was, as one newspaper put it, "a sudden underdog." Collins had carried eighteen counties, including his familiar strongholds of Dade, Broward, Hillsborough, and Pinellas, but the turnout, reduced by rain at Miami, was disappointing. Except for Leon, Faircloth carried every county north or west of Alachua. Gurney, having trampled Goldner with 80 percent of the Republican primary vote, had the advantage for the rest of the campaign.[21]

Not for the first time or the last, the returns belied most of the pre-election polls. The *Miami Herald*'s reporter thought Collins had lost a big lead to the Faircloth television blitz that he could not afford to counter. Collins said he regretted having heeded the party chairman and would pull no more punches. The choice in the runoff, he said, would be between "back-pedaling down a pork chop–flavored, dead-end street" or "going forward to good, new days of goodwill between men of common striving for excellence in all phrases of human effort."[22]

Collins was startled by criticism from an unexpected source: his former speechwriter John Perry, now on the staff of the Center for the Study of

Democratic Institutions in Santa Barbara, California. Addressing a convention of pollsters, Perry said Collins erred in listening to them. In 1956, he said, Collins had ignored "every single poll" showing that he would be defeated over the racial issue. Now, he said, Collins was "heeding the polls, conducting his campaign so as to offend as little as possible of what the polls, once again, indicate to be a substantially conservative sentiment in Florida." Perry accused Collins of avoiding strong stands on Vietnam and on urban problems because he "has decided that he *does* have to get elected" this time.[23]

Perry's criticism, reported at length by the Florida press, hurt Collins so deeply that he was still resentful eight years later. He believed that it eroded his liberal support without helping him among conservatives. There was little he could say at the time, though, without inviting attention to the internal struggle among his advisers.[24]

Collins's papers for 1956 contain only the early and favorable Dade County poll, but Grotegut did in fact lean heavily on polls in 1968. Three weeks before the primary, for example, he advised a Jacksonville supporter that poll data from that conservative city would factor into their strategy, including a "slant [in] our television and radio advertising toward law and order and the other issues you mention."[25]

The Selma photograph circulated widely in North Florida, where George Wallace, the former Alabama governor, had secured 226,000 signatures to place him on Florida's 1968 presidential ballot. Collins and Faircloth traded bitter personal attacks, along with charges over who was tougher or softer on crime. At Jacksonville, Faircloth supporters circulated posters showing a city in flames with the slogan, "Stop Riots, Elect Faircloth" and published a three-column newspaper advertisement saying in bold type, "DON'T LET THE BLOCK [*sic*] VOTE CONTROL YOUR SENATOR." The reference to bloc voting was so patently racist that Faircloth had to repudiate the ad. Remarking on a Collins campaign trip to the Panhandle, Faircloth said, "If he goes any farther he'll be back in Alabama where he started."[26]

Despite the rancor, both candidates tried to appear outwardly calm, poised, and confident. But the *St. Petersburg Times,* in the course of an unusual series of three editorials desperately promoting Collins, said he had not "seemed quite comfortable" attacking Faircloth, "which reveals one of the best reasons of all for supporting him."[27]

Collins planned to spend what little money he had in the final days on television and on trying to boost his turnout, but he again rebuffed a proposed televised debate, this one in Miami on election eve. "Never once have I condoned civil disobedience or lawlessness of any nature by anyone," Collins said in his final paid television appeal; it was his job at Selma "to strive to avoid disorder and violence and I did exactly that." Money was so short that he closed his St. Petersburg office.[28]

Collins won, but barely. Fewer voters turned out for the second round; among those who did, Collins lost votes from May 7 and Faircloth gained, so that Collins won the Democratic nomination by a margin of merely 2,993 votes out of the 818,385 that had been cast. Faircloth had mortally wounded him. Collins lost Orange, Alachua, and three other counties he had carried May 7, while gaining only Pasco, narrowly. Most ominously, his lead in Leon County shrank to 555 votes. Faircloth refused to concede until the afternoon of the next day and waited a week to say that he would vote for Collins in November and would do nothing to "actively prevent" his supporters from supporting the entire Democratic ticket. That was the extent of his support for Collins against Gurney.[29]

Collins cracked a wry joke about his first "Texas landslide," a reference to Lyndon Johnson's intensely disputed 87-vote margin in a 1948 Senate race. At his law office the morning after the runoff, Collins celebrated by blowing a loud blast on a conch shell. No one else felt joyful.[30]

He owed his nomination in large measure to Gurney, who had let the closet Republicans know that he preferred Collins for his November opponent. "My wife and I voted for you because it was Gurney's desire," a Live Oak voter told Collins. "We did not want Earl Faircloth because he had the aura of being a conservative," said James L. Martin, Gurney's administrative assistant at the time. (Pepper had confided to Gurney that Faircloth was "just as liberal as I am.")[31]

It was obvious even to Collins that his campaign needed a drastic overhaul. He fired Grotegut, whom he blamed for the campaign debt and for prodding him to remain hawkish on Vietnam, an issue on which "He was considerably firmer . . . than I was." Only two of the original workers were kept. In late October, a desperate moment, Grotegut hounded Collins for some of his back pay. Collins told him his timing was "ghoulish."[32]

Richard A. Pettigrew, a thirty-eight-year-old attorney and liberal legislator from Miami (who would become House Speaker three years later) replaced Grotegut at a fraction of his salary. It was a "sad experience, he said, "because there wasn't much that I could do." He had a dispirited candidate and a campaign organization that could not raise much money even though polls showed Collins leading Gurney. Regarding Vietnam as the major policy problem, he negotiated a new position of "de-Americanizing the war." That was what President Richard Nixon eventually did, but the idea did not help Collins. "Gurney took sides, either go in and win or get out. That fell on both sides of our position," Pettigrew said. Two years later, Collins said in a speech that the war "has been wrong from the beginning, and the wrong will continue as long as we remain involved."[33]

Collins found Mary Call crying because one of their oldest friends and campaign supporters, Eleanor Mizell McMullen, had sent word that she and her husband, his former law partner, would not back him this time on account of his views on race. The law firm itself was sharply conflicted. Duby Ausley, Charles's son, drew a salary from the firm while spending a month or more working full-time for the Collins campaign.[34]

In early August, Collins and thirty-five of his old friends and campaign workers met at Duby Ausley's home in Tallahassee. To encourage candor, the candidate was barred from part of the discussion. In a three-page summary, Ed Price told Collins that the low turnout and voter apathy had been "partially our fault, due to a failure to aggressively present positive issues." The consensus: The old Collins needed to reemerge—the man who would rather live with himself than win an election. But that would no longer be enough, Price said. Collins needed also to attack Gurney by making an issue of missed committee votes and by trying to link Gurney to Kirk, who had become an uncommonly controversial governor even by Florida standards.[35]

Gurney and Kirk were indeed close, partly because of an enmity between the governor and Cramer, whom Kirk accused of trying to displace him as the nominee against High. Kirk snubbed Florida's senior Republican office-holder by choosing Gurney to be master of ceremonies at his inauguration.[36] A chance event that day would cast a long shadow over Collins two years later.

A sudden downpour having caught Gurney unprepared, he put on a cheap plastic raincoat that a state trooper gave him. Someone took a picture and gave Martin a print; he and Gurney recognized something ineffable in the photograph, which they saved at the last moment from a studio where their advertising consultant intended to have the raincoat airbrushed out. The photograph became the one visual image that many Floridians remember from the campaign. It appeared in Gurney's newspaper ads, television spots, and, most effectively, on 550 billboards. The somewhat grainy picture showing a ruggedly handsome man in what appeared to be a trench coat could have been the cover photograph for a spy novel. Collins campaign staffers believed that the billboards, coupling Gurney's rugged image with sloganry such as "It's time to fight crime," put Gurney ahead.[37]

Another critical problem was that Collins's support was what politicians call "soft." His pollster, Pat Caddell, warned in mid-August that "many people are supporting Collins out of recognition rather than strong commitment."[38]

Collins tried to hammer Gurney over Vietnam, missing votes in Congress, and his total opposition to Johnson's antipoverty programs, but events overwhelmed him. In August, the memorably disorderly Democratic convention, where Chicago police attacked demonstrators outside and inside the hall, reinforced Gurney's law-and-order issue. Collins also did poorly in the first of their four televised debates; he looked much older and less attractive than Gurney, who projected vigor despite unremitting pain from a World War II combat injury. At Martin's suggestion, Gurney began calling Collins "Liberal LeRoy." Gurney built a fund-raising lead of more than $170,000 with a month to go and was able to spend three times as much as Collins in a single week. Within the Collins campaign, it appeared to Dan Millott, a young volunteer, that "everything was on a shoestring."[39]

The campaign was more about image and much less issue-driven than Collins's campaigns of 1954 and 1956. Nothing seemed to work for him. At a rally at Florida State University, where Collins called Gurney "war hungry" for advocating invasion of North Vietnam, Laos, and Cambodia, fewer than two hundred people showed up, most of them probably under the voting age of twenty-one. Gurney's self-discipline was simple and effective. As Martin described it, "We tried to stick to about three things: law and order, crime, and taxes. The next day it would be crime, law and order, and taxes."[40]

Almost everyone in the Collins campaign understood it was going badly. After Collins had received only polite applause at a Lakeland event, Ed Price concluded that the audience had already made up their minds. He and Mary Call agreed that Collins's prospects looked desolate. Collins felt it too. After Charles Bennett introduced him at a rally at Jacksonville, Collins privately told the congressman, "I sure appreciate your doing this. I hope it doesn't hurt your popularity."[41]

Collins received no help from the Democratic national ticket and only a pitiful $13,000 from the Florida Democratic Party. He suffered from the plunging popularity of the lame duck president who had appointed him to two offices, but at the risk of confirming the "liberal" label, he taped a television spot with U.S. Sen. Edward Kennedy, D-Mass, in which they denounced Gurney for wanting a "broader, wider war."[42]

It was time for Strom Thurmond's revenge. The South Carolina senator, who had switched to the Republican Party to support Goldwater in 1964, campaigned across North Florida with Gurney. A Gurney campaign staffer was George W. Bush, the future forty-third president, who served as a traveling aide for the candidate during a two-month break between basic training in Texas and his Air National Guard flight schooling at Moody Air Force Base in Georgia.[43]

Collins had the editorial support of about half of the urban press, notably excepting Pensacola, Ft. Lauderdale, Palm Beach, and Orlando. Twenty-two smaller dailies and weeklies backed Gurney. The *Orlando Sentinel* savaged Collins as hard under a new publisher as it had under Andersen in 1954, repeatedly referring to him as "Liberal LeRoy." One editorial, repeating the retracted Associated Press report from Columbia, said that Collins's "carefully cultivated liberalism of the late '50s and the 60's failed him. . . . He rose no further in the Great Society than a third-rate job that took him to Selma."[44]

The unkindest cut was by Collins's hometown newspaper. On the Sunday before the election, the *Tallahassee Democrat* said it was recommending neither Senate candidate "because we feel they offer such a clear choice of opposite political philosophies that the people neither need nor want much advise [*sic*] from us about how to vote." That this was simply a pretext was obvious from Malcolm Johnson's endorsement of Richard Nixon in a presidential race where the choices were equally clear.[45]

Though he understood it was a lost cause, Collins said he "still thought there was one chance in ten . . . right up to election day." He pinned that last hope on his signature campaign technique, a half-hour film shot documentary-style in black and white. "To Reach for Tomorrow" was televised during the final ten days of the campaign. Napolitan had insisted on it despite the skepticism of other campaign staffers that few voters would watch and that the money would be better spent on spot media. Collins loved the film, which featured him and daughter Darby, walking barefoot on the beach, in a candid and unrehearsed conversation about generational conflict. "Pretty good film," said one reporter at a preview screening, "but nobody's going to sit there for a half hour and watch it." Having staked everything on the film, Collins lacked the money to advertise it. By then, Gurney had outspent him $714,422 to $533,222, a disparity that was greater than it looked because Collins had to spend more to win the nomination.[46]

"This election is in the bag. We've got it made," Gurney predicted four days before the election. On November 5, he swept all but four of the sixty-seven counties with nearly 56 percent of the vote—1,131,499 for Gurney to 892,637 for Collins—to become Florida's first Republican senator since Reconstruction. Among Collins's four counties—Alachua, Dade, Hillsborough, and Monroe—only Dade had given him an emphatic margin, and by less than he had hoped.[47]

All that evening, as despair flooded his Tampa headquarters from almost everywhere else, Collins focused on each new return from Leon County. Resigned to losing the state, he was desperate for one last vote of confidence from his old friends and neighbors. But he lost Leon too, with 48 percent of the vote. It was an almost unbearable agony.[48]

Collins's voice quivered, though his eyes may have been the only dry ones in the room at his Tampa headquarters, when he conceded to Gurney shortly before 11 p.m. "This is the end of my political road," he said. "I think Florida was following a national trend—a trend which is generally referred to as a deeper conservatism. It seems to be a mood of the times. Frankly, I thought my record as governor and my personal affinity for the people of the state would allow me to overcome a handicap of this nature."[49]

Gurney's own analysis was accurate. As he saw it, the Democrats paid the price for eight decades of one-party rule. "They gather around one man and they suffer this terrible schizophrenia between liberals and conservatives," he said. "As long as you've got that, the Republicans can come in and pick up the pieces." And Collins had blundered by attacking him. "At that moment, he blew whatever image he had as Florida's elder statesman and the great former governor. I knew we had it."[50]

Florida's was one of five Senate seats the Republicans gained that day. Incumbent Democrats lost in Oregon, Maryland, and Pennsylvania. No Republican senator lost.[51]

"It wasn't the time that I could have won," Collins said in an oral history interview four years later. He believed that Faircloth had cost him the Senate seat by exposing his vulnerability to charges of liberalism.

"Actually, I was terribly disappointed," he said. "I wish I could have gone to the Senate and I think I could have made a strong senator. . . . But I think it was one of those things . . . a political leader ought to be able to face. The time may come when he won't win, and he may not win because he's done some things that he really should have done. But if you've got to win at the cost of not doing things you should do, what kind of victory do you have?"[52]

Chapter 31

Floridian of the Century

"Like Claude Pepper before him, Collins left the mainstream of his constituency," Malcolm Johnson wrote in the *Tallahassee Democrat*. "It was the civil rights issue that was the undoing of LeRoy Collins." Collins sent a four-page rebuttal. "Disappointed, yes. But bitter, never!" he wrote. "I wish you had used the word 'defeat' because frankly, while indeed I was defeated, I do not feel that I have been 'undone.'" Collins expressed pride in his record, hope that in time his principles would prevail, and comfort in knowing that there were "people in every walk of life who believe with me and in me." He had his law practice, his family, his friends, his fishing. "I am, indeed, a rich, rich man, still reaching for tomorrow," he said.[1]

Condolences poured in, Lyndon Johnson's among them: "I hope you can take more than a little satisfaction in knowing that you have served your State and your Nation with great distinction and ability. No election can ever take that away from you."[2]

But more disappointments were in store, the first just four months later when a coalition of students and professors failed to get Collins considered seriously for the vacant Florida State University presidency. "The last person we need in authority at FSU is a liberal politician with no academic background whatsoever," said an anonymously quoted member of the Board of Regents. Collins publicly disclaimed interest but encouraged the student leaders privately.[3]

He had an undisclosed campaign debt of some $125,000, enormous for the time. The accounts were so disordered that his final report, inaccurately reflecting a small surplus, was filed more than two months late. At Jacksonville, Bill Durden, who had left the bench to practice law, personally assumed a $10,000 note for local expenses that contributions had failed to match. A fund-raiser featuring Sen. Birch Bayh of Indiana raised a modest amount.[4] Having no invitation to rejoin his old law firm, and still pained by Leon County's rejection, Collins left Tampa for Miami to run Royal Castle System Inc., a struggling fast-food chain that had been founded by his friend and former Road Board appointee William D. Singer. But his heart was not in selling hamburgers.[5]

Collins hoped to pay off the debt by publishing a memoir, coauthored with Robert Akerman, a Florida Southern College professor. They titled it "The Man in the Middle: A Story of America's Race Crisis," but one publishing house that had expressed interest called for unacceptable changes including a racially provocative title. "The whole thing is too quiet and reasoned and even-tempered," one editor wrote to the author John D. MacDonald, a friend who had raised money for the campaign.[6]

Collins abandoned the memoir. At Nelson Poynter's suggestion, he wrote and privately published one of a different nature, *Forerunners Courageous: Stories of Frontier Florida*, that he described as "ninety percent history and 10 percent fiction." Collins had been collecting some of the stories for years and said he would have written the book even if he had no debt to defray because "I had fun doing this." It included the history of the Grove and a soul-baring free-verse account, "Growing Up," of racial prejudice in Tallahassee. Aided by sales to friends, *Forerunners* substantially settled the debt.[7]

Collins made an uncomfortable appearance in Washington to support G. Harrold Carswell's ill-fated nomination to the U.S. Supreme Court. After working briefly in the Collins firm, Carswell had been confirmed easily as the United States attorney for North Florida, as a federal district judge, and to the Fifth Circuit Court of Appeals. With a seat on the nation's highest court at stake, liberal senators and civil rights organizations began dissecting his record—which even a supporter conceded to be "mediocre"—for evidence of racism. Among other issues, Carswell (and Collins) had been among the contributors who helped convert Tallahassee's municipal country club to private ownership in 1956 in what appeared to be a segregation strategy. The most damaging evidence turned up in a long-forgotten speech by Carswell, as a political candidate in Georgia in 1948, saying, "I yield to no man as a fellow candidate, or as a fellow citizen, in the firm, vigorous belief in the principles of white supremacy, and I shall always be so governed."[8]

Carswell, telling the Senate Judiciary Committee that the views he had expressed then were "obnoxious and abhorrent" to him now, had Collins as his leadoff character witness. Collins insisted that Carswell "is no racist. He is no white supremacist. He is no segregationist." But Sen. Edward Kennedy's staff, leading the fight against Carswell, told other opponents that Collins had conceded that his heart was not in the fight. Nonetheless, Collins telephoned Roger Wilkins hoping to persuade him to lobby his uncle, NAACP executive director Roy Wilkins, on Carswell's behalf. Wilkins laughed. "I said, 'Governor, there's only two things wrong with that proposition. I couldn't move my Uncle Roy on this issue if I wanted to, and, number two, I don't want to.' I said Carswell doesn't belong on the Supreme Court."[9] Most senators did not think so either, and Carswell's nomination failed with fifty-one senators voting no. On hearing that Carswell had blamed "ultra-liberals" in the Senate, Collins denounced Carswell's "demagoguery."[10]

Meanwhile, Collins had wearied quickly of the hamburger business and returned to the Grove, this time to stay, late in 1969. He had built a beach house on Dog Island, southwest of the old family cottage on the mainland at St. Teresa. Dog Island, accessible only by boat, was his retreat from politics; his "lifesaver," as daughter Mary Call described it. "Man had his origins in the sea," Collins remarked in 1970, "and I think that the sea is a good place to go for renewal." He often went there alone, because, as his wife complained, his boat "only has one speed—wide open." Collins also acquired a fifty-acre farm with a pond in nearby Georgia, where he often fished.[11]

There would never be an invitation to rejoin the law firm he had helped to establish. The younger members objected privately that he would bring in less money than he took out. Collins, hurt by the snub, assumed incorrectly that it was another reprisal for his views on race. Within a few months, however, a casual inquiry through a friend led to his joining the rival law firm of Ervin, Pennington, Varn, and Jacobs. "We were flattered to have him come, we knew he was a good man," said partner Robert M. Ervin, a former Florida Bar president and brother of the Supreme Court justice and former attorney general Richard Ervin, who would join the firm later. Collins was "of counsel," which allowed him to choose his cases. Ervin said that a lawsuit Collins persuaded skeptical partners to accept became "one of the most lucrative cases we ever had." Collins remained with the firm for twenty years, until his death.[12]

But some detractors claimed his legal experience was too thin for service on the Florida Supreme Court. His last great disappointment came during his fourth year with the Ervin firm. Despite heavy lobbying by supporters, including a personal appeal from Ervin to the chairman of the new Supreme Court Judicial Nominating Commission, Collins did not get even a courtesy interview. The nominating process was a reform introduced by the new governor, Reubin Askew, whose office dismayed some Collins supporters by refusing to intervene on his behalf. Some commissioners argued that Collins had been absent too long from the practice of law. "I think that was mostly humbuggery," wrote Daytona Beach newspaper publisher Herbert Davidson after a commission member briefed him on the closed-door deliberations. "I believe you must have had some real enemies on that commission and that they were certain that if your name had been submitted Reubin would have picked you."[13]

The eventual appointee, Circuit Judge Ben F. Overton of St. Petersburg, had been a key ally of the nominating commission chairman, Dixie Beggs, in persuading a reluctant Supreme Court to adopt a stricter code of judicial ethics. Beggs may have believed that Overton would have no chance with Askew if Collins were to be another nominee. Collins said nothing publicly, but he was deeply hurt. However, he did not let the disappointment permanently impair his relationship with Askew.[14]

Collins had been one of a group of political confidants who met with Askew at the Grove to advise him how to discourage an expected overture to be Democratic presidential nominee George McGovern's running mate in 1972. (Collins again lent his home and advice to Askew at a strategy session when Askew was planning what turned out to be an unsuccessful campaign for the 1984 Democratic presidential nomination.) Also in 1972, following a U.S. Supreme Court decision that effectively invalidated all death penalty laws, Askew appointed Collins to a commission to recommend whether Florida should enact a new law, and if so, how. Collins argued passionately but unsuccessfully against reenactment.[15]

In 1974, Askew appointed Collins to the first Florida Commission on Ethics, where he advocated strict enforcement of the ethics code, indulged his passion for exacting draftsmanship, and chaired a committee that recommended unavailingly that the Legislature strengthen the commission's investigative powers. But he did not share Askew's belief that public officials should disclose all their financial interests. He considered it an invasion of privacy and obtained a commission opinion that he was not required to identify Ervin firm clients whom he did not personally represent.[16]

En route to a meeting, Collins played a practical joke, asking the taxi driver if he had heard of LeRoy Collins. Yes, the man said, and he would like to meet him. "Put it there, buddy," Collins said, holding out his hand. The startled driver ran off the road, but no one was harmed.[17]

Court-ordered reapportionment cleared the way for a new constitution in 1968 that provided for mandatory population-based redistricting every ten years. It incorporated another of Collins's early visions in a provision unique to Florida that establishes a thirty-seven-member Constitution Revision Commission to propose amendments directly to the people at periodic intervals. Collins asked Askew for one of the governor's fifteen appointments to the first commission. There was no question this time; on July 6, 1977, Askew introduced Collins to the others as "one of the finest governors that any state ever had at any time." Chesterfield Smith, the principal architect of the new constitution, said Collins was "the greatest public servant that Florida ever had."[18]

Collins waged three personal crusades over the ensuing nine months: for abolition of the Cabinet system, for a one-house legislature, and for replacing the death penalty with mandatory life sentences for murderers. The commission disagreed on all but the first. On December 8, 1977, Collins knew he would lose the debate but spoke for an hour to make his case for posterity that Florida should put the death penalty "behind us in a dark closet that will always stay closed." Relating how he had been persuaded against witnessing an execution, Collins declared, "If there is anything in this state that the governor should not see, it should not be going on."[19]

Voters rejected all of the commission's recommendations, partly because of controversy over an unrelated casino gambling initiative and because Cabinet supporters had maneuvered the commission into recommending abolition instead of a smaller-Cabinet compromise that would have had more appeal to voters. Collins had sponsored the alternative at Askew's request, but it failed on a tie vote.[20]

The commission's work was not wasted. Many of its proposals were embodied in subsequent legislation and constitutional amendments. Among these, notably, are a three-member mini-Cabinet adopted in 1998 and a 1980 privacy amendment that the Florida Supreme Court construed to guarantee a woman's right to an abortion.

Collins never thought about retiring and kept the busiest public-speaking schedule of Florida's six living former governors. He also took up jogging, switching his route to a nearby cemetery after Mary Call objected that he was wearing out the lawn at the Grove. "I get a joy out of this that goes beyond the physical," he said. He said he did his best thinking while jogging, but he eventually wore out his knee as well and settled for walking.[21]

Ed Price arranged for Collins to join him on the board of directors of Tropicana Inc., a major producer of frozen citrus concentrate. In 1972, there was yet another commencement speech at Randolph-Macon, this time for Darby's class, which he said would be his last, "for now I have run out of daughters." Another Askew appointment put him on the board of Florida Legal Services Inc. He declined an invitation to review a biography of Edward Ball because of "a very long entrenched bias against Mr. Ball," whom he assumed felt the same way about him. Collins served briefly on a newly created National Advertising Review Board—for which *Broadcasting* attacked him again—before deciding the panel was powerless.[22]

Collins was keenly interested in young people. Interviewed by Julia Sullivan Chapman, a University of South Florida graduate student in history researching the Community Relations Service, he subsidized her travel to Washington and had the agency's confidential files opened to her. Susan Cary, a United Farm Workers organizer who consulted Collins on a political matter, went to law school at his recommendation. Collins contributed $5,000 to the Florida Historical Society to establish a prize fund for students writing on history; one of the awards bears his name.[23]

Collins became fast friends and a fishing companion of the state's young attorney general, Jim Smith, a conservative Democrat, whom he endorsed for governor in 1986. Their friendship survived not only Smith's advocacy of the death penalty but his subsequent switch to the Republican Party. "I think the best thing about Governor Collins was his ability to bring out the best in you," Smith said. However, Collins was slow to forgive his son for becoming a Republican and a potential Senate candidate against a Democratic incumbent in 1988. The younger Collins declined to run soon after the news broke, acknowledging that the GOP sought him because of his father's reputation, "which he has earned and I have not."[24]

Collins was outraged by a 1980 Florida Supreme Court decision invalidating the anti-Klan law on the premise that it made even holiday masks potentially illegal. He recruited sponsors for a new law prohibiting the wearing of masks when intended to intimidate the exercise of civil rights. "While many Floridians may have forgotten the evils of the hooded night riders carrying their threats and demands for people to leave town, or not to vote in public elections, or to change their positions on public issues, there are many of us who still remember," he wrote in an op-ed article solicited by the *St. Petersburg Times*.[25]

Much had changed in Florida since 1968, and it became widely acknowledged that Collins had deserved better from the voters. Many thought so because of the circumstances that limited Gurney to a single term. He abandoned his reelection campaign after his indictment in July 1974 on federal conspiracy, bribery, and perjury charges alleging that he and several aides extorted money from real estate developers seeking mortgage approvals from the Federal Housing Administration. Gurney was acquitted in two trials that left his career and finances in ruins.[26]

The man he had defeated was accumulating more honors and awards than any other Floridian. In 1978, when the Florida chapter of the American Civil Liberties Union recognized him for his stand on civil rights, a message from Vernon Jordan of the National Urban League said he had been a "lone voice in the wilderness crying out for justice and fairness." In December 1988, Florida State University announced the establishment of the Collins Center of Public Policy (now the LeRoy Collins Institute) as an endowed research arm of its law school. At a retirement ceremony for the state's director of natural resources, Collins was credited for Florida's extensive park system. In May 1989, the Florida Economics Club at Tallahassee honored him with its first life achievement award. "The best measure of a public official is not while he is in office, but in the years that follow," Stephen O'Connell said on that occasion. "Today he is the most respected, admired, and loved man ever to hold office in our state."[27]

Collins's last years were financially secure. In 1981, the City of Tallahassee bought for a park some land for which Collins and a partner had taken out a large mortgage nearly thirty years earlier. Each received $332,750 in cash and income tax deductions worth $64,750. Replying to a friend who asked teasingly whether it was not an "obscene" profit, Collins said, "Not when it happens to you."[28] In 1985, he and Mary Call sold the Grove to the state for $2,285,500 with a contract allowing them to lease it back for the duration of her life. When his son observed that he would have to leave the Grove if he survived Mary Call, Collins said he would not want to live there without her. The Grove, which predates Florida's Capitol, is the only Tallahassee antebellum structure that has not been moved or extensively modified, and eventually will be a museum.[29]

In 1983, Collins began a series of commentaries for Florida Public Radio on issues ranging from Florida's environment to foreign policy. Three years later, *St. Petersburg Times* editorial page editor Robert Pittman recruited Collins to write a series of weekend columns rich in political lore, personal and Florida history, his convictions on public issues, and human interest. He wrote, edited, and rewrote them as exactingly as he had his public speeches. There were eighty-three columns between January 1986 and July 2, 1990, when Collins wrote briefly but optimistically of the cancer that was killing him. Characteristically, he devoted half the column to his beloved retreat at Dog Island. "The sand dunes, the storm-twisted trees, sea oats waving, the stretching sea and sky, are all so therapeutic," he wrote. "The unspoiled naturalness of the place is a beacon of local care for holding on to God's plan in dealing with such precious resources of nature."[30]

Collins had injured a shoulder pulling weeds on Dog Island. Insisting on surgery to repair it, he checked into Tallahassee Memorial Hospital in May 1989 for a presumably routine procedure. Two days after the operation he complained of shortness of breath and an X-ray was ordered. Both lungs were riddled with inoperable cancer. He had not felt even slightly ill; now he heard that he had perhaps six months to live. The cancer had originated in a malignant polyp removed from his colon three years earlier. "They say they got everything," he had said then. There would be no false expectations this time. "My doctor is very encouraging—not that I will overcome the cancer, but that the quality of my life and the time of it will have a good run yet," he wrote to a friend in January 1990. Collins said he would hardly know he had cancer were it not for the chemotherapy, which "reminds me of it very forcefully."[31]

There was one last grand party for his eighty-first birthday in March 1990, with a treasure hunt that led Collins to a gift awaiting him inside an unused gatehouse at the Grove. Intended by the family to symbolize life and hope, it was a black Labrador puppy that he named "Amazing Grace."[32]

Despite his weakened condition, Collins insisted on waiting at the end of his driveway in September of that year to watch President George H. W. Bush arrive for a visit to Gov. Bob Martinez at the governor's mansion next door. At Martinez's suggestion, the president walked back to greet Collins, who was moved by the gesture. That was the last the public saw of him.[33]

Collins insisted on being taken twice to Dog Island during his final months. He managed the stairs at the house and even a short swim. "If we can go down there I can beat this thing," he said. Fighting to the end, he said that he wanted "very heroic" measures to be taken, although he contradicted the instruction by consenting to Hospice care at home. "I'm not afraid of dying," he told his family, "but I don't want to leave you all. I just wish I had ten more years." Following a visit by a clergyman, Collins asked whether death was imminent. "I don't think so, Dad," Mary Call Proctor said. "Goodness," Collins replied, "this thing is poorly organized." James Clendenin was also fatally ill. Collins sent word to the retired editor that "If I was a good governor or a bad governor, I was better because you were there."[34]

Five days before his death, Collins was determined to get out of his wheelchair and walk back to his bed, simply to show his son that he still could. "The nurse was on one side and I was on the other and we were both carrying a lot of weight, but he just wanted to show us that he still had a lot of fight left," said LeRoy Jr.[35]

Collins invited Ed Price to the Grove to ask him to speak at his funeral. "But I want it clearly understood, I want no weeping and wailing, I want no mourning at the bar. I want a celebration," he said. Hundreds of people sent cards and letters for his eighty-second birthday, which he was too ill to observe. He died peacefully two days later, at 2:45 p.m. on March 11, 1991, with his wife and two of their daughters reading Psalms by his side.[36]

The Florida House of Representatives unanimously declared him "Floridian of the Century." During tributes in the Senate, Sen. Arnett Girardeau of Jacksonville, one of fourteen African Americans serving in the Legislature, said he had remained in Florida only because of Collins, who "stood tall and in many instances he stood alone."[37]

Collins was buried in the Call family plot behind the Grove in a private ceremony attended by family members and close friends. Sand from Dog Island was sprinkled in his grave. Later that day, more than a thousand people attended a public memorial service at St. John's Episcopal Church. It was a celebration of his life, as Price had promised. Price recounted their last conversation, by telephone, three weeks earlier. "He said, 'Ed, I'm going to tell you goodbye. I want you to know that I'm ready,' and in that soft-spoken voice, always thinking of someone else, the last words he said were, 'God bless you.'"[38]

Collins was eulogized throughout the state and in Congress. "Tallahassee just won't be Tallahassee for me without Roy," Allen Morris said. "It will be like another city."[39]

Chapter 32

The Glory of Government

Collins devoted his public life to a philosophy utterly opposite the view of some present-day cynics that government is an instrument of evil. He denounced such attitudes as "a repudiation of the greatest political effort of man during his long course of enlightened progress." The government must be strong, he said, because "it takes strength to prevent brutality, to avoid evil, and to defend against oppression." In one of his last interviews, he spoke of the opportunity to help people as "the glory of government."[1]

Collins saw his legacy embodied in a younger generation of idealistic leaders who often claimed him as their inspiration. There has not been another overtly racial campaign like that of 1968. Two years later, Reubin Askew, a racial liberal who profoundly admired Collins, defeated Faircloth in the Democratic gubernatorial runoff primary and went on to oust Claude R. Kirk Jr. just four months after a theatrical but unsuccessful attempt by the incumbent governor to obstruct desegregation of the Manatee County public schools.[2]

The idealism that animated Collins's crusades for community colleges, fair apportionment, and a modern state constitution—the three greatest institutional reforms for which he is credited—carried over to his disciples. Richard A. Pettigrew, who had tried to rescue his Senate campaign, helped to pass the new constitution and was the chief sponsor of a massive reorganization act that ensued.

There has been an ironic epilogue to the reapportionment struggle: computer-assisted redistricting so precise as to ensure the reelection of every eligible incumbent in the 2004 elections. An initiative campaign is aimed at barring such gerrymanders. The initiative process is another of the constitutional reforms inspired by his struggle with the Pork Chop Gang.

"Remember that feisty Florida legislature back in the early 70s," remarked Leo Sandon, a professor of religion at Florida State University. "I think a lot of those guys saw themselves as in the league of LeRoy Collins. He pretty much inspired a generation of young progressives into self-consciously taking the torch."[3]

Any balanced evaluation of his record pertaining to civil rights must acknowledge that it was mixed, that for a time Florida practiced "Moderation *AS* Massive Resistance."[4] Florida's 1956 pupil-assignment law helped to forestall any significant degree of elementary and secondary school desegregation until long after it had become commonplace in the Upper South and Border States. It took Title VI of the Civil Rights Act of 1964—which mandated desegregation in programs receiving federal education funds—to wear down Florida's institutionalized resistance to integration of primary and secondary schools.[5] But on the other hand, desegregation in higher education, though slow, scarcely made a ripple. There were no riots like those that had obstructed the integration of public universities in Georgia, Alabama, and Mississippi. Apart from St. Augustine, Florida dutifully complied with the public accommodation provisions of the 1964 Civil Rights Act. It is highly improbable that the record would be so largely peaceful had Johns won in 1954 or Lowry in 1956.

William R. Jones, a professor of religion and director of the Afro-American Studies Program at Florida State University, asserted in a 1995 article that Collins's civil rights legacy should be judged by a harsher standard than the prevailing view. "Even though Collins did express sympathy in later speeches and writings for the unfinished business of equalizing the economic and educational attainments of black Americans, the effect of his leadership was to keep the system rolling along in a changed form," Jones wrote. C. U. Smith, an African-American sociologist at Florida A&M University who disagrees with Jones, asserts that what mattered about Collins was "that he was able to change, and [that] he was able to state that change" in the face of overt hostility among whites. "In the end, Collins redeemed himself," said the Rev. Henry Marion Steele, son of the Tallahassee bus boycott leader. State Rep. Arthenia Joyner of Tampa, a Florida legislator who as a student joined the lunch-counter sit-ins and was jailed later for trying to desegregate Tallahassee's movie theaters, says Collins's Jacksonville broadcast "gave us some good feeling to know that the leader of the state supported our efforts."[6]

Though the landmark civil rights acts of 1964 and 1965 owed primarily to the physical courage of demonstrators who risked and sometimes lost their lives, the moral courage Collins voiced in his memorable speeches in Jacksonville and Columbia, South Carolina, contributed to the political consensus for the legislation. "I read that speech now," Collins said of the Jacksonville address seventeen years later, "and it seems so puny."[7] But in the context of its times, it was revolutionary rhetoric for a Southern governor.

Collins was an inspiration to liberal editors such as Eugene Patterson, Ralph McGill's protégé and successor. "He made our job at the newspaper, mine and Mr. McGill's at the *Atlanta Constitution*, so much easier," Patterson said. "We had somebody to quote . . . shaming Marvin Griffin, the segregationist buffoon who was the governor of Georgia." Patterson said that Collins's example also inspired other governors, notably Ernest Vandiver and Carl Sanders of Georgia, with the courage "to differ from the bawling, bellowing, bull-headed segs in Alabama, Mississippi, Louisiana, Arkansas." All three forfeited their political futures, but as Patterson observed, leadership is not "a matter of winning for yourself, it's a matter of leading the folks."[8]

Collins was succeeded for ten years by three governors who were at best indifferent to civil rights, but none attempted to roll back what had been achieved. Kirk's Manatee County escapade was the only attempt to defy a federal court; he called it off after three days to avoid fines of $10,000 a day.[9]

With Askew's election, the Collins philosophy prevailed again at Tallahassee, personified by a new governor who regarded Collins as the example "that I consciously tried to follow."[10] Askew called on Floridians to accept busing as a lesser evil than segregation. He was the first governor to appoint African Americans to a significant number of offices; among them was the first black justice of the Florida Supreme Court.

"I think I have pursued public service because of LeRoy Collins," said Janet Reno, then attorney general of the United States, at the dedication of Leon County's LeRoy Collins Library.[11] When the Legislature convened in 1996, Speaker Peter Wallace of St. Petersburg sent to the archives for the original interposition resolution and read to the House what Collins had written on it. "Today I have that document in my hand," Wallace said, "and I can tell you that it feels alive with the history of that time and with the courage of the man who wrote so boldly across it."[12]

Republican Gov. Jeb Bush, despite holding strikingly different views on the proper role of government, has referred to Collins as Florida's greatest governor. In an interview, Bush cited Collins's "integrity and his commitment to principle" and his determination "to move Florida from a Southern agriculture state to an industrial one, . . . it "shaped our future significantly."[13]

Arriving for work one day, Bush observed something out of place in the corridor outside his Capitol office where portraits of the eight most recent former governors are displayed. Upon the arrival of the newest portrait, the Collins portrait had been sent to storage. Bush ordered it returned to an alcove immediately outside his reception room where he has his picture taken with schoolchildren and other visitors, and where he intends for the Collins portrait to remain in perpetuity.[14]

Collins relished telling a story about that portrait. Visiting the Capitol long after he had been governor, he saw a group of school children looking at it. "You know," said their teacher, "I think he passed away." Collins, grinning, spoke up: "Oh no, M'am, I want to assure you he's very close alive."[15]

Chapter 33

Epilogue

Collins profoundly regretted that he had been unable to stop the plunder of Florida's submerged lands. Not long before his death, he said that on flights to and from Tampa he always faced away from the airplane window to avoid seeing what he called the "monstrous desecration" of Boca Ciega Bay.[1] In 1967, the reapportioned Legislature passed effective controls that Kirk signed into law.

In 1962, two of Willis McCall's deputies were accused of fabricating plaster casts of footprints and tire tracks to send two black men to death row on rape and robbery charges. The accusations, recalling the Irvin case, were backed by an FBI conclusion that the plaster casts had been made of footprints with no feet in the shoes. But the statute of limitations had expired, and McCall reinstated the deputies.[2] He remained Lake County sheriff until June 1972, when a grand jury accused him of fatally injuring a black prisoner by kicking him with a cowboy boot. Askew promptly suspended him, earning a private compliment from Collins, who said, "You did one of the things I always wanted to do."[3] Askew refused to lift the suspension even after a jury acquitted McCall of second-degree murder. McCall ran for reelection that fall but lost to a Republican, Guy Bliss, who said the people "just had enough of his type."[4]

Prison reports described Irvin as a "polite and courteous" inmate, a "consistently good worker" who hoped for and deserved parole. But the Parole Commission was slow to forget that it had opposed the commutation and did not release him until January 1968, nearly nineteen years after his arrest. He died of natural causes thirteen months later during his first visit home since his conviction.[5]

The first black to attend the University of Florida was not the first to graduate. George Starke withdrew after a year and a half, the pressure of being a pioneer having been too great. He made a career in business and eventually joined the University of Florida alumni association. W. George Allen, a military veteran who would become the university's first black law graduate, enrolled the year after Starke left. The university would not admit him to its married student housing facilities. "A few of the students were ugly," Allen said. He dropped one class after hearing the professor say that small claims courts were for "poor white trash and niggers." But most students were supportive, and Allen formed lasting friendships with several of Florida's future political leaders.[6]

The murders of Harry and Harriette Moore, the nation's first civil rights martyrs, were never solved.

John B. Orr Jr., who had been defeated for advocating desegregation, lost a comeback race for the Florida Senate. His career and several of his seven marriages were marred by alcoholism, but he joined Alcoholics Anonymous in 1966 and was elected Dade County mayor in 1972. He died of cancer two years later.[7]

With Hildy Ellis legally adopted, it was safe for the family to leave Florida for Washington, D.C., where she was told why Collins was a household hero. "If I grew up with any prejudices," she said, "it was against the judiciary of Boston and the State of Massachusetts." She held nothing against the church or her natural mother, whom she eventually met and with whom she remained in touch. Frances Ellis died at Silver Spring, Maryland, thirteen years after the adoption. Hildy lost her father four years later.[8]

The voluntary codes that Collins had extolled at the National Association of Broadcasters were undone by the Justice Department in what Newton Minow called "a moment of massive stupidity." The government considered them to violate the antitrust laws. In 1967, the Federal Communications Commission declared tobacco advertising to be subject to the fairness doctrine, entitling antismoking advocates to free air time. Collins predicted accurately that it would shift tobacco advertising into other media the government could not regulate. The tobacco industry contrived a law banning tobacco advertising from the public spectrum so that broadcasters no longer would be required to air the highly effective antismoking public service messages.[9]

Virgil Hawkins really did want to be a lawyer, not just a "human crowbar" for the NAACP, as one newspaper had denigrated him.[10] He finally left

Florida to earn a degree from the New England School of Law in 1964, only to find that Florida refused to let him take its Bar examination because the school was not accredited until after he had graduated. Hawkins had long since accepted the death of his dream when the Florida Supreme Court admitted Justice Richard Ervin's brother Ben Ervin to the Bar, despite four examination failures, on the premise that military service kept him from enrolling in a Florida school in time to be automatically licensed upon graduation. Hawkins won a similar dispensation when Justice Joseph W. Hatchett Jr., the African American whom Askew had appointed to the Supreme Court, reminded his colleagues of its "lawless defiance" of the U.S. Supreme Court. On February 9, 1977, at the age of seventy, Virgil Hawkins was sworn in to the Bar, but it became painfully evident that he should not have attempted to practice alone. Eight years later, facing his second set of Bar ethical grievances and a criminal charge of misappropriating his nephew's trust fund, Hawkins resigned to avoid disbarment. "When I get to heaven," he told the court, "I want to be a member of the Florida Bar." A few months before his death from a stroke, Hawkins told an interviewer: "I know what I did. I integrated schools in Florida. No one can take that away from me." On the petition of Harley Herman, a white Lake County lawyer, the Supreme Court posthumously restored Hawkins to good standing in the Bar "so that the errors in judgment made by Hawkins in his unsuccessful attempt to begin to practice law as a man in his seventies, do not overshadow the value of his service to humanity."[11]

Collins regretted what he and other Florida officials had done to Hawkins. At a chance meeting with Herman, the former governor thanked him for the posthumous reinstatement. The Legislature bestowed Hawkins's name on the University of Florida's third-year law clinic, where students train to represent indigent clients. In 1999, to commemorate the fiftieth anniversary of his lawsuit, the court ceremonially apologized for its "great mistake" in having barred Hawkins from the university. Two years later, the University of Florida, on a unanimous vote of the Faculty Senate, granted Hawkins its first posthumous degree.[12]

The Legislature—now under Republican control—suspended the runoff primary for the 2002 and 2004 elections. The ostensible reason was that with the primaries having been moved to September, election supervisors did not have enough time to accommodate three rounds of voting in an eight-week span, but the action also suited Republican campaign strategy that year. In

2005, the Legislature voted over scattered bipartisan opposition to repeal the runoff permanently. The Associated Press wrote its epitaph on June 22:

"Florida's runoff primary election, which catapulted some of the state's most renowned politicians into office, became a historical footnote Wednesday when Gov. Jeb Bush signed a bill eliminating it."[13]

To nearly everyone who had a hand in that, the 1954 Collins-Johns race—the most significant of all Florida's runoffs—was merely a historical abstraction. Only a few were old enough to remember or care how differently Florida might have fared had that election gone the other way.

Notes

Chapter 1. "I Will Do the Right Thing"

1. Strickland, Davis, and Strickland, 108–10; Eugene C. Patterson interview, Jan. 21, 2004.

2. *Tampa Tribune*, June 18, 1953.

3. *Plessy v. Ferguson*, 163 U.S. 537 (1896). Congressional Quarterly, *Guide to the U.S. Supreme Court*, 589–91. *Miami Herald, Tampa Tribune*, May 18, 1954.

4. John Perry interview, July 16, 2001; e-mail to the author, July 19, 2001; *St. Petersburg Times*, Mar. 4, 5, Apr. 8, 1954; LeRoy Collins, interview with Tom Wagy, Apr. 10, 1976, tape recording in possession of the author.

5. *St. Petersburg Times*, Mar. 6, 1954.

6. *Miami Herald*, May 18, 1954.

7. Florida State Archives (hereafter, FSA), series 776, carton 116.

8. *Tampa Tribune*, May 19, 1954.

9. Morris, *Florida Handbook*, 6th ed., 291–92, 294.

10. *St. Petersburg Times*, Jan. 9, 1957.

11. Ibid., Mar. 21, 1960.

12. Speech to Leadership Conference on Civil Rights, Sept. 11, 1964, University of South Florida LeRoy Collins Papers (hereafter, USF), box 64.

13. Wagy, *Governor LeRoy Collins of Florida*, 197. (Hereafter, all references to Wagy are to this work unless otherwise indicated.)

14. Mary Call Collins interview, July 18, 2003.

15. *St. Petersburg Times*, Mar. 13, 2001.

16. Remarks to Daytona Beach Junior College dedication, Florida State University LeRoy Collins collection, post-governor speeches and interviews (hereafter, FSU post-governor speeches), box 1, folder 10; *Florida Handbook*, 29th ed., 622, USF box 331.

Chapter 2. "This Is Where I Stood"

1. *The Florida Handbook*, 23rd ed., 566, 575.

2. *Florida Statistical Abstract 2002,* 211; Colburn, "Florida Politics in the Twentieth Century" in Gannon, *A New History*, 345; *Florida Handbook*, 5th ed., 148; *Fisel v. Wynns*, 667 So. 2d 761 (1996); *St. Petersburg Times* LeRoy Collins column (hereafter, Collins column), Feb. 16, 1987; unpublished memoir in personal papers of Murray Wadsworth.

3. Wagy, 7–8.

4. Collins oral history, May 11, 1981, FSU post-governor speeches, box 6, folder 20.

5. Ellis and Rogers, *Favored Land*, 79, 120; Paisley, 38–39, 74, 99.

6. Ellis and Rogers, *Favored Land*, 7, 10.

7. *Florida Handbook*, 29th ed., 466–67; Coles, 147.

8. Brown, Canter, Jr., "The Civil War," in Gannon, *A New History*, 243–44.

9. Coles, 316, 327–60.

10. Speech to Delta Sigma Rho/Tau Kappa Alpha, Indianapolis, Ind., Mar. 31, 1964, USF box 39; Collins column, Mar. 10, 1986; Collins, *Forerunners Courageous*, 69–71.

11. Hazel Richards, interview with Tom Wagy, Oct. 6, 1975, tape in possession of the author.

12. Bailey, 2–15.

13. Williamson, 22.

14. *New York Times*, Aug. 26, 2001.

15. Williamson, 21–22.

16. Woodward, 7–26, 31–64.

17. Shofner, "Custom, Law, and History," 289–91.

18. Williamson, 176; Branch, *Parting the Waters*, 54–55.

19. *Plessy v. Ferguson*, 163 U.S. 537 (1896).

20. Ellis and Rogers, *Favored Land*, 81, 121.

21. Brown, "The Civil War," 232.

22. Collins, *Forerunners Courageous*, 88–89.

23. Vandiver, 5; Colburn and Scher, *Florida's Gubernatorial Politics*, 13.

24. Colburn, "Rosewood and America," 175–92.

25. Stetson Kennedy, remarks to conference, "The Civil Rights Movement in Florida," University of South Florida, St. Petersburg (hereafter, USF conference), June 2–5, 2004.

26. *Tallahassee Democrat*, July 7, 1937; Florida Department of Corrections, www.dc.state.fl.us/oth/deathrow/execlist2.html.

27. *Tallahassee Democrat*, July 20, 21, 1937.

28. *Florida Times-Union*, May 28, 1941.

29. Wagy, 21.

30. Shofner, 293; Green, 45–46; W. Dexter Douglass interviews, Sept. 10, 2001, May 21, 2002.

31. David, 283–97; Allen Morris Papers, Florida State University, box 244, folder 6.

32. Douglass interviews.

33. Ibid.

34. *Tampa Tribune*, Oct. 1, 1953.

35. LeRoy Collins, undated memoir, personal files of Murray Wadsworth.

36. Wagy, 7.

37. Ibid.

38. Collins column, Mar. 23, 1987.

39. Wagy, 9–10.

40. Ibid.

41. Ibid.

42. Richards interview; Mary Call Collins, oral history interview, FSU post-governor speeches, box 6, folder 20.

43. Richards interview.

44. LeRoy Collins, interview with Lucy Morgan, Nov. 17, 1989, notes in her possession; Collins and Akerman, 32.

45. Collins column, June 5, 1989.

46. Collins oral history interview with Elizabeth Messer (Tallahassee Junior League), Nov. 24, 1975, FSA M77-164

47. J. D. Williamson interview, May 20, 2002.

48. Collins column, Mar. 30, 1987.

49. Collins and Akerman, 10.

50. Murray Wadsworth interview, June 12, 2001.

51. Mary Call Collins interviews, Sept. 20, 2001, Jan. 7, 2004.

52. Wagy, 10.

53. Collins columns, Mar. 30, 1987, June 5, 1989.

54. Collins column, Mar. 30, 1987.

55. Collins and Akerman, 16.

56. Collins column, Mar. 30, 1987.

57. Messer interview.

58. Collins column, Mar. 30, 1987.

59. Collins, *Forerunners Courageous*, 87–88.

60. Wagy, 11; Wagy, *A South to Save*, 16; Messer interview.

61. Speech to Tallahassee Chamber of Commerce, Dec. 12, 1957, USF box 21; LeRoy Collins, interview with Tom Wagy, Sept. 17, 1979, tape in possession of the author; LeRoy Collins Jr. interview, June 6, 2001.

62. Collins, *Forerunners Courageous*, 91–94.

63. Ibid.

64. LeRoy Collins, speech to Alabama Council on Human Relations, Jan. 30, 1965, USF box 64.

65. Collins, *Forerunners Courageous*, 93–94.

Chapter 3. A Young Man in a Hurry

1. Collins and Akerman, 17; Messer interview, 31.

2. LeRoy Collins, speech to Florida Blue Key, Nov. 11, 1955, USF box 21; Mary Call Collins interviews, Sept. 20, 2001, July 18, 2003; FSU post-governor correspondence, box 13, folder 3.

3. *Tallahassee Democrat*, Mar. 23, 1953.

4. Mary Call Collins interviews, Sept. 20, 2001, July 18, 2003.

5. Collins column, Feb. 8, 1988.

6. James, 60.

7. Wagy, 13.

8. University of Florida, letter to the author, May 28, 2002.

9. Messer interview, 31.

10. Ibid.

11. Wagy, 13.

12. Collins column, June 5, 1989.

13. Collins column, Feb. 8, 1988; Langum and Walthall, 125–47. (Cumberland Law is now part of Samford University at Birmingham, Alabama.)

14. Wagy, 14; Collins column, Feb. 8, 1988.

15. Collins and Akerman, 19.

16. Langum and Walthall, 146.

17. Collins column, Feb. 8, 1988.

18. Ibid.

19. Langum and Walthall, 81, 113–17.

20. Wagy, 14; Collins column, Feb. 8, 1988.

21. Murray Wadsworth interview; *Tallahassee Democrat*, Aug. 30, 31, 1932; Mary Call Collins interview, Feb. 23, 2004.

22. Wagy, 14; Collins column, Mar. 7, 1988; Mary Call Collins interview, May 21, 2001; Collins and Akerman, 20; LeRoy Collins, interview with Loranne Ausley, July 21, 1987, transcript in possession of the author; Wagy, 23; *St. Petersburg Times*, May 29, 1989.

23. Collins and Akerman, 28–29; LeRoy Collins, oral history interview with Idella Moore, May 11, 1981, FSU post-governor speeches, box 6, folder 20.

24. Ausley interview.

25. Collins column, Mar. 7, 1988.

26. James Corbin interview, Mar. 29, 2004.

27. Wagy, 17; Messer interview.

28. Menton, 13–18.

29. Doherty, 156–58. Collins, *Forerunners Courageous*, 155; ibid.

30. Menton, 58–61.

31. Ibid., 67; Wagy, 23.

32. Collins, *Forerunners Courageous*, 197; FSU, post-governor biography files, box 1, folder 3; Wagy, 23; Mary Call Collins interview, Sept. 19, 2002; *St. Petersburg Times*, May 29, 1989; Collins and Akerman, 22; Menton, 67.

33. Mary Call Collins interview, Mar. 31, 2001.

34. Wagy, 15; Collins and Akerman, 23.

35. Wagy, 24–26; Collins and Akerman, 24.

36. *Tallahassee Democrat*, June 6, 1934; Wagy, 27.

Chapter 4. Every Man for Himself

1. Mormino, "A History of Florida's White Primary," 134–37; Iorio, 297–303; Key, 620; *Tampa Tribune*, May 4, 1909.

2. Congressional Quarterly, *Presidential Elections*, 125–44.

3. Bass, 27.

4. Key, 83–105; *Florida Handbook*, 29th ed., 678–79.

5. Danese, *Claude Papper and Ed Ball*, 25–36.

6. Morris, *Reconsiderations*, 3rd ed., 157–63.

7. Mormino, "A History of Florida's White Primary," 134–37.

8. Key, 99.

9. Colburn and Scher, *Gubernatorial Politics*, 2.

10. Ibid., 348; Akerman, 4–6; Egerton, *Speak Now Against the Day*, 34–35.

11. Wagy, 19.

12. Colburn and Scher, *Gubernatorial Politics*, 352.

13. Key, 86–87.

14. Rogers, "Fortune and Misfortune," 293.

15. *St. Petersburg Times*, Nov. 3, 1924.

16. Klein, 383–85.

17. Colburn and Scher, *Gubernatorial Politics*, 20–21.

18. Rogers, "Fortune and Misfortune," 294–99; Klein, 84–85.

19. Colburn and Scher, *Gubernatorial Politics*, 15, 21–22.

20. Rogers, "The Great Depression," 305–6.

21. Klein, 74.

22. Ibid., 84–85.

23. Morris, *Reconsiderations*, 2nd ed., 108; Doyle E. Carlton Jr. interview with G. Pierce Wood, July 30, 1997, USF Oral History Program.

24. Ellis and Rogers, *Favored Land*, 91; *Sarasota Herald*, May 9, 1935.

25. Collins and Akerman, 30; Mary Call Collins interview, Sept. 20, 2001.

26. *Tallahassee Democrat*, May 22, 28, 1935; Colburn and Scher, *Gubernatorial Politics*, 166.

27. House *Journal*, May 30, 1935, 1422; Morris, *Reconsiderations*, 2nd ed., 203.

28. Allen Morris in *Miami Herald*, Feb. 26, 1941.

29. House *Journal*, May 30, 1935, 1422–25.

30. Wagy, 26; *Florida Times Union*, Apr. 12, 1935; *St. Petersburg Times*, Apr. 25, 1935; *Jacksonville Journal*, May 17, 1935.

31. Collins column, Sept. 26, 1988.

32. Ellis and Rogers, *Favored Land*, 133.

33. *Miami Herald*, June 23, 1940.

34. *Tallahassee Democrat*, May 26, 31, 1937.

35. LeRoy Collins, interview with Idella Moore, May 11, 1981, Gov. Bob Graham's Oral History Program, FSU post-governor speeches, box 6, folder 20; *Tampa Tribune*, May 5, 6, 1937.

36. House *Journal*, May 4, 1937, 398.

37. *Tallahassee Democrat*, May 4, 1937.

38. Akerman, 22; *St. Petersburg Times*, June 1, 1937; Morris, *Reconsiderations*, 2nd ed., 166–67.

39. *Florida Times-Union*, Apr. 27, 1937; House *Journal*, Apr. 28, 1937, 242, May 4, 1937, 839.

40. *Tallahassee Democrat*, June 8, 1937.

41. *St. Petersburg Times, Tampa Tribune*, July 24, 1938.

42. Morris, *Reconsiderations*, 2nd ed., 204; Morris, *Miami Herald*, Feb. 9, 1941.

43. *Orlando Reporter Star*, Nov. 16, 18, 1938.

44. Wagy, 27–28.

45. Ibid.; LeRoy Collins, interview with Tom Wagy, Nov. 19, 1975, tape in possession of the author; Morris, *Reconsiderations*, 2nd ed., 256–57; *Tallahassee Democrat*, May 8, 1940.

46. *Tallahassee Democrat*, May 5, 1940; FSU Florida Senate papers, speeches, box 1, folder 7; Wagy, 28.

Chapter 5. The Grove

1. Wagy, 27.

2. Richards interview.

3. Mary Call Collins interview, Sept. 20, 2001.

4. *Tallahassee Democrat*, Sept. 16, 23, 1932; Wagy, 24; LeRoy Collins, interview with Tom Wagy, Sept. 17, 1979; Collins column, Aug. 8, 1988.

5. Wagy interview.

6. Talbot D'Alemberte interview, Jan. 29, 2002.

7. Mary Call Collins interview, May 8, 2001; LeRoy Collins interview with Lucy Morgan, notes in possession of the author.

8. Ellis and Rogers, 91; William Durden interview, Apr. 25, 2002; William Killian interview, Sept. 4, 2002.

9. LeRoy Collins Jr. interview.

10. Ibid.; Mary Call Collins interview, May 21, 2001.

11. Menton, 44–55; Collins, *Forerunners Courageous*, 176–87.

12. *Forerunners Courageous*, 185–99; Mary Call Collins interview, May 21, 2001; Canter Brown Jr. interview, Feb. 7, 2001; McGill, "LeRoy Collins" in *Southern Encounters*; USF box 53, folder "Collins–personal."

13. *Forerunners Courageous*, 185–87; Mary Call Collins interview, May 21, 2001.

14. *Forerunners Courageous*, 200–203; Mary Call Collins interview, July 22, 2003.

15. *Florida Times Union*, May 27, 1941, Feb. 27, 1942; *Miami Herald*, June 1, 1941; Mary Call Proctor interview, Jan. 5, 2005.

16. LeRoy Collins to John G. Hodges, Dec. 14, 1943, USF box 53, folder "personal"; Mormino, "G.I. Joe Meets Jim Crow," 29; Evans, 346–61.

17. *Fort Pierce News-Tribune*, Jan. 24, 1943; Mormino, "World War II," 323–31, 337.

18. *Florida Times-Union*, May 27, 1943; Allen Morris, interview with Tom Wagy, July 13, 1977, tape in possession of the author.

19. Wagy, 30.

20. LeRoy Collins to Brandon Collins, June 14, 1944, USF box 53, folder "personal."

21. *Orlando Sentinel*, May 7, 1944; LeRoy Collins to Henry S. Harris, May 15, 1944, USF box 53, folder "personal."

22. LeRoy Collins to Fuller Warren, Aug. 8, 1944, USF box 54; Collins to Ray Carroll, July 18, 1944, USF box 53, folder "personal."

23. Wagy, 30; Collins-Messer interview.

24. Mary Call Collins interview, Nov. 11, 2003.

25. LeRoy Collins, remarks at Ney Landrum retirement ceremony, Feb. 16, 1989; Ney Landrum to LeRoy Collins, Feb. 22, 1989, FSU post-governor speeches, box 11, folder 5.

26. USF box 54; Collins to Commander J. W. Henry, Apr. 10, 1946, USF box 54.

27. Charles Ausley to LeRoy Collins, June 30, 1945, USF box 54; Klein, 142–45.

28. Wagy, 31; LeRoy Collins, interview with Loranne Ausley, July 21, 1987, copy in possession of the author; LeRoy Collins, interview with Tom Wagy, Nov. 19, 1975.

29. LeRoy Collins Jr. interview, Mar. 24, 2004; LeRoy Collins to Lewis Langdon, Apr. 11, 1946; LeRoy Collins to G. Edward Friar, Apr. 16, 1946, USF box 54.

30. LeRoy Collins to Frank T. Maxson, Apr. 16, 1946, USF box 54.

31. LeRoy Collins to Lt. R. S. McHugh, Sept. 19, 1946, USF box 54.

32. Collins to Dan McCarty, July 19, 1946, USF box 54.

33. USF box 54.

34. Wagy, 30; FSU, LeRoy Collins Florida Senate papers, correspondence, box 1.

35. LeRoy Collins Jr. interview.

36. Ibid.

37. LeRoy Collins to J. Wen Lundeen, May 23, 1944, USF box 53; Mary Call Collins interview, Sept. 19, 2002.

38. Murray Wadsworth interview, June 12, 2002.

39. Harry Douglas interview, Apr. 16, 2002.

Chapter 6. Reform, Sales Tax, Scandals, Segregation

1. Colburn and Scher, *Gubernatorial Politics*, 34; David Colburn, e-mail to the author, Apr. 2, 2004; Pepper, 117–20, 206–7.

2. Colburn and Scher, *Gubernatorial Politics*, 244–47; Wagy, 31–32.

3. USF box 52.

4. Leo Wotitzky interview, Apr. 1999.

5. *Miami Herald*, May 3, 1947.

6. Millard Caldwell, interview with Tom Wagy, July 13, 1977, tape in possession of the author.

7. Wagy, 32.

8. Strickland, Davis, and Strickland, 108–10; Akerman, 39–40; Bartley, *The New South*, 149, 166.

9. *Statistical Abstract of the United States, 1954*; *Florida Handbook*, 5th ed., 293.

10. *Miami Herald*, May 18, 1947.

11. Ibid., Apr. 25, May 7, June 3, 1947.

12. Ibid., May 15, 30, 31, June 4, 7, 1947.

13. *Smith v. Allwright*, 321 U.S. 649 (1944); Akerman, 26; Kluger, 299–300.

14. Senate *Journal*, May 8, 1947, 333; *Miami Herald*, May 9, 1947; Akerman, 27.

15. Danese, "Disenfranchisement," 118; Mormino, "A History of Florida's White Primary," 136–37; Mathews and Prothro, 153; Senate *Journal*, May 13, 1947, 333, May 14, 1947, 450; House *Journal*, May 20, 1947, 835; Akerman, 26–27; *Miami Herald*, May 9, 10, 1947; *Florida Times Union*, May 2, 3, 1950; Green, 90.

16. Mathews and Prothro, 148; Carleton, 419–21; Roady, 290.

17. Ralph Turlington interview, June 12, 2001.

18. *Missouri ex rel. Gaines v. Canada*, 305 U.S. 337 (1938); *Sipuel v. Board of Regents of the University of Oklahoma*, 332 U.S. 631 (1948).

19. *New York Times*, May 14, Dec. 4, 1948.

20. Mary Call Collins interview, May 8, 2001; LeRoy Collins to Helen Fenton, Dec. 18, 1947, USF box 54.

21. Mary Call Collins interview, May 8, 2001; LeRoy Collins to Loomis Leedy, Nov. 3, 1947, USF box 54.

22. G. Edward Friar to LeRoy Collins, Dec. 2, 1947, USF box 54; Verle Pope, oral history interview with Julian Pleasants, Feb. 20, 1973, Sam Proctor Oral History Collection.

23. Key, 88, 93.

24. Ibid., 102; FSU, Allen Morris Papers, box 245, folder 9; *Florida Handbook*, 29th ed., 675–79.

25. Senate *Journal*, Apr. 5, May 23, 1949.

26. Colburn and Scher, "The Fuller Warren Years," 398–99; *Miami Herald*, Apr. 4, 1949.

27. House *Journal*, Apr. 5, 1949, 6–10; Morris, *Reconsiderations*, 3rd ed., 159–63.

28. Wotitzky interview.

29. Morris, *Reconsiderations*, 3rd ed., 160–62; *Tampa Tribune*, Sept. 3, 4, 5, 1949; Durden interview.

30. Allen Morris column, Sept. 24, 1949; *Tampa Tribune*, Sept. 16, 17, 25, 1949; Senate *Journal*, Sept. 23, 1949, 1156.

31. Florida Legislature, *2004 Florida Tax Handbook*, 14.

32. Senate *Journal*, Sept. 23, 1949, 1157; *Tampa Tribune*, Sept. 25, 1949.

33. Colburn and Scher, "The Fuller Warren Years," 389–408.

34. *Tampa Tribune*, May 3, 4, 1951.

35. Paulson, 220.

36. U.S. Congress, Senate Special Committee, *Hearings*, 127.

37. *St. Petersburg Times*, July 22, 1950; *New York Times*, July 16, 1950; Colburn and Scher, "The Fuller Warren Years," 389–408; *Miami Herald*, Apr. 10, 12, 1951; *Tampa Tribune*, May 29, 1951; *Tallahassee Democrat*, Apr. 12, 1951.

38. LeRoy Collins to Fuller Warren, Nov. 21, 1951, USF box 144.

39. Vandiver, 14; Colburn and Scher, "The Fuller Warren Years," 407–8; Colburn and Scher, *Gubernatorial Politics*, 139.

40. Wagy, 39; Colburn and Scher, "The Fuller Warren Years," 402.

41. Colburn and Scher, "The Fuller Warren Years."

42. Paulson and Hawkes.

43. *Tallahassee Democrat*, May 8, 1951; *Florida Flambeau*, May 11, 1951.

44. *Tampa Tribune*, May 13, 1951; Earl Dobert interview, Dec. 24, 2003; *St. Petersburg Times*, Oct. 18, 1951.

45. Senate *Journal*, May 29, 1951, 1051; veto message, HB 753, June 9, 1951, FSA series 866, box 6, folder 1951.

46. *Florida Times-Union*, Jan. 10, 1952; Green, 193–95.

Chapter 7. A Bridesmaid Again

1. *Tampa Tribune*, Sept. 7, 1949; LeRoy Collins to Walter Edge, Sept. 7, 17, 1949, USF box 62.

2. Walter Edge to LeRoy Collins, Sept. 12, 1949, USF box 62.

3. LeRoy Collins to N. Ray Carroll, Feb. 11, 1950, to John D. Pennekamp, Feb. 22, 1950, USF box 152.

4. LeRoy Collins to Henry S. Baynard, Feb. 27, 1950, to Tom A. Johnson, Mar. 1, 1950, USF box 152.

5. Roy T. Lord to LeRoy Collins, Mar. 1, 1950, USF box 152.

6. USF box 53, folder "campaign–julius parker."

7. LeRoy Collins to State Welfare Board, Jan. 24, 1944, USF box 53.

8. Trippett, 122–23.

9. USF box 146; Duby Ausley interview, June 17, 2002.

10. USF box 146.

11. USF box 152.

12. LeRoy Collins to L. C. Leedy, Mar. 23, 1950.

13. *Tallahassee Democrat*, May 3, 1950.

14. LeRoy Collins to Joan Jensen, Aug. 24, 1950, USF box 143.

15. LeRoy Collins to James L. Graham, to S. Henry Harris, Sept. 1, 1950; www.eglin.af/mil/weather/hurricanes'history.html.

16. LeRoy Collins to Spessard Holland, May 8, 1950, USF box 152; LeRoy Collins to Hal W. Adams, May 30, 1950, USF box 144; W. Dexter Douglass interview, Apr. 13, 2004.

17. "Cracker Politics," June 17, 1950, FSU Allen Morris Papers, box 245. LeRoy Collins to L. C. Leedy, June 27, 1950, USF box 144.

18. Arthur MacCarthy to LeRoy Collins, Arthur MacCarthy to Dan McCarty, July 5, 1950, USF box 143; Dan McCarty to Arthur MacCarthy, undated, USF box 143.

19. John McCarty to LeRoy Collins, Sept. 30, 1950, USF box 143.

20. LeRoy Collins to John McCarty, Oct. 5, 1950, USF box 143.

21. Mary Call Collins interview, July 18, 2003.

22. LeRoy Collins to Howell Collins, Nov. 10, 1950, to Wayne E. Ripley, Nov. 13, 1950, to Mrs. Robert F. Evans, Nov. 15, 1950; *St. Petersburg Times*, Nov. 26, 1950.

23. FSU Allen Morris Papers, box 245.

24. Walter E. Edge to LeRoy Collins, July 30, 1951, USF box 144.

25. *Tallahassee Democrat*, Sept. 9, 1951.

Chapter 8. Triumph and Tragedy

1. *Florida Handbook*, 29th ed., 678–79.

2. *St. Petersburg Times*, Mar. 2, 1954; *Florida Handbook*, 5th ed., 279.

3. *Florida Handbook*, 29th ed., 679; Manley and Brown, 348–49.

4. *St. Petersburg Times*, Mar. 29, 1952; *Tampa Tribune*, Apr. 3, 4, 6, 1952.

5. House *Journal*, 1937, 335, 467, 518; Key, 117–20.

6. FSU Allen Morris Papers, box 245, folder 15.

7. *St. Petersburg Times*, May 4, 1952.

8. *Florida Handbook*, 5th ed., 263, 280; *Florida Handbook*, 29th ed., 679.

9. *Tampa Tribune*, May 25, 1952.

10. Duby Ausley interview, June 17, 2002.

11. *Tampa Tribune*, May 25, 1952.

12. LeRoy Collins Jr. interview, Mar. 24, 2004.

13. LeRoy Collins to Dan McCarty, Sept. 26, 1952, USF box 69, folder "Dan McCarty."

14. USF box 146.

15. *Tallahassee Democrat*, Feb. 27, 1953.

16. Ibid., Mar. 3, 1953.

17. House *Journal*, Apr. 7, 1953, 10–14.

18. Ibid.

19. *St. Petersburg Times*, Mar. 15, 1953; LeRoy Collins to N. Ray Carroll, Nov. 25, 1946, USF box 52; Carroll to Collins, Feb. 11, 1950, USF box 152; Charley E. Johns to LeRoy Collins, June 6, 1950, USF box 144; *Orlando Sentinel*, May 15, 1954.

20. *Tampa Tribune*, May 23, 27, 1953.

21. Ibid.

22. *Orlando Sentinel*, May 31, 1953; *Tampa Tribune*, June 18, 1953.

23. *Orlando Sentinel*, June 3, 19, 1953.

24. Ibid., June 19, 1953.

25. *Tampa Tribune*, June 25, 1953.

26. Ibid., July 12, 19, 29, Aug. 16, 18, 20, 1953.

27. Ibid., Dec. 8, 1954.

28. *Jacksonville Journal*, June 6, 1953; *Tampa Tribune*, Aug. 16, 1953; LeRoy Collins to John McDermott, Sept. 11, 1953, USF box 144.

29. *Tampa Tribune*, Aug. 1, Sept. 18, 22, 1953; *Florida Handbook*, 29th ed., 335–36.

30. *Tampa Tribune*, Sept. 27, 28, 29, 1953.

31. *Florida Handbook*, 29th ed., 303.

Chapter 9. "Do Not Hesitate"

1. *Tampa Tribune*, Sept. 30, 1953.

2. Christie, 7–8; *Florida Handbook*, 29th ed., 320.

3. *Tampa Tribune*, Oct. 2, 7, 11, 1953.

4. Ibid., Oct. 15, 18, 20, 1953.

5. Ibid., Oct. 20, 21, 24, Nov. 11, 14, Dec. 12, 1953; Wagy, 47.

6. *Tampa Tribune*, Nov. 12, 13, 1953.

7. Ibid., Oct. 23, 25, 1953; *St. Petersburg Times*, Oct. 28, 1953.

8. Verle Pope, oral history interview with Julian Pleasants, Feb. 20, 1973, Sam Proctor Oral History Collection, FP 27.

9. LeRoy Collins interview, May 20, 1980, Governor Bob Graham's Oral History Program, FSU post-governor speeches, box 6 folder 20; Morris, *Reconsiderations*, 3rd ed., 103.

10. Pope oral history.

11. *Tampa Tribune*, Nov. 23, Dec. 12, 1953; *St. Petersburg Times*, Dec. 13, 1953; Florida Constitution (1885), art. IV, sec. 2.

12. Collins column, Dec. 26, 1988.

13. LeRoy Collins, interview with Tom Wagy, Nov. 19, 1975, tape in possession of the author.

14. LeRoy Collins to unknown correspondent, Nov. 9, 1953, USF box 144; *Tampa Tribune*, Nov. 14, 1953.

15. *Tampa Tribune*, Nov. 1, 1953.

16. Ibid., Nov. 19, 20, 24, 1953; *St. Petersburg Times*, Nov. 20, 1953.

17. *Tampa Tribune*, Dec. 12, 24, 1953.

18. Ibid., Dec. 13, 1953.

19. Ibid., Dec. 13, 1953; Jan. 13, 17, 1954; Oct. 25, 1955.

20. Ibid., Dec. 27, 29, 1953; *St. Petersburg Times*, Mar. 3, 1954.

21. *Tampa Tribune*, Jan. 6, Feb. 17, 1955.

22. *Florida Handbook*, 29th ed., 308, 678; Mary Call Proctor interview, Sept. 20, 2001; *Tampa Tribune*, May 9, 1954.

23. *Tampa Tribune*, Mar. 6, 1954; Klein, 36, 43–44, 202.

24. Christie, 8; Wagy, 36–37; Doyle Conner interview, June 28, 2002.

25. *St. Petersburg Times*, Mar. 2, 1954.

26. Christie, 9; Wagy, 36.

27. *St. Petersburg Times*, Mar. 18, 26, 1954.

28. Collins column, Sept. 19, 1988.

29. *Miami Herald*, Dec. 13, 1953; *St. Petersburg Times*, Mar. 5, 27, 1954.

30. Campaign pamphlet, undated, attributed to Edgar W. Waybright Jr., USF box 184.

31. *St. Petersburg Times*, May 22, 1954.

32. *Fort Myers News-Press*, Apr. 29, 1956.

33. *Miami News*, Mar. 7, 1954.

34. *St. Petersburg Times*, Mar. 2, 1954.

35. Wagy, 37–38.

36. John Germany interview, June 7, 2001.

37. *St. Petersburg Times*, Mar. 1, Apr. 6, 1954.

38. *Miami Herald*, Mar. 18, 1954; *St. Petersburg Times*, Mar. 28, Apr. 4, 1954.

39. Thomson, 498–501.

40. *Orlando Sentinel*, May 12, 1954.

41. *St. Petersburg Times*, Mar. 25, Apr. 1, 1954.

42. Ibid., Apr. 4, 7, 1954.

43. Ibid., Mar. 10, 30, Apr. 8, 1954; undated transcript, USF box 184.

44. *St. Petersburg Times*, Apr. 4, 1954.

45. Wagy, 37.

46. USF box 184.

47. *Tampa Tribune*, June 21, 1953.

48. Hartsfield and Roady, 63.

49. *St. Petersburg Times*, May 5, 1954; Collins column, Sept. 19, 1988; Christie, 10.

50. *Orlando Sentinel*, May 6, 1954; *Florida Handbook*, 29th ed., 678–79.

51. Christie, 10.

52. Ibid., 13–15.

53. *Tampa Tribune*, May 14, 15, 1954; Christie, 13–15.

54. Christie, 13–15.

55. *Miami Herald*, May 14, 1954.

56. LeRoy Collins, interview with David Colburn and Richard Scher, Feb. 12, 1975, Sam Proctor Oral History Project, FP 38.

57. Collins-Johns debate, transcript of videotape, FSA, V97.

58. Ibid.

59. *Miami Herald*, May 14, 1954; Collins-Johns transcript.

60. Akerman, 80.

61. *St. Petersburg Times*, May 18, 1954; *Tampa Tribune*, May 21, 1954.

62. USF box 19.

63. Ibid.

64. Hartsfield and Roady, 53; *Orlando Sentinel*, May 26, 1954.

65. Christie, 19; *Tampa Tribune*, May 26, 1954.

66. *St. Petersburg Times*, May 26, 1954; USF box 184.

Chapter 10. Interregnum

1. Kluger, 689–98.

2. *Plessy v. Ferguson*, 163 U.S. 537 (1896).

3. *Brown v. Board of Education*, 347 U.S. 483 (1954).

4. Ibid.

5. *Miami Herald*, May 18, 1954; *Tampa Tribune*, May 19, 1954.

6. LeRoy Collins, interview with Tom Wagy, Apr. 10, 1976.

7. *Southern School News*, Dec. 1, 1954; *St. Petersburg Times*, Sept. 5, 1954; Akerman, 81.

8. *Florida Handbook*, 5th ed., 202.

9. Kluger, 724–25.

10. *St. Petersburg Times*, Oct. 2, 6, 1954.

11. Killian, 77.

12. "Results of a Survey," Florida brief in *Brown II*, copy in the files of Lewis M. Killian; Lewis M. Killian interview, May 17, 2001.

13. Ibid.

14. Killian, 77–87; Lewis Killian interview.

15. Transcript of *1955 Argument*, in Lewis Killian private papers.

16. *St. Petersburg Times*, Aug. 28, 1954.

17. *Tampa Tribune*, Mar. 12, 1956.

18. *St. Petersburg Times*, Oct. 12, 1954.

19. Ibid., June 10, 18, 1954; Lewis Killian interview.

20. *Tampa Tribune*, May 28, 1954; *St. Petersburg Times*, June 1, 9, Dec. 20, 1954; Lewis Killian interview.

21. *St. Petersburg Times*, June 9, 1954.

22. J. Wayne Reitz, interview with Sam Proctor, 1988, transcribed from tape in the possession of Marjorie Turnbull.

23. *St. Petersburg Times*, Dec. 22, 23, 1954.

24. *St. Petersburg Times*, *Tampa Tribune*, May 27, 1954; *Florida Handbook*, 13th ed., 462.

25. FSU Allen Morris Papers, box 245, folder 15; *St. Petersburg Times*, Aug. 13, 22, Sept. 18, Oct. 8, 1954; *Gray v. Sanders*, 372 U.S. 368 (1963); Finkelman and Urofsky, 287.

26. *St. Petersburg Times*, June 17, Aug. 6, Oct. 21, 1954; *Tallahassee Democrat*, Nov. 9, 1954.

27. *St. Petersburg Times*, Oct. 23, 29, 30, 1954, Jan. 5, 1955.

28. *Florida Handbook*, 13th ed., 460; *St. Petersburg Times*, June 3, 10, 1954; Colburn and Scher, *Gubernatorial Politics*, 54.

29. *St. Petersburg Times*, Oct. 3, 17, 19, 25, 27, 28, 1954; Akerman, 81; *Tampa Tribune*, Sept. 6, 1949; *Florida Handbook*, 5th ed., 267.

30. *St. Petersburg Times*, Nov. 3, 1954.

Chapter 11. "So Much to Be Done. So Little Time"

1. http://www/fiu.edu/docs/briefhistory2.html.

2. Wagy, 41; *St. Petersburg Times*, Jan. 5, 1954.

3. *St. Petersburg Times*, Dec. 11, 1954, Jan. 9, 1955; FSA 776, carton 23; *Florida Handbook*, 29th ed., 286; Collins column, Feb. 20, 1989; Ina Hester Thompson, interview with Samuel Proctor, Aug. 31, 1989, FP 51; *Tampa Tribune*, July 24, 1955.

4. *St. Petersburg Times*, Jan. 4, 1955; FSU Allen Morris Papers, box 245, folder 15; *Tallahassee Democrat*, Jan. 3, 1954.

5. Wagy, 41–42.

6. *St. Petersburg Times*, Jan. 5, 1954; Collins column, June 13, 1988.

7. *St. Petersburg Times*, Jan. 5, 1954.

8. Ibid.

9. Ibid.

10. Collins column, Dec. 26, 1988.

11. *St. Petersburg Times*, Jan. 5, 1955.

12. Ibid., Jan. 5, 1955, Jan. 3, 1961.

13. Ibid., Jan. 5, 16, 1955.

14. LeRoy Collins, interview with Tom Wagy, Sept. 17, 1979.

15. FSU Collins governor's papers, news clippings, box 1; Wagy, 47; *Tampa Tribune*, Jan. 13, 1955.

16. *St. Petersburg Times*, Jan. 5, 1955.

17. Ibid., Jan. 9, 1955.

18. Wagy, 47–48; *St. Petersburg Times*, Sept. 21, 1955; Roger Collar interview, May 24, 2001; *Orlando Sentinel*, Oct. 2, 1955; John Germany interview.

19. *Florida Across the Threshold*, 193–94; Wagy, 47–48.

20. *St. Petersburg Times*, Jan. 19, 1955; *Tallahassee Democrat*, Feb. 1, 1955; Wagy, 48.

21. *Florida Sentinel*, Feb. 19, 1955; W. Dexter Douglass interview, May 21, 2002; Mary Call Collins interview, May 27, 2004.

22. *St. Petersburg Times*, Feb. 22, 1955.

23. Ibid., Mar. 18, 24, 25, 1955; Collins statement, Mar. 22, 1955, Hollis Rinehart to LeRoy Collins, J. Lee Ballard to LeRoy Collins, Mar. 18, 1955, Charley E. Johns to LeRoy Collins, Mar. 23, 1955, FSA 776 carton 6; Reitz interview; Board of Education minutes, Mar. 29, 1955,

FSA 776, carton 6; J. Lee Ballard to LeRoy Collins, Feb. 25, 1955, FSA 776, carton 6; *Tampa Tribune*, Feb. 23, 1955.

24. See generally Schnur, "Cold Warriors."

25. *St. Petersburg Times*, May 16, 1962.

26. Ibid., Apr. 1, 1955. Mallory Horne interview, May 7, 2001.

27. Havard and Beth, *Politics of Mis-Representation*, 37; *Florida Handbook*, 4th and 5th eds.

Chapter 12. "Whew!"

1. Morris, *Reconsiderations*, 2d ed., 84–85; *Miami Herald*, Apr. 9, 1947.

2. The Governor's Message to the Legislature, Apr. 5, 1955, FSU, governor's speeches, box 1, folder 44.

3. Ibid.

4. Ibid.; Havard and Beth, *Politics of Mis-Representation*, 43; *Florida Handbook*, 5th ed., 295.

5. Governor's Message.

6. www.law.fsu.edu/crc/conhist/contents.html.

7. Governor's Message.

8. Ibid.

9. Ibid.; Rogers and Denham, 252, 259–60.

10. Governor's Message.

11. Ibid.

12. Ibid.

13. Ibid.

14. Ibid.

15. *Tampa Tribune*, Apr. 6, 1955; *St. Petersburg Times*, Apr. 6, May 11, 1955.

16. *St. Petersburg Times*, Apr. 7, 8, 9, 12, 1955; *Tampa Tribune*, Apr. 8, 1955; *Miami Herald*, Apr. 10, 1955.

17. *St. Petersburg Times*, Apr. 13, 21, 23, 27, 1955; *Tampa Tribune*, Apr. 23, 1955.

18. *St. Petersburg Times*, Apr. 14, 1955; *Miami Herald*, Apr. 22, 27, 1955.

19. *St. Petersburg Times*, Apr. 26, 30, 1955; FSA 776, box 42, folder 13.

20. *St. Petersburg Times*, Apr. 27, 28, 1955.

21. Ibid., May 19, 1955.

22. House Memorial 594, 1955 session, FSA 776, box 33, folder 2.

23. *St. Petersburg Times*, May 9, 25, 1955; *Southern School News*, June 1955.

24. FSA 776, box 25; Wagy, 54.

25. *St. Petersburg Times*, May 30, 1955.

26. Collins column, Dec. 28, 1987.

27. USF box 21; FSA 776, box 29, folder 3.

28. *St. Petersburg Times*, June 5, 1955.

29. FSA box 25, folder 25; Senate *Journal*, 1449, June 1, 1955; House *Journal*, June 1, 1955, 1862.

30. *St. Petersburg Times*, Apr. 26, 1955.

31. Ibid., May 20, 1955; FSA 776, box 25, folder 25.

32. Egerton, "Controversy," 1–2, 5; Doherty, 153–80; *Tampa Tribune*, Oct. 10, 1956; Sam Gibbons interview, June 7, 2001.

33. John Germany interview; Gibbons interview; Egerton, "Controversy," 11; USF box 24.

34. Mallory Horne interview; Germany interview; Ed H. Price Jr. interview, June 4, 2001.

35. Horne interview.

36. Robert T. Mann interview, June 6, 2001.

37. *St. Petersburg Times*, May 5, 1955; LeRoy Collins, speech to Supreme Court Historical Society, Nov. 12, 1987, FSU post-governor speeches, box 6, folder 1; Canter Brown Jr. interview, Aug. 27, 2001.

38. USF box 96; John Germany interview.

Chapter 13. The Pork Chop Gang

1. *St. Petersburg Times*, Apr. 24, 1955; Gibbons interview; Collins column, Feb. 1, 1988; *Florida Handbook*, 29th ed., 102.

2. *St. Petersburg Times*, May 28, 1955; Havard and Beth, *Politics of Mis-Representation*, 51–53.

3. LeRoy Collins to W. Turner Davis, to Thomas E. David, June 1, 1955, FSA 776, box 35, folder 3.

4. *St. Petersburg Times*, June 4, 1955; *Tampa Tribune*, Mar. 2, 3, 1960; Havard and Beth, *Politics of Mis-Representation*, 364; Morris, *Reconsiderations*, 2nd ed., 202.

5. Klein, 223.

6. Ibid., 223, 228–29. *Tampa Tribune*, July 1, 1955; House *Journal*, June 30, 1955, 47–49.

7. House *Journal*, June 30, 1955, 47–49.

8. *Tampa Tribune*, July 1, 9, 1955.

9. *In re Advisory Opinion to the Governor*, 81 So. 2d. 782 (1955); *Tampa Tribune*, July 14, 15, 1955; Thomas H. Barkdull Jr. interview, June 10, 2004.

10. *Tampa Tribune*, July 10, 13, 1955; Morris, *Reconsiderations*, 3rd ed., 135.

11. *Tampa Tribune*, July 24, 1955; broadcast text, FSA 776, box 29, folder 4.

12. USF box 21.

13. *Tampa Tribune*, Sept. 6, 1955.

14. USF box 21.

15. Klein, 228–29; *Tampa Tribune*, Sept. 4, 6, 1955.

16. *Tampa Tribune*, Sept. 25, 1955; House *Journal*, Sept. 28, 1955, 117–20.

17. *Tampa Tribune*, Feb. 28–Mar. 7, 1960; Sherrill, "Florida's Legislature," 88.

18. Trippett, 191–95.

19. House *Journal*, Sept. 27, 1955, 112–15.

20. Ibid.

21. Bass and DeVries, 108.

22. *Chiefland Citizen*, Sept. 29, 1955.

23. *Tampa Tribune*, Sept. 28, 30, 1955.

24. FSA 776, box 35, folder 4.

25. Ibid.

26. Ibid.

27. *Orlando Sentinel*, Sept. 29, 1955; FSA 776, box 29, folder 3; *Tampa Tribune*, Sept. 30, 1955.

28. *Tampa Tribune*, Sept. 30, 1955.

29. Art. IV, sec. 1(b).

30. FSA 776, box 6, folder 2; *Tampa Tribune,* Oct. 26, 1955.

Chapter 14. Massive Resistance

1. Green, 206–7.

2. Ibid., 87.

3. Ibid., 127–28.

4. Green, 90–105; Fuller Warren to J. R. Hunter, July 6, 1950, Florida Parole Commission files.

5. Green, 136–47.

6. Williams, 154–55.

7. Warren Pierce to LeRoy Collins, FSU post-governor correspondence, box 7, folder 1.

8. *St. Petersburg Times*, Mar. 18, 1955.

9. Akerman and Collins, 59; J. H. Hunter to State Board of Pardons, Mar. 14, 1951; FSU, governor's correspondence, box 1.

10. LeRoy Collins, interview with David Colburn and Richard Scher, University of Florida Oral History Project, FP 38.

11. Bill Harris to LeRoy Collins, undated memorandum, "Review of the Case of State vs. Walter Irvin," FSU, governor's correspondence, box 1; William C. Harris interview, Sept. 11, 2001.

12. Willis B. McCall to LeRoy Collins, FSU, governor's correspondence, box 1.

13. Collins and Akerman, 66.

14. www.dc.state.fl.us/oth/deathrow/execlist2.html.

15. Margaret Vandiver, letter to the author, June 22, 2000.

16. *Tampa Tribune*, Dec. 15, 1955.

17. Saunders, 116–18.

18. Green, 8–9, 194–95.

19. *Tampa Tribune*, Dec. 17, 1955; Jacobstein, 29.

20. FSA 776, box 23, folder 1.

21. *St. Petersburg Times*, Nov. 30, 1954; Allen Platt to Charley Johns, Dec. 21, 1954, FSA 776, box 39.

22. Allen Platt to LeRoy Collins, Jan. 3, 1955, FSA 776, box 39; "Investigation of Allen Platt Matter," FSA 776, box 39; LeRoy Collins to Allen Platt, "rough draft," Jan. 27, 1955, FSA 776, box 39.

23. Collins to Platt, "rough draft," Jan. 27, 1955, FSA 776, box 39.

24. Mabel Norris Reese to LeRoy Collins, Feb. 14, 1955, FSA 776, box 39; *Christian Science Monitor*, Feb. 5, 1955; Collins and Akerman, 52.

25. Allen Platt to LeRoy Collins, Jan. 31, 1955, FSA 776.

26. *Orlando Sentinel*, May 8, 1955; *Tampa Tribune*, Oct. 19, 21, 1953; LeRoy Collins to Willis McCall, FSA 776, box 38, folder 7.

27. Akerman, 94–95; FSA 776, box 38, folder 7; *Tampa Tribune*, Nov. 13, 1955; *Southern School News*, December 1955; Green, 197.

28. Motley, 112.

29. *State ex rel. Hawkins vs. Board of Control et al.*, 47 So. 2nd 608 (1950), 53 So. 2nd 116 (1951), 342 U.S. 877 (1951), 60 So. 2nd 162 (1952), 347 U.S. 971 (1954).

30. *State ex rel. Hawkins v. Board of Control et al.*, 83 So. 2nd 20 (1955)

31. Ibid.

32. Brazeal, 357.

33. Herman, 79–82; *State ex rel. Hawkins. v. Board of Control et al.*, 93 So. 2nd 354.

34. Gloria Barton interview, April 2004.

35. *State ex rel. Hawkins v. Board of Control of Florida et al.*, 350 U.S. 413 (1956).

36. FSA 776, box 39, folder 2.

37. Richard W. Ervin interview, May 15, 2001; Caro, 763–64; *Tampa Tribune*, Mar. 17, Apr. 3, 1956; Killian, 87–88. *St. Petersburg Times*, Apr. 24, 1956.

38. *State ex rel. Hawkins v. Board of Control et al.*, 93 So. 2d 354 (1957).

39. "Report of the Commissioner," 22–25, 34, USF box 139.

40. 93 So. 2d 354.

41. Ibid.

42. Brazeal, 358; Motley, 116–17; *Southern School News*, August 1958.

43. Collins-Akerman, 83–84; LeRoy Collins, interview with Tom Wagy, Apr. 10, 1976; FSA 776, box 109, folder 5.

44. George H. Starke Jr. interview, June 25, 2004.

Chapter 15. Backlash

1. Bartley, *Massive Resistance*, 8–33, 41–68, 75–76, 111–14, 128–33, 283.

2. *Orlando Sentinel*, May 18, 1954; LeRoy Collins, interview with Tom Wagy, Apr. 10, 1976; Waring, 39; *Tampa Tribune*, Dec. 18, 1955.

3. McGill, "A Decade of Slow, Painful Progress," 65.

4. *Tampa Tribune*, Mar. 12, 1956.

5. Bartley, 116–17.

6. USF box 19.

7. *St. Petersburg Times*, Jan. 14, 1956.

8. Ibid., Nov. 20, 1955; *Tampa Tribune*, Dec. 7, 1955, Jan. 12, 1956; FSA 776, box 29, folder 2.

9. Wagy, 54–55; *Tampa Tribune*, Jan. 26, 1956; Collins column, Apr. 13, 1987; *Tampa Times*, Jan. 13, 1956; Jacobstein, 44–45.

10. *Time*, Dec. 19, 1955.

11. Jacobstein, 41–43; *U.S. News & World Report*, Apr. 13, 1956.

12. Memorandum to Charles S. Ausley, author unknown, Mar. 28, 1956, undated memorandum, USF box 92, folder "Lowry"; *Fort Myers News-Press*, Apr. 29, 1956.

13. *Tampa Tribune*, Jan. 11, 13, 1956; *Florida Sentinel*, Mar. 10, 1956; *St. Petersburg Times*, June 22, 2000.

14. *Tampa Tribune*, Jan. 16, 22, 1956; Jacobstein, 17–18.

15. Jacobstein, 17–18.

16. *Tampa Tribune*, Jan. 15, 1956.

17. Ben C. Willis to LeRoy Collins, Jan. 27, 1956, FSA 776, box 116; Feb. 9, 1956, FSA 776, box 116.

18. Williamson, 408–9; Cash, 124–27.

19. *Tampa Tribune*, Feb. 2, 1956.

20. FSA 776, box 116.

21. Frederick E. Kidder to LeRoy Collins, Feb. 3, 1956, Collins to Kidder, Feb. 13, 1956, FSA 776, box 116, folder 10.

22. LeRoy Collins monologue, Apr. 10, 1976, Sam Proctor Oral History Program, FP 38.

23. "Statement on Segregation," undated, FSA 776, box 116.

24. LeRoy Collins, interview with Tom Wagy, Apr. 10, 1976; George Bedell, e-mail to the author, Jan. 14, 2003, interview, Jan. 22, 2003; Harry Douglas interview, June 20, 2003.

25. *Atlanta Constitution*, Jan. 28, 1956.

26. *St. Petersburg Times*, *Tampa Tribune*, Feb. 8, 1956; USF box 21.

27. *St. Petersburg Times*, Feb. 8, 1956; *Tampa Tribune*, Feb. 8, 11, 1956.

28. *St. Petersburg Times*, Feb. 17, Mar. 30, May 5, 1956; *Tampa Tribune*, Feb. 23, 25, 1956; *Leesburg Commercial*, Apr. 22, 1956; *Orlando Sentinel*, Apr. 28, 1956.

29. FSA 776, box 23, folder 2.

30. *Tampa Tribune*, Feb. 21, 1956; Collins and Akerman, 67.

31. *Tampa Tribune*, Feb. 27, 1956; Jacobstein, 31; LeRoy Collins to Dewey R. Villareal Jr., Mar. 21, 1956, FSA box 776, box 23, folder 2.

32. George Brautigam to Robert Fokes, Mar. 9, 16, 1956, USF box 95; Jacobstein, 21–32; FSA 776, box 42, folder 4; *Miami Herald*, Mar. 17, 21, 1956.

33. *Tampa Tribune*, Feb. 21, 1956.

34. Poll report, Dec. 20, 1955, USF box 65.

35. *Ervin vs. Collins, et al.*, 85 So. 2d 852 (1956).

36. *Tampa Tribune*, Mar. 6, 1954; FSA 776, box 29, folder 2.

37. *Tampa Tribune*, Mar. 11, 1956.

38. Ibid., Mar. 16, 17, 1956; FSA 776, box 29, folder 2; *New York Times*, Mar. 17, 1956.

39. *Tampa Tribune*, Mar. 6, 17, 1956.

40. Kallina, 174–75.

41. *Tampa Tribune*, Mar. 17, 19, 1956; *Miami Herald*, Mar. 18, 1956; FSA 776, box 116.

42. Collins statement, Mar. 21, 1956; FSA 776, box 116.

43. Ibid.; *Tampa Tribune*, Mar. 22, 1956.

44. *Tampa Tribune*, Mar. 23, 1956.

45. Branch, *Parting the Waters*, 213; Bartley, 65; Kluger, 322, 665, 674–75, 753; Wagy, 97–98; Congressional Quarterly, *Revolution in Civil Rights*, 3–4; letter to LeRoy Collins, Mar. 31, 1956, www.presidency.ucsb.edu.

46. Thos. B. Stanley to LeRoy Collins, Mar. 27, 1956, FSA 776, box 116, folder 11.

47. *Tampa Tribune*, Mar. 27, 1956.

48. Jacobstein, 11; USF box 19.

49. *Tampa Tribune*, Apr. 3, 1956.

50. Ibid., Apr. 3, 5, 1956; Collins television text, Apr. 6, 1956, *St. Petersburg Times* library; Jacobstein, 25–26.

51. Jack Peeples interview, Jan. 18, 2003.

52. Jacobstein, 37.

53. *Tampa Tribune*, Apr. 8, 1956; broadcast script, Apr. 6, 1956, *St. Petersburg Times* library.

54. USF box 19; *Tampa Tribune*, Apr. 5, 1956.

55. Transcript, FSA 776, box 29, folder 4; *Tampa Tribune*, Apr. 11, 20, 1956; Jacobstein, 43–45; Barlett and Steele, 188–200; "Howard Hughes: Patron of Science?" www.cbsnews.com/stories/2003/11/21/60minutes/main584945.shtml; Collins column, Apr. 20, 1987.

56. Jacobstein, 37, 39.

57. *Tampa Tribune*, Apr. 13, 19, 1956; *St. Petersburg Times,* July 7, 1974.

58. John Perry, e-mail to the author, Jan. 29, 2003; J. Stanley Marshall, quoting Collins, speech to Trinity United Methodist Church Luncheon Forum, Tallahassee, Fla., Nov. 12, 2001.

59. Jacobstein, 65; *Tampa Tribune*, Apr. 24, 1956; *St. Petersburg Times*, Apr. 14, 15, 1956.

60. Jacobstein, 47, 59; *Tampa Tribune*, Apr. 22, 1956; Smathers oral history.

61. *Tampa Tribune*, Apr. 27, 1956.

62. Grotegut to LeRoy Collins, Apr. 26, 1956, USF box 95.

63. Speech text, USF box 19; *Tampa Tribune*, Apr. 29, 1956. *St. Petersburg Times*, May 1, 1960.

64. *St. Petersburg Times, Tampa Tribune*, May 5, 1956.

65. *Tampa Tribune*, May 3, 5, 1956; Jacobstein, 32–33.

66. Jacobstein, 57.

67. Telecast text, USF box 19.

68. Danese, *Claude Pepper and Ed Ball*, 213–15; Jacobstein, 56; campaign documents, USF box 94; *Washington Post*, May 7, 1956.

69. *St. Petersburg Times, Miami Herald, Tampa Tribune*, May 9, 1956; Harry Douglas interview, Apr. 16, 2002.

70. Thomas H. Barkdull Jr. interview, June 9, 2005.

71. *Tampa Tribune*, May 10, 1956.

72. *St. Petersburg Times*, May 11, 1956.

73. "Tabulation of Official Vote, Florida Primary Elections, May 8, 29, 1956," R. A. Gray, secretary of state, 1956; *Florida Handbook*, 6th ed., 307; Saunders, 149–51; *Tampa Tribune*, Feb. 14, 1956.

74. *Tampa Tribune*, May 10, 1956; *Washington Post*, May 11, 1956.

75. Jacobstein, 71.

76. *Tampa Tribune*, May 10, 1956.

77. Klein, 310.

Chapter 16. Pressure

1. *St. Petersburg Times*, May 17, 1956; *Tampa Tribune*, June 24, 1956.

2. Raby, 9–13; C. U. Smith interview, Feb. 28, 2002.

3. Raby, 11–20, 25–26; Branch, *Parting the Waters*, 120–38; Collins statements, June 2, 4, 1956, FSA 776, box 29, folder 2.

4. Raby, 23–24.

5. Statement, July 2, 1956, FSA 776, box 79, folder 4.

6. Raby, 32–33.

7. Ibid., 30–31; USF box 139.

8. Raby, 56; Schnur, 49–57.

9. FSA 776, box 29, folder 2; *Tampa Tribune*, July 2, 5, 10, 13, 1956; Steve Trumbull to LeRoy Collins, July 16, 1956, FSA 776, box 35, folder 2; House *Journal*, July 23, 1956, 5–7.

10. *Tampa Tribune*, May 11, 16, June 28, 1956; Collins statement, June 11, 1956, FSA 776, box 29, folder 4; Havard and Beth, "Representative Government," 44.

11. FSA 776, box 42, folder 1.

12. House *Journal*, July 23, 1956, 7–14; Bartley, *Massive Resistance*, 78; *St. Petersburg Times*, *Tampa Tribune*, July 17, 1956.

13. Chapter 31380, *Laws of Florida* (1956), 30–35.

14. *St. Petersburg Times*, *Tampa Tribune*, July 17, 1956.

15. LeRoy Collins to Mary Call Collins, July 13, 1956, Proctor family files, copy in possession of the author.

16. House *Journal*, July 23, 1956, 7; *Tampa Tribune*, July 24, 1956.

17. *Tampa Tribune*, July 24, 25, 1956; Akerman, 112; LeRoy Collins, interview with Tom Wagy, Apr. 10, 1976.

18. *Tampa Tribune*, July 25, 1956; *St. Petersburg Times*, July 27, 1956.

19. "Jack Orr Without Tears," *Miami Magazine*, August 1974; *St. Petersburg Times*, July 27, 1956.

20. *Miami Magazine*, August 1974; *Tampa Tribune*, July 28, 31, 1956; Tom Orr interview, Mar. 23, 2001.

21. *Southern School News*, November, December, 1956.

22. *Tampa Tribune*, July 25, 26, Aug. 2, 1956; *St. Petersburg Times*, Aug. 2, 1956; Collins column, July 4, 1988.

23. FSA 776, box 29, folder 4.

24. *St. Petersburg Times*, July 27, Aug. 1, 1956; *Tampa Tribune*, July 29, 1956.

25. *St. Petersburg Times*, Aug. 1, 22, 1956; Schnur, 314; FSA 776, box 29, folder 4.

26. Braukman, 7–8; Schnur, 310–14, and see throughout.

27. *Tampa Tribune*, Aug. 2, 1956; Ben C. Willis to LeRoy Collins, Aug. 1, 1956, FSA 776, box 35, folder 2; chapter 31401, *Laws of Florida*, 1956; chapter 498, *Laws of Florida*, 2004.

28. *St. Petersburg Times*, Aug. 9, 16, 1956; *Tampa Tribune*, Aug. 7, 16, 1956.

29. *Tampa Tribune*, Aug. 14, 1956; *St. Petersburg Times*, Aug. 7, 1956; Wagy, 152.

30. USF box 21.

31. FSA 776, box 33, folder 2.

32. *Southern School News*, Sept. 1956.

33. Downey-Anderson, 464–72; *Tampa Tribune*, Sept. 30, Oct. 4, 1956.

34. *St. Petersburg Times*, Sept. 29, 1956; Deborah Coggins interview, July 9, 2001; *Tampa Tribune*, Oct. 5, 1956.

35. LeRoy Collins to C. K. Steele, Sept. 28, 1956, FSA 776, box 33, folder 2.

36. Saunders, 151–56; *St. Petersburg Times*, Oct. 29, Nov. 4, Dec. 13, 1956; Caro, 699–709.

37. *Tampa Tribune*, Oct. 23, 1956; *Florida Handbook*, 6th ed., 294–99; LeRoy Collins to LeRoy Collins Jr., Nov. 7, 1956, USF box 458, folder 3.

38. Havard and Beth, "Representative Government," 53.

39. *Tampa Tribune*, Jan. 22, July 19, Oct. 10, 11, 1956; Sam Gibbons interview, June 7, 2001.

40. *Tampa Tribune*, Oct. 9, 17, Dec. 7, 1956; Collins statement, Dec. 8, 1956, FSA 776, box 29, folder 4; Gibbons interview; *St. Petersburg Times*, Apr. 28, 29, 1959; Resolution of the State Board of Education, Dec. 18, 1956, FSA 776, box 6; Egerton, "The Controversity," 1–4.

41. Raby, 45–50.

42. *St. Petersburg Times*, Dec. 30, 1956.

Chapter 17. Turning Point

1. Raby, 48–51; *St. Petersburg Times*, Jan. 1, 2, 1957; Wagy, *Spokesman*, 78; Collins statement, Jan. 1, 1957, FSA 776, box 109.

2. Raby, 52; *New York Times*, Jan. 4, 7, 1957.

3. Frank Moore, interview with Tom Wagy, Oct. 8, 1975; LeRoy Collins, interview with Tom Wagy, Apr. 10, 1976, tapes in possession of the author.

4. Wagy, *Spokesman*, 79; Lil Classen, e-mail to the author, Oct. 23, 2003.

5. *St. Petersburg Times*, Jan. 9, 1957.

6. Ibid.

7. Ibid.

8. Ibid.

9. Harry Douglas interview, Aug. 23, 2004.

10. *St. Petersburg Times*, Jan. 9, 1957.

11. Ibid.; LeRoy Collins, interview with Tom Wagy, Apr. 10, 1976.

12. *St. Petersburg Times*, Jan. 9, 1957; *Washington Post*, Jan. 9, 1957; *Christian Science Monitor*, Jan. 15, 1957; *Time*, Jan. 21, 1957, 15; *Southern School News*, February 1957.

13. *Southern School News*, February 1957; *St. Petersburg Times*, Jan. 9, 1957.

14. A. Leon Lowry and Saul Nickerson to LeRoy Collins, undated letter received Jan. 10, 1957, USF box 49; *St. Petersburg Times*, Jan. 9, 1957; Robert T. Mann to LeRoy Collins, Jan. 10, 1957, USF box 49.

15. Raby, 54; FSA 776, box 109, folder 3; *St. Petersburg Times*, Jan. 12, 1957.

16. LeRoy Collins to Luther Hodges, Jan. 14, 1957, FSA 776, box 116, folder 12.

17. *New York Times*, Jan. 7, 1957.

18. Raby, 54–58.

19. Ibid., 62; Minutes, meeting of Governor's Advisory Commission on Bi-Racial Problems, Jan. 29, 1957, FSA 776, box 117, folder 1.

20. Governor's Message to the Legislature, Apr. 2, 1957, Florida State Library; Raby, 62–63; Minutes of the Governor's Advisory Commission, Mar. 5, 26, 1957, FSA 776, box 117, folder 1.

21. Minutes, Apr. 30, 1957, FSA 776, box 117, folder 1.

22. USF box 21; Thomas B. Manuel to LeRoy Collins, Mar. 6, 1957, FSA 776 box 4, folder 14; *St. Petersburg Times*, May 19, 1957; Joe Grotegut to LeRoy Collins, Mar. 8, 1957.

23. Speech text, Feb. 5, 1957, USF box 21.

24. *Tampa Tribune*, Mar. 22, 23, 24, 1957; *New York Times*, Mar. 23, 1957.

25. Florida Constitution (1868), art. XII, secs. 8, 10; *Tampa Tribune*, Mar. 29, 1957; *St. Petersburg Times*, Feb. 11, 1956, May 7, 1957.

Chapter 18. The Right to Be Loved

1. Collins column, Feb. 17, 1986; *Boston Daily Globe*, May 24, 1957; *St. Petersburg Times*, May 24, 1957.

2. *Christian Science Monitor*, Mar. 19, 1957; *Boston Daily Globe*, May 24, 1957; *New York Times*, May 26, 1957; *St. Petersburg Times*, Apr. 4, 1957; Collins column, Feb. 17, 1986.

3. Art. IV, sec. 2.

4. *Kentucky v. Dennison*, 24 How. 66 (1861).

5. Collins column, Feb. 17, 1986; Mary Call Collins interviews, Sept. 19, 2002, July 18, 2003.

6. Harry Douglas interview, June 20, 2003.

7. *Florida Catholic*, Mar. 29, 1957; USF box 25.

8. USF box 31.

9. Memorandum to media, May 21, 1957, FSA 776, box 190, folder 3; *Miami Herald*, May 24, 1957.

10. Hildy Ellis interview, July 31, 2001.

11. *Miami Herald*, May 24, 1957; Collins column, Feb. 17, 1986.

12. Collins column, Feb. 17, 1986.

13. *In the Matter of the Application of the Commonwealth of Massachusetts*, May 23, 1957, FSA 776, box 109.

14. Ibid.

15. *Miami Herald, St. Petersburg Times*, May 24, 1957.

16. *Miami Herald*, May 24, 1957; Ellis interview; Douglas interview.

17. *New York Times*, May 24, July 9, 1957; Collins column, Feb. 17, 1986. USF boxes 25–33; Douglas interview.

18. *St. Petersburg Times*, June 12, 1957; *New York Times*, July 9, 1957; *Christian Science Monitor*, July 10, 1957.

19. *Puerto Rico v. Branstad*, 483 U.S. 219 (1987); Congressional Quarterly, *Landmark Decisions,* 497.

Chapter 19. "An Evil Thing"

1. Governor's Message, State Library of Florida; *Tampa Tribune, St. Petersburg Times*, Apr. 3, 1957.

2. Governor's Message, State Library of Florida; Stephenson, 128–36.

3. Governor's Message, State Library of Florida.

4. LeRoy Collins to LeRoy Collins Jr., Apr. 4, 1957, USF box 458, folder 3.

5. *St. Petersburg Times*, Apr. 5, 9, 1957.

6. Ibid., Apr. 16, 1957; Richard W. Ervin interview, May 15, 2001.

7. Colburn and Scher, *Florida's Gubernatorial Politics*, 226; *St. Petersburg Times*, Apr. 18, 19, 1957.

8. *St. Petersburg Times*, Apr. 21, 1957.

9. *Southern School News*, June 1957.

10. House Concurrent Resolution 174, 1957, FSA 222, carton 238.

11. Havard and Beth, *The Politics of Mis-Representation*, 80–81; Klein, 406–7.

12. *Florida Flambeau*, Apr. 26, 1957.

13. *St. Petersburg Times*, Apr. 27, 1957; Ralph Turlington interview, June 12, 2001.

14. *St. Petersburg Times*, May 7, 9, 1957; Akerman, 123; Schnur, 73; *Miami Herald*, May 26, 1957.

15. *St. Petersburg Times*, May 3, 4, 17, 1957; *Miami Herald*, May 25, 1957; *Tampa Tribune*, Mar. 4, 1959.

16. *St. Petersburg Times*, May 9, 23, 1957; Robert T. Mann interview, June 6, 2001; FSA 776, box 109, folder 3; Mallory Horne interview, May 7, 2001.

17. *Miami Herald*, May 26, 1957; *St. Petersburg Times*, May 15, 1957.

18. *Miami Herald*, May 26, 1957.

19. Ibid.; LeRoy Collins to John Knight, May 27, 1957, USF box 19.

20. FSA 776, box 58, folder 6.

21. *Miami Herald*, May 24, 1957; *St. Petersburg Times*, May 28, 1957.

22. *St. Petersburg Times*, May 26, 30, 31, June 1, 1957; Havard-Beth, *Politics of Mis-Representation*, 60–61.

23. *St. Petersburg Times*, May 30, 31, 1957; *New York Times*, May 31, 1957.

24. *St. Petersburg Times*, Apr. 18, 1958; Stephenson, 136–42; Ken Woodburn, "Florida Grows Up," http://sustainable.state.fl.us/fdi/fscc/news/state/woodburn.html.

25. *St. Petersburg Times*, June 2, 5, 6, 9, 1957.

26. *Florida Handbook*, 3rd ed., 180; *St. Petersburg Times*, June 9, 12, 1957; *Tampa Tribune*, Nov. 14, 1957.

27. LeRoy Collins to the Hon. Doyle E. Conner, June 6, 1957, FSA 776, box 102, folder 8.

28. Frederick B. Karl interview, July 3, 2003; House *Journal*, May 14, 1957, 1045–47; June 7, 1957, 2269; *St. Petersburg Times*, June 8, 1957.

29. *St. Petersburg Times*, July 8, 2001; Reubin Askew interview, Sept. 10, 2004.

30. *St. Petersburg Times*, June 6, 1957; FSA 776, box 103, folder 1, box 102, folder 8; *Tampa Tribune*, Apr. 23, 1959.

31. William L. Durden interview, Apr. 25, 2002; William L. Killian interview, Sept. 4, 2002; FSA 776, box 109, folder 3.

32. *Florida Handbook*, 29th ed., 335–39; *St. Petersburg Times*, Feb. 12, June 11, 1958, May 19, 1959; FSA 776, box 109, folder 4.

33. Ed H. Price Jr. interview, June 4, 2001.

34. Guyte McCord Jr. interview, May 20, 2002; Collins column, Jan. 27, 1988.

35. Joe Grotegut memorandum, Oct. 29, 1957, FSA 776, box 109, folder 4; Wagy, 44.

36. Transcripts, Oct. 31, Dec. 12, 1957, USF box 21; *St. Petersburg Times*, Dec. 22, 1957.

37. Saunders, 155; press conference, Jan. 16, 1958, USF box 21; *St. Petersburg Times*, May 16, 2004.

38. Darby Collins interview, Aug. 20, 2003.

39. Mary Call Collins, in correspondence from Juanita Mathews to LeRoy Collins, July 8, 1957, USF box 458, folder 3.

Chapter 20. Little Rock

1. Wagy, *Spokesman*, 91; Collins column, Dec. 7, 1987; Congressional Quarterly, *The Presidency A to Z*, 262; Caro, 467–70.

2. Bartley, *Massive Resistance*, 265; Sherrill, *Gothic Politics*, 82–86.

3. Wagy, 90; Sherrill, *Gothic Politics*, 85–89; Branch, *Parting the Waters*, 222–33; Kluger, 753–54.

4. Wagy, 89–90.

5. Wagy, 89–90, 92; Collins column, Dec. 7, 1987; John Perry interview, July 19, 2001; *Atlanta Constitution*, Sept. 23, 1957.

6. Branch, *Parting the Waters*, 223–24; *Tampa Tribune*, Sept. 24, 1957.

7. Speech text, FSU governor's papers, speeches and interviews, box 3, folder 13.

8. Ibid.

9. Ibid.

10. Ibid.

11. *Atlanta Constitution, Tampa Tribune, St. Petersburg Times, Washington Post*, Sept. 24, 1957; Wagy, 94–95.

12. *St. Petersburg Times*, Sept. 24, 1957; LeRoy Collins, interview with Tom Wagy, Apr. 10, 1976.

13. *Atlanta Constitution*, Sept. 24, 1957; Collins statement, FSA 776, box 109, folder 4.

14. *Tampa Tribune*, Sept. 25, 1957.

15. Ibid., Sept. 26, 1957.

16. Ibid.; John Perry interview, July 19, 2001.

17. Senate Memorial 19-X, Senate *Journal*, Oct. 1, 1957, 2; House *Journal*, Oct. 1, 1957, 26–29.

18. LeRoy Collins to Marvin Griffin, Sept. 30, 1957, FSA 776, box 116, folder 12; *Tampa Tribune*, Sept. 25, 26, 1957; *New York Times*, Oct. 1, 1957.

19. Collins column, Dec. 7, 1987; *New York Times*, Oct. 2, 1957; Luther Hodges statement, Oct. 3, 1957, FSA 776, box 116, folder 12; Collins statement, Oct. 1, 1957, FSA 776, box 109, folder 4.

20. Wagy, 98; Collins column, Dec. 7, 1987.

21. *St. Petersburg Times*, Nov. 23, 1957; Bartley, *Massive Resistance*, 273–75, 331–32; http://www.encyclopedia.com.

Chapter 21. Failure?

1. LeRoy Collins, interview with Tom Wagy, Apr. 10, 1976; *Tampa Tribune*, Sept. 8, 1957; Wagy, 106.

2. *Tampa Tribune*, Sept. 28, Oct. 3, 1957.

3. House *Journal*, Sept. 30, 1957, 4–6; Havard-Beth, *Politics of Mis-Representation*, 61; Council of State Governments analysis, undated, FSA 776, box 59, folder 8.

4. *Tampa Tribune*, Sept. 22, 1957.

5. Ibid., Oct. 3, 1957.

6. *Washington Post, Tampa Tribune*, Oct. 10, 11, 1957; *St. Petersburg Times*, Oct. 12, 1957.

7. FSA 776, box 102, folder 1; box 109, folder 4.

8. Senate Joint Resolution 90-X, 1957; *Tampa Tribune,* Oct. 9, 31, 1957.

9. H. T. Enns Jr. to LeRoy Collins, Oct. 16, 1957, FSA 776, box 59, folder 7; LeRoy Collins to Beth Johnson, Nov. 12, 1957, ibid.; Martin Andersen to LeRoy Collins, Oct. 28, 1957; Collins to Andersen, Oct. 31, 1957, FSA 776, box 59, folder 6; LeRoy Collins to J. C. Council, Nov. 8, 1957; Council to Collins, Nov. 12, 1957, FSA 776, box 59, folder 7.

10. *St. Petersburg Times,* Nov. 5, 1957; Jan. 10, 1958; USF box 21; USF boxes 1, 22.

11. *Rivera-Cruz v. Gray, Pope v. Gray,* 104 So. 2d 501 (1958).

12. FSA 776, box 59, folder 7; special message on the Constitution, Apr. 9, 1959, FSU governor's speeches, box 3, folder 14; Wagy, 108–9; *St. Petersburg Times,* Apr. 11, June 6, 1959; Press conference transcript, Apr. 18, 1959, FSU governor's speeches, box 2, folder 20; Havard-Beth, *Politics of Mis-Representation,* 66.

13. Havard-Beth, *Politics of Mis-Representation; Tampa Tribune,* Apr. 16, 1959.

14. *St. Petersburg Times,* Oct. 13, 1959.

15. *Tampa Tribune,* Oct. 30, 31, 1959; LeRoy Collins, interview with Tom Wagy, Nov. 19, 1975, *St. Petersburg Times,* Oct. 19, 25, 1959.

16. Statement, Nov. 2, 1959, FSA 776, box 109.

17. Havard-Beth, *Politics of Mis-Representation,* 67; *St. Petersburg Times,* Nov. 4, 1959; FSU, post-governor speeches, box 10, folder 7.

18. *Colegrove v. Green,* 328 U.S. 549 (1946); *Baker v. Carr,* 369 U.S. 186 (1962); *Swann v. Adams,* 378 U.S. 553 (1965); MacManus, 172–73; Wagy interview, Nov. 19, 1975; Collins column, Feb. 1, 1988; John Perry interview, July 16–17, 2001; Hugo Black Jr., e-mail to the author, Sept. 21, 2004.

Chapter 22. Spotlight

1. USF box 20; *New York Times,* Sept. 20, 1957; Transcript, *Meet the Press,* May 25, 1958. Washington: National Broadcasting Co., 1958.

2. *Charleston News & Courier,* Nov. 18, 1957; *Time,* Nov. 25, 1957, 32; Rivers, 470–73; *St. Petersburg Times,* Dec. 28, 1957; LeRoy Collins to William L. Rivers, Jan. 24, 1958; Rivers to Collins, Jan. 26, 1958, USF box 20; LeRoy Collins to William K. Williams, Jan. 8, 1958; Collins to Joe Grotegut, Feb. 13, 1958, FSA 776, box 116, folder 13.

3. Collins, "How It Looks from the South," 90–99.

4. Speech text, Feb. 1, 1958, FSU governor's speeches, box 1, folder 43.

5. *Meet the Press,* May 25, 1958. (Collins was the first governor to simultaneously chair the national and Southern conferences.)

6. *Southern School News,* October 1958.

7. LeRoy Collins, interview with Joe B. Frantz, Nov. 15, 1972, FSU post-governor speeches, box 7, folder 22; John Perry, e-mail to the author, July 14, 2004; Wagy, 125–26; *St. Petersburg Times,* Sept. 26, 1958, July 26, 1959.

8. Frantz interview; Wagy, 122–28; *Christian Science Monitor,* Sept. 24, 1958.

9. *St. Petersburg Times,* Mar. 14, 1958; press conference, Mar. 13, 1958, USF box 22.

10. *New York Times,* Mar. 17, 1958; FSA 776, box 116, folder 13.

11. *St. Petersburg Times,* Apr. 16, 1958.

12. FSU governor's speeches, box 1, folder 28; LeRoy Collins to Roy Baden, Dec. 29, 1959, FSA 776, box 136, folder 8; Ed H. Price Jr. interview, June 4, 2001.

13. *St. Petersburg Times*, Dec. 31, 1959; news conference, Jan. 30, 1958, USF box 21; Bill Killian to LeRoy Collins, Sept. 23, 1958, USF box 96.

14. FSA 776, box 136, folders 24, 25, 26.

15. News conferences, June 12, 19, 1958, USF box 22; statement, June 27, 1958, FSA 776, box 109, folder 5.

16. *St. Petersburg Times*, Oct. 15, 1958.

17. News conference, Nov. 13, 1958, FSU governor's speeches, box 2, folder 18; Collins statements, Nov. 18, 1958, FSA 776, box 109, Nov. 25, 1958, FSA 776, box 109; *Florida Times-Union*, Nov. 11, 1958; Paul Skelton Jr. interview, Aug. 9, 2002.

18. News conference, Apr. 15, 1959, FSU governor's speeches, box 2, folder 20; *Tampa Tribune*, Apr. 17, 23, May 15, 1959; Louie L. Wainwright interview, Aug. 7, 2002.

Chapter 23. The Last Session

1. Collins column, June 27, 1988; William B. Killian interview, Sept. 4, 2002; Mary Call Collins interview, Sept. 4, 2002.

2. Susan Cary interview, Sept. 27, 2002; Florida Constitution Revision Commission, transcript of proceedings, vol. 11, Dec. 8, 1977, 23; William L. Durden interview, Apr. 25, 2002; John Perry interview, July 16–17, 2001; *Where He Stood*, WFSU-TV, 1991; Margaret Vandiver, letter to the author, June 22, 2000.

3. Vandiver, ibid.

4. *Horne v. State*, 101 So. 2d 864 (1958); *Florida Times Union*, Jan. 13, 1959.

5. Collins column, June 27, 1988; Collins-Akerman, 65–66; www.dc.state.fl.us/oth/deathrow/execlist2.html.

6. Dessie Horne Williams to LeRoy Collins, July 27, 1964, FSU post-governor correspondence, box 1, folder 8.

7. William B. Killian interview.

8. *Tampa Tribune*, Jan. 20, 21, Feb. 4, 1959; Bartley, *Massive Resistance*, 248–50; Kluger, 778.

9. Press conference, Dec. 18, 1958, FSU, governor's speeches, box 2, folder 18; *Southern School News*, November 1958; *Miami Herald*, Sept. 26, 1958.

10. LeRoy Collins to Herbert M. Davidson, Dec. 23, 1958, USF box 20.

11. *Tampa Tribune*, Jan. 16, 17, 1959; *St. Petersburg Times*, May 2, 1959.

12. *St. Petersburg Times*, Mar. 25, 1959; LeRoy Collins to Homer Brinkley, Mar. 30, 1959, USF box 96.

13. Speech text, Jan. 26, 1959, USF box 22; press conference, Feb. 12, 1959, USF box 23; *Tampa Tribune*, Jan. 31, Feb. 12, Mar. 7, 1959.

14. *Miami Herald, St. Petersburg Times, Tampa Tribune*, Feb. 19, 1959; press conferences, Feb. 19, 26, 1959, USF box 23; *Tampa Tribune*, Feb. 25, 1959; *St. Petersburg Times*, Mar. 15, 1959.

15. Press conference, Jan. 8, 1959, FSU, governor's speeches, box 2, folder 20; John Germany interview, June 7, 2001; Jack Peeples interview, Jan. 18, 2003.

16. House *Journal*, Apr. 7, 1959, 23.

17. Ibid.

18. Ken Driggs, "Florida Executions List," Mar. 2, 2001, copy in possession of the author.

19. *Tampa Tribune*, Apr. 26, 29, 1959; Ed H. Price Jr. interview, June 4, 2001.

20. Durden interview; *Tampa Tribune*, May 6, 1959; *New York Times*, June 7, 22, 1959; *Washington Post*, June 14, 1959; *Tampa Tribune*, May 26, 1959.

21. Akerman, 134–35; Collins column, Apr. 14, 1986; veto message, USF box 23.

22. *Tampa Tribune*, Apr. 10, June 5, 1959; press conference, June 6, 1959, FSU, governor's speeches, box 2, folder 20.

23. Jack Peeples interview.

24. Joseph Grotegut to William Durden, June 5, 1959, FSA 776, box 124, folder 7.

25. Peeples interview.

26. Wagy, 116; Perry interview.

27. Request for advisory opinion, June 8, 1959, FSA 776, box 135, folder 5; press conference, June 6, 1959; *Tallahassee Democrat*, June 8, 1959; *St. Petersburg Times*, June 11, 1959; FSA 776, box 102, folder 9.

28. *New York Times*, June 23, 1959.

29. LeRoy Collins to Mary Call Collins, various letters, July 1–9, 1959, USF box 456, folder 1.

30. Wagy, 116–17; Collins correspondence, ibid.

31. Perry interview.

32. Transcript, interview with Premier Khrushchev, July 7, 1959, FSU, governor's speeches, box 2, folder 41.

33. Collins correspondence.

34. *Washington Post*, Aug. 16, 1959; memorandum, Apr. 18, 1956, FSA 776, box 53, folder 3; Harry Douglas interview, June 20, 2003; *Washington Post*, Dec. 15, 1959.

35. Mary Call Collins interviews; *Tallahassee Democrat*, Dec. 19, 1959.

Chapter 24. "Moral, Simple Justice"

1. "Integration, Third and Critical Phase," *New York Times Magazine*, Nov. 27, 1960, 111–13.

2. *Miami Herald*, Aug. 25, Sept. 9, 1959; Philip Meyer, panel discussion, "Covering the Movement: The Media in Florida, USF conference; *Florida Across the Threshold*, 68.

3. *St. Petersburg Times*, Sept. 10, 1959; press conference, Sept. 10, 1959, FSU governor's speeches, box 3, folder 1; speech text, Sept. 18, 1959, box 2, folder 13.

4. Raby, 81–83; Richard W. Ervin to Richard Gerstein, Sept. 30, 1959, FSA 776, box 48, folder 15.

5. Patricia Stephens Due, "The Tallahassee Movement," USF conference, June 3, 2004; *Tampa Tribune*, Oct. 28, 1959.

6. Branch, *Parting the Waters*, 271–75.

7. Raby, 88–94; Due, "The Tallahassee Movement."

8. Raby, 96–99; Arthenia Joyner interview, Apr. 3, 2002.

9. Press conference, Mar. 3, 1960, FSU, governor's speeches, box 3, folder 2.

10. Killian, 106.

11. *Tallahassee Democrat*, Mar. 17, 1960; statement, FSA 776, box 109, folder 8; *St. Petersburg Times*, Mar. 13, 1960; *Tallahassee Democrat*, Mar. 17, 1960; Tallahassee Chamber of Commerce to LeRoy Collins, Mar. 17, 1960, Thomas Beasley to LeRoy Collins, Mar. 15, 1960, USF box 96.

12. Killian, 105; *Tallahassee Democrat*, Mar. 17, 1960.

13. Killian, 110–17; Raby, 104–5, 114–15.

14. Raby, 102–5; Killian, 114–15; Lewis Killian interview, May 17, 2001.

15. Killian, 114; Lewis Killian interview.

16. Killian, 115, Lewis Killian interview; speech text, Mar. 15, 1960, USF box 23.

17. Speech text, Mar. 17, 1960, FSU governor's speeches, box 3, folder 8.

18. Statement, FSA 776, box 109, folder 8; Perry interview; Jim Southerland interview, June 11, 2002.

19. Collins diary, USF box 96; abstract, FSA 776, box 109, folder 8; *St. Petersburg Times*, Mar. 21, 1960.

20. *St. Petersburg Times*, Mar. 21, 1960.

21. Ibid.

22. "Remarks by Gov. LeRoy Collins," Mar. 20, 1960, FSA 776, box 109; Durden interview, William B. Killian interview.

23. Colburn and Scher, oral history, Feb. 12, 1975.

24. William Killian interview.

25. Edmonds, 58; *Tallahassee Democrat*, Mar. 22, 1960.

26. Duby Ausley interview, June 17, 2002.

27. *Tallahassee Democrat*, Mar. 21, 1960; *Florida Times-Union*, Aug. 30, Sept. 3, 1960; *Florida Handbook, 1963–1964*, 197.

28. Wagy, 137.

29. Akerman, 168; USF box 40.

30. *Washington Post*, Mar. 23, 1960; *U.S. News & World Report*, Apr. 4, 1960.

31. USF box 47.

32. Press conference, Mar. 31, 1960, FSU governor's speeches, box 3, folder 2; Douglas interview; *Miami Herald*, May 12, 1960.

33. *Christian Science Monitor*, Aug. 2, 1960; confidential memorandum, May 14, 1960, FSA 776, box 117, folder 4; Raby, 118, 133.

34. Colburn and Scher oral history Feb. 23, 1975; LeRoy Collins, oral history interview with Elizabeth Messer, Nov. 24, 1975.

Chapter 25. "Reaction, Retreat, and Regret"

1. Wagy, 143; *Christian Science Monitor*, May 26, 1960.

2. Akerman, 179.

3. *St. Petersburg Times*, Sept. 3, 1959, Jan. 8, 1960; Wagy, 140; Millard Caldwell, interview with Tom Wagy, July 13, 1977, tape in possession of the author; Ed Price interview.

4. *St. Petersburg Times*, May 1, 1960; *Florida Handbook*, 29th ed., 680.

5. *St. Petersburg Times*, May 9, 1960.

6. Ibid., May 10, 12, 16, 22, 1960.

7. Ibid., May 15, 19, 21, 1960; Senate *Journal*, May 16, 2003, 27.

8. Wagy, 140–41; *St. Petersburg Times*, May 20, 21, 24, 1960; news conference, May 20, 1960, FSU, governor's speeches, box 3, folder 2.

9. Akerman, 179; *Florida Handbook, 1963–64*, 199.

10. Price interview; *St. Petersburg Times*, May 25, 1960.

11. *St. Petersburg Times, Miami Herald*, May 25, 26, 1960; *St. Petersburg Times*, June 2, 1960, Feb. 14, 1962.

12. Woodie A. Liles to Joe Grotegut, Jan. 15, 1960, FSA 776, box 125, folder 9.

13. *St. Petersburg Times*, Jan. 8, Dec. 4, 1960, Mar. 11, 1961; press conference, Jan. 7, 1960; FSU governor's speeches, box 3, folder 2; William B. Killian interview; Mary Call Collins interview, Mar. 31, 2001; William L. Durden to William B. Killian, Jan. 14, 1960, FSA 776, box 126, folder 15; Robert Pittman interview, Oct. 20, 2004.

14. *Florida Across the Threshold*, 131–33.

15. FSA 776, box 117, folder 4.

16. Press conference, Sept. 1, 1960, USF box 24; Akerman, 184–89, 195.

17. *St. Petersburg Times*, Oct. 14, 1960.

18. *Gray v. Bryant*, 125 So. 2d 846 (1960); Durden, Killian, Peeples interviews.

19. Speech text, Sept. 26, 1960, USF box 24.

20. Jane Aurell interview, May 21, 2001; John Aurell interview, May 15, 2002; *Life*, Oct. 17, 1960, 135–38; LeRoy Collins to Hugh Moffett, Nov. 3, 1960, USF box 457, folder 2.

21. *Florida Handbook*, 29th ed., 676–77; *St. Petersburg Times*, Nov. 10, 1960.

22. Press conference, Dec. 29, 1960, USF box 331; Allen Morris, interview with Tom Wagy, July 13, 1977, tape in possession of the author.

23. *Florida Across the Threshold*, 54–86; SAS to Bill Durden, Nov. 17, 1960, USF box 98.

24. Press conference, Dec. 29, 1960, USF box 331; Joe Grotegut to Steve Turnbull, Apr. 22, 1955, FSA 776, box 29, folder 3.

25. Press conference, Dec. 29, 1960; *St. Petersburg Times*, Dec. 30, 1960.

26. Diary entry, USF box 96.

27. *St. Petersburg Times*, Jan. 4, 1961.

28. Ibid.; FSU governor's papers, speeches, and interviews, box 1, folder 22.

29. *St. Petersburg Times*, Jan. 4, 1961.

Chapter 26. "A Big, Loud, Noisy Show."

1. Press conference, Apr. 7, 1960, FSU governor's speeches, box 3, folder 2; LeRoy Collins to Robert L. Plunkett, May 3, 1960, FSA 776, box 60, folder 1.

2. *New York Times*, July 13, 1960; Jim Southerland interview, June 11, 2002; John Perry interview, July 11, 2002.

3. *St. Petersburg Times*, Mar. 19, 1960.

4. LeRoy Collins, oral history interview with Joe B. Frantz, Nov. 15, 1972, FSU post-governor speeches, box 7, folder 22; Wagy, 153–56.

5. Wagy, 147; John Perry interview, July 11, 2002; press conference, May 20, 1960, FSU governor's speeches, box 3, folder 2.

6. *New York Times*, May 20, 25, 1960; *St. Petersburg Times*, May 22, 1960; Frantz interview; Transcript, Hale Boggs Oral History Interview I, Mar. 13, 1969, by T. H. Baker, Internet copy, LBJ Library.

7. LeRoy Collins to Adlai Stevenson, Feb. 13, 1959, copy in the possession of John Perry; *Christian Science Monitor*, July 7, 1960; John Perry interview, July 19, 2001.

8. Press conference, June 2, 1960; LeRoy Collins to R. A. Gray, June 13, 1960, USF box 1; John Perry interview, July 11, 2002.

9. Wagy, 143.

10. *Television*, May 1961, 69.

11. Morris, *Proceedings*, 72; Wagy, 158; *New York Times*, July 3, 1960; White, 158–59.

12. *New York Times*, July 4, 1960; Wagy, 158–61.

13. Wagy, 158–61; Morris, *Proceedings*, 49; *Washington Post*, July 13, 1960.

14. Morris, *Proceedings*, 55–56; Mary Call Collins interview, May 23, 2001.

15. Wagy, 161; Eleanor Roosevelt to LeRoy Collins, July 26, 1960, FSU post-governor correspondence, box 13, folder 13.

16. Morris, *Proceedings*, 60–61, Perry interview; *Washington Post*, July 13, 1960.

17. Morris, *Proceedings,* 74–97; Wagy, 163.

18. Wagy, 162; *New York Times, Wall Street Journal*, July 12, 1960; Morris, *Proceedings*, 103–5.

19. Wagy, 163; Morris, *Proceedings*, 106–59.

20. Morris, *Proceedings*, 143; White, 165–67.

21. *New York Times*, July 14, 1960; Morris, *Proceedings*, 143–47.

22. Morris, *Proceedings*, 143–47.

23. *New York Times*, July 14, 1960; Morris, *Proceedings*, 169; LeRoy Collins, interview with Ronald J. Grele, Nov. 1, 1965, John F. Kennedy library, FSU post-governor speeches, box 7, folder 16; Wagy, 196.

24. Wagy, 168; White, 175–77; LeRoy Collins, undated memorandum, FSU post-governor speeches, box 7, folder 12; Morris, *Proceedings*, 219; LeRoy Collins to Bob Delaney, July 28, 1960, USF box 19.

25. LeRoy Collins, oral history interview, Nov. 24, 1975, FSA M77-164, box 1; Frantz interview; Wagy, 167.

26. Morris, *Proceedings*, 177, 211; *Broadcasting*, July 18, 1960, 9.

27. Harry Douglas interview, Apr. 16, 2002; *New York Times*, July 15, 1960.

28. Mary Call Collins interview, May 21, 2001; Douglas interview.

29. Press conference, FSU governor's speeches, box 3, folder 3; LeRoy Collins to James O. Powell, Aug. 5, 1960, USF box 20.

30. *Florida Times-Union*, Aug. 6, 1960; press conferences, Aug. 11, 1960, USF box 24, Aug. 18, 1960, FSU, governor's speeches, box 3, folder 3.

31. *St. Petersburg Times*, Aug. 19, Oct. 22, 1960; Wagy, 173–75; *Florida Times-Union*, Aug. 27, Sept. 2, 1960; *New York Times*, Aug. 23, 1960.

32. Congressional Quarterly, *Presidential Elections*, 145–46.

Chapter 27. Dog Eat Dog

1. Baughman, 14–31, 40–44; *Broadcasting*, Mar. 14, 1960.

2. *Television*, May 1961, 68–69.

3. *New York Times*, Mar. 4, 1970; USF box 456, folder 1; J. Brown Farrior to LeRoy Collins, Aug. 2, 1960, Collins to Farrior, Sept. 16, 1960, USF box 458, folder 3; USF box 456, folder 1.

4. Philip L. Graham to LeRoy Collins, Aug. 25, 1960, USF box 458.

5. John S. Hayes to LeRoy Collins, Sept. 15, 1960, USF box 458; FSU governor's speeches, box 2, folder 2, box 3, folder 7; FSA 776, box 109, folder 7.

6. *Television*, May 1961, 71; *Broadcasting*, Oct. 3, 1960, 27–29, Nov. 26, 1962, 5; *St. Petersburg Times*, Oct. 11, 1960.

7. *Public Papers of the Presidents of the United States: John F. Kennedy, 1961*, 719; Darby Collins interview, Aug. 20, 2003.

8. Darby Collins interview, Aug. 20, 2003.

9. Newton Minow interview, Oct. 9, 2001; Herbert Block, *Straight Herblock*, 43; *Broadcasting*, Jan. 9, 1961, 102.

10. LeRoy Collins to Mary Call Proctor, undated, Proctor family files.

11. *Broadcasting*, Feb. 6, 1961, 102.

12. *New York Times*, Mar. 16, 1961; John Perry, quoted in Lucoff, 31; *Television*, May 1961, 72; USF box 38.

13. *New York Times*, Mar. 16, 1961; *Washington Post*, Mar. 17, 1961; *Broadcasting*, Mar. 20, 1961.

14. *Broadcasting*, May 15, 1961, 58–60; USF box 38; *Variety*, May 10, 1961; *Broadcasting*, May 15, 1961, 32.

15. *Broadcasting*, Aug. 21, 1961, 61, 138; Feb. 5, 1962, 42; Nov. 19, 1962, 62; Lucoff, 78–79; LeRoy Collins to Walter P. Fuller, Oct. 9, 1963, USF Walter Fuller Papers, box 7, file "LeRoy Collins."

16. Minow interview; speech texts, Sept. 29, Oct. 13, 1961, USF box 38; *Broadcasting*, Oct. 2, 1961, 98; Mar. 26, 1962, 162; Apr. 9, 1962, 122; *New York Times*, Apr. 3, 5, 1962.

17. Mann, Darby Collins interviews; LeRoy Collins to Palmer and Mary Call Proctor, undated, Proctor family files; LeRoy Collins to Jane Aurell, Oct. 29, 1962, Collins family papers, copy in possession of the author.

18. Speech text, Nov. 19, 1962, USF box 38; Lucoff, 126–27.

19. *Broadcasting*, Nov. 26, 1962, 24–26, 30, 98; *New York Times*, Nov. 28, 1962.

20. *Broadcasting*, Nov. 26, 1962, 98, Jan. 21, 1963, 31–34, 36, 48; *St. Petersburg Times*, Mar. 13, 1963.

21. Speech text, Jan. 23, 1963, USF box 39; *Broadcasting*, Jan. 28, 1963, 38; text, FSU post-governor speeches, box 10, folder 1; *New York Times*, Dec. 3, 1963.

22. Speech text, Dec. 3, 1963, reprinted in *Congressional Record*, July 20, 1964, 15735–37; see also Senate Committee on Commerce, *Hearing on Nomination of LeRoy Collins*, 88th Cong., 2d sess., 1964, S. Serial 53, 50–53, hereafter, *Collins Nomination*.

23. *Tampa Tribune*, Dec. 4, 1963; *New York Times*, Dec. 4, 1963; Wagy, 179.

24. *Raleigh Times, Greenville Piedmont*, Dec. 7, 1993.

25. Frantz interview; *Waterbury Republican*, Dec. 8, 1963; *Washington Post*, Dec. 10, 1963; *Broadcasting*, Dec. 16, 1963, 116.

26. *Broadcasting*, Jan. 20, 27, 1964; Jan. 20, 1964, 98.

27. *Broadcasting*, Feb. 3, 1964, 36–37; speech text, Jan. 28, 1964, FSU post-governor speeches, box 9, folder 5; Lucoff, 237.

28. Mary Call Collins interview, Sept. 20, 2001; Frantz interview; Grele interview.

29. Patterson, 121; Collins column, Jan. 18, 1988; Congressional Quarterly, *Revolution in Civil Rights*, 4, 53.

30. Colburn, *Racial Change and Community Crisis*, 1, 26–27, 66, 105; Branch, *Pillar of Fire*, 335–36; Akerman, 333.

31. Congressional Quarterly, *Revolution in Civil Rights*, 4, 53.

32. Frantz interview; *Broadcasting*, June 29, 1964, 9, July 27, 1964, 90; *Collins Nomination*, 17.

Chapter 28. Selma

1. Caro, 212–15, 832, 862–63, 990–92.

2. Conversations between Lyndon B. Johnson and Luther Hodges, June 19, 1964, 2:28 p.m., citation # 3787, June 19, 1964, 2:59 p.m., citation # 3829, and between Lyndon B. Johnson and James Eastland, June 23, 1964, 3:59 p.m., citation # 3836, Recordings and Transcripts of Conversations and Meetings, LBJ Library (hereafter, LBJ Library).

3. Hodges conversation, # 3829, LBJ Library; Frantz interview; Mary Call Collins interview, Nov. 19, 2004.

4. Michael Beschloss, *Taking Charge: The Johnson White House Tapes, 1963–1964* (New York: Simon and Schuster, 1997), 433.

5. Ibid.

6. Conversations between Lyndon Johnson and Luther Hodges, June 25, 1964, 11:56 a.m., citation # 3896; June 23, 1964, 4:14 p.m, citation # 3839, Lyndon Johnson and Walter Jenkins, June 26, 1964, 6:23 p.m., citation # 3931, Lyndon B. Johnson and Al Friendly, June 26, 1964, 6:30 p.m., citation # 3932, LBJ Library.

7. Frantz interview; *Where He Stood* (1991); LeRoy Collins interview, Southern Oral History Program, May 19, 1974, SOHP A-49; Mary Call Collins interview, Mar. 31, 2001; Collins column, Jan. 18, 1988.

8. http://www.lbjlib.utexas.edu/johnson_archives.hom/speeches.hom/640702.html; Bill Moyers, e-mail to the author, Apr. 11, 2001.

9. www.georgiaencyclopedia.org; *Time*, July 17, 1964, 25–26; Colburn, *Racial Change*, 110; *Washington Post*, July 17, 1964; Colburn and Scher, *Race Relations*, 166–67.

10. Bass and Thompson, 180; *Collins Nomination*, 1–55.

11. *Collins Nomination*, 1–55; Bass and Thompson, 273–86; *New York Times*, Dec. 18, 2003.

12. Bass and Thompson, 199–200; *New York Times*, July 10, 1964; *Congressional Record*, July 20, 1964, 15735–41.

13. LeRoy Collins, interview with Tom Wagy, Apr. 10, 1976; Mary Call Collins interview, July 18, 2003.

14. LeRoy Collins Jr. interview, June 6, 2001.

15. *New York Times*, July 24, 1964; www.africanaonline.com; *Meet the Press*, Aug. 2, 1964.

16. Chapman, 30, 34, 116; LeRoy Collins, interview with Julia Sullivan Chapman, undated, tape in her possession, transcribed by the author.

17. Chapman, 44, 69–70, 72.

18. Wilkins, 142–45; John Perry interview, July 16–17, 2001; Roger Wilkins interview, Oct. 16, 2002; LeRoy Collins, Feb. 12, 1975, interview with Colburn and Scher.

19. Perry interview.

20. Speeches to American Municipal Congress, July 27, 1964, to Leadership Conference on Civil Rights, Sept. 11, 1964, to Alabama Council on Human Relations, Jan. 30, 1965, USF box 64; to Virginia Teachers Association, Oct. 30, 1964, quoted in Fanning, 132–37.

21. Alabama Council speech, Jan. 30, 1965.

22. Ibid.

23. Lewis, 312–13; Branch, *Pillar of Fire*, 522; Congressional Quarterly, *Presidential Elections*, 68–69, 123–47; Garrow, 25–42.

24. Garrow, 35–42; Lewis, 313–14.

25. Lewis, 323–47; Garrow, 61–87; Collins-Akerman, 139, 347.

26. Lewis, 323–47; Garrow, 61–87; Chapman, 49–50; Collins-Akerman, 139–45.

27. Chapman, 49–50; Collins-Akerman, 145–46; Garrow, 86–87.

28. Collins-Akerman, 145–46; Garrow, 86–87.

29. Wagy, 185; Collins-Akerman, 146–47.

30. Garrow, 86; Collins-Akerman, 147–48; Collins column, June 27, 1988.

31. Garrow, 86–87; Lewis, 348; Collins-Akerman, 149–50; *New York Times*, Mar. 10, 1965; Wagy, 188.

32. Garrow, 91; *New York Times*, Mar. 10, 1965; Perry interview; *Washington Post*, Mar. 11, 1965; *Christian Science Monitor*, Mar. 13, 1965.

33. *St. Petersburg Times*, Dec. 10, 1978; Collins-Akerman, 143; Garrow, 99; Lewis, 362.

34. *New York Times*, Mar. 26, 1965.

35. Garrow, 97–101.

36. Johnson, 252–53.

37. *Public Papers of the Presidents of the United States: Lyndon B. Johnson, 1965*, vol. 1, entry 107 (Washington: Government Printing Office, 1966), 281–87.

38. Ibid.; emphasis added.

39. Lewis, 353–54.

40. Congressional Quarterly, *Revolution in Civil Rights*, 67–71; Chapman, 64.

41. Garrow, 112–14; Collins-Akerman, 151–52.

42. Collins-Akerman, 151–52; *Tallahassee Democrat*, Mar. 23, 1965.

43. Collins-Akerman, 153–54; Mary Call Collins interviews.

Chapter 29. Watts

1. LeRoy Collins to Sue Evans, undated, FSU post-governor correspondence, box 13, folder 13.

2. Conversation between Lyndon Johnson and Robert McNamara, Nov. 17, 1964, citation

3787, LBJ Library; *Washington Post*, June 22, 1965; Frantz interview; *New York Times*, July 8, 1965.

3. Speech to Conference on Human Relations and the Future of the Metropolitan Community, July 1, 1965, FSU post-governor speeches and interviews, box 2, folder 22.

4. http://www.usc.edu/isd/archives/la/watts.html; *New York Times*, Aug. 17, 19, 1965; Wilkins, 163–64.

5. Wilkins, 164; *New York Times*, Aug. 24, 1965; *Wall Street Journal*, Oct. 6, 1965; Wilkins interview.

6. Wilkins, 166–67; Wilkins, Perry interviews.

7. Perry, Wilkins interviews; Wilkins 166–67.

8. Wilkins, 168.

9. Ibid., 169.

10. Ibid.; *Washington Post*, Aug. 26, 1965.

11. *New York Times*, Aug. 29, Sept. 5, 1965; *Washington Post*, Aug. 29, 1965; Collins-Akerman, 158–67.

12. LeRoy Collins Jr. interview, June 6, 2001.

13. *New York Times*, Nov. 21, 1965; *St. Petersburg Times*, Nov. 17, 1965; Collins-Akerman, 171; *St. Petersburg Times*, Nov. 23, Dec. 9, 1965.

14. LeRoy Collins to Mary Call Proctor, Oct. 30, 1962, Proctor family files; Glenn Marshall Jr. to LeRoy Collins, Dec. 9, 1965, USF Box 380; G. E. Finch to LeRoy Collins, Dec. 7, 1965, USF box 280.

15. *Washington Post*, Jan. 3, 1966; Sherrill, "The Power Game" and *Gothic Politics*, 137; John Germany interview; *George A. Smathers, United States Senator, 1961–1969*, Oral History Interviews, Senate Historical Office, Washington, D.C.

16. Collins-Akerman, 167–70; Chapman, 85–90; Harry McPherson Oral History Interview V, Apr. 9, 1969, by T. H. Baker, Internet copy, LBJ Library; Frantz interview; *New York Times*, Dec. 15, 1965.

17. *Tampa Tribune*, May 3, 1966; *Tallahassee Democrat, St. Petersburg Independent*, May 25, 1966.

18. *New York Times*, June 30, 1966; Lyndon B. Johnson to LeRoy Collins, Sept. 13, 1966, FSU post-governor campaigns, box 1, folder 2.

19. LeRoy Collins to Hank Drane, Nov. 16, 1967, USF box 380.

20. Darby Collins interview; LeRoy Collins Jr. interview; *Tampa Tribune*, Oct. 2, 1966.

Chapter 30. The Last Campaign

1. *Tampa Tribune*, May 3, 1966; *New York Times*, May 20, 1966; Pepper, 280; assorted correspondence among Louis E. Wolfson, Claude Pepper, and LeRoy Collins, August 1966, USF box 280.

2. Richard N. Friedman, undated memorandum, USF box 281; Radford Bishop memorandum, Aug. 1, 1966, FSU post-governor campaigns, box 1, folder 7.

3. *Florida Handbook*, 29th ed., 677, 684; *Florida Handbook, 1967–1968*, 308, 317; Kallina, 30.

4. *Miami News*, Feb. 7, 1967; LeRoy Collins to Charlie Hesser, Feb. 17, 1967, USF box 380, folder "press: Miami."

5. Dubose Ausley interview, June 17, 2002; *Florida Times-Union*, Dec. 21, 1967; *Washington Post*, Jan. 24, 1968.

6. *Florida Handbook*, 6th ed., 289; Joe Napolitan to Joe Grotegut, Oct. 23, 1967, USF box 117; poll data, USF box 282; www.eac.gov/election_resources.

7. *Tampa Times*, July 13, 1967; Buddy MacKay interview, Oct. 19, 2002.

8. Speech draft, Apr. 7, 1967, FSU post-governor speeches, box 6, folder 30; speech text, box 7, folder 19; Espey, 120–25; "A Memorandum on Opinion toward Vietnam," Nov. 3, 1967, USF box 282.

9. *St. Petersburg Times*, Aug. 21, Oct. 4, 1967; Collins-Akerman, 190; Espey, 68, 93; McClenahan, 27; memorandum, Oct. 23, 1967, USF box 117.

10. Wagy, 192–93; *Miami Herald*, Oct. 30, 1967; *St. Petersburg Times*, Mar. 21, 1960.

11. Congressional Quarterly, *Revolution in Civil Rights*, 84, 87; *St. Petersburg Times*, Oct. 24, 1967; LeRoy Collins to Larry King, Nov. 3, 16, 1967; Larry King to LeRoy Collins, Nov. 8, 1967; USF box 380.

12. Espey, 75–76, 86–87.

13. John Aurell interview, May 15, 2002; LeRoy Collins Jr. interview, June 4, 2001; Joseph Napolitan to Joe Grotegut, Jan. 5, 1968, USF box 117.

14. Faircloth text, Dec. 8, 1967, copy in possession of the author.

15. USF box 280, folder "hate file"; *Winter-Haven News Chief*, Mar. 11, 1968.

16. Undated document, copy in possession of the author; speech text, Jan. 25, 1968, FSU post-governor speeches, box 7, folder 19.

17. Espey, 88; McClenahan, 28; *St. Petersburg Times*, Feb. 9, 1968; Faircloth newsletter, Feb. 5, 1968, USF box 387.

18. LeRoy Collins to Joe Grotegut, Mar. 5, 1968, USF box 115, file "applicants—film producers"; Clark Hoyt, interview with the author, Nov. 12, 2003; Joe Grotegut to LeRoy Collins, Mar. 14, 1968, USF box 115, folder "memos."

19. Joe Grotegut to LeRoy Collins, Mar. 27, 1968, USF box 115, folder "advertising, finances"; Joseph Grotegut to Sherwin Simmons, Mar. 29, 1968, USF box 115, folder "advertising, tv"; Joseph Napolitan to Joe Grotegut, Apr. 10, 1968, USF box 117; memorandum, Apr. 25, 1968, USF box 115, folder "office procedures"; *St. Petersburg Times*, May 2, 1968.

20. *St. Petersburg Times*, Apr. 6, 1968; McClenahan, 37.

21. *Florida Handbook*, 12th ed., 460; *St. Petersburg Times*, May 9, 1968.

22. *St. Petersburg Times*, May 13, 1968; Espey, 93–94.

23. Speech text, John L. Perry to the annual conference of the American Association for Public Opinion Research, May 9, 1968, Santa Barbara, Calif. Copy in possession of the author.

24. *St. Petersburg Times*, May 11, 1968; LeRoy Collins, Wagy interview, Apr. 10, 1976.

25. Joseph Grotegut to Charles Commander III, Apr. 19, 1968, USF box 281.

26. *New York Times*, May 20, 1968; *St. Petersburg Times*, May 22, 23, 26, 1968; USF box 480; *Florida Times-Union*, May 21, 1968; Espey, 101.

27. *St. Petersburg Times*, May 20, 1968.

28. USF box 380, folder "press: Miami"; *Florida Times-Union*, May 19, 1968; Espey, 103; *St. Petersburg Times*, May 25, 1968.

29. *Florida Handbook*, 12th ed., 460; Espey, 106–7; *St. Petersburg Times*, May 29, 30, June 6, 1968.

30. *New York Times*, May 29; *Christian Science Monitor*, June 1, 1968; *Collins-Akerman*, 197.

31. James L. Martin interview, Aug. 3, 2001; Espey, 87; J. Philip Griffin to LeRoy Collins, Oct. 14, 1968, USF box 280.

32. *St. Petersburg Times*, July 18, 1968; Espey, 116–17; Joe Grotegut to LeRoy Collins, Oct. 22, 1968, FSU post-governor campaigns, folder 7.

33. Richard A. Pettigrew interview, Feb. 8, 2002; speech text, May 25, 1970, FSU post-governor correspondence, box 11, folder 10.

34. Collins interview, *Where He Stood*; Mary Call Collins interviews, Mar. 31, 2001, Feb. 23, 2004; Duby Ausley interview.

35. Memoranda, July 24, Aug. 3, 1968, FSU post-governor campaigns, box 1, folder 7.

36. *St. Petersburg Times*, Jan. 4, 1967; Kallina, 29, 135.

37. Martin interview; Espey, 140; Ted Phelps interview, Oct. 19, 2002.

38. Undated analysis, USF box 282.

39. Espey, 123–26, 129; *St. Petersburg Times*, Oct. 15, 1968; Martin interview; Dan Millott interview, Sept. 5, 2002.

40. *St. Petersburg Times*, Sept. 29, 1968; Martin interview.

41. Ed Price interview, June 4, 2001; Vince Rio III interview, June 21, 2001.

42. Wagy, 196; *St. Petersburg Times*, Oct. 3, 1968, Mar. 15, 1970.

43. Martin interview; Gizzi.

44. McClenahan, 63–64; *St. Petersburg Times*, Oct. 27, 1968; *Orlando Sentinel*, Oct. 22, 23, 25, 1968.

45. *Tallahassee Democrat*, Nov. 3, 1968.

46. Espey, 148; Millott, Pettigrew interviews; Joe Napolitan to LeRoy Collins, Aug. 13, 1968; "To Reach for Tomorrow," FSU post-governor campaigns, folder 7; *New York Times*, Nov. 6, 1968.

47. *St. Petersburg Times*, Nov. 2, 6, 1968; *Florida Handbook*, 12th ed., 460–63.

48. Price, Millott interviews; Dan Millott, letter to the author, Sept. 5, 2002.

49. *St. Petersburg Times*, Nov. 6, 1968.

50. *Miami Herald*, Nov. 7, 1968.

51. *Washington Post*, Nov. 6, 1968.

52. Frantz interview.

Chapter 31. Floridian of the Century

1. *Tallahassee Democrat*, Nov. 6, 1968; LeRoy Collins to Malcolm Johnson, Nov. 13, 1968, FSU post-governor correspondence, box 1, folder 7.

2. Lyndon B. Johnson to LeRoy Collins, Nov. 9, 1968, FSU post-governor correspondence, box 13, folder 13.

3. *St. Petersburg Times*, Feb. 20, 1969; Gary Pajcic interview, Oct. 3, 2001; Canter Brown Jr. interview, Aug. 27, 2001.

4. Espey, 116–17; *St. Petersburg Independent*, Feb. 27, 1969; Bill Durden interview; *Miami News*, Nov. 17, 1969.

5. *Wall Street Journal*, Feb. 26, 1969; Brown interview.

6. Robert Akerman interview, June 5, 2002; Knox Burger to John D. MacDonald, Sept. 23, 1969, MacDonald to LeRoy Collins, Sept. 28, 1969; Collins to MacDonald, Oct. 7, 1969, FSU post-governor correspondence, box 1, folder 7.

7. Menton, 87; *St. Petersburg Times*, Sept. 14, 1971; Will Varn Jr. interview, June 3, 2002.

8. U.S. Congress, *Carswell Hearings*, 23; *Washington Post*, Jan. 29, 1970; *New York Times*, Jan. 20, 1970.

9. *Hearings*, 23, 75; Harris, 37–38, 55, 58; Roger Wilkins interview.

10. *Congressional Quarterly's Guide*, 720; *St. Petersburg Times*, Apr. 30, 1970.

11. LeRoy Collins Jr. interview, Mary Call Proctor interview, Jan. 5, 2005; *St. Petersburg Times*, Mar. 15, 1970, Dec. 29, 1977, Mar. 5, 1989.

12. Dubose Ausley interview, Oct. 31, 2001; Steve Uhlfelder interview, Jan. 9, 2003; Robert M. Ervin to LeRoy Collins, Sept. 28, 1970, FSU post-governor correspondence, box 8, folder 4; Robert Ervin interview, Mar. 17, 2002.

13. Herbert M. Davidson to LeRoy Collins, Jan. 31, Mar. 6, 1974; FSU post-governor correspondence, box 5, folder 4; Robert M. Ervin to E. Dixie Beggs, Jan. 31, 1974, FSU post-governor correspondence, box 13, folder 3.

14. Ben F. Overton interview, Mar. 31, 2005; Fred Karl interview, July 3, 2003; Murray Wadsworth interview, June 12, 2002.

15. *Miami Herald*, July 4, 1972; James Apthorp memorandum, July 6, 1982, FSU post-governor speeches and interviews, box 11, folder 17.

16. Steve Uhlfelder interview, Jan. 9, 2003; *Advisory Opinion to LeRoy Collins*, CEO 74–55, Florida Commission on Ethics, Nov. 15, 1974.

17. Bonnie Williams interview, Oct. 15, 2003.

18. Debate, Florida Constitution Revision Commission 1977–78 (hereafter, CRC), vol. 1, p. 4.

19. CRC, vol. 7, 4–68, vol. 11, 3–96; Talbot D'Alemberte interview, Jan. 29, 2002.

20. *St. Petersburg Times*, Apr. 28, 1978; D'Alemberte interview.

21. LeRoy Collins interview with Tom Wagy, Sept. 17, 1979; Mary Call Proctor interview.

22. Ed Price interview; speech text, May 9, 1972, FSU post-governor speeches, box 11, folder 16; LeRoy Collins to Samuel Proctor, Aug. 11, 1976, FSU post-governor correspondence, box 5, folder 1; FSU post-governor correspondence, box 11, folder 13; *St. Petersburg Independent*, Nov. 20, 1972.

23. Julia Sullivan Waters interview, Aug. 2, 2002; Susan Cary interview, Sept. 27, 2002; FSU post-governor correspondence, box 5, folder 2.

24. Jim Smith interview, Oct. 3, 2001; *St. Petersburg Times*, Aug. 20, 1987; LeRoy Collins Jr. interview.

25. *St. Petersburg Times*, Jan. 11, 1981; LeRoy Collins to Ken Tucker, Mar. 3, 1981; George Stuart to LeRoy Collins, Aug. 10, 1981, FSU post-governor correspondence, box 5, folder 2; FS 876.155, 2004.

26. *New York Times*, July 24, 1974; *Washington Post*, Aug. 7, 1975, Oct. 28, 1976.

27. *St. Petersburg Times*, Dec. 15, 1978, Dec. 22, 1988, May 20, 1989; FSU post-governor speeches, box 11, folder 5.

28. FSU, post-governor speeches, box 11, folder 5; Elston S. Roady interview, May 16, 2001.

29. Leon County, Fla., official records book 1159, p. 151; LeRoy Collins Jr. interview; *The Grove: A Brief Historical and Architectural Evaluation*, Department of State files, Tallahassee.

30. *St. Petersburg Times*, July 2, 1990.

31. Mary Call Proctor interview; *St. Petersburg Times*, July 24, 1986; LeRoy Collins to Eugene Zimmerman, Jan. 10, 1990, FSU post-governor correspondence, box 11, folder 2; LeRoy Collins, interview with Lucy Morgan, Nov. 17, 1989, notes in possession of the author; Raymond Bellamy, interview with the author, May 11, 2005.

32. Mary Call Collins interview, Sept. 19, 2002.

33. Bob Martinez interview, Nov. 20, 2003; *St. Petersburg Times*, Sept. 7, 1990.

34. Mary Call Collins interviews, May 20, Sept. 20, 2001; Mary Call Proctor interview.

35. LeRoy Collins Jr. interview, June 8, 2001.

36. Price interview; *St. Petersburg Times*, Mar. 11, 1990.

37. House *Journal*, Mar. 12, 1991, 114–15; Senate *Journal*, Mar. 14, 1991, 103–6.

38. *St. Petersburg Times*, Mar. 15, 1991.

39. *Tallahassee Democrat*, Mar. 13, 2001.

Chapter 32. The Glory of Government

1. Speech to National Automobile Dealers Association, Feb. 5, 1962, USF box 38; Speech to Citizens Constitution Committee, Oct. 8, 1956, USF box 21; *Where He Stood*, WFSU Television, 1991.

2. Kallina, 169–75, 196–97.

3. Leo Sandon interview, Aug. 28, 2001.

4. Brian Ward, informal remarks, "Moderation and Massive Resistance" (seminar discussion), "The Civil Rights Movement in Florida," USF Conference (hereafter, USF seminar).

5. *Southern School News*, June, 1965.

6. Jones, 27; C. U. Smith interview, Jan. 28, 2002; Henry Marion Steele, "The Tallahassee Movement," USF seminar; Arthenia Joyner interview, Apr. 3, 2002.

7. *Tallahassee Democrat*, Oct. 9, 1971.

8. Eugene C. Patterson interview, June 6, 2001.

9. Kallina, 174.

10. Reubin Askew interview, Sept. 26, 2001.

11. *St. Petersburg Times*, Mar. 19, 1993.

12. House *Journal*, Mar. 6, 1996, 8–9.

13. Jeb Bush interview, Jan. 27, 2003.

14. Ibid.

15. Jim Smith interview.

Chapter 33. Epilogue

1. Stephenson, 136–42.

2. Green, 207.

3. Reubin Askew interview, May 7, 2001.

4. *Washington Post*, June 13, Nov. 10, 1972.

5. Parole Commission files; letter to Department of Corrections, Mar. 14, 1969.

6. George H. Starke interview, June 25, 2004; W. George Allen interview, Sept. 9, 2002.

7. *St. Petersburg Times*, June 17, 2001; "Jack Orr Without Tears," *Miami Magazine*, August 1974.

8. Hildy Ellis interview, July 31, 2001.

9. Newton Minow interview; *New York Times*, June 13, 1967; John F. Banzhaf III interview, Aug. 26, 2003; *Washington Post*, Aug. 11, 1969.

10. *Tampa Tribune*, Oct. 15, 1957.

11. *St. Petersburg Times*, Mar. 21, 1976; Herman, 27–40; *The Florida Bar, Re: Virgil Darnell Hawkins*, 532 So. 2d 669 (1988).

12. Harley Herman interview, May 1954; *St. Petersburg Times*, May 26, 1999, May 16, 2004.

13. *St. Petersburg Times*, June 23, 2005.

Bibliography

Akerman, Robert Howard. "The Triumph of Moderation in Florida Thought and Politics: A Study of the Race Issue from 1954 to 1960." Ph.D. diss., American University, Washington, D.C., 1967.

Attorney General of Florida. "Results of a Survey of Florida Leadership Opinion on the Effects of the U.S. Supreme Court decision of May 17, 1954, Relating to Segregation in Florida Schools." Appendix A to brief in *Brown v. Board of Education* (Brown II), 349 U.S. 294 (1955).

Bailey, Fred Arthur. "Free Speech at the University of Florida: The Enoch Marvin Banks Case." *Florida Historical Quarterly* 71 (July 1992): 2–17.

Barlett, Donald L., and James B. Steele. *Empire: The Life, Legend, and Madness of Howard Hughes*. New York: W. W. Norton, 1979.

Bartley, Numan V. *The New South 1945–1980*. Vol. 11, *A History of the South*. Baton Rouge/Austin: Louisiana State University Press and the Littlefield Fund for Southern History, University of Texas, 1995.

———. *The Rise of Massive Resistance: Race and Politics in the South during the 1950s*. Baton Rouge: Louisiana State University Press, 1969.

Bass, Jack. *Unlikely Heroes*. New York: Simon and Schuster, 1981.

Bass, Jack, and Walter DeVries. *The Transformation of Southern Politics: Social Change and Political Consequence since 1945*. New York: Basic Books, 1976.

Bass, Jack, and Marilyn W. Thompson. *Ol' Strom: An Unauthorized Biography of Strom Thurmond*. Atlanta: Longstreet, 1998.

Branch, Taylor. *Parting the Waters: America in the King Years, 1954–62*. New York: Touchstone, 1988.

———. *Pillar of Fire: America in the King Years, 1963–65*. New York: Simon and Schuster, 1998.

Braukman, Stacy Lorraine. "Anticommunism and the Politics of Sex and Race in Florida, 1954–65." Ph.D. diss., University of North Carolina, Chapel Hill, 1999.

Brazeal, B. R. "Some Problems in the Desegregation of Higher Education in the 'Hard Core' States." *Journal of Negro Education* 27 (1958): 352–60.

Byron, Dora. "Courage in Action: On a Florida Newspaper." *Nation*, December 1, 1956.

Carleton, William G. "Negro Politics in Florida: Another Middle-Class Revolution in the Making." *South Atlantic Quarterly* 57 (1958): 419–34.

Carlton, Doyle E., Jr. Interview by G. Pierce Wood. July 30, 1997. Transcript. USF Oral History Program, University of South Florida, Tampa.

Caro, Robert A. *The Years of Lyndon Johnson: Master of the Senate.* New York: Alfred A. Knopf, 2002.

Cash, W. J. *The Mind of the South.* Garden City, N.Y.: Doubleday, 1954.

CBSNEWS.com. "Howard Hughes: Patron of Science?" November 23, 2003. www.cbsnews. com.

Chapman, Julia Sullivan. "A Southern Moderate Advocates Compliance: A Study of LeRoy Collins as Director of the Community Relations Service." Master's thesis, University of South Florida, 1974.

Christie, Terry L. "The Collins-Johns Election, 1954: A Turning Point." *Apalachee* 6 (1967): 5–19.

Clark, James C. "Civil Rights Leader Harry T. Moore and the Ku Klux Klan in Florida." *Florida Historical Quarterly* 73 (October 1994): 167–82.

Clark, Roy Peter, and Raymond Arsenault, eds. *The Changing South of Gene Patterson: Journalism and Civil Rights, 1960–1968.* Gainesville: University Press of Florida, 2002.

Colburn, David R. "The Push for Equality: All Eyes on Florida, St. Augustine 1964." *FORUM: The Magazine of the Florida Humanities Council* (Winter 1994/1995): 22–29.

———. *Racial Change and Community Crisis: St. Augustine, Florida 1877–1980.* Gainesville: University of Florida Press, 1991. First published 1985 by Columbia University Press.

———. "Rosewood and America in the Early Twentieth Century." *Florida Historical Quarterly* 76 (Fall 1997): 175–92.

Colburn, David R., and Richard K. Scher. *Florida's Gubernatorial Politics in the Twentieth Century.* Tallahassee: University Presses of Florida, 1980.

———. "Florida Gubernatorial Politics: The Fuller Warren Years." *Florida Historical Quarterly* 53 (April 1975): 389–408.

Colburn, David R., and Lance deHaven Smith. *Florida's Megatrends: Critical Issues in Florida.* Gainesville: University Press of Florida, 2002.

Coles, James David. "Far from Fields of Glory: Military Operations in Florida during the Civil War 1864–1865." Ph.D. diss., Florida State University, 1996.

Collins-Johns Debate: May 1954. Florida State Archives (photographic), V97.

Collins, LeRoy. *Forerunners Courageous: Stories of Frontier Florida.* Tallahassee: Colcade Publishers, 1971.

———. "How It Looks from the South." *Look*, May 13, 1958.

———. "How We Solve Our Teen-Age Problem." With Glenn D. Kittler. *Saturday Evening Post*, April 21, 1956.

———. "Legalized Gambling." *Parade*, March 1, 1959.

Collins, LeRoy, and Robert H. Akerman. "The Man in the Middle: A Story of America's Race Crisis." Typescript. LeRoy Collins Papers, Florida State University, 1969.

Congressional Quarterly. *Congressional Quarterly's Guide to the U.S. Supreme Court.* Washington: Congressional Quarterly, 1979.

————. *The Presidency A to Z*. Washington: Congressional Quarterly, 1992.

————. *Presidential Elections 1789–2000*. Washington: CQ Press, 2002.

————. *Revolution in Civil Rights: 1945–1968*. 4th ed. Washington: Congressional Quarterly, 1968.

D'Alemberte, Talbot "Sandy," and Frank Sanchez. "A Tribute to a Great Man: LeRoy Collins." *Florida State University Law Review* 19 (Fall 1991): 255–64.

Danese, Tracy E. *Claude Pepper and Ed Ball: Politics, Purpose, and Power*. Gainesville: University Press of Florida, 2000.

————. "Disenfranchisement, Women's Suffrage and the Failure of the Florida Grandfather Clause." *Florida Historical Quarterly* 74 (Fall 1995): 117–31.

David, Jack E. "Whitewash in Florida: The Lynching of Jesse James Payne and Its Aftermath." *Florida Historical Quarterly* 68 (January 1990): 277–97.

Davis, David Brion. "Free at Last: The Enduring Legacy of the South's Civil War Victory." *New York Times*, August 26, 2001.

Doherty, Herbert J. *Richard Keith Call: Southern Unionist*. Gainesville: University of Florida Press, 1961.

Doherty, P. C. "Development and Impact of Legislative Involvement on Selected Aspects of State University System Operations." Vol. 1. Ph.D. diss., Florida State University, 1991.

Downey-Anderson, Charlotte. "The 'Coggins Affair': Desegregation and Southern Mores in Madison County, Florida." *Florida Historical Quarterly* 59 (April 1981): 464–72.

Edmonds, Bill. "Civil Rights and Southern Editors: Richmond, Little Rock, Tallahassee." Master's thesis, Florida State University, 1996.

Edmonds, Rick. "The Push for Equality: Journey to the Selma Bridge, LeRoy Collins." *FORUM: The Magazine of The Florida Humanities Council* (Winter 1994/1995): 30–33.

Egerton, John W. "The Controversity: One Man's View of Politics in the Making of a University." Typescript. University of South Florida Special Collections, 1960–66.

————. *Speak Now Against the Day: The Generation before the Civil Rights Movement in the South*. Chapel Hill: University of North Carolina Press, 1995.

Ellis, Mary Louise, and William Warren Rogers. *Favored Land Tallahassee: A History of Tallahassee and Leon County*. Norfolk, Va.: Donning Company, 1988.

————. *Tallahassee Leon County: A History and Bibliography*. Tallahassee: Florida Department of State, 1986.

Entin, Jonathan L. Review of *Before His Time: The Untold Story of Harry T. Moore, America's First Civil Rights Martyr*, by Ben Green. *Florida Law Review* 52 (2000): 497–514.

Espey, Ruth F. "The Anatomy of Defeat: The 1968 United States Senatorial Campaign of LeRoy Collins." Master's thesis, University of South Florida, 1974.

Evans, Jon. "The Origins of Tallahassee's Racial Disturbance Plan: Segregation, Racial Tensions, and Violence during World War II." *Florida Historical Quarterly* 79 (Winter 2001): 346–63.

Fanning, Sandra L. "A Study of Changes in Racial Attitudes as Revealed in Selected Speeches of LeRoy Collins, 1955–1965." Master's thesis, University of South Florida, 1969.

Farris, Charles D. "Effects of Negro Voting upon the Politics of a Southern City: An Intensive Study, 1946–48." Ph.D. diss., University of Chicago, 1953.

Finkelman, Paul, and Melvin I. Urofsky. *Landmark Decisions of the United States Supreme Court*. Washington: CQ Press, 2003.

Florida Across the Threshold: The Administration of Governor LeRoy Collins. Tallahassee: Office of the Governor, 1961.

Florida Department of State, Division of Historical Resources (formerly Division of Archives, History and Records Management). *The Grove, A Brief Historical and Architectural Evaluation*. Tallahassee, 1982.

The Florida Handbook. Edited by Allen Morris. Tallahassee: Peninsular Publishing Co., 1947–69.

Florida Legislature. *2004 Florida Tax Handbook*.

Florida Statistical Abstract 2002. Gainesville: University of Florida, 2002.

Fortune. Notes on the Business Landscape. February 1958.

Gannon, Michael, ed. *The New History of Florida*. Gainesville: University Press of Florida, 1996.

Garrow, David J. *Protest at Selma: Martin Luther King, Jr., and the Voting Rights Act of 1965*. New Haven: Yale University Press, 1978.

Germany, John. Interview by Harris Mullen. August 13, 1996. Transcript. USF Oral History Program, University of South Florida.

Gizzi, John. "Launching George W. in Politics." *Human Events*, January 1, 1999.

Grafton, Samuel. "New Boom, New Blueprint, for Florida. *New York Times Magazine*, September 20, 1959.

The Grove, Tallahassee, Florida, Historic Structures Report. Tallahassee: Florida Department of State, 1992.

Green, Ben. *Before His Time: The Untold Story of Harry T. Moore, America's First Civil Rights Martyr*. New York: Free Press, 1999.

Halberstam, David. "Claude Kirk and the Politics of Promotion." *Harper's*, May 1968.

Hall, Kermit L. "Civil Rights: The Florida Version." *FORUM: The Magazine of The Florida Humanities Council* (Winter 1994/1995): 10–13.

Harris, Richard. *Decision*. New York: E. P. Dutton, 1971.

Hartsfield, Annie Mary, and Elston E. Roady. *Florida Votes 1920–1962*. Tallahassee: Institute of Governmental Research, Florida State University, 1963.

Havard, William C., and Loren P. Beth. *The Politics of Mis-Representation: Rural-Urban Conflict in the Florida Legislature*. Baton Rouge: Louisiana State University Press, 1962.

———. "The Problem of Apportionment in Florida." In *Reapportionment and Representation in Florida*, edited by Susan A. MacManus. Tampa: University of South Florida, 1991, 21–76.

Herman, Harley. "Anatomy of a Bar Resignation: The Virgil Hawkins Story. An Idealist Faces the Pragmatic Challenges of the Practice of Law." *Florida Coastal Law Journal* 2 (Fall 2000): 77.

Hollifield, Marilyn J. "Being the First at Leon High School." *FORUM: The Magazine of the Florida Humanities Council* (Winter 1994/1995): 34–35.

Howard, Walter T. "Vigilante Justice and National Reaction: The 1937 Tallahassee Double Lynching." *Florida Historical Quarterly* 67 (July 1988): 32–51.

Iorio, Pam. "Colorless Primaries: Tampa's White Municipal Party." *Florida Historical Quarterly* 79 (Winter 2001): 297–318.

Jacobstein, Helen L. *The Segregation Factor in the Florida Democratic Gubernatorial Primary of 1956.* Gainesville: University of Florida Press, 1972.

James, Edwin H. "No Man's Collar but His Own." *Television Magazine,* May 1961.

Jefferson v. Sweat, 76 So. 2d 494 (Fl. Sup. Ct. 1954).

Jerome, Paul. "St. Augustine: Watershed Beach." *Flavour* (Spring 2002): 8, 28.

Johnson, Lady Bird. *Lady Bird Johnson: A White House Diary.* New York: Holt, Rinehart, and Winston, 1970.

Jones, William R. "The Disguise of Discrimination: Under Closer Scrutiny, Gains Were Ephemeral." *FORUM: The Magazine of the Florida Humanities Council* (Summer 1995): 22–27.

Kallina, Edmund F., Jr. *Claude Kirk and the Politics of Confrontation.* Gainesville: University Press of Florida, 1993.

Kearney, Deborah K. "The Florida Cabinet in the Age of Aquarius." *Florida Law Review* 52 (2000): 425–56.

Kennedy, Stetson. *After Appomattox: How the South Won the War.* Gainesville: University Press of Florida, 1995.

Key, V. O., Jr. *Southern Politics in State and Nation.* New York: Vintage, 1949.

Killian, Lewis M. *Black and White: Reflections of a White Southern Sociologist.* Dix Hills, N.Y.: General Hall, 1994.

Klein, Kevin N. "Guarding the Baggage: Florida's Pork Chop Gang and Its Defense of the Old South." Ph.D. diss., Florida State University, 1995.

Kluger, Richard. *Simple Justice: The History of* Brown v. Board of Education *and Black America's Struggle for Equality.* New York: Random House, 1977.

Knebel, Fletcher. "One Man's Progress . . . and the Fight Ahead." *Look,* April 14, 1959.

Langum, David J., and Howard P. Walthall. *From Maverick to Mainstream: Cumberland School of Law, 1847–1997.* Athens: University of Georgia Press, 1997.

Lawson, Steven F., David R. Colburn, and Darryl Paulson. "Groveland: Florida's Little Scottsboro." *Florida Historical Quarterly* 65 (July 1986): 1–24.

Lewis, John. *Walking with the Wind: A Memoir of the Movement.* In collaboration with Michael D'Orso. New York: Harcourt Brace, 1998.

Lucoff, Manny. "LeRoy Collins and the National Association of Broadcasters: Experiment in the Public Interest." Ph.D. diss., Florida State University, 1971.

MacManus, Susan, ed. *Reapportionment and Representation in Florida.* Tampa: Interbay Innovation Institute, 1991.

Manley, Walter W., II, and Canter Brown Jr. *The Supreme Court of Florida, 1917–1972.* Vol. 2. Gainesville: University Press of Florida, 2006.

Mathews, Donald R., and James W. Prothro. *Negroes and the New Southern Politics.* New York: Harcourt, Brace, and World, 1966.

McClenahan, Heather C. R. "Florida in Black and White: Newspapers, Race, and the 1968 U.S. Senate Campaign." Master's thesis, University of South Florida, 1994.

McGill, Ralph. "A Decade of Slow, Painful Progress." *Saturday Review,* May 16, 1964.

————. *Southern Encounters: Southerners of Note in Ralph McGill's South.* Edited by Calvin M. Logue. Macon, Ga.: Mercer University Press, 1983.

Menton, Jane Aurell. *The Grove: A Florida Home through Seven Generations.* Tallahassee: Sentry Press, 1998.

Mohl, Raymond A. "Whitening Miami: Race, Housing, and Government Policy in Twentieth-Century Dade County." *Florida Historical Quarterly* 79 (Spring 2001): 320–23.

Mormino, Gary R. "G.I. Joe Meets Jim Crow: Racial Violence and Reform in WWII Florida." *Florida Historical Quarterly* 73 (July 1994): 25–31.

————. "A History of Florida's White Primary." In *Sunbelt Revolution: The Historical Progression of the Civil Rights Struggle in the Gulf South, 1866–2000*, edited by Samuel C. Hyde Jr., 133–50. Gainesville: University Press of Florida, 2003.

————. "World War II." In *The New History of Florida*, edited by Michael Gannon, 323–41. Gainesville: University Press of Florida, 1996.

Morris, Allen, comp. *The Florida Handbook.* Tallahassee: Peninsular Publishing Co., 1947–69.

————, comp. *Official Report of the Proceedings of the 1960 Democratic National Convention and Committee.* Washington: National Document Publishers, 1964.

————. *Reconsiderations: Second Glances at Florida Legislative Events.* 2nd ed. Tallahassee: Office of the Clerk, House of Representatives, 1982.

————. *Reconsiderations: Second Glances at Florida Legislative Events.* 3rd ed. Tallahassee: Office of the Clerk, House of Representatives, 1985.

Motley, Constance Baker. *Equal Justice under Law: An Autobiography.* New York: Farrar, Straus, and Giroux, 1998.

The Nation. "The Old Slave Market." June 15, 1964.

The New Republic. "Thaw in the South." December 17, 1959.

Nordheimer, Jon. "Florida's 'Supersquare'—A Man to Watch." *New York Times Magazine*, March 5, 1972.

Padgett, Gregory B. "Push for Equality: A Bus Boycott Takes Root and Blossoms." *FORUM: The Magazine of The Florida Humanities Council* (Winter 1994): 14–17.

————. "The Tallahassee Bus Boycott." In *Sunbelt Revolution: The Historical Progression of the Civil Rights Struggle in the Gulf South, 1866–2000*, edited by Samuel C. Hyde Jr., 190–209. Gainesville: University Press of Florida, 2003.

Paisley, Clifton. *From Cotton to Quail: An Agricultural Chronicle of Leon County, Florida, 1860–1967.* Gainesville: University of Florida Press, 1968.

Paulson, Darryl. "Campaign Finance in Florida: Who Gave It, Who Got, Who Knows?" In *Money, Politics, and Campaign Finance Reform Law in the States*, edited by David Schultz, 213–37. Durham: Carolina Academic Press, 2002.

Paulson, Darryl, and Paul Hawkes. *Desegregating the University of Florida Law School:* Virgil Hawkins v. the Florida Board of Control. *Florida State University Law Review* 12 (1984) 59–70.

Pepper, Claude Denson. *Pepper: Eyewitness to a Century.* With Hays Gorey. New York: Harcourt Brace Jovanovich, 1987.

Phillips, Kevin P. *The Emerging Republican Majority.* Garden City, N.Y.: Anchor Books, 1970.

Pleasants, Julian M. "Claude Pepper, Strom Thurmond and the 1948 Presidential Election in Florida." *Florida Historical Quarterly* 76 (Spring 1998): 439–73.

Porter, Gilbert L. "The Status of Educational Desegregation in Florida." *Journal of Negro Education* 25 (1956): 246–53.

Poston, Ted. "The Story of Florida's Legal Lynching." *Nation*, September 24, 1949.

Prescott, Stephen R. "White Robes and Crosses: Father John Conoley, the Ku Klux Klan, and the University of Florida." *Florida Historical Quarterly* 71 (July 1992): 23–37.

Raby, Glenda Alice. *The Pain and the Promise: The Struggle for Civil Rights in Tallahassee, Florida*. Athens: University of Georgia Press, 1999.

Rivers, William L. "Governor Collins of Florida: The Fine Art of Moderation." *Nation*, December 21, 1957.

Roady, Elston E. "The Expansion of Negro Suffrage in Florida." *Journal of Negro Education* 26 (1957): 297–306.

Rogers, William W. "Fortune and Misfortune: The Paradoxical Twenties." In *The New History of Florida*, edited by Michael Gannon. Gainesville: University Press of Florida, 1996.

———. "The Great Depression." In *The New History of Florida*, edited by Michael Gannon. Gainesville: University Press of Florida, 1996.

Rogers, William W., and James M. Denham. *Florida Sheriffs: A History 1821–1945*. Tallahassee: Sentry Press, 2001.

Sandon, Leo. "Thomas LeRoy Collins: The Courage to Change." Seminar reading. Collins Center for Public Policy, Tallahassee, 1989.

Saunders, Robert W., Sr. *Bridging the Gap: Continuing the Florida NAACP Legacy of Harry T. Moore 1952–1966*. Tampa, Fla.: University of Tampa Press, 2000.

Schnur, James Anthony. "Cold Warriors in the Hot Sunshine: The Johns Committee's Assault on Civil Liberties in Florida, 1956–1965." Master's thesis, University of South Florida, 1995.

Sessums, T. Terrell. Interview by Harris Mullen. August 22, 1996. Transcript. USF Oral History Program, University of South Florida, Tampa.

Sherrill, Robert. "Florida's Legislature: The Pork Chop State of Mind." *Harper's*, November 1965.

———. *Gothic Politics in the Deep South: Stars of the New Confederacy*. New York: Grossman Publishers, 1968.

———. "The Power Game: George Smathers: The Golden Senator from Florida." *Nation*, December 7, 1964.

Shofner, Jerell H. "Communists, Klansmen, and the CIO in the Florida Citrus Industry." *Florida Historical Quarterly* 71 (January 1993): 300–305.

———. "Custom, Law, and History: The Enduring Influence of Florida's 'Black Code.'" *Florida Historical Quarterly* 55 (January 1977): 277–98.

Smathers, George A. Oral History Interviews, Senate Historical Office, Washington D.C.

Smith, Charles U., ed. *The Civil Rights Movement in Florida and the United States: Historical and Contemporary Perspectives*. Tallahassee, Fla.: Father and Son Publishing, 1989.

Stephenson, R. Bruce. *Visions of Eden: Environmentalism, Urban Planning, and City Building in St. Petersburg, Florida 1900–1995*. Columbus: Ohio State University Press, 1997.

Statistical Abstract of the United States. Washington: U.S. Census Bureau, 2002.

Strickland, Michael, Harry Davis, and Jeff Strickland, eds. *The Best of Ralph McGill: Selected Columns.* Atlanta: Cherokee Publishing, 1980.

Thomson, H. Bailey. "Orlando's Martin Andersen: Power behind the Boom." *Florida Historical Quarterly* 79 (Spring 2001): 492–516.

Time. "Florida: A Place in the Sun." December 19, 1955.

Trippett, Frank. *The States: United They Fell.* Cleveland: World Publishing, 1967.

U.S. Congress. Senate. Committee on Commerce. *Hearing on Nomination of LeRoy Collins.* 88th Cong., 2d sess., 1964. S. Serial 53.

———. Committee on the Judiciary. *Hearings on Nomination of George Harrold Carswell.* 91st Cong., 2d sess., 1970, S. Rep. 521–29.

———. Special Committee to Investigate Organized Crime in Interstate Commerce. *Hearings, Part 1.* 81st Cong., 2d sess., 1950.

Vandiver, Margaret. *Lethal Punishment: Lynchings and Legal Executions in the South.* New Brunswick, N.J.: Rutgers University Press, 2006.

Velie, Lester. "Secret 'Mr. Big' of Florida." *Collier's,* October 5, 1951.

Wagy, Thomas R. *Governor LeRoy Collins of Florida: Spokesman of the New South.* Tuscaloosa: University of Alabama Press, 1985.

———. "Governor LeRoy Collins of Florida and the Little Rock Crisis of 1957. *Arkansas Historical Quarterly* 38 (Summer 1979): 99–115.

———. "A South to Save: The Administration of Governor LeRoy Collins of Florida." Ph.D. diss., Florida State University, 1980.

Waring, Thomas R. "The Southern Case Against Desegregation." *Harper's,* January 1956.

Where He Stood. Tallahassee, Fla.: WFSU TV (1991). Video recording.

White, Theodore H. *The Making of the President 1960.* New York: Atheneum Publishers, 1961.

Wilkins, Roger. *A Man's Life: An Autobiography.* New York: Simon and Schuster, 1982.

Williams, Juan. *Thurgood Marshall: American Revolutionary.* New York: Times Books, 1998.

Williamson, Joel. *The Crucible of Race: Black-White Relations in the American South since Emancipation.* New York: Oxford University Press, 1984.

Woodward, C. Vann. *The Strange Career of Jim Crow.* New York: Oxford University Press, 1954.

Index

Page numbers in italics refer to illustrations and maps.

Martin A. Dyckman is a retired associate editor of the *St. Petersburg Times*, where he specialized in commentary on Florida government and politics.

Books of related interest from the University of Florida

Anna Madgigine Jai Kingsley: African Princess, Florida Slave, Plantation Owner
Daniel L. Schafer

Claude Pepper and Ed Ball: Politics, Purpose, and Power
Tracy E. Danese

Florida: A Short History, Revised Edition
Michael Gannon

Florida's Megatrends: Critical Issues in Florida
David R. Colburn and Lance deHaven-Smith

Government in the Sunshine State: Florida since Statehood
David R. Colburn and Lance deHaven-Smith

The Invisible Empire: The Ku Klux Klan in Florida
Michael Newton

Jacksonville: The Consolidation Story, from Civil Rights to the Jaguars
James B. Crooks

Land of Sunshine, State of Dreams: A Social History of Modern Florida
Gary R. Mormino

Making Waves: Female Activists in Twentieth-Century Florida
Jack E. Davis and Kari Frederickson

Maximum Insight: Selected Columns by Bill Maxwell
Bill Maxwell

Napoleon Bonaparte Broward: Florida's Fighting Democrat
Samuel Proctor

Radio and the Struggle for Civil Rights in the South
Brian Ward

South of the South: Jewish Activists and the Civil Rights Movement in Miami, 1945–1960
Raymond A. Mohl

"The Ticket to Freedom": The NAACP and the Struggle for Black Political Integration
Manfred Berg

For more information on these and other books, visit our Web site at www.upf.com.